D1711854

STRATEGIC BEHAVIOR IN
BUSINESS AND GOVERNMENT

The Little, Brown Series in
Strategy and Policy

Charles E. Summer,
Editor

STRATEGIC BEHAVIOR IN BUSINESS AND GOVERNMENT

Charles E. Summer

University of Washington

Little, Brown and Company
Boston   Toronto

TO CAROL

FOREWORD

THE LITTLE, BROWN SERIES IN STRATEGY AND POLICY consists of a group of books addressed to problems of increasing importance to large complex organizations in business and government. Existing books in such fields as organizational behavior, management, administrative behavior, and operations research have dealt with decision making inside organizations, and with human behavior inside organizations. Existing books in political science have dealt with discrete, partial, and piecemeal decision making as it occurs in the political arena. But as industrial societies become ever larger and more complex, there is a general feeling in both academic and practicing management circles that "something is missing."

In a purely scientific (descriptive) sense, there is a great deal of action taking place at the very highest levels in corporations and government agencies that these micro (internal) approaches have not explained. General managers, policy makers, strategists, top managers, or whatever you wish, are in fact making decisions and engaging in forms of human leadership which are not explainable by theories of decision making that apply at the middle and lower levels of organizations, and which are not explainable by theories of leadership in small face-to-face groups. One thing that "is missing" is a description of how top level managers go about two things: decision making and human leadership. Books in this series will show that the making of global, gestalt, holistic, comprehensive decisions that relate the entire organization to the society around it is a far different matter from the more meticulous, analytical, fragmentary decision making that must occur later as strategic decisions are implemented. Scientific analysis, from cost-benefit analysis to market research, has its place in policy making but only after the strategic decisions have found, identified, and formulated the global problem. Though policy analysis has an important place in strategy formulation and implementation, it is precisely because of the importance of problem finding and problem focusing that the terms "strategy formulation" and "policy formulation" have come to be commonly used in the literature. Books in this series will indeed recognize the importance of science and policy analysis in the whole process of strategic decision making. Most of them include tools, techniques, and analytical methods that are relevant to strategy and policy formulation. But these methods of science interact with conceptual logic and even with ethical principles. Only in ineffective practice would they precede a definition of the strategic problem that, from society's viewpoint, requires focus and attention.

A second thing that "is missing" in much of the social science literature is a normative approach. Social scientists are quite right in trying to discover how managers *do* behave rather than how they *should* or *ought to* behave. In this respect they are obeying the canons of science. But that leaves a vital question demanded by society and by professional managers unanswered: How ought managers behave in relation to the needs of society? Society profoundly depends upon large productive organizations, from medical clinics that meet the demand for human health to commercial banks that meet the demand for loans to build shelter. Not only does the standard of living in society depend upon technical and economic leadership; the cultural welfare of society depends upon cultural leadership—a leadership which takes into account the intangible values (e.g., freedom, justice, ecological balance, fraternity) of society. These are matters that most social scientists have either deliberately ignored or perhaps hidden in a mass of factual techniques and assumptions.

For example, "good" science of organizational behavior explains how supervisors should act in order to promote the self-actualization and growth of human beings. "Good" accounting, finance, and operations research show how managers should rationalize resources to achieve efficient production and achieve a level of minimum waste of resources. But we have little "good" strategy and policy literature that shows how top level managers either *do* or *ought to* go about 1) defining and formulating the standard of living missions of society, 2) adjusting the organization's production system so that both standard of living and cultural values are taken into account, 3) exercising a kind of leadership that is acceptable to the organization and to society, and 4) insuring the health of the corporation or the government agency itself so that it survives and continues to serve society.

In general, these are the problems that the field of strategy and policy study. As we move into the last part of the twentieth century, in which industrial society is forced to depend on ever larger and more complex organizations to satisfy its needs, this field will become more important. The first three books in the series approach these problems in different ways. But they are similar in that they study the actions and behavior of top managers, strategists, and policy makers. They focus on the global management of total organizations as they relate to their social environments. They study this behavior in two ways: how strategists *do* behave and how managers *ought to* or *might* behave in order to be more effective in solving strategic problems.

In this last respect, much of the literature that deals with top level managerial behavior is critical. It shows the malfunctioning of large organizations when they fail to serve society. Or it shows the abuses which top leaders have inflicted on organizations, society, and the public trust. Though such malfunctioning and such abuses do indeed exist in society, there is also a great deal of effective organizational behavior and effective strategic leadership which occurs. These books concentrate on this neglected side of organizational and leader performance.

Finally, all three books view strategy formulation, policy making, and leadership as a dynamic process, in which general managers interact with social forces inside and outside the organization in a *never ending process of organizational development and change.* They do not depict organizations as static, mechanistic forms that exhibit the negative side of bureaucracy. nor do they view strategists as persons who mastermind some rational plan to satisfy needs for status, technical elegance or psychological dominance. Rather, strategists are continually coping, sometimes in a comprehensive and logical (stable) way and sometimes in a partially logical (unstable) way, to steer big organizations through their evolutionary life cycles in ways that satisfy social demands.

Of the first three series books, two are addressed primarily to strategy and policy in business corporations, while one focuses on these problems in both business corporations and government agencies. Forthcoming books are committed to adding to knowledge in both the private sector and in the government sector.

John H. Grant and William R. King, in *The Logic of Strategic Planning*, give an overview of strategic planning as it is done in both single product and multi-product enterprises. They show problem formulation as a conceptual and logical process (to define the company's product and market mission) and a collateral analytical process (i.e., they give tools and techniques for analyzing product portfolios and for investigating financial, marketing, and human resources). This book is one of the most complete summaries of "the state of the art" of strategic planning as it is accomplished in business corporations.

In *Strategies for Diversification and Change*, Milton Leontiades covers existing descriptive models of how corporations progress from simple, one-product companies to very complex corporations serving many market constituencies. He focuses on diversification, by means of unrelated acquisitions, as the dominant current process of corporate development—a process where practice has thus far preceded theory. As I have in my book, he also stresses the long, evolutionary, trial and error development of the corporation. This is a process in which strategists interact with various constituencies in society to plot a path of growth. Both books are separated into two parts, the first descriptive (how corporations actually behave) and the second normative (some ways they might behave to better satisfy demands from constituencies). In the latter part of the book, as he applies a proposed growth path model, Leontiades shows that planners accomplish one other important thing as they match their planning systems to their overall strategic missions: they devise an organization network that somehow copes with the masses of information needed in strategic planning without causing an information overload on the organization or "future shock" to strategists themselves.

Finally my own book, *Strategic Behavior in Business and Government*, as the title implies, shows that there is a great deal of strategic planning done in government in the United States but that much of this has gone unrecognized. The secretary of Health, Education and Welfare behaves in a way strikingly similar to the way the president of General Motors behaves when planning global, comprehensive strategies and when implementing them by an intricate rationalization of internal resources. Furthermore, the health or education industries in this country evolve their organization structures in very much the same way as companies in the electronics industry or the automobile industry evolve theirs. This is true of organizations which range from Hewlett-Packard Corporation to Group Health Hospitals or the Boston Symphony Orchestra.

These three books are intended for use by students in advanced undergraduate courses and masters level courses in schools of business administration (all three books) and public administration (one book). They are also intended for use by professional executives in business and government who are engaged in the difficult but challenging work of strategic planning and policy formulation.

As time goes on, other books in the series will continue to focus on the strategic viewpoint. The field of strategy and policy will become more and more important as society demands of its leaders both a degree of stability and order and a degree of flexibility and disorder. Time will tell whether or not the giant organizations of today, managed in part by strategists and policy makers, can walk the difficult tightrope in a way that is acceptable to society.

Charles E. Summer
Series Editor

CONTENTS

xi

STRATEGIC BEHAVIOR IN
BUSINESS AND GOVERNMENT

PART I

SOCIETY, ORGANIZATIONS, AND STRATEGISTS

CHAPTER 1

Organizations: A Strategic View

Organizations, Society, and Strategists

Productive organizations—manufacturing companies, hospitals, commercial banks, symphony orchestras, school systems, and the like—have much in common whether they happen to be corporations in the private sector of society or government agencies in the public sector.

First, they are of enormous importance to society. They have a strong impact on the social welfare. Second, they come into being and grow only if they can maintain a balance of exchange favorable to society. In return for giving something to society they receive resource support and political support to survive and grow. Third, they move through life cycles. They all proceed through the same first three stages of life: from inception to growth to signs of breakdown. At the third stage, a particular organization might proceed in one of two directions. If it can maintain, through time, its contribution to society, it will enter a stage of readjustment and growth. If it cannot maintain its contribution to society, it will enter a stage of stagnation and disintegration. Fourth and finally, one key factor that determines the life cycle of all organizations, at each stage of development, is the leadership pattern displayed by general managers or strategists. How these general managers formulate strategies and policies, and how they use strategy and policy as instruments of influence and power, will to a large extent determine whether the organization enjoys a long and useful life or whether it disintegrates in a shorter span of time. Some organizations may disintegrate early in growth and development (Stage 2), because they cannot continuously align their products and resources with changing society

3

Others disintegrate later, when signs of breakdown appear (Stage 3), because they cannot solve cultural conflicts.

This book is devoted to explaining and clarifying the process of organizational evolution and the role general managers or strategists play in such evolution. In the first two chapters we will summarize the argument. In Part II we will show that those organizations which successfully progress through a long growth and development stage do so because strategists are able to align the organization's primary missions, or *task missions*, with the demands and expectations of an ever-changing society. In Part III we will show that growth and development result in large, complex organizations, so large and so complex that (1) it is difficult to maintain alignment between society's needs and effectiveness in the primary mission, and (2) it is difficult to meet the challenges of an increasing number of constituencies which object to the organization on cultural grounds. These difficulties and challenges, taken together, move the organization to Stage 3, a time of conflict, or, as Toynbee called it, a "time of troubles."

Parts II and III are descriptive. We can prove empirically, by use of extensive case histories, the main argument. We can prove that some organizations are successful in the growth and development stage and that they then enter a conflict stage. We can prove that one key factor in this success is the leadership pattern of general managers. But what happens during and after the breakdown stage must be normative and speculative. Industrial societies of today, containing organizations of a size and complexity never before seen, are truly experimental. Can such organizations indeed continue to maintain their alignment with constituencies and minimize the cultural challenges they face? Or will all of them, conforming to the history of civilizations, move from conflict and signs of trouble to full scale disintegration? We do not know. Rather, in Part IV we will speculate about how strategists might adjust their leadership patterns to cope with disjointed and unsuccessful accomplishment of primary missions, and to cope with cultural challenges from outside constituencies and internal employees.

Throughout the whole span of organization development and evolution, this book will examine the behavior of three actors in the strategic arena, or the strategic system, each of which affects the others:

1. *Society*, which turns out to be a diverse network of constituencies, each of which makes demands on productive organizations.
   Organizations themselves, which supply the demands of society, \d receive resource and political support in return.

4

3. *General managers or strategists* who formulate strategies and policies that shape organization goals.

If the behavior of these three actors is truly *interdependent*, if each depends on the others, there must be some starting point for describing "who does what to whom." The next section will select the natural starting point, the goals of productive organizations as they are derived from basic needs in society. Needs in society are the root causes why organizations come into being in the first place (stage 1 in evolution), and they are the root causes that determine each successive stage in the life cycle.

The Goals of Productive Organizations:
A Static View

Though we will see later that organization goals are dynamic and changing, in this section we will picture them as if they were static. We will view them at one point of time in the organization's long process of development.

Chapters 3–9 will provide down-to-earth, empirical details of organization goals, describing in case histories what they are and how they originate. However, there are so many different goals, set by so many constituencies of the organization, that we need some way to begin to understand them. We need an understanding of their *content*, what they are. We also need an understanding of *who sets them*, and how they are set.

From a strategic viewpoint, one portion of the literature in social sciences has been misleading as to what these goals are. Strategists, as professional persons who must deal with all facets of an action problem, must accept and deal with multiple and conflicting goals of all types. So many, in fact, that the world sometimes looks like a buzzing confusion of goals. Researchers in social sciences, on the other hand, specialize in disciplines that *focus* only on one limited type of goal. For example, specialists in psychology focus on human psychological satisfaction at work. Specialists in economics, or its applied branches such as accounting, finance, and operations research, focus on economic productivity or economic efficiency. To thoroughly understand any one class of organization goals, social scientists must obey the canons of their discipline, deliberately shutting out the rest of the world when they frame hypotheses. The focus of the problem, the hypothesis, then determines what kind of evidence they will look for. Unfortunately, general managers, like lawyers, doctors, judges, and statesmen, cannot do this. They cannot use *ceteris paribus* ("other things being equal") to eliminate the confusing number of goals. And they cannot turn their organizations into controlled experiments, or controlled field observations, gathering data on only one aspect of the world's value goals, and "controlling out" all others.

The following summary is a first attempt to make sense of the myriad conflicting goals that must be taken into account by strategists when they make decisions, when they formulate a comprehensive strategy for the organization, or when they formulate policies, or "pieces" of the comprehensive strategy.

We begin with the fact that all organizations come into being and survive because they satisfy the expectations or demands of society. Therefore, the goal of any organization is to contribute to "the social welfare" or to the "quality of life in society." But such a theoretical abstraction gives little indication of what the social welfare is or who society is. In reality there is no such thing as "the social welfare." Social welfare means many things to many people. Nor is there any real entity known as "society." The social fabric is made up of many diverse groups, each with its own *needs and self-interest*, its own *expectations*, and its own *ethic*, where ethic is defined as what the organization ought to do to be a good organization.

Social Needs, Expectations, Demands

The starting point for understanding both the content of organization goals (what they are) and their source (who sets them) is the social expectation matrix or social demand matrix shown in Exhibit 1-1.

At the top of the diagram, we see that everyone in society would agree that every bank, every hospital, every art museum, and every manufacturing company should contribute to the social welfare, to the quality of life in society.

The two column headings indicate what is being expected or demanded. Column (T) is the demand for effective task performance, the demand that the organization be successful in its primary mission. Hospitals are expected to perform surgical operations. Commercial banks are expected to make loans to homeowners and businesses. Museums are expected to produce historical exhibits. Column (C) shows the demand for cultural performance. The hospital is expected to produce effective surgical operations (T), but it is also expected either to contribute to certain cultural values (C), or at least to refrain from negatively affecting such values in society.

The two row headings show whether the constituencies are de-

6

EXHIBIT 1-1

Social Expectations Matrix: The Goals of Productive Organizations

The demand for contribution to social welfare (quality of life in society)

		T The demand for task performance	C The demand for cultural performance
E	The demand for (external) effectiveness	The demand for high quality, low price utility. This is made by task constituencies: con- sumers, clients, and resource suppliers.	The demand for contribution to a wide range of cultural values in society. This is made by cultural constituencies— groups not directly connected with the organization's primary task.
I	The demand for (internal) efficiency	The demand for efficient rationalization of internal resources. This is made by task constituencies: consumers, clients, and resource suppliers.	The demand for contribution to employee satisfaction, or to the quality of work life inside the organization. This is made by two groups of internal members—administrators and work-level employees.

manding that the organization accomplish some goal in the outside world (Row E, the demand for external effectiveness) or something inside the organization (Row I, the demand for internal efficiency).

Combining columns and rows, the squares in the matrix show not only the content of various goals, but the constituencies that demand each goal. For example, in cell TE we see that the demand is that the hospital be effective with patients in the outside world. This is the demand for effective task performance. Chapters 3 and 4 will show that this demand is made by task constituencies: consumers, clients, patients, customers, and various resource suppliers such as tax-payers or stockholders.

Cell TI is the demand for efficient task performance. The hospital must also be efficient in allocating its internal resources in such a way that it does indeed serve the outside world. In Chapter 5 we will break this demand into more specific demands by use of a classifica-tion system. It will reduce philosophical concepts such as "the demand for efficient task performance" to a lower level of specificity by breaking it down into two more specific demands: the demand for efficient design of long-term structural (fixed) resources (TI.1) and

7

the demand for efficient design of shorter-term operating (dynamic and changing) resources (TI.2).

But even at this intermediate level, the concepts are too broad and general. They are not operational for doing research on policy-making and they are not operational (useful and practical) to real strategists in business and government who must actually design and allocate resources. Therefore, the demand for efficient fixed resources (TI.1) will be further reduced to: the demand for an efficient structure of physical capital (TI.11, buildings, equipment, machinery) and the demand for an efficient structure of human organization (TI.12, organization structure). Likewise, the demand for efficient work level operating processes will be broken down into: the demand for efficient technical procedures and sequences (TI.21, work flows, processes) and the demand for efficient human work efforts (TI.22, work design, reward systems, selection and development systems).

A similar classification is needed to understand more specific demands which make up the broad demand for cultural performance. Cell (CE), the demand for effective cultural performance, covers the entire range of intangible values demanded by interest groups outside the organization.

Chapters 6 and 7 will show that these range all the way from the demand for freedom and autonomy (CE.1) to demands for justice (CE.2), and demands for ecological balance in nature (CE.6). There is virtually no limit to the number of groups in society that expect organizations to accomplish these goals, or to the number of variations in the value themes demanded by each group. Cell CE also includes constituencies who value technology and economics but who are not directly connected to the organization's primary task as consumers or resource suppliers. For example, some groups in the cultural environment want a healthy economy, with large gross national income so that they can find employment.

Finally, cell CI is the demand for cultural efficiency. By this slightly unusual term, we mean simply that internal employees have personal needs and demands, connected with the internal culture of the organization. These needs are different from the task demands in TI. Chapter 8 will show that some represent self-interests of middle managers or administrators (CI.1). Chapter 9 will show that some represent demands of work-level employees (CI.2).

At this point, both the demands themselves, and the constituencies doing the demanding, appear to be somewhat dry and theoretical. They do not appear as active or dynamic. We shall have to wait for case histories to understand the real impact they have on

8

organizations and on strategic decision making. Suffice it to say that they are, when acted out in real situations, the deep and profound needs of mankind. Groups that have these needs and make these demands are serious about them. These groups also have diverse means to enforce their demands, rewarding the organization and its strategists by increasing their support or penalizing the organization and its strategists by withholding support.

There is a final reason why such a classification must be injected even though it may seem tedious at this point. The field of strategy and policy formulation is one in which both researchers and practicing managers are *forced* to deal with the general and specific at the same time. Policy makers in fact operate on real world facts, events and people. They cannot become theoreticians who deal only with global concepts. At the same time, however, they cannot possibly make sense of the vast complexity of facts surrounding a policy decision without some way of aggregating them into a conceptual framework that is broad enough to encompass the total policy situation. Tedious or not, the classification in this book is one attempt to be general and specific at the same time.

Organization Goals: A Social Science View

The description of social welfare as composed of task effectiveness, cultural effectiveness, task efficiency, and cultural efficiency is not new in social science literature. Parsons, as early as 1956, envisioned the entire society, including all branches of government and industry, as having to solve four types of functional problems: (1) the definition of ultimate value goals (TE, CE), (2) the adaptation of resources to meet those goals (TI), (3) the provision of some form of role specialization and reward system (TI) to integrate human beings with resources to achieve those goals, and (4) the recognition of existing patterns of culture (all four dominant demands) in *all* decisions as a way of "integrating" or securing the support of all persons connected with the system.[1]

More recently, two social psychologists, Katz and Kahn, realized that there are many different frames of reference for evaluating an organization's total contribution to the social welfare. These frames correspond roughly to the four dominant responsibilities we have described. Katz and Kahn conclude that all four are indeed relevant to the quality of life in society and that all four must be included in any assessment of whether a given organization is doing a "good" or "bad" job of contributing to social welfare.[2]

9

Systems, Dependence, Power, and Exchange:
Forces behind Organization Goals

At one time, the study of *management* was concentrated solely on the *internal* task responsibilities, TI in the social expectations matrix. It explored many task techniques (PERT diagrams for coordinating activities, capital budgets to coordinate the investment in buildings and equipment) to ensure that the internal rationalization system produced some product or service. But this type of study assumed away the ultimate humanistic value of the product to society (TE), many of the cultural demands of society (CE), and most of the cultural demands of internal employees (CI). Like economists, management theorists assumed that all of these matters would automatically be taken care of by the unseen hand. The rise of government as owner and operator of many productive organizations, along with a number of unintended cultural consequences of the free-market economy, has meant that all four dominant demands must be included in decision making.

A most powerful development in organization theory dawned on the academic world shortly after World War II. With the publication of MIT mathematician Norbert Weiner's work on cybernetics, it became obvious that no organization could survive without support and feedback from its environment.[3] *All* organizations are *open systems*. All must, in order to survive, give something to the environment and receive something from it in exchange.

Applying this principle to organizations, Emerson, a sociologist, recognized that the organization depends on a network of other organizations for support, and that, in turn, these other organizations depend on the focal organization for some output.[4] Dependency, it turns out, is the reverse way of stating a *power relationship*. Each party has power over the other, and it will be the policymaker's job somehow to arrange real activities (what product or service output to produce, what internal rationalization or throughput processes to use, and what resource inputs to acquire, so that they in effect pay off in value received to *external* constituencies.

Another way of stating the exchange relationship between the organization and its constituencies is that used by Herbert Simon.[5] All organizations, whether private corporations, government agencies, or nonprofit institutions, must give some *inducement* to each of those groups which *contribute* something to the organization. Translated into terms of the expectations matrix, a shoe manufacturing company offers as inducements to customers the utility of a pair of

10

shoes (TE), produced efficiently at a low price by rationalizing the company's internal operations (TI). A fire department offers a call service (TE) to provide safety to homeowners, which is produced efficiently at a low cost to taxpayers (TI) through rationalization of internal operations and equipment (TI). In return, the shoe customers, acting directly, or the taxpayers, acting through city government as a third-party payer, contribute money needed by the two organizations. At the same time, internal employees (firemen, clerks) contribute labor, effort, and time (TI), and the fire department and the shoe company offer as inducement fair wages or a high quality of work on the job (CI).

This same exchange relationship may be applied to intangible cultural values. Seattle City Light, an electric utility, plans to adjust its internal technology (TI) by raising the Ross Dam 12 feet.[6] This increase in hydroelectric technology will provide cheaper kilowatts to customers (TE), and provide clean air (as contrasted with oil or coal technologies) to those who demand ecosystem balance (CE).

The notion that organizations must satisfy a diverse group of external interests in exchange for support from those interests is so important that some researchers in sociology[7] and in business administration[8] have concluded that the *ultimate* measure of whether an organization is effective or ineffective is simply the degree to which it can satisfy the many constituencies in its task environment. The most recent and forceful statement of this position in regard to business corporations has been put forth by Harvard sociologist Daniel Bell.[9] According to Bell, the justification or legitimacy of a corporation, in the eyes of the public, formerly hinged on the notion of private property, because shareholders were psychologically involved in the product as well as the firm's internal operations. Today, not only do shareholders, "have no real psychological ties, they move in and out of corporate stock to get a return on their money. . . . This is a fundamental structural change. . . . Whereas formerly corporate power was justified by ownership, now the justification is *performance*, which includes making good cheap products (TE, TI) meeting the needs of people and serving the community (CE, CI)."[9] We might add that the present analysis does not go as far as Bell in eliminating shareholders as part of the cultural constituency or environment. As we will show in Chapter 3, taxpayers who support government agencies, and shareholders who support private corporations, represent simply a different constituency, which must be included with others in order to legitimate the institution, whether it be a commercial bank, the HEW, or a city water department.

11

Primary Goals and Collateral Goals

In the previous discussion, we referred to the primary mission of hospitals (to render a service such as a medical operation) and commercial banks (to render a service of loans to persons who want to buy a home). This suggests that the task performance goals (T) of organizations in some way are more important than cultural performance goals (C), or that they take some kind of priority in the sequence of strategic decision making. Both are sometimes true and sometimes not, depending on the *time frame* in which one views the organization:

Over the entire life cycle of the organization, T is indeed more important. In comprehensive strategy formulation (which takes this time span into account), T also takes sequential or focus priority. The reason: without such priority, the organization would never accumulate enough resources from society to survive and grow. This argument will be substantiated later.

In the first two stages of the life cycle of organizations (inception, and growth and development), case histories in this book will show that more of the organization's time, effort, and resources are devoted to task performance (T) and that cultural performance (C) has not yet become a relevant problem. This argument will be substantiated in Chapter 6.

In the later stages of the life cycle, those organizations which succeed in turning breakdown (stage 3) into further growth (stage 4) must do this by somehow optimizing, or trading off conflicting goals. In policymaking at this stage, *either* goal may receive priority of focus. This argument will be substantiated in Chapters 10 and 11.

We shall have to wait for Chapters 6, 10, and 11 to understand the latter two points more fully. Here, we will explain the first point: that over the entire life cycle, organizations that survive and grow are the ones that respond to the ultimate value demand: the demand for task performance. In the last analysis, society expects a hospital to devote most of its efforts to surgical operations. It must not devote most of its time, resources, and attention to producing symphony orchestra concerts or to making money loans to people who want to buy a home. A simple test of the truth of this statement is: "If you had the choice between First National Bank of Chicago, the Boston Symphony, and the Mayo Clinic, which would you choose if you needed a surgical operation?" or "If you walk into Symphony Hall in Boston to buy a ticket for a performance, and the ticket person should try to interest you in a surgical operation or a bank loan, what would you conclude in your own mind?"

Though these are simpleminded questions, your reaction to them (confusion, if you think deeply about the questions) points up some powerful reasons why, over the life spans of organizations, task performance takes precedence over cultural performance.

One reason, referred to by the abstract term "specialization," is more complicated than first meets the eye. The greatest economists have pointed out that entities such as hospitals, banks, gasoline stations, and child-care centers are not accidents of history. They are social institutions that have *evolved* to produce what human beings in society need. No organization, however big, can do all things for all people.[10] If one doubts the reasoning of economics, there is even greater evidence when the powers of anthropology are brought to bear on the evolving nature of society. In "Biological Foundations of Ethics and Social Progress," a noted zoologist has shown direct analogies between (1) the structure of animal species at any one point of time, and their evolution (through genetic variation, reproductive isolation, and natural selection); and (2) the structure of production organizations in society at any one time, and their evolution (through changes in their goals, their specializations, and their natural selection).[11] The ecology of organizations is in many respects similar to the ecology of plants and animals. Both organization systems and natural species exist as specialists (i.e., they are differentiated and have different functions in relation to the rest of the world). Both are ever evolving, changing, or mutating in their environments.

A second reason for the priority of task goals, to be more clearly understood in Chapter 6, is not a matter of functional interdependence (i.e., how one organization serves functions for other organizations and constituencies) but of cognitive, or intellectual, necessity. This is why the simpleminded and somewhat bizarre-sounding questions earlier were "confusing." The argument here is that both constituencies outside the organization and strategists inside the organization learn certain images about what an organization is. Without these images, persons would not know how to go about focusing their daily behavior, that is, to use productive organizations as instruments for need satisfaction. You do not go to Symphony Hall if you are ill and need medical attention. You do not go to a bank if in need of placing a child in a day-care center. Strategists in the Department of Health, Education, and Welfare do not focus their time and attention on weapons to protect the United States from enemy attack. Strategists in the Defense Department do not focus their minds on how to create health maintenance organizations across the United States.

Final evidence for the importance of task goals in the long-term

13

evolution of organizations comes from the relationship between the organization and those who supply the resources so vital for its survival and growth. This relationship can be demonstrated by first asking another seemingly bizarre question, predicting your reaction, and then showing evidence that resource suppliers in the real world take actions similar to yours.

Here is the background of the problem. We are all familiar with the fact that corporations such as Mobil Corporation give money (as a resource supplier) to philanthropic and charitable organizations. Mobil, for example, sponsors *Masterpiece Theatre* on the Public Television Network. This program provides works of considerable literary and dramatic merit for the public.

This act on the part of Mobil can be looked at in three ways. First, the company, whose primary mission is producing oil products (to supply heating oil for homes or gasoline for driving automobiles) is making a transfer payment of money to another productive organization, which specializes in a service to another constituency, persons who want to view great works of drama. Second, the goal of drama production is an auxiliary goal for Mobil. Third, Mobil is transferring some of its resources because, among other reasons, it will receive social support from the public, or political support from the government, in exchange for its contribution to the auxiliary goal.

If you were a stockholder of, or a bank lender to, Mobil (both resource suppliers), you might take one of several views of this contribution. You might interpret it as a fair and legitimate exchange: "Society gives Mobil a license (charter) to make a profit for me, Mobil should give something back to society, provided that, Mobil still puts most of its money into producing oil." Or, you might view it as a means of getting additional support from outside: social support of the public and political support from governmental agencies. Still another view is as an inappropriate action: "Mobil should stick to what it knows best, the producing of oil products," or "Mobil should not give away my money; I should do that when I get dividends."

Regardless of the differences in these reactions, they all have one thing in common: they show that resource suppliers expect Mobil's primary and most important goal to be producing oil, and that this goal should take precedence over auxiliary goals.

The central importance of task performance may be even more pronounced in the case of government organizations. To show this, we must take another hypothetical situation. Suppose that you are a taxpayer, supplying money for operation of a city government, or

14

that you are a city council member representing the taxpayers when you vote on the comprehensive budget for city departments. You find out that the water department has used part of its budget to make a contribution to the sanitation department, which collects garbage in the city. The sanitation department has made a contribution to the welfare department, for operation of day-care centers for children. The police department has contributed to a local art museum which, as a private foundation, depends on donations.

What will be your reaction as a resource supplier (as either a taxpayer or as a member of a city council which budgets funds)? You will probably simply be confused at such "unusual" actions. On deeper thought, you would probably take a position similar to that of the zoologist as explained earlier. These priorities are somehow "not right." Organizations have grown up as certain species which are differentiated (specialized) from one another. We hold each responsible first and foremost for its own goal in society, that is, for its primary functional mission, its main task.

This hypothetical case is currently being acted out in reality by most state utilities commissions, which are charged with determining how much citizens will pay for their electricity and telephone service. Whereas formerly the contributions of a Bell Telephone Company, or a private electric company, were allowed to be passed on to the consumer in higher rates, today the commissions are saying to utilities, in effect, "Telephone service is your ultimate mission. That is what your main resource suppliers (your customers) expect of you. You may not require them to pay for anything other than for telephone service. Museums have their own supporters. If your stockholders want to contribute to museums, that is their business and you may pay such contributions out of profits." Most persons who contract with the telephone company for telephone service, and pay bills for telephone service, would probably agree with the commissions.

Organizational Levels

Thus far, the terms "strategists" and "general managers" have been used interchangeably to denote a group of persons at the highest levels of organization who are most influential in setting its major goals. In all large, complex organizations in the history of the world, such a group has in fact existed.[12] Particularly in the case histories in Chapter 5, the existence of a group of general managers is seen as a natural thing. For example, in Sears, Roebuck, operating as it does with branches throughout the United States, it is obvious that

15

the many thousands of persons necessary to operate the enterprise must specialize. Some specialize in managing one store, others in managing one division (e.g., the hardware department or the ladies clothing department). Equally obviously, some specialize in trying to keep up with the multitude of demands happening outside of the Sears organization, so that the company as a whole can adjust and be successful. Not every one of the thousands of employees can do everything at once.

Case histories in government will show the same natural division of labor. In the Department of Health, Education, and Welfare, there are 300 separate lines of activities (programs), ranging from those which render a service to citizens who cannot read and write to those which render service to elderly citizens who need nursing home care. Each of these programs may have branches across the nation, just as Sears has branch stores across the nation. Not all of the thousands of employees in the HEW can do everything. Some specialize in keeping up with the myriad external demands made in one region, and in trying to arrange resources in that region to meet the demand. Others specialize in trying to match internal resources to external demands for a certain program (nursing homes) while others specialize in the same function for another program (school systems). The organization of the Department of Health, Education, and Welfare is discussed in Chapters 4 and 5.

The most basic reason for such a division of labor is not that there are "elites," persons who are "better" than others (though, as Chapter 8 will show, people who believe this way become a problem for the organization). The ultimate cause again lies in the viewpoints of evolution and anthropology: the internal parts of an organization are not accidental, they have arisen because each part has a functional relationship to the others. Each part must perform its particular function or the whole organization will never be able to achieve any of its goals. Certainly no one part can accomplish the entire task. Any person who is not convinced of this principle should reserve judgment until after studying cases describing both business corporations and government agencies.

To simplify the understanding of organizations, and the role strategists play in them, we will at times refer to three specialized levels in the organization:

1. *The strategic group:* those persons who formulate broad strategies and policies to align the organization with the outside world.
2. *The middle management (administrative) group:* those persons

16

who take the broad strategy and *elaborate it* into more concrete and detailed actions, and who help experiment, in policy formulation, to change the strategy.

3. *The work-level group:* those persons who take the actions elaborated at the administrative level and elaborate them still further into real actions. Over the life cycle of an organization, they also experiment, by trial and error, in the policy formulation process, thus changing the strategy. This is the way that the *perceived* strategy (the one first envisioned at the strategic level) is translated into *real or objective* strategy. This will be seen in great detail in Chapter 5. Typical of this group are doctors in a hospital, salesmen who sell shoes in Sears, Roebuck, mechanics on the production line in a General Motors plant.

This classification parallels that made by Talcott Parsons, though he used the terms "institutional level," "managerial level," and "technical level."[13]

In discussing these levels of organization throughout the book, we will be looking at them primarily in their functional relationships to each other inside the organization, and their functional relationship to society outside the organization. We will not look at one or the other as some kind of elite—a group that is "superior" or "inferior" to the others. For example, if employees of a hospital demand higher and higher salaries for their own self-interests, while hospital patients and taxpayers are demanding lower and lower costs for hospital care, which group is the "elite"? If managers in an electric utility are building more dams to supply cheap electricity to customers while members of a wildlife federation are demanding fewer and fewer dams because they destroy wildlife in a region, which one is the "elite"? In Part IV we will have to deal with this question.

In focusing on functional relationships between society, strategists, and the organization, we will not, however, ignore power and influence. Rather, we will show that over the entire life span of an organization, the power and influence of the organization itself and of the strategic group depend on how well the three parties to strategic behavior—society, strategists, organizations—adjust to each other. If strategic leadership is successful in creating such an integration, or adjustment, the power and influence of the organization and of the strategic group will be increased. If it is not successful, the power and influence of both the organization and the strategic group will, in evolutionary terms, disintegrate.

Evolution and Development of Organizations

From a strategic view, one of the most important characteristics of organizations is that they arise, grow, enter troubled times, and then proceed either to solve the trouble (thus entering a new stage of growth) or fail to solve the trouble (thus entering a stage of disintegration). This characteristic is important because strategic action and leadership, of all of the specializations in society, are concerned with the course of history, as well as with current developments. Civilizations have depended on strategists, not other professions, for guiding the historical development of the society. This requires not only that strategists have a sense of history as a stream of past events (how the organization got the way it is in society), but even more important, that strategists view the *future as history* (how the organization will or might progress through future stages in its life cycle).

In Part IV we will deal with the functions of strategists as they differ at various stages in the life cycle. Before we can understand these functions, however, we need some notion of what the stages in an organization's life cycle are. In this book we will draw on the principles, concepts and sequences from Arnold Toynbee's massive *Study of History*.[10]

The Toynbee Model

Before describing the stages in an organization's life cycle, we must answer one question: Of all the theories of evolution available in the social sciences, why should this one be more appropriate? There are four reasons why Toynbee's study of the history of civilizations is relevant to the work of strategists.

First, the model resulted from the study of longer time cycles than most others in the social sciences. In Chapter 3 we will show, for example, that in economics, for the most part, the view is limited to much shorter time cycles. Cultural anthropology has addressed the entire life cycles of organizations, but deliberately limited itself to the study of primitive societies. Longitudinal studies in the sociology of organizations typically deal with cycles of a few months, a few years, or in rare cases a few decades.

Second, Toynbee's model resulted from a study of an entire, interconnected culture. It shows, for example, that at the same time that the organization attempts to get control of its physical environment (things, technologies, engineering artifacts, tangible objects in nature) it is attempting to get control of its human environment

18

(various groups and organizations both outside and inside the organization). Economics (and its applied branches such as accounting, finance, operations research) has focused on the "thing" side of life, ignoring the "people" side. Psychology and sociology have focused on the "people" side of life, ignoring the "thing" side.*

Third, Toynbee studied *large* organizations that were also *complex*, where complexity is defined as richness in number of parts of the technical system and the human system. The field of organization development has tended to concentrate on small organizations—the behavior of individuals in small face-to-face groups, or the relationships between groups at the factory, office, or community level.

Fourth, Toynbee's model shows that the creative and conceptual behavior of strategists determines whether an organization survives, grows, or declines. Other models in the social sciences have either ignored the central role of strategic leadership or emphasized one of the other parties in the strategic arena.

One final point must be made regarding the use of the Toynbee model. Toynbee pointed out that *all* organizations eventually die. When the breakdown point comes, there are built in reasons why both strategists and other constituencies engage in dysfunctional behavior that breeds more conflict. This propels the organization directly into the final stage of life, disintegration. However, he found that some organizations not only live longer and more useful lives than others, but that during any one stage the degree to which the organization benefited mankind varied. The key to whether or not an organization performed better or worse on these dimensions depended on what strategists did at the third stage, where there were signs of breakdown. At that point some organizations entered a phase of realignment, adjustment, and growth, whereas others sank more quickly into disintegration. In this book we will distinguish between realignment (stage 4) and disintegration (stage 5).

STAGE 1: INCEPTION   Initially, all organizations come into being because a certain group of persons—strategists—have a certain type of vision. This vision has two principal characteristics. First, it is logical. It connects several ideas into a logical whole. These parts are

* The early work of the Tavistock Institute in London indeed focused on both the technical system of organizations and the human system of organizations in studying textile mills in India and coal mines in England. However, since that work, the field of organization development has moved in the direction of psychology and sociology, that is, concentrating on *human* organization development. Tavistock's original "sociotechnical system" has gradually been turned into a "sociosystem."

(1) opportunities or threats in the environment (physical challenges in nature, political challenges in human society), (2) things the organization might *do* to control the environment (these "outputs" or "missions" cover everything from fighting wars to producing ocean-going ships) and (3) technical and human arrangements inside the organization that would accomplish the mission (these internal resource arrangements include everything from devising production processes to marshalling workers to do the work). Second, the vision is creative. It is creative because the human mind conceptualizes things and events in the future that do not now exist.

Toynbee thus saw a budding civilization composed of the same three actors in the strategic arena mentioned earlier. Some external world (society, both technical and human), an organization (internal technical and human parts), and strategists (the persons who connect the two).

Two simple examples—one from a private corporation and one from a nonprofit organization—will show this process.

In 1938 Bill Hewlett and David Packard were two people trained in electronic engineering. For both "thing" reasons (they wanted to make money) and "human" reasons (they wanted to influence their world and accomplish something in it), they decided to form a company. During the next 12 years, they had a number of logical and creative visions. They knew that the astronomers at Mt. Hamilton Observatory needed some way to move their telescopes more accurately. They envisioned a certain output goal: a control device. They also envisioned certain internal organization structures and processes that would produce the device. For example, they envisioned a series of steps on a production line. They then envisioned an organization design that would keep track of money. Mrs. Packard became the first bookkeeper.

As the company grew over the years, they replicated the same kind of logical vision time and again, a vision that connected society "out there" with an organization (network of logically related resources) "in here." They produced a device that would keep accurate scores on a scoreboard in a bowling alley. They produced a low-frequency audio device to make Walt Disney's motion picture, *Fantasia*. They produced an electrocardiograph to measure the condition of the human heart. Their product/markets thus encompassed telescope movers for astronomical observatories, scoreboards for bowling alleys, audio speakers for movie theaters, and electrocardiographs for hospitals.

As the company became larger and larger, and more and more complex, Hewlett and Packard felt that it was getting so amorphous

20

that they could no longer quite make sense of the whole strategic arena, customers and markets outside, thousands of machines, workers, and administrators inside. They suffered an information overload, a "future shock." They needed somehow to visualize what the company *now* was. They did what we will see successful strategists do in Chapter 5; they formulated a global, gestalt type of logic, somehow to put all of the pieces together in a logical whole. They decided that the company would focus all its future efforts, all its future time, and all its future technical resources, on electronic instrumentation products. This would not only build on the *distinctive competence*[15] they themselves, and their organization (thousands of specialized workers, thousands of customers) had *learned* over the years, but it would form a super-hypothesis of how the whole thing would operate. Since they knew that no organization could ever do all things for all persons (technically impossible, and utterly confusing to the human mind), this global strategy would also shut out of their thinking the rest of the world, enabling them to concentrate on, and focus all resources on, a specific logical vision.

Today, 42 years later, Hewlett-Packard is one of the largest electronic instrumentation firms in the world, with diverse product/markets including pocket calculators for engineering students, pocket calculators for real estate agents, and pocket calculators for financial officers. Its customer resource suppliers (private purchasers, government purchasers) have rewarded it well ($1.1 billion in sales in a recent year). Its noncustomer resource suppliers (bankers who lend money, individuals and pension plans that invest in its stock) have been equally supportive. Its employees have *co*-operated their part of the strategy.

The second example concerns a nonprofit organization much smaller than Hewlett-Packard, and only in its fourth year of development. The strategists in this case are Bill Kemsley, one of the editors of *Backpacker Magazine*, and Jim Kern, a hiking enthusiast from Florida. Their vision: The American Hiking Society.

Seven years ago, Kemsley began to get letters from people who enjoy hiking, expressing a need for an organization that would perform services for hikers. Some of these suggested educational seminars, dealing with such matters as geological formations or weather prediction. Others suggested that hikers were being impeded in their endeavors by high prices for clothing, or government regulations that limited their movements in the wilderness.

Kemsley's reasoning at this point shows the truth in the viewpoint of cultural anthropology. Organizations are not accidents of history, but arise to *specialize* in the many needs of society. Kemsley states,

21

"I knew that the Sierra Club, for instance, is so involved with general environmental issues that they don't have the time for narrower interests such as hikers." We might add at this point that the Sierra Club strategists had developed *their* focus in the world, and that focus did not, in Kemsley's opinion, include sufficient specialized attention to the needs of hikers.

Kemsley also knew that attempts had been made to start a hiking organization before but that these somehow did not attract "active and imaginative leaders" and did not "provide services which attracted enough members to provide strength in numbers." It is clear that Kemsley knew what the strategic arena was, and the function of strategists in that arena. He not only refers to a constituency as the source of support, but to the fact that the future American Hiking Society would have to provide enough service output to the members to gain their support in a fair exchange. Finally, he clearly saw the role of strategists, citing their characteristics as "active and imaginative leaders."

As it turns out, Kemsley attracted another person to join the strategic group, Jim Kern, who worked hard to build the internal resources necessary to produce the services. Kern called a meeting of other interested people, and drew up a global strategy aimed at the welfare of hikers and a step-by-step program for developing services. When Congress introduced a bill to tax sleeping bags, tents, and stoves, the AHA did analysis to find out what the tax would do to the hiking industry. As Kemsley puts it, "We got the bill withdrawn."

STAGE 2: DEVELOPMENT AND GROWTH   These two small case histories are simple, but they are appropriate to describe the beginnings of organizations. Case histories in Chapters 3–5, which describe the process of development and growth, are much more extensive. So important are those case histories to any real understanding of the second stage of evolution that we can only summarize briefly the organizational view of this stage in Chapter 1, and strategists' work in this stage in Chapter 2. Full understanding will be left to the study of Chapters 3–5.

In summary, the criterion of growth, the measure of whether or not an organization is growing, is the mastery of a succession of challenges. Those organizations which are meeting a succession of challenges successfully are growing. Those which are not are not growing.

But what causes some organizations to do this while others do not? The answer is somewhat a chicken-and-egg sequence of events. As the organization progresses through time, it develops a *distinctive* competence, making it possible to meet the next *challenge*, but in meeting this challenge, the organization learns *more competence*, and so on and on.

But what is competence? There are two kinds: external, having to do with outputs to society (richness in product/markets) and internal, having to do with matters inside the organization (richness in parts, resources, technology, and human talents). Let us look first at *external competence*.

We noticed in Hewlett-Packard Corporation that after the telescope moving device (an output to society), the corporation received enough support from the outside world to use these resources in meeting still other challenges in the outside world. In meeting each challenge, the company saw opportunities not only to render *more* services to the outside world but to receive in exchange more resources to repeat the process. In Chapters 4 and 5 we will see that the Department of Health, Education, and Welfare progressed through the same series of events, to the point where it now has over 300 programs to benefit mankind, and a great deal of political, social, and monetary support from the outside world.

The American Hiking Society is still in its infancy. It has not developed a richness of outputs to constituencies. It relies on two or three services to hikers. We might predict that if this organization continues to grow, it will develop a richer contribution to society and gain even more approval and support from outside. This might be accomplished by increasing the variety of services to one constituency, by increasing the number of constituencies which benefit from one service, or both.

In this process, the organization gains another very important attribute, one of the two kinds of *self- determination*. The more it satisfies society on the outside, the more society *allows* it to grow. Society, by its support, gives the organization freedom, discretion, and autonomy to go on growing. If we view the process at any one point of time, we see that society grants the organization *legitimacy*. If we view it as progress over time, we see society granting the organization *autonomy* to grow.

The second type of competence is *inner competence*, a growth in the richness and complexity of internal parts, resources, technologies, human talents, and learned abilities to operate. In more practical terms, Chapter 5 will show that these parts break down into things like capital machinery and buildings, organization structures, work processes, motivation and reward systems, and the like. In that chapter, we will see that organizations such as Sears, Roebuck, the Boston Symphony, and the United States Office of Education

23

indeed become rich in the number and diversity of internal resources necessary to meet outside challenges.

If one organization has a rich diversity of resources and talents, while organizations around it (which are also competing for their place in society) have a very narrow and restricted internal competence, the first organization will be able to gain much more autonomy, that is, command over what it can do to develop external competences (meet new challenges), and therefore it will gain even more autonomy from society. This is the chicken-and-egg process of growth and development.

Picture today one hospital without an ordinary x-ray machine and another with such a machine; the first hospital without trained talent in the emergency room and the second with such talent. Or picture one airplane manufacturer without a wind tunnel and a second with a wind tunnel. In each case, the first organization is relatively *undeveloped*. A piece is missing in its development of complexity and richness so necessary for further growth. The same could be said for a grocery store without refrigeration to store meat, and without a trained buyer to buy fresh produce. Finally, the same could be said of a police department without any patrol cars or without any access to trained talent to take fingerprints.

This concept of growth and development is not new. Psychologists have long viewed human growth as a process of adding new and diverse parts to the human personality. Infants have very simple personalities with few "parts." They have no skills with which to master the world, no knowledge frameworks to gain self-determination, and no attitudes and beliefs to act as decision rules. If they were thrown into mature society they would, lacking growth "inside," fail to find their way in the "outside." On the other hand, as human beings grow through experiences, they acquire more richness of skills, of knowledge frameworks, and of attitudes and beliefs. Only then can they master themselves and then turn to coping with the outside world.

Economists who study the development of nations also know well this concept of growth. A nation with very simple agricultural implements and very simple human talents is an *underdeveloped* nation. This nation is in need of growth if it is to master itself and its destiny in the world. Of course, a nation may choose not to grow, but the price it pays is less control over its own destiny. A human being may be impeded from growing, by obstacles thrown up by parents or vindictive competitors. But the underdeveloped human being has less control over him- or herself, and less means of getting what he or she wants in the outside world.

According to Toynbee, then, there are two interrelated causes of growth: increase in richness and complexity of the organization's internal system and use of this system to meet a succession of outside challenges. In his theory, the matching of these two competences, through time, cannot occur by accident. In Chapter 2, and Chapters 3–5, we will see that this matching is done by strategists, who *align* the internal resources of the organization and its outputs with needs and demands of society.

STAGE 3: CONFLICT, BREAKDOWN, TIME OF TROUBLES   In Stage 2, the organization proceeds through a series of successful experiences in its environment which *integrate* its internal competences with the forces in the outside world. It does so in part because strategists are able to envision both missions in the outside world and resource networks inside the organization, and match the two.

In Stage 3, signs of conflict appear. The types of conflict and their causes are covered in detail in Part IV. In Chapters 6 and 7 we will see that two things happen in the outside world to create an external alignment or effectiveness problem. First, as the organization grows larger and larger, it impinges on more and more groups that it did not affect before. By acting out its growth in the outside world, (sociologists have called this enacting its domain or environment), it runs into objections to what it is doing. The very process of successful task alignment means that the organization creates for itself a wider cultural environment.* There is then a conflict between the previous alignment created in Stage 2 (products, missions, internal resources) and a diverse set of groups who are interested in *other* values. Second, the outside world does not "stand still." It is ever changing in both its technological fabric and its human and social fabric. This means that strategists and organizations, to continue developing, must be dynamic. In other words, the original task alignment itself becomes out of date and must be modified if growth is to continue.

During this stage there develops also an internal or efficiency problem. As Chapter 8 will show, strategists themselves begin to turn inward. They stop having comprehensive visions of how the whole organization exists in society and how to accomplish missions in society. Instead, they regard the existing internal organization and its goals as ends in themselves. They demand that the status quo be maintained, rather than that the organization try to adjust itself

---

*In the language of Organization Theory, the organization and its strategists *enact* a successful task alignment in the growth stage of development. As growth actually occurs, this aligment automatically brings into being (enacts) a wider cultural environment.

to a changing society. Middle-level administrators, lacking a sense of organizational direction, and stressing their own self-interests, fall into conflict. As we will see in Chapter 9, work-level employees, who formerly respected the strategists and the organization when both were coping in a real way, and in a way that was accomplishing something of value in society, begin to feel alienated. They, too, lose their sense of direction. They, too, fall into endless conflict with administrators and strategists about *internal* matters, unaware of the kind of accomplishment that the organization originally pursued. At this point, it is as if the entire organization is "contemplating its navel," rather than actualizing itself in the wider society.

STAGE 4: REALIGNMENT AND GROWTH   Stage 3 is the time in an organization's life when its future in society can go in one of two directions. If somehow strategists can regain their ability to see the forces at work, and to put them together in a way that renews the organization's competence both in external affairs and in internal resources, a new stage of realignment and growth will follow. If not, full-scale disintegration will set in.

As pointed out earlier, there are two major problems that must be faced, (1) cultural alignment of the organization with the needs of new constituencies that either object to, or do not care about, the original task alignment, and (2) task realignment itself which, because of the "inward" orientation of strategists and employees, has become out of date with a changing society.

In Part IV of this book we will speculate about the kinds of strategic leadership that would be required for organizations to recover from the troubles and conflict that appear in stage 3. We will recognize the *causes* of these conflicts as they are depicted in Chapters 6–9, as well as the successful ways of realigning tasks shown in Chapters 3–5. We will also draw on some of the errors that Toynbee found were made by strategists in the time of breakdown—errors that actually contributed to further disintegration rather than to readjusting and reviving the organization.

STAGE 5: DISINTEGRATION   As already mentioned, Toynbee's civilizations all disintegrated. In this book organizations are not seen as good per se and as deserving to live forever. I believe they should live as long as they serve society. Those which do so should live longer; those which do not should disintegrate. It was also mentioned before that organizations differ in both the length of *time* and the *degree* to which they serve society. Part IV of this book is addressed to increasing that length of time and that degree.

26

Evolution:
Organization Theory Models

Particularly in Chapter 10, we will also draw on one theory of organizational evolution developed in modern organization theory, the Population-Ecology model. The essence of this theory, like that of others already mentioned, stems originally from Darwin's *The Origin of Species* and from Herbert Spencer's application of Darwin's concepts to the evolution of social organizations. Like the zoologist Emerson (referred to earlier), organization theorists view organizations as embedded in a natural environmental (ecological) system. It is within this ecology that organizations act out the vital process of variation. They experiment by varying their own nature (their TE and TI goals) in a constant effort to find a combination of outputs and resources that will match the ecology (demands) of the outside world. They discard those experiments that do not fit the outside world. They retain their distinctive competences, the products and services that turn out to be effective and the internal resources that turn out to be efficient. For organizations that survive and grow, the whole life process of change in the corporation or agency may be viewed as a process of mutation.

Aldrich's Population-Ecology theory,[16] and Campbell's Socio-Cultural theory,[17] are powerful instruments by which managers in business and government can understand the true nature of the strategic problem: the problem of long term alignment between the organization on one hand and its outside environment on the other. There is, however, one important difference in the theory presented in this book and the theories mentioned above. They tend to be deterministic, to show that organizations are in effect at the mercy of their outside worlds, responding to, rather than creating new environments. As Weick proposed,[18] Chapters 3–6, using the clinical method and actual case histories, hopefully will prove that organizations do indeed have great influence over their environments. They create (enact) strategies which govern their own destinies. They can be proactive as well as reactive. Finally, it is the act of conceptual leadership—of strategy formulation and policy formulation—which is the force within most organizations that enables them to do this.

Notes

1. Talcott Parsons and Neil Smelser, *Economy and Society*, The Free Press, 1956.
2. Daniel Katz and Robert Kahn, *The Social Psychology of Organizations*, Wiley, 1978, Chapter 8.

3. Norbert Weiner, *The Human Use of Human Beings*, Doubleday, 1950.

4. Richard M. Emerson, "Power-Dependence Relations," *American Sociological Review* 27 (February 1962): 31–41. For a review of subsequent literature, see Karen S. Cook, "Exchange and Power in Interorganizational Relations," *The Sociological Quarterly* 18 (Winter 1977): 62–82.

5. Herbert Simon, *Administrative Behavior*, The Free Press, 1976 edition, pp. 110–22.

6. The Ross Dam, Appendix.

7. Jeffry Pfeffer and Gerald Salancik, *The External Control of Organizations*, Harper & Row, 1978, pp. 24–27. These authors apply the concept of value markets only to the external environment of the organization—the TE and CE quadrants of the expectations matrix. The present analysis applies the concept to *both* external and internal value markets, including employees as demanders of cultural goal outputs.

8. Yair Aharoni, Zvi Maimon, and Eli Segev, "Performance and Autonomy in Organizations: Determining Dominant Environmental Components," *Management Science* 24:9 (May 1978): 949–59.

9. Daniel Bell, Address at Pacific Lutheran University, January 7, 1978.

10. Alfred Marshall, *Principles of Economics*, Macmillan Company, 8th ed., 1920, especially Book IV, Chapters 7–13.

11. A. E. Emerson, "The Biological Foundations of Ethics and Human Progress," in *Goals of Economic Life*, edited by Dudley Ward, Harper, 1953, pp. 277–305. The same ideas are inferred in works from other disciplines. For example, in *Politics, Economics and Welfare* (Harper, 1953), political scientists Robert Dahl and Charles Lindblom show that organizations which are effective in satisfying needs of individuals and groups over time will be perceived as legitimate. Talcott Parsons, a sociologist, takes the same position, namely, that organizations which somehow adjust their internal processes and structures to serve vital functions for society will be more significant in society. They will be perceived as legitimate and will receive more social support (*Structure and Process in Modern Societies*, The Free Press, 1960).

12. Robert Michels, *Political Parties*, The Free Press, 1949.

13. Parsons, *Structure and Process*.

14. Two volumes abridged by D. C. Somervell, Oxford University Press, 1957.

15. This concept is taken from Philip Selznick, *Leadership in Administration*, Harper, 1957.

16. Howard E. Aldrich, *Organizations and Environments*, Prentice-Hall, 1979.

17. Donald Campbell, "Variation and Selective Retention in Socio-Cultural Evolution," *General Systems*, 16, 69–85, 1969.

18. Karl E. Weick, *The Social Psychology of Organizing*, Addison-Wesley, 1979, p. 153.

CHAPTER 2

Strategic Leadership

IN CHAPTER 1 we argued that one of the key causes of the success of organizations is the leadership role of strategists. Those organizations which are successful in increasing their own competences, in meeting external challenges successfully, and in receiving support from society in return, will have longer lives and contribute more to society. They will accomplish these things in part because of certain leadership patterns acted out by their strategists. It is our purpose in this chapter to summarize the roles strategists play in organizational development and growth. Part IV will deal with the role strategists play in mature organizations, those organizations which have reached a stage when signs of conflict and trouble appear.

In this book we will approach strategic leadership from two traditions. In the growth stage of organization development, we will describe leadership behavior. Case histories in Part II show the actual behavior of successful strategists as they contribute their part in the strategic arena. Case histories in Part III will illustrate the kind of conflict that strategists actually face when signs of breakdown and conflict appear. At this point, in Part IV we will take a normative position. Rather than finding empirical evidence of certain leadership patterns, we will speculate about the kind of pattern that might solve problems in large, complex organizations in today's world. There are two reasons for this change in approach. First, the world has never witnessed the growth of organizations with such complex technical and human systems as those we have today. Second, as a result of the newness of these conditions, there is no clear record of leadership action, either successful or unsuccessful, which can be reported. What we will do in Part IV, then, is to speculate about the future.

Ethical Responsibilities of Strategists

This chapter will contain broad guidelines, to be elaborated in later chapters, as to how leaders actually act out, and might act out, their decision-making work, their influence role, and their power role.

Two things are necessary in leadership. One is a practical view, the other is a philosophy, a sense of purpose. Each plays its part in successful leadership. Without some sense of one's place in the order of things, one may find practical techniques to be dangerous. One may apply them as cookbooks are applied, dumping ingredients such as "policy formulation" and "strategy formulation" into the pot without ever understanding what the meal is all about. Cooking, under such circumstances, becomes a drudgery. And such a strategist may fall into one of Toynbee's *inappropriate* kinds of leadership. He or she may try to pour new wine in old bottles, believing that those who eat the meal will not know the difference. Or, he or she may become so focused on the *techniques* of cookery that he or she forgets altogether about those who are going to eat the meal.

There are four general philosophies that deal with the relationship of the strategic group to the rest of the world. One deals with the relationship of strategists to society, one of the actors in the strategic system. Another deals with the relationship of strategists to the organization, the other actor in the system. A third deals with the whole question of "social responsibility of managers," a subject very much on the public's mind in today's society. A fourth deals with the strategist's relationship to himself or herself, what part his or her own decisions should play in shaping society and organizations.

Ethical Responsibilities in Society: The Integrator Role

In most general terms, strategists' most fundamental function in society is somehow to *integrate* the organization (its outputs to society and its internal structures and processes) with the needs and demands of society (a network of constituencies each of which has its own needs and ideas about what the organization *ought* to do). We can change the words "function in society" in this sentence to "responsibility," and say also that strategists' responsibility to society is to integrate the organization with the needs of society.

30

But what is responsibility? Is it something that one *has* to perform because one is held responsible by somebody else? Is this the meaning of "duty"? In one respect, yes. The exchange view of organizations shows us that, if strategists do not play this role, not only can current rewards and punishments be exercised by various constituencies, but the long-term development of the organization will mean that there eventually will be no organization to integrate.

Or is responsibility something that comes from within? In part that is also true. As we will see, successful strategists who can perform their more practical work of strategy and policy formulation learn the values in society. They internalize various demands as they go about the day-to-day experimentation that policy formulation involves.

The idea that managers are or should be integrators is not new. Follett, writing earlier in this century, proposed that managers perform this same essential function when dealing with conflict between work-level employees and administrators.[1] More recently, Lawrence and Lorsch, studying conflict at the administrative level, proposed that the central function of higher-level managers is to integrate the needs, viewpoints, and orientations of middle managers on the one hand, with the requirements of technical efficiency on the other.[2] Kotter and others, addressing the theory and processes of organizations, showed that managers use certain technologies (internal organization structure, measurement and control systems, reward systems, and selection-development systems), as *instruments* to integrate the needs of administrators and work-level employees into the firm's required technical operations.[3] In one sense, the entire field of *human* organization development has grown up to show managers how to integrate the internal resource system of the organization (TI in the expectations matrix) with the needs of employees (CI in the matrix).[4]

Whereas those studies focus on the role of *administrators* as they attempt to integrate conflicting parts of the *internal* administrative system, others have focused on the role of *strategists* as they attempt to integrate the internal demands on organizations (TI, CI), with the external society (TE, CE). Philip Selznick's *Leadership in Administration*,[5] Kenneth Andrews' *Concept of Corporate Strategy*,[6] Chester Barnard's *Functions of the Executive*,[7] Charles Lindblom's *Policy Making Process*,[8] and Henry Mintzberg's *Nature of Managerial Work*,[9] all have a common thread. They focus on the role of strategists as they try to cope with the entire range of demands, both inside and outside the organization, and as they try somehow to build an organization that will, through evolutionary time, serve society, receive support in return, and therefore survive and grow.

Ethical Responsibility in Organizations:
The Competence Role

Another way of viewing the ultimate responsibility of general managers is to focus on their crucial function in relation to the organization. If the integrator role shows that organizations are instruments for the betterment of society, the organizational building role shows that strategic leadership is the primary instrument that builds organizations. If one observes the leadership behavior of the strategic group in Sears, Roebuck, the leadership behavior of the strategic group in the Boston Symphony Orchestra (Chapter 5), or the leadership behavior of Mr. Champion, undersecretary of Health, Education and Welfare (Chapter 4), we can see an emphasis on building the internal competences of organizations, their internal technical systems, and their human systems, to face the future.

This is why cell TI in the social expectations matrix is labeled a *goal* of productive organizations, rather than simply a *means* to achieve the ultimate goal of producing products and services (TE). In Chapter 3 we will see that internal task efficiency (TI) is indeed vital to the production of useful products and services (TE). But here we are stressing the strategists' responsibility to the organization. (The long-term development of competences [TI] is an important end in itself.) Reasoning behind this goes back to Chapter 1. Unless the organization can continuously increase in its own internal competences, it will not survive to meet successive challenges in society.

Social Responsibilities:
The Pluralistic Role

There is great concern in today's society about the social responsibilities of general managers. The problem is expressed in such terms as, "a loss of leadership," or "a failure of leaders to discharge their responsibilities to the public."

This problem surfaced first in the private sector. Corporations are believed by many to produce products that are not "good" for society, to arrange their internal operations in a way that is not "good" for employees, or to pay off their stockholders in profits that are not deserved (notice the implication that there is not a fair exchange between value given to society and value received from society). There are great debates on whether or not the ultimate goal of

32

business corporations is *effective and efficient task performance*, *effective cultural performance*, or *efficient human performance* (i.e., contribution to the satisfaction and growth of employees). Businessmen are bombarded not only by constituencies' very real demands, but by various paradigms from the social sciences, each of which gives one or the other of these goals ultimate value.

The controversy is not limited to business corporations. Government agencies are coming increasingly under attack from various constituencies. Citizens demand a health care system that will deliver "good" hospital services (defined as effective treatment at low cost) but at the same time charge that services are performed poorly or inefficiently. When strategists in the federal government designed a merit rating system with which they intended to reward productive employees (and therefore to contribute to better services at lower costs), it was labeled "authoritarian," "theory X," a return to the days of inhuman management practices.

In one sense, government and business are converging, becoming alike. Both are being held responsible for the full range of task performance demands and cultural performance demands. It is a central thesis of this book that they *are* becoming more alike. But they have started from different ends of the value spectrum. Government is accused of concentrating too heavily on cultural responsibilities while neglecting its responsibility for productive output and efficiency. Business, on the other hand, is accused of concentrating too much on products and efficiency while neglecting cultural demands.

If we use the social expectations matrix from Chapter 1, case histories will show that these expectations, from the viewpoint of the constituencies involved, are *ethics*. They are beliefs about what the organization *ought* to do to satisfy the needs of the various constituencies. "Responsibility" in this sense means that strategists are expected to take into account the needs of constituencies as *the constituencies* (not the strategists) define them. Such a view of ethics means that there are four ethical responsibilities required of strategists by society:

A1. The ethic of effective task performance.
A2. The ethic of efficient task performance.
B1. The ethic of effective (external) cultural performance.
B2. The ethic of efficient (internal) cultural performance.

This pluralistic view of ethics is an important starting point which strategists can use to make sense of the general theme "social responsibility." It is useful because it at least identifies what ethics (plural) are involved, and whose ethics *must* be taken into account (according to the social exchange point of view) or whose ethics *ought to be* taken into account (according to the viewpoint in Part IV of this book).

The Strategic Ethic:
The Judgment Role

The pluralistic viewpoint of ethics just presented raises two other difficult questions. First, what about the *strategists' ethics?* Are strategists pawns in all of this, who must somehow follow the rule that might makes right, proposing policies that somehow please the constituencies that have the strongest rewards and penalties? That is what the social exchange theory leads to. Second, even if we can propose some way of trading off, balancing, reconciling, or optimizing the various demands of society, what is the ultimate decision rule by which we tell right from wrong?

Answers to these two questions should emerge in this book. To the first, we propose that the central ethical function of strategists in society is indeed to make judgments that reconcile conflicting ethics. The answer to the second question will be discussed in Part IV.

Work Responsibilities of Strategists:
Formulating Alignments

Philosophies are one aspect of strategic leadership. They give a person not only cognitive guidance for further action, but emotional motivation (arousal) to marshall the energy to engage in further action. But if we stop with philosophy alone, it is like going to church on Sunday and then, not knowing how to translate sermons into action, very likely sinning on Tuesday, Wednesday, and Thursday.

Somehow we must begin to get closer to the specific things and people strategists cope with—what they "integrate," or what competences they build. We must also get closer to how they go about integrating or building the processes they use.

We will now move down the ladder of abstraction one step closer to reality. We will see how leadership philosophy is translated into real things and real people and what processes leaders use to do this. In Chapters 3–5 we should move all the way to reality. Those chapters will show real strategists coping with real technologies and social groups.

Here, then, is a middle-range model of the work responsibilities of strategists. It deals with *what* strategists align to reach the philosophical goal of integration and *how* they go about aligning.

What Is Being Aligned: Content

We have already seen that the social expectations matrix presented in Chapter 1 can be interpreted in two ways. From an exchange view, it shows what groups are dependent on the organization and what their needs and self-interests are. It also shows that these groups might either support or withdraw support from the organization. From the viewpoint of ethics, it shows what different groups believe the organization *ought* to achieve to satisfy their self-interests, and therefore, to be a good organization.

To convert this matrix to terms that are actually *operational* for the strategist, we must translate it into those things that actually make up the world around the strategic group, those which it can at least partly manipulate or control.

It turns out that those things are on the left side of the matrix. We shall see that when strategists in the nursing home industry try to grapple with intangible values, whether a particular demand for task effectiveness (service output to elderly persons), for task efficiency (x-ray equipment to carry out the work inside the nursing home), or cultural efficiency (satisfying work for nurses inside the nursing home), the *only* means strategists have of trying to satisfy these demands is to "work on" or "change" the *product or service* (TE) offered by the nursing home or the *design of internal resources and processes* in the nursing home (TI).

The same is true for strategists in Sears, Roebuck and Company. If there is a demand for justice in promoting disadvantaged persons who work for Sears (CI, the demand for equal opportunity), the only thing Sears strategists have to work on is the work design inside the company, including reward systems, promotion systems, and the like. If automobiles in the parking lot of the Sears store in Atlanta are polluting the atmosphere with exhaust fumes, and citizens object (CE, the demand for ecological balance and human health), the *only* thing Sears strategists have to work with is the structure of physical capital (in this case, a parking lot) that is part of the total company operating alignment. Task alignments in the organization will be more clearly understood in Chapter 5. There, they will be broken down into still more identifiable systems of technology and systems of human organization.

In summary, what the strategist aligns is a framework of:

1. Product/markets or service/constituencies of the organization (TE, Chapter 4).
2. The network of internal parts of the organization: its physical capital, its administrative organization, its technological or work processes, and its work-level organization design (Chapter 5).

Importance of Recognizing Content

Why is it important to recognize the fact that *task* elements are the only ones which strategists work on? The first reason has already been given. It is the only thing they *can* work on, at least in their roles as strategists.

The second reason is to emphasize that when successful strategists work on task performance, they are not, as some think, simply hardheaded economists or engineers, focusing on the mechanical side of life and unaware of the human side. Nor are they efficiency experts or bureaucrats (in the "bad sense") somehow imbued with the idea that stopwatches and rule systems are the end values in life. Chapters 6–9 will show that at times managers indeed act this way. So do work-level employees, and so do resource suppliers outside the organization. But in attributing these types of dysfunctional behavior to strategists as a group one ignores the behavior of strategists who do in fact start with humanistic demands to formulate product policies of the organization (TE), to formulate the markets these products serve (TE), and to formulate internal resources that align with society's demands (TI).

Organization Builders

Another important way of viewing the work responsibilities of strategists is to recognize that they are *organization builders*, or, more accurately, builders of *organization competences*. Whereas the previous section shows what strategists work on at any one time, it ignores the fact that organizations do not come into the world as full-blown, clockwork mechanisms, instantly ready to do the world's work. Instead, they develop very slowly. The learning curve needed to build competences of the type Toynbee refers to may cover many decades, even centuries.

In this view, it is the entire organization that is the operational workshop of the strategist. In the last analysis, the strategist is developing two kinds of organizational competences:

1. A *social competence:* a set of output goals to society, a set of products matched with markets, or services matched with client constituencies (TE).
2. A *resource competence:* a complex network of internal resources (TI), that will in fact produce those output goals.

Somewhat more accurately stated, successful strategists are able to build into the organization a *distinctive* competence,[10] one that somehow carves out a niche in the world that is different from that of

36

other organizations. The German automotive manufacturer, Bosch A.G., produces a fuel injection system that is different from those of other manufacturers. This concept of distinctive competence is important for two reasons. First, it determines how *valuable* the organization is to society, and therefore how much society will *support* the organization in return for its contribution. Second, it determines how much power and influence the organization has in the outside world. In a competitive situation, we can easily see that an industry with a very high distinctive competence will command both resource support and political support.

For example, the energy producing industry has branches with distinctive competences to produce electricity (utility companies), to drill wells (oil companies), or to mine ores (coal- and uranium-producing companies). These organizations, regardless of whether they are owned by governments in Europe or by private corporations in the United States, are in one way or another going to get resource support and political support from society.

Third, from the cultural anthropology view, distinctive competence determines which organizations will, in a survival-of-the-fittest sense, survive and grow. Those organizations which can develop a *comparative advantage*, a set of competences better than other organizations', will survive and grow. Those which have little to offer in the way of specialization and comparative advantage will disintegrate.

Strategy Formulation

A *strategy*, viewed at one static point of time, is a broad, comprehensive, holistic, gestalt network of *policies* which pictures products or services to be rendered to the outside world (TE), and a logically related network of internal resources (TI) necessary to produce that product or service. It is a conceptual framework in the strategist's mind.

In the inception stage, when there *is* no real, objective strategy, no actual products and services or resources yet in existence, this vision is rather simple. It is a hypothesis predicting how the whole system *should* operate.

We have already seen the visionary strategy of Hewlett and Packard and the strategy of Kemsley and Kern as they conceived the Hewlett-Packard Corporation and the American Hiking Association.

As the organization grows through Stage 2, things get more complicated. Both technologies ("things") and social conditions ("people") are unpredictable. The real world never works like broad visions indicate.

37

Suppose that Hewlett and Packard had envisioned a certain way to produce the telescope device. That is, they had formulated a certain production policy. Suppose further that six months later the factory engineer comes in and says that it will not work and explains why. Or suppose that Mrs. Packard, the bookkeeper, discovers that the materials visualized in the production policy will violate the regulations of the Occupational Safety and Health Act. The production vision would then be prohibited by the United States government. What happens then? One choice is to change the *product* policy, to abandon the telescope device altogether. Another choice is to change the *production* policy, to envision a new production line that will work technically, or the use of materials that will not violate government regulations. Of course, this may affect the financial policy, because the capital equipment may cost more than the production equipment originally visualized.

This hypothetical case shows some vital characteristics of what a strategy is, and of how strategies are formulated. Strategies are indeed logically connected networks of policies. But they are only *approximations* of reality, to be tested in the real world of policy formulation.

Strategy and Policy: A Two-way Process

We have just seen that strategy formulation and policy formulation influence each other. Which comes first? At the *very beginning*, in stage 1, strategy precedes policy. After that, it is anybody's guess. Sometimes strategists adjust their strategic whole and try to make specific policies fit it. At other times they adjust their visions to the realities of the world.

This fact is made clear in Chapter 5. There, we will see strategists engaging in a kind of heuristic decision making to focus first on one part of the organization's task (an individual policy) and then on another (another policy). This will be called *task heuristics*. In longer time periods, strategists sometimes make major breakthroughs, trying to change a comprehensive network of interrelated policies in a period of crisis, or, if the crisis is great enough, trying to readjust the whole complex system at once. Chapter 6 will show that the same thing happens when strategists have to cope with cultural demands on the organization. One group may be demanding equal employment rights, another group may be demanding that the product be changed for health reasons, still another may be demanding that the production line be changed to give human beings more work satisfaction and growth. In these cases, the strategist is forced to switch the focus of policymaking to take into account these unpredictable

38

events, and to change the entire strategic vision. This will be called *cultural heuristics*.

In any event, this relationship between policy formulation and strategy formulation shows that policy formulation is a way of *learning*. It also develops real competences—learned ways of doing things that *work*.

The way strategies relate to policies also throws light on one of the great puzzles in history. Do heroes make history (do strategic visions shape the world) or does history make heroes (do the realities of practical experiences shape strategists' visions)? The answer is, both. Strategic vision shapes policy formulation but policy formulation shapes strategic vision.

Policy Formulation

By this time it is evident that policy formulation is a slow, evolutionary, trial-and-error discovery process that accomplishes two things at once. It works out the increments or pieces of the strategy, taking into account the strategic whole. It starts from a synopsis of the whole situation and proceeds to elaborate the details. At the same time, it serves as a learning device for increments and pieces that are *workable*, thus changing the synopsis of the whole.

One author has described this process as a *series of successive approximations*.[11] The comprehensive strategic vision is never achieved in the real world. Instead, it is *approximated* as the organization grows and develops.

Perceived Versus Objective Strategy

In the field of organization theory, current research addresses what sometimes seems to be a complicated question. The question is: are strategies in the last analysis subjective visions in the mind of top management or are they objective products, services, equipment, buildings and work processes, entities that can be seen, touched and verified? Are they private perceptions in the minds of certain people or are they the brute facts of reality?

The concepts of strategy formulation and policy formulation just presented answer this question. Real life strategies of a corporation or government agency emerge, over time, from *both* the vision of managers and from the forces of nature that cannot be predicted or controlled. To argue from a purist standpoint that either of these factors is dominant in world affairs is a fruitless endeavor.

Influence and Power Roles of Strategists

In Part IV we will discuss more fully the influence and power roles in strategic leadership. In broadest terms, strategists approach the

39

uask of influencing other parties in the strategic arena in three ways: (1) they align the organization, over long periods of time, with the diverse needs and self-interests in society, (2) they use this alignment *itself* as a means of influencing the behavior of constituencies, and (3) because alignments are never perfect, they use whatever power and authority they have to enforce imperfect alignments.[12]

Task Alignments as Power and Influence

The strategic alignment, and the incremental policy alignments, if successful, are the central instruments of power and influence available to strategists in business and government.

Though we shall have to wait for Chapter 10 to understand this more fully, at this point here we can state the essentials of the argument. Briefly, organizations that are *really* aligned to society's diverse needs have power: they naturally attract both physical resources and political support in exchange for their contributions. They also have a certain kind of influence: an influence based on legitimacy in the eyes of constituencies.

As a result of this legitimacy, the balance of power in society confers autonomy on the strategic group. Constituencies in effect delegate political authority to that group to continue what has been, in the past, a successful institution, corporation or agency. They also reward effective performance by giving leaders intellectual discretion to make decisions in the future.

There is another force which causes society to delegate authority and discretion to the strategic group. Constituencies may consciously *reason* that the organization is doing an effective job and that therefore it, and its strategists, have authority to proceed. But constituencies may also have an intuitive *feeling* or *belief in* strategists' actions, without ever being too clear about why. This is charismatic authority. It will be explained further in Chapter 10. It results not only from actions of the leader, but from the needs of followers for stability and security (which strategy formulation provides) and at the same time for dynamism and change (which policy formulation provides).

Initiative Influence and Resource Power

Strategists in organizations that are reasonably well aligned have other sources of influence and power which grow out of their formal and informal activities in the system. They are specialists, who know

40

a great deal about the system. This, plus the fact that others in the system have less legitimacy status, means that they have a certain power to initiate change that is not possessed by others in the system. Political scientists have called this kind of power "feasibility power" because strategists are most likely to know how to respond to the diverse demands of society with alternatives that are actually *feasible*, rather than with alternatives that are unworkable.

Strategists also have a kind of power that is obvious to all, resource power or the power to invoke sanctions. The sources of such power are the official offices or positions strategic group members occupy. The amount of resource power possessed by top managers varies greatly between societies, between organizations and between different time epochs in the same society or organization. Part IV will argue that if other forms of power and influence have been used to the maximum (task alignments, charisma, initiative), conscious use of sanctions becomes a residual concept. Successful strategists use sanctions to enforce alignments only after other sources of influence and power have been exhausted. If other actors in the strategic system are already cooperating because they want to cooperate, together they form an important *zone of support* which requires no use of sanctions. On the other hand, since it is impossible ever to achieve complete integration of the organization in society (i.e., to reconcile all conflicting demands being made), there remains a residual *zone of opposition*, a set of constituencies which for one reason or another oppose strategies and policies. It is in this zone that successful strategists in both business and government use whatever sanctions they have to secure compliance.

Ethics and Power

Lord Acton's famous words, "Power tends to corrupt and absolute power corrupts absolutely," signal a warning as we approach the subject of ethics and power. The ethical use of power is not a subject which can be covered in three easy lessons and it cannot be discussed in the required depth in this introductory chapter. Part IV will argue two things. First, successful strategists (i.e., those who influence organizations into real social alignment) derive a final additional form of power from the processes of strategy formulation and policy formulation, a kind of power that comes not from society around the organization but from within the belief system of the strategic group. This power is a willingness and self-confidence to use all means at its disposal (task alignment, charisma, initiative, sanctions) to keep the organization in long term alignment with the needs of society.

41

Because such a feeling (self-confidence, willingness to use other forms of power) is in the last analysis based on belief in one's own ethical righteousness, it can be called ethical power. We see it in individuals who, because of it, simply marshall the energy and willingness to act.

But what separates this kind of self-righteousness from that possessed by those people who, in the name of God and nature, have actually done great harm to society? Is there any reason why self-righteous strategists are any different from zealots and dictators who have distorted strategic visions? Chapter 10 will provide two answers. There are certain reasons why successful strategy and policy leadership serve as correct devices to protect the ethics of society. In addition, there are certain normative guidelines that will help leaders to keep their ultimate goals reasonably in line with society.

Finally, what happens at the third stage of organization evolution, the stage when conflict appears and signs of breakdown occur? By definition, this stage is one in which the organization's zone of opposition expands, in which the organization is getting out of alignment. This may be caused by the sheer number of cultural constituencies that are affected negatively as the organization grows or by the fact that products and services rendered get out of date with needs of consuming task constituencies.

What kind of ethical guidelines are appropriate under such conditions? Should strategists use sanctions to bring things back into alignment? The answer is no. As Chapters 6–9 show, this would only *increase* the opposition of those who challenge the organization. It would bring things one step closer to Stage 5, disintegration.

Notes

1. Mary Parker Follett, "Constructive Conflict," in *Dynamic Administration*, Edited by H. C. Metcalf and L. Urwick, Harper, 1940.

2. Paul Lawrence and Jay Lorsch, *Organization and Environment*, Harvard Business School, Division of Research, 1967.

3. John P. Kotter, L. A. Schlesinger, and V. Sathe, *Organizations*, Richard D. Irwin, 1979.

4. For example, see Chris Argyris, *Intervention Theory and Method*, Addison-Wesley, 1970.

5. Harper, 1957.

6. Dow-Jones Irwin, 1971.

7. Harvard University Press, 1938.

8. Prentice-Hall, 1968.

9. Harper, 1973.

10. This concept is taken from Selznick, *Leadership in Administration*.

11. This concept is taken from Barnard, *Functions of the Executive*.

12. This concept of leadership follows that in Lindblom, *Policy Making Process*.

PART II

TASK ALIGNMENT IN GROWTH AND DEVELOPMENT

PRODUCTIVE ORGANIZATIONS that survive and grow do so in a long evolutionary life cycle, the strategic cycle. We have seen that the first stage in this cycle is inception. Strategists visualize or conceptualize a comprehensive strategy composed of two things at once: (1) a set of products or services that they believe will secure support from outside consumers and resource suppliers (a network of product/market or service/constituency policies) and (2) a set of broad internal resources for producing the product or service (a network of resource allocation policies).

As organizations pass the inception stage they must convert visions and concepts to reality. It is one thing to have visions. But as most businessmen-entrepreneurs who have failed after the first stage can attest, it is quite another thing to elaborate and operationalize the vast number of details necessary to build an *institution*, a viable and successful corporation or government agency.

Another way of saying this is that in the second stage of the strategic cycle strategists face the problem of real *task performance* and alignment. Not only must the demands of persons "out there" (TE) be analyzed more specifically, but the resources "in here" must be cast in terms of complicated technologies. Realistic resource allocation policies must be formulated: capital equipment and buildings must be designed (TI.11), organization structures must be specified and developed (TI.12), operating processes must be engineered (TI.21), and job descriptions (work roles) must be developed for those who will actually carry out the work (TI.22).

It is the purpose of Part II to explain the problem of task performance and show how it is solved. Chapter 3 will concentrate on the demands of outside constituencies (TE). It will show that both business strategists and government strategists are subject to the same demands. Over the strategic life cycle, there are three demands of key importance in survival and growth. These are the demand for low price utility (TE.1), the demand for highest use products and services (TE.3), and the demand for efficiency or low cost utility (TE.4). In addition, strategists in some private corporations are subject to a demand that has been central in the study of free enterprise economics (TE.2). This demand for high price utility is indeed important in the economists' "short run" and "long run." And it complicates matters for strategists in firms that are monopolies or that are in monopolistic competition. However, in the *strategic run* this demand is overriden by the power of the other three. In the strategic life cycle all businesses and all government agencies are alike. They are subject to the three key demands.

Chapter 3 will also explain the institutional structure of government organizations which produce goods and services. Though government-owned industries with concise organization structures are well-known entities in Yugoslavia, Britain, and Russia, they are not so well known in the United States. We shall look at city and state industries, national industries, federal industries, and quasi-government industries. In Chapter 4, we shall see that federal industries are relatively newly developing in the United States. Like many other things in this culture, they simply "evolve." And they have striking strategic similarity to General Motors, AT&T, or IBM. Strategists in Washington formulate the broad product, constituency, and internal resource allocation policies in health care or education, for example. Then middle managers in states and cities elaborate these into detailed resource allocation networks.

Chapter 4 will concentrate on the behavior of strategists as they formulate products and services for a specific constituency (TE.1). Whereas we analyze the behavior of constituencies in Chapter 3, we want to see the behavior of general managers in Chapter 4. We will see that such behavior in a food store chain is similar to that in a federal industry (the education industry), a national industry (the Post Office, the Social Security Administration), and a quasi-government organization (the Port of Seattle). Finally, Chapter 4 will show that there is actually some demand in the United States to treat the whole national society as a productive organization. Were the federal budget to be made in the spirit of "zero-based budgeting," or were certain legislative proposals such as the Economic Planning Act of 1975 instituted, the federal government could be analyzed as a giant conglomerate, prioritizing goals according to the demands for low cost utility (TE.1), for highest use services (TE.3), and for most efficient use of scarce resources (TE.4).

Chapter 5 continues to explore what now becomes the long, laborious, complex process of comprehensive task alignment. As the organization's life cycle proceeds, an almost impossibly complex set of internal resources must be assembled. Capital structures, organization structures, operating work processes, and job designs must all be logically related to each other and to the ultimate goal, the production of some useful product or service for human beings that constitute a market or a constituency. Although in the literature of policy and strategy this process is usually depicted as either a synoptic, rational, "masterminded" plan by top managers or as an incremental, piecemeal, disjointed, "muddling" coping by diverse interest groups, we shall see that in real case histories (as opposed to

45

closed system either/or theories) the process consists of both kinds of behavior at once. Throughout the task alignment stage this is a chicken-and-egg phenomenon. Strategists have broad conceptual visions. But these do not often work in reality. No strategist can predict the behavior of all constituencies. No strategist can predict the functioning of internal technologies (i.e., how the machines, the organization structure, the processes for getting out the work, or job descriptions assigned to workers will work). As a result, the master-minded visions of strategists interact with real people and technologies. There is a process of learning, adaptation, trial-and-error discovery, and piecemeal (incremental) adjustment. During this process of piece-by-piece decision making (which we call *policy-making*), the behavior of strategists is to change their comprehensive visions or strategies, their gestalts, their holistic picture of ends (products/services) and means (internal resource configurations). This behavior we call *strategy formulation*.

In summary, Part II depicts the stage of task alignment. In it we see which constituencies demand which ultimate value outputs from the firm or agency. We also see what strategists and policymakers *do* to comply with these demands. They engage simultaneously in strategy formulation (gestalt, holistic, comprehensive task alignment) and policy formulation (piecemeal, incremental formulation of task policies).

CHAPTER 3

Society's Demands for Task Alignment

Utility: The Ultimate Goal

In Chapter 1 powerful forces that bring productive organizations into being and support organizations as they grow and develop were explained. The first of these forces is the demand by human beings for products and services that meet deep psychological needs.

Economists have long held that all human beings seek physical products or invisible services that have an attribute called *utility*. Utility, in the last analysis, is the want-gratifying power of some good or service. At the same time, cognitive psychologists have pointed to the fact that material objects and services are *instrumental* to more basic needs. The hungry person finds utility in food. Food is an instrument for the satisfaction of a basic need: nourishment. The human being needing protection from raw nature finds utility in a house. The house is instrumental for the satisfaction of basic needs: shelter and warmth. The person who needs friendship and love finds that there is utility in a telephone call. Such a service is instrumental to a basic social need. A person who needs security finds utility in the operation of a police patrol. Such a service is instrumental to basic safety needs. This same utility is found in an insurance policy (instrumental to family security), a mortgage loan from a bank (instrumental to security of shelter), a day-care service for children (security for protection of loved ones), or a sanitation/garbage service (the maintenance of physical health).

In this sense, the primary and ultimate goal of *all* productive organizations, whether the Chase Manhattan Bank, the City of Detroit Sanitation Department, the Family and Child Service Association of Los Angeles (a Community Chest affiliate), General Motors Corporation, or the police department in Atlanta, is the

47

production of utility by means of a product or service to a certain constituency. The same might be said for the police department in Buenos Aires, the Commissariat of Agricultural Equipment in Moscow (Russian equivalent of a single farm equipment company producing tractors for growing wheat), or the Matsushita Electric Company in Tokyo.

Traditional economics has also regarded utility as the ultimate goal in the free enterprise paradigm. Utility and marginal utility are the *starting points*, the ultimate value goals, of all theories following this paradigm. Unfortunately, today the two leading basic textbooks on economics state bluntly that the purpose of business organizations is to make a profit, whereas the purpose of government organizations is to render a service.

The position taken in this book, and one that will be supported by case histories, is that *all* organizations are subject to the demand for utility. Over the long strategic life cycle, no organization can survive without supplying utility to customers and clients. If the organization fails to achieve this goal, resource suppliers from the outside will eventually cut off the support so necessary to survival.

Full comprehension of the reasons why the demand for low price utility (TE.1) prevails over the demand for high price utility made by stockholders in monopoly firms (TE.2) must wait until one has studied Chapters 3–6. For the present, we shall simply acknowledge three reasons. First, over the strategic life cycle of an organization, survival, growth or decline depends on massive innovation in the entire task alignment (TE/TI). Stockholders are one, but only one of the constituencies whose self-interests must be satisfied. Other groups in the responsibility matrix must be satisfied, too.

Second, even in what the economists have called the "short run" and the "long run," corporations that are in situations approximating pure competition have stockholders whose interests are in harmony with the consumer, very much as Adam Smith predicted in his theory of the "unseen hand."

Third, economic forces are not the only ones that ensure the dominance of low price utility. This chapter will show that *social* and *political forces* operate to enforce this demand over the organization's life cycle.

Low Price Utility (TE.1): Case Histories from Business

In this section, we will examine several case histories showing that goods and services indeed satisfy basic human needs, that business

48

corporations and nonprofit organizations in fact respond by inventing products and services that possess utility, and that both consumers and resource suppliers have certain ways to enforce their demands. They support those organizations which satisfy the demand for low price utility. They bring sanctions against those companies which do not. These sanctions may be economic (the withholding of money), social (the shaping of public opinion), or political (the invoking of rules by government).

Because it is sometimes difficult to trace the connection between utility in different types of goods and services, we will devote separate attention to:

Gasoline and kilowatts of electricity: a consumer soft good and consumer service

Mopeds and paper tissues: a consumer durable good and a consumer soft good

Audio speakers and retail stores: a consumer durable good and a consumer service

Electric motors, packing cartons, computers, stoves for camping vehicles: industrial goods

Consumer Goods and Services in Time of Crisis

In an affluent society such as the industrialized West, perhaps the real value of consumer products is never realized with bold impact except in time of crisis. Two of such crises have been covered by serious research, the Northeast power blackout of November 1965,[1] and the gasoline and fuel oil crisis of 1973–74.[2] The objective of the research was to discover the human value of a kilowatt of electricity (in the case of the power blackout) or a gallon of gasoline or fuel oil (in the case of the oil crisis).

A kilowatt of electricity, it turns out, is a very powerful thing in a humanistic sense. During the Northeast power blackout, Mrs. Monserrata, 35 years old, gave birth by flashlight to a second of her twins at Mount Sinai Hospital. Captain George of Air Canada and Captain Lofstedt of Scandinavian Airlines, each saw Kennedy Airport suddenly go dark as they approached for a night landing. One had 80 human beings aboard and the other 89. Each of these passengers, as human beings, had different ultimate reasons for traveling, ranging from visits with loved ones to attending to their careers and work. At the Walpole (Mass.) prison, 300 inmates tossed chairs about and ripped plumbing from the walls. In Syracuse, an Eastern Ambulance Service ambulance, receiving an emergency call, could not leave through the electrically controlled garage door. Theodore

49

Brophy found his train stalled between New York and his home town. Mr. Vange Burnett, a 52-year-old hotel guest from Florida, was found dead at the bottom of an elevator shaft with a partly burned candle near his hand. Radio and television programs were cancelled. For six days major New York newspapers could not start their presses. U Thant, secretary general of the United Nations, and his staff, were trapped for five hours on the 38th floor of headquarters, and undersecretary Bunche injured his leg coming down 34 floors in darkness. Temperatures were below freezing. The blackout covered 80,000 square miles (from Toronto to Vermont, Rhode Island, Massachusetts, Connecticut, New York, and New Jersey) and affected 30 million people in the United States and Canada. Nine months after the blackout, the birth rate in New York City rose to an unusually high statistical percentage, which could not be accounted for by random error.

Space does not permit full description of the many effects of the oil crisis of 1973–74. Gasoline is a chemical compound produced by enormously complicated internal operating technology at the refinery. In the automobile's engine, at 40 miles per hour, gasoline vapors equal to one drop of liquid enter each of six or eight cylinders 13 times per second. It must begin burning in each cylinder at exactly the right time, causing, in effect, 13 explosions in that cylinder-second. At the time, there were 220,000 filling stations in the United States, each selling this product. According to California state officials, 19,000 persons there temporarily lost their jobs because of oil shortages. In Oakland, one filling station operator was rationing gasoline at four gallons per customer. When he declined to sell one customer more fuel, he was shot and killed. Ellen Jackson, of Oakton, Virginia, could not get to a store for groceries for her family (the nearest one was three miles away). Garrett Oppenheim, a crippled resident of Rockland County, New York, felt that, as the shortage worsened, he would be unable to get to his work as an editor of a medical magazine. "If it gets worse, I'd be stranded. No shopping, no errands, no visiting friends. After I got a hand-controlled car, people were honking at me instead of making way for me on the street. The car puts me in a competitive position with everyone else. Because of it I have more self-respect. To have gasoline and the car threatened is a dreadful feeling." A federal Office of Economic Opportunity survey showed that the poor and elderly were hit particularly hard by the shortage of home heating oil. The Maine OEO office moved to establish emergency fuel depots for these people. As one psychologist interpreted it, "the meaning of it all is that people see gasoline now in terms of basic survival. Whenever you have anything with that kind of value on it, people are going to fight for it. They do things they would not ordinarily do."

A recent research study conducted in England simulates a time of crisis. In it, five young couples simulated life as it was lived by Iron-Age Celts who lived near London 2200 years ago. They lived together in a house made of sticks, grass, and mud, lit only by fire and the daylight that came through two low doors. They grew vegetables, raised boars, cows, chickens, and goats, and kept a polecat for catching rabbits. They shaped pottery, forged tools, built cartwheels, wove cloth, cured the skins of animals. They had no soap, running water, coffee, or newspapers. They found some enjoyment in this life, but there were "things we longed for, like beer, and books to read, and warm baths, and comfortable shoes."[3]

Mopeds and Paper Tissues

The following examples may seem pedestrian when discussed so briefly. The purpose of presenting them is simply to become accustomed to diagnosing the product output goal in terms of ultimate meaning to human beings. That is, to think of products in terms of *utility*.

Consider the case of mopeds, two-wheeled, single cylinder vehicles, something of a hybrid between bicycles and motorcycles.[4] They weigh only 80 pounds, will travel 25–30 miles per hour, and average 160 miles per gallon of gasoline. Fifteen million of these vehicles are used by men and women in Europe today, in traveling to work, and in recreation. They are found in great numbers on the streets of Amsterdam and in the parks and recreation areas throughout Holland. Thirty-three states in the United States have approved these vehicles for use without the complicated licensing of motorcycles. They are quiet (less noise pollution) and easy to handle, allowing the person to pedal at times and use the motor at other times. The fact that 15 million persons in Europe use them is ample evidence that they indeed serve as instruments for recreation, for sheer enjoyment of leisure, for physical exercise, or for going to work. The greatly increased use of bicycles in the United States is evidence that this product also fulfills such needs. They are also instrumental to physical fitness and health.

Or, consider the consumer products of Scott Paper Company, and try to visualize the ultimate values produced for human beings: bathroom tissue, household towels, table napkins, facial tissues, food wraps, sanitary napkins, and baby wipes. These products may be traced to the need for human health, or human comfort as compared to that of persons living in preindustrial society.

Audio Speakers, Retail Services, and Symphony Concerts

Utility is also found in consumer durable goods, as contrasted with services (electricity) and soft goods (gasoline). Matsushita Electric in Tokyo produced 60 million audio speakers each year in 12 speaker factories in 11 countries. For those seeking joy in beauty, specifically the beauty of music, the utility of this product can range from sheer recreation to positive self-actualization.

Retailing services provide what economists call time-and-place utility. Products and services are of no value if the consumer is located in Texas in June and the product is located in Ohio in August. Hence, for example, Recreational Equipment Company, through both retail stores and mail-order operations supplies 380,000 human beings with backpacks, tents, sleeping bags, mountain safety equipment, and clothing.

Even in the arts we find the demand for low-cost utility in consumer services. The symphony orchestra industry is an organization that provides higher order needs of human beings, the need for aesthetic beauty, for tranquility, and for self-actualization. In a recent article the *Economist* of London reported that, though the orchestras of the world are faced with increasing cost of musicians' salaries, and are in serious financial difficulty, those who make policies for these orchestras do not dare to raise prices of tickets because the public believes that orchestra music must be available to large numbers of people at low prices. This same responsibility is found in a strategic planning case history of the Boston Symphony Orchestra,[5] to be presented in Chapter 5.

Industrial Goods and Services

One problem faced by organizations is that it is sometimes difficult to trace the *utility* in industrial goods, those goods which are not produced directly for the consumer, but for other producers who in turn satisfy the final consumer. If the organization produces iron ore, its product is sold to steel mills, which in turn produce hundreds of different products for sale to other producers: automobile companies, aluminum cookware companies, lawnmower companies, dental instrument companies, and so on. To complicate matters further, the cookware company may sell to wholesalers, who sell to retailers, who in turn sell to consumers.

Economists have called the modern system with its many complex chains of production, a system of "roundabout production," meaning that the production of final utility is often roundabout through diverse input-output connections. In fact, one of the policy analysis tools available to industrial goods producers in both business and government is the input-output analysis first conceptualized by Harvard economist Leontief. Long production chains are often called "Leontief chains." Some examples will help to show how utility can indeed be traced.[6]

Matsushita Electric also produces 50 million electric motors a year, from heavy-duty 100-hp motors that supply power for factories, to motors sold to producers of refrigerators, clothes dryers, air conditioners, dish washers, ice crushers, sewing machines, and pumps for deep-water wells. Wheat farmers use the latter for producing wheat, which is in turn put through a long Leontief chain before it satisfies the need for prevention of hunger. Matsushita's motors are used by a producer of minced onions in Paris, for a machine that picks tea leaves in Russia and India, and for making clothing in New York's garment district. One can see that the original product fans out to a large number of product/market constituencies.

Boise Cascade Corporation, an Idaho wood products company, produces 3 billion "composite cans" for transporting to consumers the basic utility found in hundreds of products from orange juice to motor oil, home insulation caulking, and motor oils. These cans were developed to combine paper, foil, and plastic laminate in such a way that labor costs, basic metal usage, and cost of shipping weight were all reduced, thus lowering prices of the utility to consumers.

Philips Industries of Holland produces a minicomputer to be used by the City of Amsterdam to control its drinking-water-purification process, a dust-monitoring device used in Austria's largest steel works to reduce air pollution, and a gas-monitoring system of twenty stations used by Mexico City for measuring pollution.

IBM produces computer services for 81 of the nation's largest banks, 62 of the largest insurance companies, more than 1200 employee credit unions, 80 automobile finance companies, and 5100 miscellaneous manufacturing companies. A series of computations that in 1952 cost $1.26 to perform can be done in 1978 for seven-tenths of one penny; 180 times less than 15 years earlier or 400 times cheaper if inflation is taken into account. These computers are used in business, schools, hospitals, and municipal governments. More specifically, the fire department in Wichita, Kansas stores information on 400 invalids who live in the city and who may need special help. This information is relayed to firemen while they are speeding to a fire. A computer-based system in Hampton, Virginia, dispatches police over a 54-square-mile area to persons who telephone "emergency," in half the time taken before the system was installed. A patient in a small hospital in Texas receives a computer-analyzed electrocardiogram from a large hospital in Houston, enabling treatment to begin immediately.

In analyzing the structure of the recreational vehicle industry, Harvard casewriters found that there are 1000 companies that supply components: Coleman and Magic Chef supply stoves, for example. There are 704 manufacturers of mobile homes, including Winnebago, the largest. These 704 manufacturers in turn sell through 10,000 dealers: 7000 mobile home dealers, 350 truck dealers, and 2650 farm equipment dealers.[7]

If one thinks deeply about these few cases, the utility in industrial products and industrial services becomes meaningful. It indirectly has a profound effect on society's standard of living. Each firm contributes its own utility (TE.1). The gross national product is the sum of products produced by all firms in society. In the end, the term *standard of living* takes on a humanistic meaning. It is difficult for the untrained analyst to trace the connections between a seemingly mechanistic thing like an electric motor or a computer and the basic needs of humanity. Yet for responsible strategy formulation, involving a choice between which products to produce for which consumers, such an analysis may well be imperative.

Enforcement of Demands: Business Corporations

Since there is a need for low price utility, what kind of mechanisms do constituencies use for enforcing the corresponding managerial responsibility? What means do they use to influence managers to align product and service outputs with the needs of human beings? Two different constituencies, consumers and resource suppliers, utilize different methods. In competitive industries, consumers may simply stop buying, thus cutting off outside funds support for the firm. In monopolistic firms, when competition does not satisfy the demand, there are other methods of enforcement:

Citizens and informal groups may try to publicize their demands in the media.

Citizens may form more formal organizations that use the theme "consumerism" to publicize demands, do scientific analysis on products, or engage in lobbying. Lobbying then becomes a political pressure on government to enforce the demand.

Government itself may take action by passage of antitrust laws, or, as we shall see, by various methods of "moral suasion."

54

Finally, if prices of the product are too high, or the quality of utility out-of-date with consumer demands, new industries with new life cycles will arise to serve the consumer with more utility, lower prices, or both.

Examples of each of these enforcement methods are presented in the following paragraphs.

Price Competition

Consumers in competitive industries also act as resource suppliers. They use the power of money to enforce their demands on the organization. Different cultures have different degrees of competition, and within one culture (the United States, for example) different industries have differing degrees of competition. And competition has at least three forms, two of which ("short run" and "long run") economists have accounted for in their paradigm. One form, "strategic competition," has mostly been ignored by economists.

The fact that there is still a great deal of "short-run" competition in United States industry is known by anyone who has shopped for a suit or dress at different department stores, compared offerings of auto dealers, or watched supermarket advertisements in the newspaper. Most homeowners who buy storm windows or have new water pipes installed secure competitive bids from contractors. Purchasers of industrial products notoriously make their decisions on the basis of which company can supply the technical characteristics of a product (for example, a machine that manufactures shoes) to the middle company in the Leontief chain (a shoe manufacturing company) at the lowest cost. The shoe retailer, then, seeks the shoes from that shoe manufacturer who can supply the shoes with the most *utility* at the *least cost*.

Actions of Consumers and Pressure Groups

Turning now to enforcement by means other than competition, we see that individuals and small informal groups may use the press as a leader. Consider this letter to the editor of *Business Week*, written by a citizen, Elbert Smith, of Hollywood, Florida:

> I own a number of rental apartments that are, most unfortunately, furnished with Westinghouse appliances. Over the past five years, the failure rates, poor service, and ridiculous prices for replacement parts leave me with little sympathy for Westinghouse, even if it disappears. Matter not why Westinghouse left the appliance business, I bought a label which I respected, and got stung instead.[8]

At a more formal level, the Louis Harris opinion research organization represents consumers through the press. It reported in 1977 that 50 percent of American consumers believe that they are getting a worse deal than a decade ago, that 61 percent believe that the quality of products has fallen, that 63 percent wanted to complain about a product within the last year and that 47 percent actually did complain.[9]

Using policy analysis as a technique, *Consumer Reports* regularly performs scientific tests on hundreds of products each year. It publishes these for all to see. These tests cover both *utility* and *cost* of products ranging from peanut butter and life insurance to lawnmowers and liquid floor polishers.[10]

Actions of Government

Government in the United States and other industrialized countries has taken an increasingly proactive role in representing consuming constituencies, in effect requiring private companies to comply with the demand for low cost utility. They have done this in two ways, one of which deals with the *quality* or *usefulness* of products, the other of which has to do with the *price* of products and services (their cost to the consumer).

Responding to the demand for high quality utility, as presented by powerful lobbying groups such as that headed by Ralph Nader, the United States government in 1972 passed the Consumer Product Safety Act. In England, the National Consumer Council was not established until 1975. This council is officially recognized by the government to represent consumers, as the Confederation of British Industry represents management and the Trade Union Confederation represents labor, before the Economic Development Council, which advises the government on total economic strategy for the nation.[11]

The Swedish government in 1971 established the National Board for Consumer Policies, with 250 employees to perform policy analysis and elaboration. The director-general of the board also holds the position of consumer ombudsman in the government.[12]

Private sector policymakers have indeed learned from these actions of constituencies. In a poll of 3600 businessmen conducted by the *Harvard Business Review*, 84 percent believe that consumerism is a serious and permanent movement stressing product quality and prices, and that it must be taken into account in policy formulation.[13]

Government not only represents the consumer by ensuring

56

quality. It has for many years reinforced the consumer's demand for a low price utility. One of the most vivid clashes between any private corporation and the United States government was that precipitated when the U. S. Steel Corporation raised its price of steel in 1962. The president of the United States, John F. Kennedy, reacted with the full weight of the government. He used various tactics from Internal Revenue Service investigations to having his personal contacts call customers of the corporation so that they would boycott purchases from U. S. Steel. Diagnosis of this complex case[14] shows that the corporation had not innovated its steel-making processes (TI), and therefore could not offer its product at as low a price as its competitors, the German and Japanese steel companies. Because of the great length of time necessary to change the entire company, U. S. Steel's only shorter-term alternative seemed to be to raise its prices to the American consumer and hope for tariff protection from Japanese companies. But the president of the United States acted as representative of the steel-consuming constituency, and this did not work either. The corporation was forced to rescind its price increase. Its strategists were forced to put more emphasis on developing new capital equipment and new steel-making processes that would produce steel at a lower cost to consumers.

So strong is the government's desire to prevent inflation that sometimes low cost utility (TE.1) overrides the demand for human health and safety (CE). Chapter 7 contains a case history in which one arm of government, to protect this cultural value, sought to change the type of lawnmowers produced by the lawnmower industry. Injuries were being inflicted by existing mowers. However, in order to create a new product which did not threaten human life and health (CE), it was found that companies that produce mowers would have had to add significantly to the price of the product (TE). Using impartial research agencies to verify how much this would cost the public, another government agency intervened at this point. It proposed that the new product not be implemented unless some way be found to prevent the price increase.

Finally, the entire range of antitrust laws were enacted to prevent collusion in raising prices in manufacturing industry. In typical strategy-structure sequence, Congress set up the Federal Trade Commission to elaborate rules to implement the broad goal, that is, to prevent this kind of price increase. In the same way, state agencies regulate the prices to be charged by public utilities. Prices for natural gas and electricity may be raised only if they are justified on the basis of cost of production. No utility company may therefore reap monopolistic profits by charging "too much" for a kilowatt of electricity.

Strategic Competition: The Evolution of New Industries

Most authors in economics (at least the economics of the Western world) have studied two things. First, they have studied the "short-run" behavior of managers. The "short run" is the length of time it takes to sell products already produced. Second, they have studied the "long-run" behavior of managers. The "long run" is the length of time it takes to change the internal capital equipment (TI.11) or the operating process (TI.12) in the firm to produce the same product more efficiently. In both cases, economists have assumed that firms continue to produce the same product for the same customer constituencies (though the number of customers may increase or decline). Economists have invoked the logical construct ceteris paribus: "other things being equal (such as consumer tastes changes, or innovation of new products changes) managers will behave in this fashion."

In making these assumptions, economists have by and large ignored the "strategic-run" behavior of both consumers and managers—the massive and complex changes in comprehensive alignments that we are about to examine in Chapters 3–5. And yet, strategic behavior is perhaps the most powerful instrument managers use to increase the task performance of the corporation, to respond to consumers' demand for utility, and, by adding quantity and variety to the gross national product, to contribute to the material welfare of society. The "quality of life" in society, from this viewpoint, is the standard of living so dearly pursued by under-developed nations and so closely guarded by industrial nations.

Not all economists have ignored this fact. Two branches of the discipline, the economics of industrial organization and the economics of national economic development, have indeed been concerned with understanding how innovation contributes these values to society.

In studying industrial organizations some economists have directly attacked the question, "How much of the increase in the standard of living (the increase in total utility provided to all consumers) is due to innovation in products (TE) or in processes (TE)?" In asking this question, economists are asking for answers like the ones described previously in this chapter: Matsushita Electric's electric motors and audio speakers, or IBM's computer. They are also trying to find out the impact of innovations, innovations that result in enormous benefit to consumers. These range from the humble machine that takes the pits out of olives to the capital innovation at the Metropolitan Museum that brings aesthetic learning to millions of persons seeking historic and artistic satisfaction.

They include lowering the cost of hospital services and the production of high-quality hamburgers consumed at the rate of thirty-seven million each day by a constituency in the United States.

Economists in industrial organization have found, for example, that 36 percent of the increase in total utility produced in the nation is due to innovation of internal production processes (TI).[15] But they have never been able to measure the productivity (increase in the standard of living) caused by innovation in product outputs (TE). Like most competent social scientists, they cannot write about things they cannot measure. Their predicament must not cloud the fact that they, too, have somewhat ignored a most powerful cause of material welfare in society.

As a preliminary to discussing more complex case histories, here are three common sense examples. It costs much less for a human being in Los Angeles to talk with a family member in New York than it did ten years ago, even though inflation has advanced 110 percent. Both the speed of placing the call (a time utility) and the voice quality reproduced (a quality utility) have improved. Thirty years ago no major hotel in Houston, Texas, had central air conditioning, whereas today all hotels (and a majority of private homes) have an air conditioning system. In addition, innovation of the heat pump has lowered the electric bills of consumers (TE.1) while conserving society's scarce energy generating resources, oil and gas (CE). Thirty years ago, the only blankets on the market were made of wool. Expensive blankets were of soft wool, less expensive ones were of coarse wool. Today, blankets are produced of velour, or of open-weave thermal fibers. Their price is far lower than before. Their utility for human beings seeking warmth or comfort is greater.

We shall see in Chapter 4 that two economists and one economic historian have squarely faced the fact that strategic behavior has indeed been a major factor in the increasing quality of life of the western world. Joseph Schumpeter found such behavior to be a central cause of economic development of individual corporations and of the national economic society. More recently, Edith Penrose presented similar arguments. Alfred Chandler went even further. He found that it was not Adam Smith's "invisible hand" of short-run and long-run competition that has given the United States one of the highest standards of living in the world. Instead, it was a highly visible hand—the hand of strategists who could perform the process of comprehensive strategic alignment. It was not Alfred Marshall's "short run" or "long run" that caused the economic welfare of citizens of the United States but the evolutionary and strategic life

59

cycle of Sears, Roebuck, the DuPont Corporation, or 100 other corporations whose history was laboriously recorded.

Finally, there is another case history that shows the power of strategic alignment. It is one in which strategists in government *failed* to formulate strategic alignment. They did so deliberately by (1) creating a legal monopoly based on one kind of service output to two market constituencies and then (2) prohibiting this industry from innovating into a new kind of service which was demanded by the constituencies. At the same time, the strategists tried very hard over many years to *make* the industry supply out-of-date services which did not align with the demand for high quality low cost utility (TE.1). In the end, the TE.1 force won out. Not even government, supplying enormous resources, could stop the engine of innovation as it was fueled by consumer demands.

The case history is of the railroad industry. Railroads supply a transportation service to two constituencies: persons needing freight transported and those seeking transportation as passengers. In 1887, companies in the industry were obeying stockholder demand for high price utility to customers (TE.2). The stockholders wanted more revenues that contributed to profits and dividends. In that year Congress, representing customers, invoked the demand for low cost utility (TE.1). It passed an act specifying that government officials would henceforth regulate rates (prices) charged. It created the Interstate Commerce Commission to elaborate the rules and oversee the rate structure.

Over the long history of the industry, the ICC also held the service/market constant. Its rules would not allow company strategists to enter the trucking business (for freight constituencies), the bus transportation business (for passenger constituencies) or the airline business (for both). As new industries arose to supply either high quality utility (faster, safer, or more punctual transportation) or lower price utility the consumer demand for innovation first appeared as weak. Later it grew stronger and stronger. It has taken a long time for the railroads to decline to their present state especially since the government has tried desperately to keep them healthy. As consumers refused to support them the government poured hundreds of millions of dollars of subsidies into their operations. In the end, consumer demand (TE.1) won out. As we shall see, taxpayers have their demands, too. They demand that their resources be spent for services that have the highest payoff for society. Railroad subsidies have not met this test. As this book goes to press, AMTRAC, the government-sponsored organization set up to maintain passenger services, is preparing to discontinue 40 percent of its routes which have the lowest consumer demand.

Government Organizations for Production of Utility

The want-gratifying power of most government services is self-evident. Such services as education, water supply, health care, welfare services, and highway construction are generally recognized as satisfying basic human needs. The examples that follow illustrate the kinds of organization that is established to produce these services.

In the United States, government organizations differ in terms of where (at what level) three functions are performed: formulation of broad strategic alignments (the strategic level), elaboration of broad strategies into more specific details (the administrative level), and performance of the actual operations and work necessary to carry out the alignment (the operating or work level). They also differ as to which type of governmental unit (local, state, national) performs these functions. In national industries, for example, Congress acts as strategist and creates an agency or industry to carry out the administrative and work-level functions. In federal industries, on the other hand, Congress still acts as strategist, but the administrative and work level functions are performed by states, counties, and cities. In local government (city, county, state) industries, the local government performs all three functions. It formulates broad strategies, carries out administrative work to elaborate these into more detailed alignments and then performs the actual operating work necessary to carry out the alignment. We shall look briefly at the following types of industries:

In local government industries, legislative bodies establish broad strategic goals for different industries (water, sewer, public parks, etc.). Like a conglomerate in business, city councils decide the service mix to be offered. Individual industries then act as middle managers or administrators, elaborating broad goals into detailed programs. The agency also does the operating work.

In national industries such as the Post Office or Social Security Administration, the same three levels (strategic, middle-management, and work levels) are arranged similarly. Congress establishes broad service goals but the agency itself does both program elaboration and the operating work.

In federal industries, Congress sets broad strategic goals. It then creates departments or agencies to act as middle managers to give programs more detail. The operating work is done by state agencies or city agencies that are not part of the federal departments.

Finally, in quasi-government agencies, such as port authorities and turnpikes, legislative bodies assign broad goals to some agency that not only performs the middle-managementand work functions but also has fiscal autonomy.

City and State Industries

At the city level, New York City offers certain services to a generic market constituency: all the human beings within the geographic confines of the city. In that city, 31,000 policemen perform traffic, foot, and detective patrols for physical and mental security of citizens; 12,500 firemen stand shifts at firehouses and respond to fires with complex equipment; 12,000 garbage collectors man trucks which prevent hazards to physical health; and 7000 judges, court stenographers, and probation officers arrange trials for persons apprehended by the police.

At the same time, New York City offers specialized services to more specific constituencies. Eighteen thousand people are engaged in serving those human beings who want a college education, 40,000 people are serving those who want elementary and high school education, and 47,000 people are serving those who are physically ill in New York City's 18 city-owned hospitals.[16] Four thousand people plan and operate the recreational and cultural services of the city: zoos, museums, and parks.

A city or state government *as a whole* can be viewed as a conglomerate, producing a wide range of services to different constituencies. For example, states and not cities have traditionally both planned and operated four-year colleges and universities for those constituencies who need and want advanced education. They have provided highway patrols for those traveling outside cities and counties who need protection from accidents. They have provided services in the form of state parks for those seeking recreation.

National Industries

One of the largest national industries has been the Post Office. Forty-four thousand local post offices and 700,000 workers render a communication service for millions of people who have individual needs for communicating with other human beings. The Defense Department has provided security from foreign threats by both elaborating broad goals (naval services, air services) and actually "doing the work."

Another national industry is engaged in receiving applications for social security benefits, processing these applications, deciding on the amount of payments due to each person, and doing the operating work of mailing checks. The Social Security Administration employs 73,000 persons and pays out $54 billion to those elderly or disabled persons in need of financial security. Economists would say that the SSA is engaged in making transfer payments. By this they mean that the SSA transfers funds from taxpayers to certain service/market constituencies.

The SSA serves specific constituencies with different kinds of utility. One constituency is the aged. Transfers are made from the younger to the older. Another is the sick. Transfers are made from the well to the sick. Another is those with poverty level incomes. Transfers are made from those who have sufficient food and shelter to those who do not. A final example is the family with dependent children but no wage earning father or mother. Transfers are made to persons who are in such a situation.

Often one can learn the strategic service or product mix of an organization by looking at its organization structure. This is not accidental. It is because Congress formulates service alignments for certain constituencies by passing laws. It then either creates a new agency to execute this broad goal or assigns the goal to an existing agency. Listed here are various parts of the Social Security Administration, each designed to offer a different service to a different constituency.

The Bureau of District Offices is the *operating level* of this national organization. Each branch office throughout the 50 states, the Virgin Islands, and Puerto Rico actually faces the public (the constituency) to process individual benefits.

The Bureau of Retirement and Survivors Insurance is a middle-management, administrative, or "corporate staff" agency that plans, innovates, elaborates, and supervises benefits to elderly persons who are not disabled, or to their survivors. It has six program offices in Birmingham, Chicago, Kansas City, New York, Philadelphia, and San Francisco. These offices explain the strategy to the branch offices and take into account problems that arise at branches in adjusting the strategy.

Two of the SSA strategic programs operate not as national but as federal industries. They translate the broad goals enacted by Congress into more detailed programs. They then contract with states, cities, or private organizations to carry out the actual work processes. The Bureau of Disability Insurance, headquartered in Baltimore, plans, elaborates and supervises benefits to disabled persons. It works with state government agencies that actually certify persons as disabled.

The Bureau of Health Insurance, also in Baltimore, performs a similar function in relation to state, city, and private organizations. It acts as middle manager or administrator in certifying which persons get medical services under Medicare. It then contracts with state, city, or private organizations to do the work.

The Bureau of Data Processing performs an auxiliary service for all other program headquarters. It actually keeps the records of all persons, the earnings premiums they pay into the system, and the benefits they receive, and it mails checks to individuals.

Federal Industries

In Chapter 4 we will discuss the recent origin of federal industries in the United States. Only since the 1960s has the federal government become *proactive* in creating a host of new services and a host of new constituencies in the fields of education, welfare services, and health services. In Chapter 5 we will look at the overall comprehensive strategy for these industries in the United States. Here we will abstract from two case histories, one from the nursing home industry and one from the hospital industry. The purpose at this point is to illustrate the provision of utility to consuming constituencies (TE.1). To conserve space, we shall also be able to preview how these industries plan their *comprehensive* alignments, how they logically relate goals (TE) with internal resources (TI).

The broad service goal (TE.1) is set by Congress. This goal is elaborated into more detail by a federal cabinet department. This department also specifies policies in the internal structural resource alignment (TI.1). Finally, states and cities must then take the planned alignments and execute these with operating processes and work designs (TI.2).

THE NURSING HOME INDUSTRY   In 1962, Congress passed Public Law 92-603, the Social Security Amendment Act, covering a wide variety of services to be offered to various constituencies. Title XIX provided for grants to states for certain medical assistance programs. One of these programs was defined as producing nursing home care. The act defined the services to be offered to two constituencies (TE.1; two types of *clients*): clients requiring skilled nursing service (SNCs) and clients requiring intermediate care (ICCs). It identified two types of *institutions* that will perform operating work (A2.1): skilled nursing facilities (SNFs) and intermediate care facilities (ICFs).

To specify in more detail the service itself, the act continued: ICFs "do not require the degree of care provided in a hospital or a skilled nursing facility (SNF), but require care above the level of room and board which can be rendered only by an institution, as contrasted with home care." They must also "meet such standards as are prescribed by the Secretary of Health, Education and Welfare."

64

Fourteen years later, on Thursday, July 1, 1976, the *Federal Register* published the standards that had been elaborated by the Social and Rehabilitation Service, a subunit of HEW. This department *itself* had been created by the secretary of HEW to carry out (analyze, elaborate) the service/constituency policy formulated by Congress. There are nine pages of standards. One set specified the quality of services to be rendered by SNFs to their constituencies. Another set specified quality of services rendered by ICFs to their constituencies, for example, the number of skilled nurses required per patient (TI.2).

Reacting to these plans and goals (to obtain budget funds) the state legislature of Washington passed a law providing for the licensing of nursing homes in smaller geographic constituencies, using standards set in Washington, D. C. The State Department of Social Services now contracts with 277 nonprofit and governmental nursing homes (TI.1) providing care for 16,000 human beings. These 277 institutions are part of the vast organization structure necessary to execute the total service strategy in the nation. They must also observe a procedure, set by the HEW, which ensures low cost utility: their operations must be inspected by the State and their charge per patient per day must be certified as "reasonable."[17]

THE HOSPITAL INDUSTRY   In 1973, the federal government planned another industry in a way that follows the classic strategy/structure pattern found by Chandler in the development of private corporations. It visualized a strategy of a certain kind of service, aimed at a certain constituency. It then implemented this strategy by a combination of (1) organization design (TI.12), (directing what organization structure should be used to implement the strategy), and (2) money resource allocation (TI.11) as a motivational technique for compliance.

The 1973 Health Maintenance Act was passed by Congress to create a particular type of hospital (health maintenance organization, or HMO) patterned after the famous Kaiser Foundation Hospital in San Francisco. The institution differs from other hospitals in several respects. It is supported by insurance (sold to individuals, or to companies paying medical insurance for their employees or provided by medicare). Its service mix includes *all* of the services required for complete health maintenance. As the HEW elaborated the goals, for example, it specified that any group may form an HMO, but in order to get federal funds for an HMO hospital, the hospital's organization structure would have to include a department of human relations. Further, this department must include specific

65

subservice specialties: (1) mental health service, (2) medical social work, (3) health education, (4) preventive medicine such as nutritional counseling, (5) family planning, and (6) baby-care counseling.[18] Provided with this strategic service plan, and an organization design to implement the service plan, the HMO in Long Beach, California, in fact started a project to elaborate further, for its own constituency, this departmental design. We see here an elaboration of organization structure (TI.12) at three levels. The federal law (strategic goal) decreed that there would be institutions across the country of a certain type: HMOs. The HEW regulations (administrative elaboration) decreed that there should be a "second level" within the HMO composed of a number of departments, one of which was "human relations." They also elaborated a "third level" within the human relations department consisting of six specialized sections.

Quasi-Government Industries

In addition to city, state, national, and federal industries, governments have established certain organizations that have some of the characteristics of private enterprise. They raise their own funds through bond issues, and they sell a service to some consumer constituency. The Pennsylvania Turnpike Authority, for example, can issue bonds without prior approval from the legislature. It sells transportation by charging tolls to three constituencies: private motorists, trucking companies, and bus transportation companies. Yet these quasi-government industries have other characteristics of city or national industries. Their product/service goals are set by legislative bodies.

In Chapter 4 we will look at the strategic planning process as carried out by one such organization, the Port of Seattle Authority. The points to be made here are that (1) these industries tend to have more discretion in selecting their task alignments and (2) they are in part answerable to consumers who pay fees or bondholders who supply money, rather than solely to some higher agency which collects taxes and then budgets funds.

The Demand for Highest Use (TE.3)

In the case of private corporations, economists have postulated a principle that determines how a resource supplier (the buyer or consumer) make his or her choice between competing products. At the same time, the resource supplier enforces this choice by registering

66

his or her "vote" for which organization survives and grows and which organization declines or dies. It is the purpose of this section to show that resource suppliers to government organizations behave according to the same principle. Their method of bringing pressure to bear on government strategists are, however, different.

The private sector principle is the law of marginal utility. In briefest terms it predicts that a consumer will support (buy from or vote for) that organization which supplies him or her with the highest *marginal* utility. "Marginal" refers to a *comparison* of the product with *other* products the consumer might buy. Stated in another way, the consumer is demanding that the corporation produce a product which has, for him or her, the "highest usefulness." Accordingly we shall call the demand on government organizations the *demand for highest use* (TE.3).

Chapter 4 will contain case histories that describe the behavior of resource suppliers and also the behavior of government officials as they respond to this demand. For example:

The press, certain interest groups, and certain elected officials demand that the federal government stop spending money on services they see as "frivolous" or "unnecessary" and concentrate on those that are "essential."

Government officials, responding to public outcry, have passed "sunset laws," which specify that government agencies should "go out of business" unless they can justify their whole service mix rather than simply asking for budgets in the future to support programs that have been offered in the past.

In the fiscal crises in New York and Cleveland one of the demands of resource suppliers (bondholders, the federal government, citizens themselves) was that city officials *prioritize* their services, weeding out the "less useful" and keeping the "most useful."

In the so-called "taxpayer revolt" in California, as well as in the national demand for a constitutional amendment to curtail federal spending, one of the demands most frequently heard was that both state and federal governments must cut unnecessary programs and emphasize most needed programs.

The whole movement for "accountability" in the public school system demands that strategists offer what seem to resource suppliers to be the most vital services (reading, for example) and curtail the less vital (courses which teach how to dribble a basketball).

These case histories will show that resource suppliers to government industries behave similarly to their counterparts in private industry.

Enforcement in Business: (TE.4)

It is well known in the economics of private enterprise that three different resource suppliers (consumers, stockholders, lenders) demand that the organization rationalize internal resources to produce the product at low cost. From the viewpoint of outside resource suppliers, this is the demand for low cost utility (TE.4). From the viewpoint of strategists, it is the responsibility for efficiency (TI). You may wonder why, with all of the other complexity in organization goals, this distinction must be made. It is because the same phenomenon (the rationalization of internal capital structure, organization structure, production processes, and work roles) is viewed in two heuristic ways by the external resource supplier and the strategist. For resource suppliers, the ultimate end is low cost utility. Efficient production is the means. For the strategist, efficient allocation of internal resources is a major goal in everyday work life, equal in importance to establishing output goals. In fact, as we will see in Chapter 8, some strategists "go overboard" and become "bureaucrats." Focusing on internal efficiency alone, they forget the inevitable long-run connection between service to the public and arrangement of internal resources. Victor Thompson has called this disease, "bureausis."

We have already seen that *consumers* demand low price utility, made possible by low cost production. This is true in the short and long run in competitive industries. It is true over the strategic life cycle for both competitive and monopolistic industries.

Stockholders of both competitive and monopolistic firms make the demand for efficiency. Since profits are determined by subtracting costs from revenues $(P = R - C)$, the lower the costs the more profits are left for distribution of dividends. Stock underwriting firms, doing research for potential stock buyers, publish analyses to show the strategic alignment. These analyses are strikingly similar to the comprehensive alignments described in Chapters 4 and 5. To protect investors, not only do they assess the potential success of the company in its product market (TE.1), but they also examine critically the internal resource capabilities (TI) of the firm. Furthermore, to protect investors even more, the Securities and Exchange Commission requires stock underwriters to present a *prospectus*. This prospectus must give information on both the product to be produced, the market to be served, the kinds of capital equipment to be used (TI.11), the organization structure (TI.12), the operating processes (TI.21) and the kinds of work designs required (TI.22).

Lenders have similar self-interests. Bankers who make short-term or intermediate-term loans to corporations have lower risks if the firm has a realistic comprehensive alignment. In fact, Wells Fargo Bank of San Francisco now includes the subject of "strategic risk analysis" as part of its training for loan officers. The bank's top officers reason as follows. One reason the borrower may fail to repay the loan is that the corporation's strategy is out of alignment. Either the inherent appeal of the company's products (TE.1) is threatened by change in consumer needs, or the inherent nature of the company's internal technology (TI) is inefficient or out-of-date. Therefore, in addition to usual financial analysis, the loan officer should perform a *strategic analysis* of both the company's goal and its internal efficiency. In designing such a training program, Wells Fargo top management required loan officers to practice analyzing some of the case histories reported in Chapters 4 and 5.[19]

Finally, insurance companies maintain large analysis departments to gather information on companies which apply for long term loans. These departments generate information on product market alignments (TE.1), on the type of structural resources the company is going to use to produce the product (TI.1) and the type of operating work processes the company proposes (TI.2). Why? Because the risk in loaning money to a large supermarket chain or a large housing developer is much less if those firms' comprehensive alignments are in order.

Enforcement in Government: (TE.4)

There is so much publicity given to inefficiencies in government that one is likely to overlook a very important movement in society, the movement toward efficiency. Resource suppliers are as strong in their demand for low cost utility when dealing with government organizations as they are in dealing with businesses. Furthermore, strategists in government respond by behaving more and more like their counterparts in business. They are rationalizing internal resources to meet the responsibility for efficiency.

Scattered throughout this book are numerous case histories that support this thesis. It would be redundant to repeat them at this point, but we shall summarize some of them very succinctly.

In Chapter 3 we have already seen how the United States government rationalized certain resources in the nursing home industry (TI.22, the work roles of nurses, and the number of nurses required per shift) and the hospital industry (TI.12, the organization structure of health maintenance organizations).

In Chapter 4 we will see how Congress and state legislatures bring pressure to bear on government agencies to be more efficient by passing sunset laws and requiring zero-based budgeting procedures. Not only do these laws reflect the demand of citizens to prioritize outputs (TE.1), but much of the public criticism that brought them about expresses another theme: that there is too much manpower in government, that manpower in government is not utilized efficiently (TI.22), or that government operating procedures (TI.21) are inefficient.

Chapter 5 will show how strategists in the Boston Symphony Orchestra, a nonprofit organization, respond to the demand for low-priced concert tickets (TE.1) by rationalizing its capital structure (TI.11, the utilization of seats in Symphony Hall) and operating processes (TI.21, by changing the schedule of concerts in Boston and New York).

The most impressive case histories showing the demand for internal efficiency are presented in Chapters 8 and 9. In 1974 Congress passed a law that forces hospitals to plan their capital (TI.11) in the most efficient way. It did this in order to satisfy three resource-supplying constituencies: (1) patients who pay their own hospital bills, (2) insurance companies that pay the bills, and (3) taxpayers who must, in the last analysis, pay for Medicare and Medicaid. Two kinds of capital are involved, expensive machines and hospital buildings. In order for a hospital to buy equipment, or build a new wing, hospital managers must file application for a *certificate of need*. No hospital may buy an $800,000 tomographic scanner (a sophisticated x-ray machine) or a $300,000 generator for radiation treatments if the hospital down the street has one that is in use only part of the time. No hospital may build a new building or add a wing if the whole geographic area's occupancy rate is below 80 percent of total beds. No hospital may add an obstetrics department unless the existing hospital in the area is delivering at least 2000 babies per year in cities over 100,000 or 500 babies a year in areas less than 100,000. The federal government is very serious about controlling the price of health care (TE.1) by forcing internal rationalization (TE.4, A.2). Unless facilities and machines are fully utilized, the government will cut off Medicare and Medicaid funds to the hospital. Government strategists estimate that curtailing construction of buildings alone will save patients, taxpayers, and private patients over $2 billion a year in maintenance costs and $80,000 a year in construction costs *for each bed*.

Capital costs are not the only hospital costs rigorously scrutinized by the government. It has moved to force efficient work designs (TI.22) for doctors who actually perform work on patients. The

70

so-called Bennett Amendment to the Social Security Act forces doctors to justify their "job descriptions"—the procedures they use to diagnose and cure patients. The goal of the legislation is to make sure that the doctor's work procedures (1) are medically necessary, (2) meet professional standards, and (3) are provided in the most economical site of treatment. This goal is accomplished by setting up 203 geographic areas of the country, each of which must have a *Professional Standards Review Organization.* Each PSRO samples the work done by doctors to determine if the methods and the time used are medically necessary, meet acceptable standards, and are provided in an economical setting.

The federal organization structure (TI.12) created to implement this strategy includes, in addition to the 203 geographic branches, the Bureau of Quality Assurance within the Department of HEW. Under such a program, Dr. Gilbertson serves his turn at monitoring the work of doctors in Bethesda Lutheran Hospital in Minneapolis. He finds that two doctors in the hospital, one executing a total knee replacement and the other performing minor surgery for a female disorder, are exceeding the customary and normal time required to keep the patient in the hospital. He recommends dismissal. Overall, average length of stay in this hospital has decreased markedly due to monitoring of doctors' work. And in Colorado, the PSRO estimates that eliminating unnecessary hospitalization in the state will save patients, taxpayers and insurance companies from $2 billion to $6 billion each year.

Health care is not the only industry in which the federal government enforces the demand for efficiency. The president has called the Civil Service Reform Act of 1978 "the most sweeping reform of the Civil Service system since it was created nearly 100 years ago," and has further said, "It will put incentives and rewards back into the federal employment of 2.8 million civilian workers . . . it will help taxpayers get what they have been paying for." Essentially, the act requires periodic appraisal of the work of each employee in terms of methods used and output achieved, the same standards already seen in the case of medical doctors and factory workers. Rather than paying persons for seniority alone, salary raises will be tied to "merit." Increases will be based on performance. This is another attempt to rationalize the work design (TI.22) so that (1) citizens as consumers get lower cost utility on government services (TE.4) and (2) citizens as taxpayers get highest use for their money (TE.3). Finally, in enacting the law with presidential leadership, Congress executed the responsibility for efficient work design (TI.22).

71

Other cases in Chapters 8 and 9 include:

Enforcement of these demands at the state level: The state of New York as it attempts to engage in productivity bargaining with unions representing state employees; the State of Pennsylvania as it enforces efficient use of manpower in colleges and universities.

Enforcement of these demands at the city level: The city of Fresno, California, as it attempts to rationalize 54 fire and water departments; the city-county of Indianapolis as it seeks to eliminate overlapping or unnecessary organization structures; the city of New York as it enforces the eight-hour work day and changes the output of teachers in the secondary school classroom.

Enforcement of these demands in foreign countries: The government of Iceland as it attempts to eliminate duplicate capital equipment in the pharmaceutical industry; the government of England as it seeks to eliminate smaller schools that duplicate expensive libraries and teaching staffs.

All of these case histories together prove that significant demands are being made on governmental organizations: the demands for low cost utility (TE.4) and the demand for efficient task performance (TI). They also show that government strategists indeed respond to such demands. They behave in ways that rationalize the internal operations of government.

Notes

1. C. E. Summer and Janice Morgan, *The Northeast Power Failure* (Appendix 1); See also, *The Night the Lights Went Out*, by the staffs of the *New York Times*, Signet Books, 1965; and Federal Power Commission, *Report to the President on the Northeast Power Failure*, Washington, December 6, 1965.

2. *Human Value of Oil* (Appendix).

3. *New York Times*, March 5, 1978.

4. United Press International, December 5, 1977.

5. *Boston Symphony Orchestra* (Appendix).

6. *Utility in Industrial Goods*, case file (Appendix).

7. *The Recreational Vehicle Industry* (Appendix).

8. February 21, 1977.

9. United Press International, May 17, 1977.

10. *Consumer Reports* 43, 7 (July 1978); 43, 8 (August 1978).

11. *The London Times*, September 13, 1978.

12. *Sweden Now*, March 1977, pp. 27–28.

13. S. A. Greyser and S. L. Diamond, "Business is Adapting to Consumerism," *Harvard Business Review*, 52:5 (September, 1974): 38–58.

14. *United States Steel Corporation* (Appendix).

15. Frederick M. Scherer, *Industrial Market Structure and Economic Performance*, Rand McNally, 1971; Solow, Robert M., "Technical Change and the Aggregate Production

Function," *Review of Economics and Statistics*, August 1957, 312–20; Caves, Richard, *American Industry: Structure, Conduct and Performance*, Prentice-Hall, 1977.

16. *New York City Fiscal Crisis* (Appendix).

17. *The Nursing Home Industry* (Appendix).

18. Josephine Gumbiner, *A Department of Human Relations*, Family Health Program of Long Beach, 1976.

19. C. E. Summer, *Strategic Risk Analysis for Bank Loan Officers*, San Francisco, Wells Fargo Bank, 1978.

Task Effectiveness: Product and Service Alignment

CHAPTER 4 will concentrate on one important aspect of the behavior of general managers, the formulation of policies that determine what products and services the organization will provide to satisfy which segment of human beings in the population. In other words, we will see how general managers align the output of the organizations with demands of consumers, clients, and resource suppliers. In business policy literature, this has been called "the product/market decision" or "formulating policy on product lines." In government it can be called "the service/client decision" or "formulating policy on services or programs."

The chapter will begin with an explanation of product/market alignment which is based on literature in six fields: business policy, organization theory, administrative behavior, management theory, political theory, and economics. The main body of the chapter contains case histories from both business and government in order (1) to prove that general managers do formulate products, services, and programs to meet the demands outlined in Chapter 3, (2) to show how managers do this, and (3) to show that the "visions" or "perceptions" of managers result in factual products and services.

The Concept of Output Alignment

In Chapter 2 we saw the exchange relationship between the organization and its task constituencies, how strategy formulation and policy formulation are means of fashioning outputs which satisfy demands, and how satisfied demands result in support from outside constituencies. There, we looked at Hewlett-Packard Corporation, The American Hiking Society, the United States Post Office, and

74

Seattle City Light Company. In each case, strategists were formulating some product (a computer which would move a telescope) or service (kilowatts of electricity, writing letters to Congress, delivery of letters and packages) which satisfied the needs of some constituency. A product/market is therefore a logical relationship between a "thing" (product or service) and "people" (a segment of human beings in the population).

In practice, this concept is difficult enough in business administration. For example, take the problem faced by general managers in an insurance company. In broadest terms, the company goal is to fashion a service (an insurance policy) that will satisfy a market segment of human beings who have the need for safety and security (TE). The insurance policy will be produced by certain internal operating processes (TI.21) such as use of actuarial mathematics to determine risk and premiums. But this is only the beginning of the service policy or decision. The environment has many subgroups with different demands. There is automobile insurance to serve one constituency, those persons who want protection of their property (collision insurance) or protection from damage they cause to others (liability insurance). There is homeowners insurance for protection from fire (fire insurance policies) or theft (personal property policies). There is marine insurance for those who own boats, and industrial accident insurance for employees in factories.

The strategist faces not only this kind of complexity, but other kinds as well. If we limit ourselves to homeowners' insurance policies, do we sell them in Indianapolis, or Indianapolis plus Dayton, or in one region (e.g., the Midwest).

Finally, suppose we have settled on selling homeowners insurance in the Midwest, what is *our* distinctive competence for the consumer? Travelers Insurance Company of Hartford is not only clear about this question but insurance buyers who shop around also know the Travelers service characteristics. The company deliberately differentiates its service from other carriers (1) by offering certain claims settlements that are a little easier for the consumer than other companies (the company is more "liberal" in getting fast custom-made service and slightly less "tight" on the money amounts), but also (2) by charging slightly higher premiums to cover the cost of this service. Some other companies are equally successful by picking a different niche in the total insurance market. If a competitor has decided on the same functional market (homeowners) and geographic market (the Midwest), that company may stress lower cost premiums coupled with a good but less liberal claims settlement procedure (their claims personnel use slightly more of a "mass production" technique and require more appraisals or estimates to arrive at the dollar payment).

In business policy, the problem just described is sometimes split into two: first, what is our industry niche (what industry do we compete in, e.g., insurance in Massachusetts) and second, what is our distinctive competence or competitive weapon (high-service, high-price or low-price, adequate-service).

An excellent example of distinctive competence decision making is that performed by strategists in the West German company, Bosch A.G. They have decided that the company will compete in the automotive parts industry, more specifically, in fuel injection systems for automobile engines. One of its customers is Mercedes-Benz. But several other companies produce the same product (a fuel injection system) for the same market (multinational, worldwide auto manufacturers). What differentiates Bosch from the others? A certain distinctive competence. The company decided that it would concentrate on highly engineered injection systems with precision tolerances and unusually long life. At the same time, Bosch's customers would pay more for these products, there would be less reliance on a sales force to push the product, and there would be fewer of these products produced than in the case of competing companies with mass-production policies. Another fuel injection producer might well have different distinctive competences: less highly engineered systems, mass produced, without exact tolerances, at a lower price, for sale to automobile manufacturers who demand this type of product. Both companies will succeed if they know their niche in the outside world and align their entire resource systems to achieve that goal.

Product Alignment in Business Policy Literature

Several explanations of strategic alignment are important in the literature of business administration. In the field of marketing, alignment has been discussed in terms of formulating the product mix, product positioning, market segmentation, product/market targeting, or market planning.[1]

In business policy literature the concept of product alignment goes back into history of the Harvard Business School.[2] There, for some thirty years prior to 1933, the business policy course was primarily concerned with integration of the *internal* operations of firms. Sales policies and manufacturing policies, for example, were related to policies in finance or manpower and personnel. In 1933, an additional objective was added, the study of "top management" or

76

"the top management point of view." This marked the beginning of emphasis on integration of the *internal* operations of a firm with the *external* task and cultural environment. As professors at Harvard worked with massive case histories over the next thirty years, they evolved a paradigm that explained the process of product/market alignment and of comprehensive task alignment. For a variety of reasons, this was never actually published until the late 1960s. For one thing, the professors believed that clinical analysis during which students discovered and internalized the process themselves, was a much superior type of learning than reading theories that someone else put down.[3] For another, the process was complex and difficult to explain unless the reader could see *reality* in case practice (the same reason why such laborious reference to case histories must be used in this book!).

Though Harvard professors had published pieces of their process framework in 1955,[4] it was not until the period 1965–73 that a comprehensive framework for strategic alignment was available to the public in published form. During that period Learned and others first published the process.[5] This was followed by two other works, one by Andrews[6] and the other by Uyterheoven and others.[7] Each of these works is today in widespread use in business and in universities.

All three of these works were influenced by the work of Alfred Chandler, whose *Strategy and Structure* was published in 1962.[8] He proved conclusively that those corporations which change their product lines to align with changing needs of customer constituencies, and which make corresponding changes in their complex internal structures, over long time cycles, not only survive but become leaders in their industries. They do so because (1) they have support from customers and other resource suppliers and (2) support is generated because strategists in the firm can visualize and implement these two kinds of changes (TE, TI). Chandler's meticulous historical research in 100 corporations shows that Sears, Roebuck and General Motors did not evolve as industry leaders by accident. There were many powder plants in the United States before 1860, some larger than that one owned by a French immigrant named DuPont. The DuPont Corporation is what it is today because at crucial times in its history its strategists drastically altered the company's product mix, always by coping with the inertia of bureaucracy. Though such inertia at times made major change difficult, it was a major resource supplier—the customer—that forced such changes to take place.

Chandler has followed this study with an even more impressive research effort. In *The Visible Hand* (1977) his thesis is that strategic alignment is the single most powerful force which has caused development and growth of individual firms.[9] It is also the most powerful force causing the development and growth of the entire national economy.

Another contribution to the alignment concept has been made by William Newman who started his career with J. O. McKinsey when the latter was chairman of Marshall Field; he later taught at Chicago, Wharton, and Columbia. Like the Harvard professors, Newman first concentrated on relating the *internal* policies of the firm[10] but later moved to show the central role of product alignment.[11]

During the 1960s another researcher explained comprehensive alignment. Ansoff not only saw that product/market alignment (TE) is a central job of top management but he saw that comprehensive alignment of internal resources (TI) is the other half of total system planning.[12] He used the term "synergy" to mean a state of affairs in which each part of the complex resource alignment (TI) fits with, is logically related to, and depends on, every other part of the system. This concept will be more clearly understood in Chapter 5. Furthermore, in successful corporations, this internal policy structure must align with the final goal (TE).

Output Alignment in Organization Theory

Like many theories in economics and management, organization theory in the 1960s concentrated almost entirely on the *internal* organization structure (TI.12) necessary to produce a given product. Burns and Stalker,[13] Woodward,[14] and Lawrence and Lorsch[15] did recognize that different organizations had to cope with different outside constituencies. The latter authors studied industries with different rates of change in consumer tastes or demands (TE.1). Container producers had slowly changing ("stable") customer demands: food companies had moderately changing customer demands, and plastics companies had rapidly changing ("turbulent") customer demands.

But this was as far as these studies went in assessing the product/ market alignment problem. They simply acknowledged that it existed. Given that "someone else" picked the product domain or niche, all the strategist had to do was to act as a computer. He or she had to read the degree of change (turbulence) created by "someone else" and then match the internal organization structure alignment (TI.12) to the reading on the barometer.

It remained for Child, a British sociologist, to introduce the

78

concept of strategic choice of products and markets full force into the world of sociology and organization theory. In a well-known article,[16] he pointed out, like Chandler, that the strategic choice process, by which strategists conceptualize, visualize, or otherwise *determine the products* to be produced *and the markets* to be served is the most critical factor in the entire field of organization theory. It is the central variable that determines internal organization design.

Chapter 1 has already covered the most important contributions of organization theory to the understanding of strategic behavior. There are four concepts of central importance. First, the concept of an organization as an *open system* that must, in order to survive, furnish outputs *to* the environment and receive life-giving feedbacks and support *from* the environment. Second, the concept of *exchange* of outputs for inputs as the only way an organization can secure support. Third, the concept of *resource dependence*, which translates the notion of exchange one step further, focusing on specific resources that the organization needs or that the constituencies need, to make the transaction viable. Fourth, the concept of *evolution*, which not only shows that organizations must align themselves over very long periods of time but also shows that they do this by using a process of mutation to align their goals with an ever-changing ecological environment.

Output Alignment: Theory of Administrative Behavior and the New Science of Management Decision

Herbert Simon's now-famous works, *Administrative Behavior* and *The New Science of Management Decision*, can be related to strategic behavior in three ways. His heuristic theory of decision making can be applied to strategy and policy decisions in a way that helps strategists understand what situation they face and how they make these decisions. His explanation of how administrators inside the firm behave is helpful in showing why middle managers often cannot "see" the whole strategic situation (TE, TI, CE, CI). Finally, Simon makes a few broad remarks of a prescriptive nature: he makes suggestions as to how to prevent administrators who are subject to these limitations from blocking strategic alignment.

The notion of heuristic decision making implies that a human being cannot make sense of the buzzing confusion around him or her without *focusing attention on* (giving priority to, giving high weight to) one ultimate goal (end) at a time. All the other factors in the situation become constraints, restrictions, or means to the ultimate end. Chapter 5 will show that in comprehensive task alignment,

79

strategists behave exactly like this. They practice technical heuristics. In the long trial-and-error policymaking processes, a problem may arise that focuses attention on the most efficient capital equipment (TI.11) to be used. But the next problem to arise may focus attention on the most efficient organization structure (TI.12), the most efficient work design (TI.22), or the best product mix to offer to customers (TE.1). In each case, all other factors are affected and must be considered as means to correct the central problem.

Chapters 6–9 will show that the same kind of process occurs when strategists face cultural demands outside the organization (CE) or inside the organization (CI). Strategists then engage in cultural heuristics. A problem may arise in which the focus (highest priority) is on a demand by environmentally concerned constituencies for clean air (CE) because the existing factory equipment (TI.11) puts out too much smoke. Two years later this means-end relationship can be reversed. The new equipment does indeed reduce smoke, but it costs so much that the price of the product to the customer escalates (TE.1). The efficiency of capital equipment (TI.11) once again becomes the focus of attention, the central goal.

Turning now to why Simon's administrators often cannot behave like strategists, we must recall that there are three levels of decision making in organizations: the strategic level, the administrative level, and the operating or work level. The administrator's span of attention is severely limited by the organization design, and by identification with his or her specialty. The time available for administrative decisions often does not permit taking so many variables into account. Notice that Simon assumes a certain time frame in administrative decisions, much shorter than the evolutionary cycle in strategic decisions. Both of these factors, identification and time restrictions, mean that most administrators simply do not make strategic decisions that include the whole range of goals demanded by all constituencies (TE, TI, CE, CI).

Finally, though Simon's work is principally devoted to how administrators *do* behave (and not to how they ought to behave) he occasionally presents prescriptions designed to overcome problems he sees. He takes a clear position that *someone* in the organization "must give proper weight to *all*" cultural values (CE) and task values (TE).[17] Because the administrator is prevented from "making correct decisions," yet "the restricted area of values with which he identifies himself must be weighed against other values outside that area," what can be done and by whom?

Simon specifies what must be done. But because he is studying administrative behavior and not strategic behavior, he gives only broad suggestions. He does not investigate who strategists are or how they exert leadership. One suggestion is to design the organization structure so that the attention of middle managers can be focused on the whole strategic situation and not on one department. A second is to locate budget decisions in an organization at a level high enough in the hierarchy that those who dispense the money are also those who "see" all the factors in a strategy problem. As a third thought in this passage, Simon refers to "decisions which precede the establishment of the organizational structure itself" and warns that in matters of "invention" it would be harmful if persons at highest levels in the hierarchy were to be biased in identifying with any one sub-part of the organization.[17]

It is a striking coincidence that what Simon speculated ought to happen at the strategic level, Chandler found did happen at the strategic level. In corporations that survived and grew to be leaders in their industries, it was at the strategic level, and through the strategic behavior of managers that three things happened: (1) strategists did indeed take into account all diverse and changing demands outside the organization, (2) budget decisions (resource allocations) were indeed made so that they implemented the strategic decisions, and (3) an organization structure was designed. This organization structure was a structure of *administrative* positions like the ones Simon described. In these positions administrators were to take a certain part of the strategy, focus their attention on that part, and elaborate the strategy into still more detailed actions to be carried out at the work level.

External Alignment in Management Theory

Two branches of literature exist that attempted to deal with top management as integrating the *internal* alignment of a firm but that also tend to ignore the problem of external product alignment.

The first was widely popular in the period 1900–30. In *Scientific Management*, Frederick Taylor took the micro approach, concentrating on management at the plant level. He was interested in work processes (TI.21) and individual job design (TI.22). He, as well as his followers, assumed that the production of steel was given, and that plant management's task was to arrange processes, reward systems, and jobs to align with producing steel.

A second branch of literature was widely popular in the United States in the period 1945–70. It still has considerable acceptance in some business schools. This was the field of "management." It was influenced heavily by the work of a French industrialist, Henri

81

Fayol. His book was published in French in 1916 but unavailable in English until 1949. It was also influenced by works of Urwick, a British army officer and retail executive, and Mooney, a General Motors executive.

The large number of management books that followed had a fundamental flaw from a strategic viewpoint. Like Taylor, they concentrated on internal operations, taking product alignment as given. Because they also concentrated on certain limited facets of organization design (TI.12, rule systems, procedures, delegation of authority), they also could not explain the human side of enterprise (cultural demands of employees), which loomed large in the literature of the 1960s and 1970s. Management textbooks of this type have gradually changed to meet these two criticisms. First, they began to include more analyses of human needs of employees (CI.2). Second, as this book goes to press, they are including more analyses of external demands, the necessity for product alignment (TE) and cultural alignment (CE), *before* they proceed to design policies as rule systems and before they explain how authority is delegated.

No summary of management literature would be complete without reference to Drucker and Sloane. Drucker's original work, *The Concept of the Corporation*,[18] focused mainly on management of internal resources. Published in 1946, it was a brilliant analysis of General Motors, using a model from political theory (e.g., "federal decentralization"). Eight years later, his *Practice of Management* moved more in the direction of comprehensive alignment. His notion of "what business are we in," colorfully illustrated with examples from the telephone company, and Cadillac and Packard automobiles, stressed product/market alignment (TE). His eight objectives of a business corporation stressed the necessity for both task alignment and cultural alignment. Market standing and innovation objectives were matters of product alignment (TE.1). The profitability objective was a matter of stockholder demands for high revenues (TE.1, TE.2, TE.3) and low costs (TE.4). Physical and financial resource objectives were a matter of capital alignment (TI.11). Manager development (CI.1) and worker attitude objectives (CI.2) were matters of cultural efficiency. It was also in this book that Drucker postulated his system for internal resource alignment. His chapter on "Management by Objectives and Self Control" had profound influence on practicing managers and on business school curricula.

Like Drucker, Alfred Sloane has had a major impact on corporate strategists as they perceive their responsibility for product/market alignment. He described the way model changes were worked out during his years as president and chairman of General Motors. Starting with the Company's product line of ten cars (products) in seven market segments in 1921, he proceeded to show that this alignment was totally "irrational." By that he meant that company strategists had not done their homework in (1) diagnosing utility demands of consumers and (2) innovating products to meet those demands. He then showed how, over the years, the company moved to rectify the situation. Anyone studying his case history is bound to be impressed with the central principle: General Motors has become the largest producer of automobiles in the world because it aligned its products with the market better than any other company. It did this by slow, often halting trial and error, coupled with a sense of strategic vision on the part of top managers.[19]

Output Alignment:
Public Policy Literature

A number of political theories explain *policy* alignment as it is practiced by policymakers in government organizations in the United States. Two theories explain *strategic* alignment. A brief review of each of these will show their usefulness in understanding behavior of strategists.

One paradigm shows constituency pressure groups as making policies. Legislatures simply act as referees in a struggle of interest groups and in effect codify into law any policy that satisfies the most influential groups.[20] This paradigm calls attention to the fact that policymakers *react* to constituencies' demands. It does not indicate the *proactive* role of policymakers as they innovate and change alignments on their own initiative. It also does not address the question of what values are important in society. A policy decision is simply that which gets the most support of influential groups.

Another paradigm is at the other extreme. In it a centralized oligarchy makes policies. There is an elite group in the United States (perhaps John K. Galbraith's "military-industrial complex") that shapes policies on its own initiative, in its own self-interests.[21] In this model the proactive role of policymakers is emphasized but the role of constituencies over the strategic time cycle is underestimated.

Two other paradigms fall in the middle road. In them policymakers shape decisions on the basis of which policies are most satisfying to constituencies. The constituencies let policymakers know what they want and the policymakers modify these demands according to what outputs are feasible and possible. Both of these paradigms show that strategic behavior is composed of behavior of two parties, policymakers and constituencies. It is a *two-way inter-active process*, so necessary for long-term strategic survival and growth of the organization.[22] As we saw in Chapter 2, heroes do not make history and history does not make heroes. They both make each other.

All of these theories have two drawbacks from the viewpoint of understanding strategic behavior. They describe *policy* decisions (ad hoc, piecemeal, incremental decisions logically unrelated to a master strategy). Though Chapter 5 will show that half of strategic behavior is policymaking, the other half is comprehensive strategy formulation. Second, they treat the output of government organizations simply as a decision—any decision—without regard to its content. They ignore what output is being produced, whether it be a useful product or service to satisfy the demand for standard of living (TE) or some intangible value such as autonomy or ecology to satisfy the demand for cultural performance (CE).

These deficiencies are rectified in two models of political behavior that correspond closely to the concept of strategic behavior explained in this book. Both contain a stress on the proactive role of top government strategists as they interpret the needs of society and innovate new ways of meeting these needs. In both it is stressed that strategists have a vision of some output they want to achieve. Both contain descriptions of a fundamental and revolutionary change in the way the United States is governed, a change that has taken place recently and with great speed.

In Wilson's "Rise of the Bureaucratic State," we see that both the president and Congress visualized "The Great Society." They used this as an overarching theme to stress that the United States must produce basic services to satisfy deep human needs. Like Chandler's strategists in the DuPont Corporation, Congress passed the laws that stated the service/markets to be served, created an organization structure of federal departments to execute this strategy, empowered administrators and middle managers to further elaborate the strategy into detailed programs, and budgeted the money to ensure compliance. As Wilson puts it:

> Beginning in the 1960's, the Federal Government, at the initiative of the President and his advisors, increasingly came to define the purposes of federal grants—not necessarily over the objection of the states, but often without any initiative from them. Federal money is to be spent on "national" goals for which, until the laws were passed, there were few, if any, well organized and influential constituencies. Whereas federal

84

money was once spent in response to the claims of distinct and organized clients, money has increasingly been spent in ways that have *created* such clients.[23]

Before this time, most grants of money were for purposes that were *initiated* by the states or by constituency groups, for such product/market constituencies as road transportation users (highways) or air users (airports).

We see, then, that the first characteristic of such organizations is that they are entrepreneurial. The most important characteristic of entrepreneurs, according to the classical economists (e.g., Schumpeter) is their ability to have a comprehensive vision or conceptual framework beginning with a need for utility on the part of a constituency (TE) and moving to a series of interconnected operations (technical processes, labor, machinery, capital funds) that would provide that utility (TI). The word also denoted a "profit-maker," but that fact should not obscure the entrepreneur's most basic characteristic. Federal government strategists have indeed fulfilled this intellectual characteristic of entrepreneurs. They may have also fulfilled the emotional characteristic: that of a risk-taking attitude to undertake new products and services to new market constituencies. They do not, however, fulfill the financial characteristic: profit-making from the sale of services.

A second characteristic of these organizations is that they design an organizational structure that some political scientists have called "cooperative federalism." The successive elaboration of goals at the state, county, and city levels, backed by the power of money grants to these geographically decentralized operating headquarters means that the various levels of government are engaged in joint ventures to execute the strategy set at the federal level. This is somewhat like the mixed economy structure except that states and cities, rather than private corporations, perform the physical work to be done.

Nathan Glazer depicts a change to the same kind of behavior on the part of the court system in the United States, and particularly on the part of the Supreme Court, except that the Court has a cultural strategy (CE, CI) rather than a task strategy (TE, TI).[24]

Political scientists have noticed a cycle over the history of the Supreme Court which causes changing leadership patterns. The Court has oscillated from a period of quietism (inactive leadership) to a period of activism (proactive leadership) and back again. As the Court reached a peak of proactive leadership it found that it had gone too far ahead of the legislative branch, and perhaps ahead of constituency opinion. The way the Court knew it had gone too far was that an explosion resulted. For example, the *Dred Scott Decision* caused a war. The overruling of the New Deal legislation in the 1930s caused Congress and the president to draw up legislation to pack the Court with justices who would follow the will of the executive and legislative branches. At such points the Court returns to quietism, content to let congresses and presidents, interacting with constituency demands, determine the policies of the nation.

Glazer traces the history of decisions of the Supreme Court over a period of years. He shows that today this cycle of leadership has been broken. He cites case histories in which the Court has ordered the Environmental Protection Agency, the nation's school systems, and the Department of Health, Education, and Welfare to invoke practices (1) that Congress did not specify and may even oppose, (2) that the agency executives did not feel were wise, and (3) that the executive departments and agencies did not know how to perform.

The last point is of crucial importance in comparing the Court's behavior with that of strategists. Glazer clearly points out that no agency knew how to create the permanently racially balanced community that Judge Weinstein ordered. The City of Boston did not know how to create a tranquil situation in public housing projects (CE) and still spend only what it could afford (TI). Yet this was exactly what Judge Garrity ordered. Other agencies did not know how to rehabilitate prisoners, or treat mental patients, as Court decisions decreed.

Four hallmarks of strategic behavior are (1) that strategists have broad goals which they visualize should be accomplished, (2) these goals are to be accomplished over very long time spans, (3) they are to be accomplished by designing an organization structure, i.e., assigning the goal as a responsibility to specific administrators, and (4) the administrators then elaborate the details of how to achieve goals. They invent, use trial and error, and otherwise "make happen." All four of these hallmarks are present in the new behavior of courts as described by Glazer.

Product Alignment in Economic Theory

In Chapter 3 we have already discussed the fact that most of traditional economics has ignored the concept of strategic competition, the process by which strategists make major innovations in products and in the markets these products are designed to serve. It also mentioned the contribution of Edith Penrose, who focused attention on this neglected subject. She explained why some firms survive and grow while others stagnate or die. She viewed firms in

86

terms of long time spans. Here we need to become more familiar with her theory.

Penrose's *Theory of the Growth of the Firm* indeed deals with output innovations.[25] She points out that those firms which can perform the process of strategic alignment, slowly inventing, elaborating, and discovering new products over time, will survive and grow. Even powerful monopolies cannot survive without meeting this test. Two of the characteristics of firms that survive and grow through consumer acceptance are actually characteristics of the firm's strategists. They are able to *see*—to create, to conceptualize, to visualize, to formulate, to align—opportunities for new products and new market constituencies. They are also *willing* to act on those opportunities. A third characteristic of firms with long life cycles has to do with the situation in which strategists operate. Strategists can act because they are in a situation without excessive rigidities. Firms that have no strategists who can see or who are willing to act and firms in which strategists cannot act will die.

It is this kind of alignment behavior that enabled strategists in Vlasic Foods Corporation,[26] an unknown corporation in Michigan, systematically to capture market after market for pickles from H. J. Heinz and other large competitors by slowly switching from processed pickles to fresh packed products, by slowly convincing hundreds of farms to grow cucumbers, by establishing 42 receiving stations in North Carolina to pack and ship cucumbers to Michigan, by gaining loyalty of distributors in Boston, by working with hundreds of supermarkets from Kansas City to Los Angeles, and by learning how to advertise pickles on television when no one had ever heard of advertising this product.

The same kind of strategic behavior enabled Timex Watch Corporation systematically to destroy other United States rivals (Hamilton, Gruen, Waltham) and even partially destroy the powerful Swiss watch cartel. It did so by gradually building a strategy—a new product with different utility for human beings, and a different internal technology learned and implemented in nine plants around the world by 17,000 workers whose special skills matched the final product output.[26]

Product Alignment:
Case Histories in Business

The first two examples in this section will show that the responsibility for strategic alignment was successfully fulfilled because strategists did indeed see, were indeed willing, and could in fact move the firm through historical evolution. Resource suppliers (customers and investors) rewarded them with resources to grow. The third example shows that the management of A&P Food Corporation were less effective, either because they could not see the necessary changes far enough in advance, because they were unwilling to risk major change, or because some rigidity in their organization prevented them from being able to act.

7-11 Food Stores, Inc.[27]

Prior to 1927, the Southland Ice Company of Dallas, Texas, operated a chain of ice service stations. At that time, gas compressor refrigerators, run by electric motors, had not been invented by such organizations as Frigidaire of Dayton, or General Electric of Schenectady. A product/market constituency, needing better nutrition and protection from health hazards of decomposing foodstuffs, was served by Southland. It manufactured ice in ice plants in 10-, 25-, 50-, and 100-pound blocks. It stored them at branch locations for sale to persons in a certain geographic area. The ice blocks were sawed at the "ice plant" with a saw very much like a carpenter's saw.

With the coming of gas compressors and electric refrigerators, the company would have died had not policymakers made a strategic decision—a decision that meant changing the product and changing the market segment constituency. They decided that the delivery branches could be converted to a service human beings need. They saw a "utility niche" or "utility domain" that was not being offered by any other company. Grocery stores of that day opened at 8:30 A.M. and closed at 5 or 6 P.M. Yet many persons, for various reasons including working late-night or early-morning shifts, needed food at other hours. The company named its new stores "7-11 Food Stores," indicating in the title that the stores would stay open from 7 A.M. until 11 P.M.

This marked the beginning of the "convenience store industry." There are today 30,000 stores of this type in the United States. Their product/market constituency (i.e., their strategic domain or strategic niche) is different from the strategic product/market of the supermarket chains such as Safeway and Jewel. They carry a different and smaller product mix, they charge slightly higher prices, they offer no car-delivery or other frills offered by supermarkets. But they free consumers from time spent in parking and shopping in large complex supermarkets.

Within this industry, 7-11 is an undisputed leader. It has 6500 stores in the United States and Canada, selling 3000 different items

88

(large supermarkets may sell 50,000). Whereas the product/market constituency of the entire industry rewards these companies with *$8.85 billion* each year, 7-11's reward (market share) is *$2.1 billion.* In one three-state region alone (Washington, Idaho, Oregon) there are 283 stores.

As the resource suppliers continued to support the company because of its strategic success (investors in both stocks and bonds of Southland Corporation have also contributed), the product/market domain expanded. In September 1978, there were 500 7-11 stores in Japan. To reward its investors, the company has paid cash dividends each year for 22 years. In 1977 it paid out $10.9 million to stockholders.

What is the strategic utility being offered? John P. Thompson, chairman of Southland says, "convenience is the key—convenience of location, convenience of time saved in shopping when compared to the time it takes to shop at big supermarkets, and convenience of the hour that some people need to shop."

Eagle-Picher Industries[27]

Eagle-Picher Industries is a Cincinnati company that began 134 years ago as a producer of lead and zinc. These basic metals were connected to the final consumer by a roundabout production process that finally ended in such things as linings for burial caskets and battery liners for automobiles. Over the years its strategists have fit Chandler's and Penrose's description of strategic behavior. They have not only seen opportunities to fill a certain utility domain/niche in society, but they have been willing and able to act on it. Today the company specializes in industrial products of a certain product/market mix. It is not an unrelated conglomerate, but carefully interrelates its 48 product lines to 48 constituencies: other companies that need basic chemicals, machines for the original equipment market (the constituency includes companies manufacturing new equipment such as automobiles), and transportation products.

In 1971, policymakers at Eagle saw that atomic energy was going to be needed to help supply the needs of electric utilities. They built a pilot plant to produce boron, a chemical much needed in nuclear energy plants. They began to assemble the needed personnel, as well as to build an organization that could learn to manufacture and sell boron. This vision became a reality in 1975 when the Energy Research and Development Administration (ERDA) concluded that the United States needed more boron. ERDA, acting in the capacity of a mixed-economy entrepreneur itself, asked 26 corporations which of them had the experience, specialization, and learning to produce boron. Not one company—except Eagle—had in fact developed the organizational culture and technology to produce it. It had taken four years to accumulate the experience capability. ERDA, a resource supplier, rewarded Eagle with a $90 million contract. Eagle, in return, fulfilled the responsibility for strategic alignment.

In 1971, Eagle policymakers executed the responsibility for strategic alignment in its plastic transportation products domain. They had been producing fiberglass exterior trim parts for automobiles such as Chrysler's Cordoba and New Yorker. They reasoned that the energy shortage was going to mean that American automobiles would have to be lighter in weight to conserve gasoline. It was not until 1978 that the United States government tax authorities began to enforce a law of Congress known as the "gas guzzler tax." This tax, in effect, means that all automobile companies must produce lighter cars. Mr. Scheffel, a policymaker in Eagle, says, "we knew 7 years ago that there were only 30 pounds of plastic in an automobile. We forecasted that this had to triple. Today there are 185 pounds. By 1981 we predict it will increase another 200%."

A&P Food Corporation[27]

The early history of the Atlantic and Pacific Food Corporation indicates that the company grew because its policymakers obeyed the responsibility for strategic alignment. The history of the company from 1960 to 1979 shows the opposite. Initially beginning as the Great Atlantic and Pacific Tea Company, specializing in the importation of tea into the United States, the company gradually changed its output (its product/market) to a type of retail store that satisfied consumers' needs from the 1920s to 1955. It had developed mass merchandising appropriate to the period, at first building convenience stores in local neighborhoods then later building supermarkets that served suburban markets. By 1960 it had 3468 stores across the nation. It had 27 manufacturing plants, producing everything from bakery products to mouthwash.

But the A&P failed to keep its products and services aligned with a changing society. By 1960, 1250 of its stores were not taking in enough revenues from the public to cover the cost of operating them. Total revenues had slipped millions of dollars. Its share of consumer retail grocery purchases decreased from 10 percent of all dollars expended on food in the United States to less than 6 percent. In 1973, it ceased to be the largest retail food company in the nation, and another organization, Safeway Stores, which *had* aligned its products and services, became the largest.

What was happening to A&P? First, it had not aligned its service with consuming constituencies (TE). It had failed to follow its customers to the suburbs, concentrating more on declining in-city populations. Whereas competitors concentrated on increased size, convenience, and variety of products in their in-city stores, A&P found itself with hundreds of small neighborhood stores without variety and without new services such as quicker checkouts and convenient layouts. Its own brands (Jane Parker and Ann Page) failed to appeal to customers who demanded a wider choice of brands.

Second, A&P had not aligned its *internal* structure and processes (TI). The *cost* of its products would not be paid by the consumer: its labor costs (in part caused by out-of-date layouts and procedures) were 12.4 percent of sales, whereas competitors' were 10.1 percent. Its overhead costs of headquarters staff was 2 percent of sales, whereas competitors' were 1.25 percent.

Faced with this failure in strategic alignment, management faced bankruptcy if something were not done. After the company lost $16.8 million dollars in the first half of 1978 it closed 1433 stores. Twenty-seven manufacturing plants were closed.

Even this did not produce results. Every time a store was closed the per unit costs of warehousing, advertising, and transportation increased (economies of scale *decreased*). Furthermore, the top policymakers found it impossible quickly to restructure the organization so that lower store managers would have the information (on pricing, promotion, new technologies, etc.) or the motivation (they had been trained another way) to execute the new strategy. In short, the long learning curve necessary to develop people in the new strategy could not take place so quickly. Those acquainted with Chandler's work will see that the strategists in A&P had not been able to do what those in Sears, Roebuck or DuPont did. They had not anticipated the long time it takes to change a complex technological system. They did not allow for the "time gap" between the point at which strategists "see" a changing society and the time it takes actually to engineer the changes into practice.

Harvard Business School Cases in Strategy: Private Corporations

Nowhere is the evidence of responsibility for strategic alignment better documented than in the enormous collection of cases of the Harvard Business School. Over the years, professors teaching business policy have sought to have students, by studying historical evidence in particular companies, relate the key outputs of a corporation to its environment. Here are a few examples:[26]

History of the watch industry, and strategies of the Swiss, the Japanese, and the American companies, and, specifically, Timex Watch Corporation.

History of the mutual funds industry, and strategy of one of the nation's largest managers and sellers of mutual funds, Wellington Corporation.

History of the recreational vehicles industry, and strategy of a leading company, Winnebago Industries, Inc.

History of the wine industry and strategy of the Taylor Wine Company.

History of the international bulk shipping industry and strategy of the Anglo Norness Shipping Company.

History of the pickle industry and strategy of Vlasic Foods, Incorporated.

History of the mechanical writing instrument industry and separate cases for the strategies of Scripto, Inc. and BIC Pen Corporation.

History of the major home appliance industry and separate cases on the strategies of Sears, Roebuck & Company, Design and Manufacturing Corporation, and Tappan Company.

History of the newspaper industry and separate cases on the strategies of The Boston Globe and Harte-Hanks chain of 47 newspapers (e.g., San Antonio Express, Cincinnati North Journal).

Careful diagnosis of all of these cases yields the same result. Strategists who can anticipate far ahead the changing needs of society and change their complex, unwieldy institutions to fit those needs (by strategic change in the *utility* rendered to their product/ service/markets) not only survive but grow in public acceptance. Those which do not keep the highest marginal utility in their product/service mix evolve over time in an opposite direction. They decline, or die.

Other Evidence of Strategic Alignment

Before leaving the subject of strategic alignment in private corporations, we should recognize four implications of a rather large amount of research that has followed Chandler's original works:

1. In all corporations, strategists act as representatives of consuming constituencies, visualizing the match between the constituency

92

and the product (TE.1), as well as the internal resources (TI) necessary to bring about the real delivery of the product to the consumer.

2. These kinds of alignment, and the role of strategists, are found in foreign countries as well as in the United States: in Germany;[28] in Britain;[29] in Italy;[30] in France.[31]

3. This literature is empirical. It is not simply "theory" about how firms and strategists behave. It substantiates this theory with what actually happens in ongoing companies.

4. Finally, most realignment of mature companies comes about because strategists are forced by outside pressures (i.e., loss of resources supplied by consumers, stockholders or bondholders). This is the force that overcomes the inertia in existing organization structures caused by powerful political persons in the organization who prefer the status quo (TI).[32]

Service and Program Alignment: Government Organizations

In this section case histories will be presented to show how strategists in government act to align service and program outputs with the needs of some constituency; that is, to satisfy the demand for utility (TE.1). We shall look at city and state industries (New York, San Francisco, California), national industries (the provision of social security benefits, the seeding of hurricanes), and a quasi-government industry (the Port of Seattle). Federal industries will be discussed in a later section.

City and State Industries

As Chapter 3 showed, cities are in one sense autonomous organizations (they plan what services are to be offered, and operate those services). In another sense they are part of federal industries (many of their programs are dictated by federal grants). The fact that strategists in city government engage in strategic service alignment is shown by three crises in recent years: the New York City fiscal crisis,[33] the California tax revolt crisis,[34] and the Cleveland, Ohio fiscal crisis.[35]

Between December 1974 and October 1975, the city of New York had to choose which of its many services were to be curtailed, and which were to be maintained. City strategists did just that. The president of the United States (a potential funds supplier in the form of a federal loan) made it explicit that the city should curtail the less

93

important services it offered and maintain the most essential services.[36] It was found that New York spends $100 per capita for police and fire protection whereas Atlanta spends $41; New York spends $151 for health care and hospitals whereas Chicago spends $30; New York spends $295 for education whereas Philadelphia spends $217; New York spends $88 for pensions for its employees whereas Los Angeles spends $21. In addition, professors at the City University of New York had, through their labor union, secured the highest salaries in the nation for certain positions, outranking those at Harvard University.[37]

In 1978, after taxpayers through a referendum cut off $134 million in property taxes to San Francisco, strategists in that city responded in similar fashion. Mayor Moscone told the citizens that every effort would be made to prioritize city services, ranking them according to usefulness to citizens.[38] Samuel Roth, a citizen of Rancho Mirage, wrote to the *New York Times*, "we who voted this cut hoped that our legislators and other public officials would get the message that we do not want to decimate the ranks of policemen, firemen and schoolteachers . . . but there are many programs and agencies which have outlived their usefulness but still spend freely from the public purse."[39]

At the state level, the same reaction was shown by the governor and other state officials. They were forced to become strategists (prioritizing the comprehensive constituencies served by the state) instead of policymakers (looking only at one service at a time). A select committee of the legislature immediately convened to divide the available funds among the priority utilities to various constituencies. Governor Brown (a Democrat) and Mr. Priolo (a Republican minority leader in the legislature) stopped their disagreements and both "agreed . . . that the package of services the State can offer will protect essential police and fire service and basic classroom instruction," while cutting back on less essential services. Brown said, "I'm going to make sure that those who are most in need are most protected."[40]

National Industries: The Social Security Administration

A clear example of strategic alignment in a self-contained organization at the federal level is the change in strategic services offered by the Social Security Administration over its strategic (evolutionary) cycle. Originally, Congress specified that this agency would have one service and one market constituency. The service was making transfer payments (issuing retirement paychecks in the proper amounts). The constituency was millions of people over the age 65. The geographic market was the nation (plus United States citizens living abroad). During the first forty years of the SSA, a vast procedural network and branch organization structure were elaborated, by making thousands of incremental decisions to execute the broad goal. All of this "learning curve" was devoted to one service and one market, which was growing in numbers.

In the 1960s, something important happened. The federal government, under leadership of the president and key congressional leaders, announced an overarching theme, "The Great Society." They saw other constituencies, human beings with needs for service outputs (Medicaid, Medicare, food stamps, retirement payments to many groups not already covered) that would provide a profound *utility* for these constituencies. Medicare is aimed at health care for the elderly; Medicaid at health care for low-income groups. Retirement benefits were extended to cover persons in smaller industries, or those working in state or local governments (originally excluded).

Organization structure again followed strategy. The responsibility for issuing medical transfer payments was centralized in the Social Security Administration. Managers in these agencies then elaborated the vast complex of procedures and subgoals necessary to carry out the new services.[41] In spite of the criticisms directed at these new strategic services, the most important phenomenon still emerges: the federal government does in fact respond to the necessity for strategic alignment.

Birth of the Hurricane Seeding Industry

This case history will show a national industry at its inception stage, when strategists in government visualize a broad service goal that will satisfy the needs of a specific consuming constituency. If the goal is approved, it will then be assigned to some government agency as the latter's responsibility to execute. Responsibility in this case means that whichever organization is delegated must then elaborate the detailed policies necessary to accomplish the broad goal.

First we must locate ourselves in the hierarchy of government organizations that have service goals. Our specific interest is the Environmental Science Services Administration (ESSA), one part of the Division of Science and Technology (DST), which is in turn one part of the Department of Commerce.

Within the Department of Commerce, the DST has been assigned a certain goal. It is supposed to represent all citizens who believe that technology should protect human beings from "raw

95

nature." In other words, it is supposed to provide services that will protect persons and their property from the vicissitudes that would have rendered life very difficult for primitive man. But even "science in the service of man" is a very broad objective to assign to any one department. For example, the science of the human body is the specialty of the Public Health Service, a part of the HEW. The science of food nutrition is the specialty of the Food and Drug Administration.

Therefore, ESSA is focused on its specialty, environmental science. Its mission is to make specific programs for various ways in which human beings might be protected from harmful environmental forces. But even this is a broad goal. The way specific programs and services were made is described below.

In the early 1970s, the assistant secretary of commerce for science and technology was thinking about how environmental science might be used in behalf of mankind. In discussion with others, he decided that, since hurricanes cause enormous damage to life and property, something ought to be done about their destructiveness. This was an act of goal elaboration. It was directed to a constituency: human beings harmed by hurricanes. (It is similar to what the leaders of the American Hiking Society did when they isolated taxes as a threat to hikers.) He then recommended that the staff of ESSA scientifically analyze some alternatives for preventing hurricanes, and whether these alternatives would *in fact* prevent hurricanes. ESSA in turn gave a grant of money to a subcontractor, the RAND Corporation, a specialist in policy analysis. RAND studied the alternative of seeding hurricanes from airplanes, drawing on intricate scientific experiments. The resulting study indeed made predictions of whether seeding would help prevent hurricanes, and of the benefits and costs that would actually result if hurricanes were seeded from airplanes. This in turn was used by the assistant secretary in making policy recommendations to be used by other government agencies or private productive organizations responsible for actually doing the work, i.e., flying airplanes and seeding.[42]

A Quasi-Government Industry: Port of Seattle

The Port of Seattle is a quasi-autonomous organization chartered by King County, Washington. In its charter, it assigned the goal of rendering services to steamship companies and railroads. These services include (1) the assembling of land, (2) the engineering design of complex ocean terminals of six types, (3) the assembling of cranes and other machinery, and (4) the operating of terminals with approximately 30 different specializations of manpower. The port is semiautonomous in that it gets most of its funds from "customers" (the ocean carriers) and from selling bonds to the public. It also receives a tax subsidy from taxpayers of King County.

Steamship companies and railroads are the immediate customers of the port, but ultimate consumers are persons in Cleveland and Chicago who receive automobiles from Japan.

As ocean vessels changed from small cargo ships to giant container ships, not only the type of terminal engineering/construction/operation but the needs of ocean carriers changed. No longer could Matson Steamship Lines afford to make Seattle the first port of call before going on to Portland or San Francisco. The $100 million ships cost $25,000 a day if idle or if they sail only partially loaded. The port went through twelve long years in converting to totally different types of terminals, with totally different types of equipment, different relations with labor unions, and a different financing method. New computer software services were invented to ensure that ships could completely load in Seattle (as opposed to having a "first port of call stop") and completely unload there as well. As a result of these strategic changes, not only did Seattle increase its relative share of the transportation business on the West Coast (at the expense of Portland, Oregon, for example) but the amount of money paid to the port by steamship carriers and shippers increased.

The port strategists also realized that a broad plan for all facets of operations had to be worked out, even though they could not give answers to some of the specific details. These details would have to be "learned" over the years, as the broad plan was gradually put into effect. For example, the new cranes and machinery would require different operator jobs, with different pay scales. Or, the computer programs that would schedule ships to yard-space locations and schedule flows of containers would have to be worked out. Nevertheless, task groups were appointed to (1) figure out the capital equipment involved (the structure of buildings and machines), (2) the amount of financing required, and the method for raising money (taxes, bonds, fees from carriers), (3) the type of human organization required (structure of job descriptions). The comprehensive plan required these organizations to learn, to experiment, and to devise the details as the major goal (a second-generation terminal in eight years) was elaborated.

In 1978, the top 12 strategists of the port (themselves specialized by engineering, labor relations, selling to the ocean carriers, etc.) spent 24 weeks formulating a strategic plan.[43] They studied the 12-year history of terminal conversion and recognized it as the "first generation" of automation of cranes and terminals. Then they looked outside the port at consumers in Chicago, shippers in Tokyo, and steamship companies in New York, Hamburg, and San Diego. They looked at developments in the railroads in the United States and Germany, the political climate in state and national governments, and the labor situation on the docks. As they assimilated all of this, they predicted that ports all over the world would go through two more generations of change, taking place about 8 or 9 years apart. Each generation had to be planned for immediately, to arrange financing, to design new engineering, to relate to the taxpayers, to gain agreement from the labor unions.

If resource suppliers, the steamship companies, bond buyers, and taxpayers of King County are to support the port 15 years from now, the strategists realized that all of these separate incremental policies —finance, labor relations, terminal engineering, etc.—had to be *comprehensively* aligned in a strategic plan. If they wait until 8, or 12 years have elapsed to do this, it cannot be done. And the resource suppliers will take their cargo traffic to San Francisco or Portland.

Federal Industries

In this section we shall look at the service or program alignment features of two cases reviewed in Chapter 3, the nursing home industry and the hospital industry. An additional case history in the education will show that top managers in all federal industries innovate services and constituencies very much as their counterparts in business innovate products and markets.

The Nursing Home Industry

In the nursing home industry, Chapter 3 showed how the Social Security Act (1962) set broad goals and assigned them to the Department of Health, Education and Welfare, how the HEW elaborated these into two different services (skilled nursing care and intermediate nursing care). Fourteen years later, in 1976, HEW elaborated nine pages of standards describing the type of care to be given in each of these two services. Later, the state legislature, in response to resources supplied by HEW further elaborated these for 277 nursing homes in the state of Washington, giving care to 16,000 human beings.

The Hospital Industry

In the hospital industry, the 1973 Health Maintenance Act envisioned a certain type of hospital, the health maintenance organization (modeled after the Kaiser Foundation Hospital in California), to render a certain diversified list of services to society. HEW elaborated this broad goal into the groups of services to be offered. So detailed were the programs that when, four years later, Long Beach, California, wished to create a hospital of this type, it had to follow HEW strategy by offering *six* separate services (e.g., patient counseling, human relations, etc.) within *one* of several major groups of services.

As this book is written, seven years after the original service/constituency was enacted by Congress, the strategic process still goes on. Hale Champion, undersecretary of Health, Education and Welfare, is doing what all strategists do: reading the demands of consumers in the environment and envisioning still greater development of the HMO throughout the nation. He calls attention to the fact that in the past year the number of persons who enrolled in group health plans at HMO hospitals increased to 7.5 million from 6.3 million in the previous year. He predicts that the number of people who get this type of care will triple from 1980 to 1990, to a total of 20 million. He also predicts that the number of hospitals of this type will increase from the present 200 to 440 in the same period. In these respects he views service innovation (TE) and the organization structure to implement it (TI. 12, 440 branch hospitals) very much as the president of Ford would view the development of a small compact car that serves the needs of 20 million people and requires an organization of five branch manufacturing plants to implement its production.

Champion continues: "To understand how important we think this is, and how much effort we will invest in it, we project a savings of $20 to $24 billion in the national health bill. Most important of all, we project superior health care along with those savings."[44]

The Education Industry

A similar pattern of strategic behavior can be found in the education industry. A fascinating case history of the Right-to-Read Program, initiated by the commissioner of the United States Office of Education in 1971 shows how the broad goal to achieve 99 percent literacy in the United States by 1980 was elaborated into subprograms over a nine-year period. For example, in 1972, 120 local reading renewal programs were planned. The regulations spelled out four types of services to be rendered to state and local agencies, which would then render the actual education programs to people with reading deficiencies. Of interest in this case is the fact that the commissioner of education did not need legislative authority to create these programs. In his words, the internal budget process was used "to take money from other programs to carry out this program."[45] This shows freedom to innovate services, very much like the freedom enjoyed by entrepreneurs in DuPont when they decided to produce plastics instead of gunpowder.

Today there are numerous examples, both informal (e.g., taxpayers or interest group demands) and formal (federal and state government intervention) of what has come to be called in the secondary education industry the *accountability movement*. There is also a vast literature on this subject.[46]

Examples of informal interest group action are the numerous parent groups demanding that their children get a certain service output from the school system. This informal behavior on the part of parents may later turn to the court system for formal action. In Fort Lauderdale, Florida, a Mr. and Mrs. Garrett sued the Broward County School Board to *prevent* their 19-year-old daughter from graduating. They alleged that she could barely read and write, that she did not have the basics in mathematics and English to give her skills for a happy and productive life, and that the school board was negligent in not giving more priority to such knowledge and skills.[47]

What these parents were objecting to was the school's neglect of one product/service while devoting resources to other, less essential services such as this one, cited in a school program brochure of the Metropolitan Detroit Board of School Studies basketball program (other programs dealt with language and reading): the objective of the "dribbling with change of hand" category is "to develop skill and speed of dribbling, hand, eye, and foot coordination, agility and ability to change direction."[48]

At a more formal level, a proposal has been introduced into Congress that would establish national examination standards. Senator Pell (R.I.), chairman of the Senate Education Committee, told participants at the National Conference on Achievement Testing and Basic Skills that he favored a voluntary national school examination emphasizing three service outputs: reading, writing, and mathematics. Joseph Carrol, superintendent of schools in Palm Beach, agreed. "I think such an examination would be useful. Knowing how to read and do mathematics is not all that different in Florida than it is in Oregon." Joseph Califano, as secretary of Health, Education and Welfare, took a step predicted by strategy and structure theory: he announced the establishment of an Office of Testing and Assessment to take the broad goal and work out details to implement it.[49]

100

The Demand for Service Alignment: National Society Level

The demand for prioritizing—for aligning the vast operations of the whole national society and somehow relating them so that scarce resources can be allocated to produce services that have highest utility for mankind—has been most evident in countries that are not as affluent as the United States. Because of their scarce resources, underdeveloped nations such as India must allocate those resources to industries and services with the greatest payoff. For national productivity reasons, nations such as France, Japan, and Sweden have devised federal mechanisms for allocating the total capital in the nation to industries that produce services most needed by society.

In the United States, the demand for strategic alignment has not arisen as strongly as in these other countries. Nevertheless, in this section we will see that such a demand does exist in the United States, and that it is being expressed in various ways. We shall first look at some demands made by interest groups, using principally the press or political leaders as their representatives. Second, we will look at two types of alignment actually used in government. Finally, introduction of a national planning act into Congress deserves attention.

To see most clearly the connection between society level strategy and the strategic behavior described in this book one might imagine the entire national government as a vast conglomerate using scarce resources to produce goods and services that the government believes would have the greatest payoff in utility (TE) for the population. Of course, as Chapter 7 will show, to most Americans this notion conflicts directly with a powerful cultural demand (CE), the demand for freedom and autonomy. That is exactly the problem faced by national strategists in this and in every other industrialized society. It is what a respected member of the President's Council of Economic Advisors meant when he authored a book entitled *Equality and Efficiency: The Big Tradeoff.*[50] The Russians have solved this tradeoff in one way, the British in another way, the Yugoslavs in another, and the French and Swedes in still others. The following case histories will show the tradeoff situation in the United States in the 1980s.

Interest Groups and National Alignment

The press, as well as certain individual congressmen, often act as leaders of a constituency that demands that "low priority" or "low

101

marginal utility" services be dropped from government and their resources added to programs of more importance. Senator Proxmire receives wide publicity for his "Golden Fleece" awards granted throughout the year to those government projects he considers of low priority. The implication is that such projects fleece the taxpayer of scarce money resources. Recently, his award went to the National Institute for Mental Health. The Institute had spent part of a $97,000 project for a university professor to study prostitution in a brothel in Cuzco, Peru. Cuzco is one of the leading tourist attractions in the Andes. In the resulting research study, only fourteen lines of information was devoted to the main goal of the $97,000 project. The fact that the National Institute immediately apologized to the senator shows that resource suppliers do in fact influence strategic alignment.[51]

Once a year, Proxmire grants a "Fleece of the Year" award. In 1978 it went to the Air Force for purchasing a fleet of 23 jet airplanes for $66 million to transport government VIPs. James Kilpatrick, a well-known newspaper columnist, adds that "this travel by V.I.P.'s is not free. It is paid for by the sweat of men and women who labor and pay taxes."[52]

This same demand is expressed by Senator Beard of Rhode Island. In November 1978, the nation was shocked by the mass suicide of American citizens who belonged to a religious cult. They had voluntarily migrated to and lived in Guyana. After the federal government spent an estimated $8 million to return the dead to the United States, Beard objected. Congressman Crane from Illinois joined him: "The American taxpayers have no responsibility to absorb one cent of the burden of dealing with the problems in Guyana."

At a more organized level, formal interest groups also engage in this kind of prioritizing. The United States Conference of Mayors, the United Auto Workers, and the Urban League recently joined in drafting "The Transfer Amendment" to present to Congress. This law would transfer $12 billion from national defense programs to other agencies such as HEW, or the Department of Housing and Urban Development.

The press in Britain has been especially strong in demanding alignment. There are a number of government organizations in Britain which the government calls "Quasi-Autonomous National Government Organizations." The London Times has labeled these "quangos" and severely criticized the low priority of their programs. It points out that were 10 quangos in 1900, 84 in 1949, and 252 in 1978.[53]

102

Zero-Based Budgeting and Sunset Laws

In the state of Georgia, the zero-based budgeting system installed in the early 1970s was clearly aimed at the responsibility for strategic alignment. It demanded that all public agencies in the state must evaluate all of their service outputs together, in relation to each other, as if they had zero-budget money. This in turn would prevent them from simply extending last year's budget from year to year. Such an "incremental" extension would, the governor held, simply result in each agency rendering a service that fit some other constituency in history (i.e., back when the program was evolving). By ranking all services under their jurisdiction, policymakers would become strategists, comprehensively aligning all services to their future utility to the public, rather than simply extending what had been done in the past.

So important is the zero-based budgeting theme at the present that a book on the subject is one of the ten best-selling nonfiction books in the nation. The publisher is announcing the tenth printing.[54] One of the nation's leading public accounting firm's seminars on the subject have drawn crowds in New York, Chicago, Boston and Houston. The president of the United States has mandated that the federal budget for fiscal year 1979 must employ the zero-based method.[55]

Another mechanism for strategic alignment of federal programs has been the introduction of so-called *sunset bills* in state legislatures. In 1977 Senator Muskie of Maine introduced a sunset bill into the national Congress. This bill would automatically terminate each federal program every six years, unless Congress decided after reviewing the program's goal that it was still of priority usefulness to the American people. The bill passed the Senate Governmental Affairs Committee, and was approved by more than half the Senate. The bill had the endorsement of the president.

The Economic Planning Act (1975); The NIRA (1933)

In 1975 a coalition of powerful Democratic and Republican senators (Humphrey, Jackson, Javits) introduced the Balanced Growth and Economic Planning Act. Its purpose was to predict the future needs of consumers and then arrive at a gross outline, or "skeleton" of the future distribution of resources between industries and firms over a fairly long period of time. The bill also contained an organization structure to elaborate detailed plans. It created in the Office of the President an Office of Balanced Growth and Planning that would

103

review the budgets of all federal agencies, and all legislation creating new agencies. The office would analyze the economy industry by industry and sector by sector, including energy, transportation, housing, health, etc. It would put together "a six year plan, embodying coherent and realizable economic and social goals."

This plan would be submitted to the president. If he or she approves, the act requires the president to submit a proposed updated plan to Congress every two years.

It is beyond the scope of this book to describe the details, merits, or drawbacks of this bill. That has been done in an exhaustive analysis by leading academics.[56] The bill indicates to us that a significant number of political leaders believe that some comprehensive strategic alignment of the nation's production of goods and services is needed—an alignment that would more nearly allocate resources to the most needed and useful product/markets.

It is significant that the other serious attempt at strategic alignment of the United States economy occurred at a time when scarce resources were not being utilized to produce *growth* in the economy. One of the reasons Congress passed the National Industrial Recovery Act in 1933 was to enable companies in industry to fix prices, so that they would have enough revenues to hire more employees, raise wages, and invent and develop new products. This effort at national alignment, declared unconstitutional in 1935, had some similarity to the systems used today in France, Sweden, and Japan.

Strategy and Structure: Behavior of Political Parties

In Chapter 5 we will look at the strategic vision of one of the most powerful leaders of the Democratic party, extending over 80 years. As he addresses the platform (strategy) committee for one year (1973), he sketches the history of relatively unchanging broad goals of the party in terms of services to be rendered to major segments of society. He sees the entire work of the Democratic party over the 80-year period as, "translating these fundamental human aspirations into *public institutions*" which elaborate new variations of services to be rendered. His explanation of the role of strategy (visions of services to be provided) and structure (creating organizations) is not unlike that found in Sloan's *My Years With General Motors.*[57] Sloan, over the 45 years from 1920 to 1965, viewed General Motors as having certain overarching missions (major types of vehicles) directed to persons with "differing fundamental aspirations" (market segments). He viewed these missions as unchanging over the years.

104

The function of General Motors strategists were (1) to create divisions within General Motors (including various coordinating mechanisms) and (2) to make sure that these divisions continued to innovate new variations of the same missions.

In this chapter we have focused on how business strategists align products with market segments and how government strategists align services with client constituencies. This is only the beginning of the comprehensive task alignment process. It remains to align the internal resources (TI) of the organization in a logical way to produce the final output goal. This will be the subject of Chapter 5.

Notes

1. Philip Kotler and S. J. Levy, "Broadening the Concept of Marketing," *Journal of Marketing*, January 1969, pp. 10–15; Philip Kotler, "A Generic Concept of Marketing," *Journal of Marketing*, April, 1972, pp. 46–54; R. Bagozzi, "Marketing as Exchange," *Journal of Marketing*, October 1975, pp. 14–31; Derek F. Abell and John S. Hammond, *Strategic Market Planning*, Prentice-Hall, 1979.

2. C. E. Summer, Interview with Professor Edmund P. Learned, in *Factors in Effective Administration*, Columbia University Graduate School of Business, 1956, pp. 187–93.

3. Charles I. Gragg, "Because Wisdom Cannot Be Told," *Harvard Alumni Bulletin*, October 19, 1940, pp. 78–84.

4. Edward C. Bursk and D. H. Fenn, *Planning the Future Strategy of Your Business*, Harvard University Press, 1965.

5. E. P. Learned, C. R. Christensen, K. R. Andrews, and W. D. Guth, *Business Policy*, 1965.

6. K. R. Andrews, *The Concept of Corporate Stategy*, Dow Jones-Irwin, 1971.

7. Hugo Uyterhoeven, R. W. Ackerman, and J. W. Rosenblum, *Strategy and Organization*, Richard D. Irwin, 1973.

8. Massachusetts Institute of Technology Press, 1962.

9. Harvard University Press, 1977.

10. W. H. Newman, *Business Policies and Management*, Southwestern, 1946.

11. W. H. Newman, "Shaping the Master Strategy of Your Firm," *California Management Review* 9:3 (Spring 1967): pp. 000–00.

12. H. Igor Ansoff, *Corporate Strategy*, McGraw-Hill, 1965.

13. Tom Burns and G. M. Stalker, *The Management of Innovation*, Tavistock, 1961.

14. Joan Woodward, *Industrial Organization*, Oxford University Press, 1965.

15. Paul R. Lawrence and Jay W. Lorsch, *Organization and Environment*, Harvard Graduate School of Business Administration, 1967.

16. John Child, "Organizational Structure, Environment and Performance: The Role of Strategic Choice," *Sociology* 6:1 (January 1972): 000–00.

17. Herbert Simon, *Administrative Behavior*, 3rd ed., The Free Press, 1976, p. 186, 219.

18. Peter F. Drucker, *Concept of the Corporation*, John Day, 1946.

19. Alfred P. Sloan, *My Years With General Motors*, Doubleday, 1963.

20. David B. Truman, *The Governmental Process*, Knopf, 1951.

21. Thomas R. Dye and H. Zeigler, *The Irony of Democracy*, Wadsworth, 1975.

22. Charles E. Lindblom, *The Policy-Making Process*, Prentice-Hall, 1968; David Easton, *A Framework for Political Analysis*, Prentice-Hall, 1965.

23. James Q. Wilson, "The Rise of the Bureaucratic State," *The Public Interest*, 41 (Fall 1975): 77–103.

24. Nathan Glazer, "Towards an Imperial Judiciary," *The Public Interest* 41 (Fall 1975): 104–23.

25. Edith Penrose, *The Theory of the Growth of the Firm*, Basil Blackwell, 1963.

26. For sources see Appendix.

27. *Strategic Output Alignment*, (case file) Appendix.

28. Heinz Thanheiser, *Strategy and Structure of German Firms*, Doctoral Dissertation, Harvard Business School, 1972.

29. Dereck Channon, *Strategy and Structure of British Enterprise*, Doctoral Dissertation, Harvard Business School, 1973.

30. Robert Pavan, *Strategy and Structure of Italian Enterprise*, Doctoral Dissertation, Harvard Business School, 1972.

31. Gareth Pooley-Dias, *Strategy and Structure of French Enterprise*, Doctoral Dissertation, Harvard Business School, 1972.

32. Bruce Scott, "The Industrial State, Old Myths and New Realities," *Harvard Business Review* 51:2 (March 1978): 133–48.

33. *New York City Fiscal Crisis* (case file) Appendix.

34. *California Tax Revolt* (case file) Appendix.

35. *Cleveland, Ohio* (case file) Appendix.

36. *New York Times*, October 30, 1975.

37. *New York Fiscal Crisis* (case file) Appendix.

38. *San Francisco Chronicle*, June 8, 1978.

39. *New York Times*, June 25, 1978.

40. *Seattle Times*, June 24, 1978.

41. For a comprehensive strategic history of the Food Stamp Program, see "Politics and Economy of Hunger," and "The Food Stamp Program—U.S.D.A.," by Beverly Brandt (Appendix).

42. Ronald A. Howard, James Matheson, and D. W. North, "The Decision to Seed Hurricanes," *Science* 176:4040 (1972) 1191–1202.

43. *Port of Seattle*, Strategic Plan, 1977 (Appendix).

44. *Federal Industries* (case file) Appendix.

45. *U. S. Department of Health, Education and Welfare*, Appendix.

46. There are at least ten books on the subject. The following articles from the *National Association of Secondary School Principals Bulletin* are also examples: Huber, "Dangers of Misapplication of Accountability," (April 1971); Ornstein, "The Promise and Politics of Accountability," (March 1974); Shami, "Dimensions of Accountability," (September 1974).

47. United Press International, June 2, 1977.

48. *Planning with PPBS*, Metropolitan Detroit Bureau, 1970.

49. *New York Times*, March 5, 1978.

50. The Brookings Institution, 1975.

51. *Seattle Times*, June 28, 1978.

52. *The Washington Star* Syndicate, 1976.

53. *London Times*, September 14, 1978.

54. Peter Pyhrr, *Zero Based Budgeting*, John Wiley, 1977.

55. Peat, Marwick, Mitchell & Company, *WNLD*, Summer 1977.

56. *The Politics of Planning*, Institute for Contemporary Studies, 1976.

57. Doubleday, 1963.

CHAPTER 5

Comprehensive Alignment: Strategy and Policy Formulation

THIS CHAPTER will first show what a comprehensive task alignment *is*. From an organization theory point of view, it is a comprehensive network of internal resources (TI) that are logically related to produce a certain product for a certain constituency (TE). Objective alignment is never achieved in reality. Instead, it is approximated over long evolutionary time cycles. Furthermore, it is achieved only in organizations that are surviving and growing. Organizations that stagnate, decline, or die do so precisely because their resources, or their products and services, get out of alignment with the demands of consumers, clients, or resource suppliers.

The main body of the chapter concerns the way objective alignment is accomplished—by *strategic management*. Strategic management involves the management of three processes:

1. *Strategy formulation*, by which general managers (strategists at the strategic level) conceptualize a *strategy:* a broad, holistic, gestalt network of logically interrelated *policies* covering both external products and markets (TE), and internal resources (TI). This is a hypothesis of how the whole system should operate.
2. *Policy formulation*, by which general managers engage in slow, evolutionary, trial-and-error discovery of how the system does operate. In this process they make piecemeal, incremental decisions (individual policies) taking into account the strategic whole. They also learn from experience, adjusting the whole. They allocate resources to two other levels in the organization: to administrators (at the middle-management or administrative level) and to supervisors (at the operating level or work level).
3. *Policy implementation*, by which administrators and supervisors

elaborate the policy being made into detailed actions. They also feed back information on the workability of policies for general managers' use in adjusting the strategy.

Viewed in another way, this chapter describes the work of general managers or strategists. Their "job description" turns out to be the first two processes. The third is described briefly, but full coverage is best left to books on implementation or administration. Our mission is to understand strategy formulation and policy formulation.

The first half of the chapter is devoted to the theory of the strategic process. The second half contains case histories. Though cases are important in all facets of strategic leadership, they are especially important in this chapter. One cannot gain an understanding of comprehensive alignment by theory alone. Only the reality shown in cases provides command of an essential principle: the perceived visions of strategists do indeed get engineered into real, objective, organizational actions. But they do so only through a complex process of comprehensive alignment—what we shall call the processes of strategic management.

The Concept of Comprehensive Task Alignment

Comprehensive task alignment of an organization has four main characteristics. First, it is *comprehensive:* a complex network of internal resources (TI) is logically related in such a way that it produces the final product or service goal (TE). Second, it is *evolutionary:* it takes place (is approximated) over all survival and growth phases of the organization's life cycle rather than at only one time. Third, it is approximated *only by organizations that are in survival and growth stages* of their life cycles. In fact, organizations stagnate, decline, or die because resources and services somehow get out of alignment, the final product cannot be produced to satisfy the outside world, and resource suppliers cut off the support so necessary for survival. Finally, alignment is achieved by the *strategic management process*, an interrelated combination of *strategy formulation, policy formulation*, and *policy implementation*.

Sociologists and economists have used the term "rationalization" to describe the process by which resources and outputs are related. In England, France, and Denmark even the newspapers and persons in the street know the meaning of rationalization. We can as easily use the term here except for one thing, to be made clear later. The alignment we are talking about is not a matter of science, as scientists interpret rational systems. It is facilitated by scientific analysis but it is more a process of conceptualization and logic. Therefore, the term "alignment" is preferable in the study of strategy and policy.

In sections that follow, we will discuss the first three characteristics of alignment. The remainder of the chapter will be devoted to case histories that show what the strategic process is and how it is carried out in real organizations.

A Comprehensive Network of Resources

Unfortunately, the internal resource system of an organization is so complex that some way must be found to answer the question of *what* is being aligned. For example, any museum, child-care program, or manufacturing company must use physical buildings, office equipment, or machines to get out the work. Any police department or commercial bank must have an organization structure that permits middle managers to work out the detailed suboperations necessary to put police patrol work into effect or to open savings accounts for depositors. We can completely understand the vast network of internal resources only after studying the case histories in this chapter. For the present, we need some classification system to make sense of it.

The following classification is stated as though an organization is comprehensively aligned at a given point of time. It is an ideal model, an abstract synopsis of what an organization would look like if it were so aligned. No organization is ever in such alignment. But as we will see in the next section, organizations that survive and grow *approximate* this alignment over long stages in their life cycles. This is the way "ideal" alignments or "perceived alignments" are translated into real, objective alignments.

TE. The products or services (the output) are aligned with utility demands of consumers and resource suppliers. These are the task goals of the organization.

TI. The internal resources (inputs, throughputs) required to produce the product are aligned among themselves and with the product (TE).

    TI.1. Structural (fixed) resources are aligned:

        TI.11. A structure of physical capital (buildings, equipment).

        TI.12. A structure of administrative (middle-management) roles (i.e., the organization design).

    TI.2. Operating (dynamic work-level) resources are aligned.

109

TI.21. A physical workflow or operating process (flow of materials or semifinished services).

TI.22. A manpower resource system (work roles or work design, manpower acquisition, training, and motivation processes).

In earlier chapters, we saw part of the comprehensive alignment in the Department of Health, Education, and Welfare as it aligned its organization structure for nursing homes and hospitals. This chapter will continue those histories. We shall also look at the alignments of Sears, Roebuck and Company, the Boston Symphony, and Timex Watch Corporation.

Evolutionary Time Cycles: An Ongoing Process

In Chandler's study of the DuPont Corporation,[1] the policy decision to enter the plastics industry (diversifying further from the original product: gunpowder) was made after lengthy investigation by the management. Following that, many years elapsed during which the details of internal alignment had to be worked out by policy formulation: buildings had to be designed, departments and divisions had to be created to engineer (design machines and production lines for) the processes, advertising techniques directed at different constituencies (ladies' stockings) never before included in the strategy had to be learned. People had to be hired and trained to fill the boxes on the organization chart.

Cooper and Schendel[2] studied the length of time it took from the moment a new product appeared in an industry until the sales of that product exceeded those of the product it was replacing. It took 14 years from the time the diesel electric locomotive was introduced until its sales exceeded sales of the steam locomotive. It was nine years from the time the ballpoint pen was introduced to the market to the time its sales exceeded those of conventional fountain pens. The first ballpoint pens blotted, skipped, and leaked in the consumer's pockets. As public interest waned in the third year, it may have looked as if strategists in the industry were making disjointed policies; manufacturing policies did not seem to align with product/market utilities. However, the survival of the ballpoint pen 17 years later shows that strategists were formulating incremental corrective policies that were indeed comprehensive (they aligned with one another).

An even greater length of time was involved from the time, in the early part of the century, when DuPont diversified from gunpowder to its first new product until the time, in the 1970s, when it was considering still further diversification. Forty-two years elapsed during which the strategists envisioned first one product and then another and experimented with internal arrangements, abandoning some and keeping others.

We saw in a previous case history that in the Department of Health, Education, and Welfare it took fourteen years from the time Congress established the service market policy for nursing homes (the Social Security Act of 1962) until the HEW spelled out, in 1976, nine pages of regulations. These regulations specified the type of capital equipment to be used (buildings, health care devices), the type of organization structure to be used (intermediate homes versus skilled nursing homes), the number of nursing positions to be used in each of the two types, and the type of manpower selection processes to be used (qualifications of human beings required to fill those positions).

We also saw that there was a nine-year elaboration cycle from the time when the United States commissioner of education visualized remedial reading programs in the United States and the time when he visualized the programs in full operation. He set as one benchmark the establishment of an organization structure (TI.12)—a set of 120 facilities in the United States—that was to be achieved at the end of two years. These 120 facilities were then expected to further refine operating processes (TI.2) to accomplish the goals of learning. As in many such federal programs, the corporate staff in Washington would actually monitor the way these lower units "discovered" teaching and learning processes. When people in a program in San Antonio, for example, discovered a particularly effective set of operating processes, they might suggest its use in programs in Wichita or Philadelphia.

A final case we have seen is the creation of health maintenance organizations by Congress. The evolutionary cycle of these hospitals included (1) attempts by a group in California to work out their own implementation of one department in the hospital (four years after Health Maintenance Act), and (2) a series of changes made by California lawmakers and state health care officials designed to correct incremental abuses that had been discovered in operating such hospitals (eight years after the initial act).

Growth Organizations Versus Declining Organizations

The third characteristic of comprehensive alignment, that it is approximated only in survival and growth stages, is covered in this

111

book only from one viewpoint. The entire book shows case histories in which strategic alignment in fact takes place in successful organizations. Case histories of stagnating, declining or dying organizations, is left to other books. However, at the end of this chapter, after we have clearly seen the role alignment plays in causing success, we will be able to throw light on how *lack* of alignment would cause stagnation or decline. We will do this simply by pointing out what would have happened to Timex Corporation, or the Boston Symphony, if they had failed to correct their mistakes by learning from experience. The A&P Food Corporation, cited in Chapter 4, also shows how lack of alignment can move a company from growth to decline.

Alignment:
A Strategic Process View

Alignment is not a theoretical matter as the previous static, point-of-time model would at first imply. In fact, the whole field of study of policymaking has grown up in response to the need for action. Schools of economics have, for example, established courses in economic policy as contrasted with economic theory. Law schools have been more concerned with law practice than they have with political theory. We must, therefore, bridge the gap between a theory or organization goals and resources on the one hand and the practical process by which these goals are engineered into reality on the other. This gap is filled by recognizing that over the long evolutionary life spans of organizations three dynamic processes are at work that cause organizations to approximate the state of ideal alignment described in organization theory. Two of these processes occur at the strategic level of organizations. They are performed by general managers or strategists. Case histories in Chapters 3–6 give detailed meaning to the following summary of strategy formulation and policymaking. The third process, policy implementation, is performed by managers at the administrative level or the operating level in organizations.

Strategy Formulation

Strategy formulation is a broad, first approximation of the comprehensive network of policies (decisions) in the comprehensive alignment. It yields a comprehensive, gestalt, holistic picture of the environment (constituencies), the task goal (product or service), and the system of internal resources. It is a tentative hypothesis, an

112

approximation, to be continuously adjusted as strategists engage in policymaking. In this chapter we are concerned with case histories to show how real strategists perform this kind of decision-making. In Part IV we will also be concerned with the intellectual and cognitive processes by which a human mind does this, and refer to the social processes a group of strategists might use to think in this manner. At this point we simply recognize that the mental process is more a matter of conceptual creativity and logic than it is one of scientific analysis and scientific experiment. It is, however, similar to what scientists do when they generate hypotheses, not what they do when they perform rigorous quantitative analyses to accept or reject hypotheses.

Policy Formulation

Policy formulation is the process of making more specific decisions (policies) about pieces or parts of the strategy: for example, a policy on products or services (TE), a policy on capital equipment (TI.11), or a policy on organization structure (TI.12). This is a long, evolutionary, trial-and-error process by which (1) the broad conceptual vision (the "perceived strategy") is translated into real, objective alignments, and by which (2) the whole organization, strategists, administrators, and workers learn from experience to approximate, change, and adjust the strategy. Here, middle-level administrators and workers perform more scientific policy analysis. They also use judgment to elaborate the broad strategy into successively more detailed actions. They, too, learn by experience and trial and error.

Fortunately, this terminology is consistent with common language often used by business managers or government officials. For example, "our product policy is to make high-quality women's dresses for marketing in Florida, California, and Texas (TE). To do this, we have a manufacturing policy of using highly engineered machinery (TI.11). Our marketing policy is to distribute through wholesalers (TI.12) and to hire salespersons who are experienced in consumer goods selling (TI.22). We grow by financing fixed assets from retained earnings rather than by borrowing from banks (TI.11)."

This quote is phrased in terms of *policies*, parts of the strategy. These have been formulated to align with each other. All of these statements together represent a strategy for the firm.

In government administration, terminology is similar. "It is our policy to provide two types of services to two different constituencies: intermediate care for those not physically ill, and skilled

113

care for those who have physical illnesses (TE). It is also our policy to have a registered nurse (TI.22) on duty at all times in those nursing homes which we classify as skilled nursing facilities, but not those which we classify as intermediate care facilities."

This quote is phrased in terms of formulated policies. Because they align (logically relate) with each other, all statements together represent a strategy that has been formulated by the Health Care Facilities Service, a division of HEW.

It is thus possible to translate the organizational view of alignment into decision-making terms. If we ask what is the decision-making role of strategists, the answer is that they formulate:

Product and service policies (TE)
Resource policies (TI)
    Structural-resource policies (TI.1)
        Capital-budget policies (TI.11)
        Organization-design policies (TI.12)
    Operating or work-process policies (TI.2)
        Physical-workflow-process policies (TI.21)
        Work-design policies and manpower-acquisition/motivation policies (TI.22)

Policy Formulation Versus Policymaking

Up to this point we have used the terms "policy formulation" and "policymaking" interchangeably. To avoid endless repetition, we will continue to use them in this way. You can tell, however, by the context in which the terms are used, that there is an important difference between these two types of decision making.

Policy formulation takes into account the strategic whole. Individual policies are formulated in light of their effect on other internal resources and their effect on the product or service output over the strategic time period. As later case histories will illustrate, this concept is very much the same as what Quinn has called "logical incrementalism" and what Wrapp has called "muddling with a purpose." All three of these concepts imply that strategists, over time, do two things at once: they formulate a holistic picture of the comprehensive alignment (a strategy) and they formulate specific parts of that alignment (individual policies). The two processes each provide information and learning for the other.

Policymaking is another matter. Though we will not deal with stagnating, declining, and dying organizations, the end of this chapter will contain some examples of policymaking that *does not* take into account long-term effects on strategic alignment. These examples strongly suggest that policymaking that *is* disjointed (i.e., is unrelated logically to other policies), if pursued over any significant period of time, would result in stagnation if not decline and death of the organization.

Strategy and Policy: Chicken or Egg?

There are an infinite variety of combinations of *sequences* between individual parts of a comprehensive alignment which any one organization might pursue over its life span. For example, when Hewlett and Packard founded their corporation, they first envisioned a product (a control device) that could serve a certain market (the astronomers on Mt. Hamilton who needed something to move their telescopes). Thus, the first step became the product-alignment decision. They hoped to increase the volume of this one product by selling to other observatories. Having solved the TE policy first, they proceeded simultaneously to make other policies: they designed a factory building and machines (TI.11), a production process to use the machines (TI.21), an organization structure of administrative positions (TE.12: Packard's wife kept the books and took care of the correspondence), and jobs to be performed by production workers and salespersons, those who did the actual operating work (TI.22). The general management function (TI.12, trying to coordinate these decisions) they reserved to themselves. Notice the decision sequence here. They started with a goal (TE—"end") and reasoned to resources to reach the goal (TI—"means"). They generated a comprehensive alignment by deductive, logical (not "scientific") synopsis.

Very soon in the company's history, the strategists made the decision to diversify into other product markets, to achieve product/market diversification. They found that they could *start* with their existing resources (TI—"means") and *then* modify the product/market (TE—"end"). They could use their resources to make a signaling device that would transmit scores to customers in a bowling alley. Within a few years, they also used their resources (TI) to diversify into other products for other markets—electrocardiographs for hospitals which wanted to measure performance of the human heart, low frequency audio equipment for Walt Disney who wanted to produce the movie *Fantasia*, etc.

This process of changing the *focus* of the problem from ends to means and back to ends was called, in Chapter 3, technical heuristics, to distinguish it from cultural heuristics which we shall see in

Chapters 6–9. Technical heuristics accomplishes task alignment but it does not always do so in the same sequence that Hewlett-Packard used (logical synopsis, reasoning from the final goal to the resource means).

Strategy and Structure

Those familiar with the Chandler concept of strategy and structure may wonder at this point how the concept of strategic alignment presented thus far compares to his fundamental work. If one reads Chandler closely, one will see that he meant not simply the design of departments and positions, though he concentrated on the evolution of work-level offices, departmental headquarters, division headquarters, and finally the general office. The last office is what this book calls the strategic level. The middle two are our administrative levels.

More importantly, Chandler showed that when managers in Sears, DuPont, and 100 other corporations formulated *strategies* they really decided on the product/market alignment (TE). When they formulated broad *structures* they not only conceptualized the job description—the role—of lower administrators (TE.12), they also conceptualized in broad terms the capital required (TE.11) and often the types of work or operating processes required (TI.21). The DuPont strategists were equally interested in the plant investments when they decided to enter the rayon business. Structure, in this sense, means a pattern of total resources, not merely jobs and positions.

Policy Implementation

Policy implementation is the *elaboration* of policy decisions at the administrative (middle-management) levels and work levels of the organization. It is here that the more detailed and specific analyses of actions are worked out. Like strategy formulators, administrators and work-level managers engage in a cycle of activities that is both an intellectual and social. They perform thousands of technical analyses, from financial and accounting analyses to operations research and systems research. All of the technical subjects in the modern business school curriculum are (or should be) relevant. Cost-benefit analysis and welfare-economic analysis should also be relevant. On the cultural side of organizational life, the whole range of social psychological concepts, small-group process concepts, and human-organization development techniques are used. Management by

116

objective and program planning and budgeting are in wide use. As Lorange and Vancil[3] have shown, and as various corporations (e.g., General Electric, IBM, the Swedish company Alfa Laval) have discovered, there are even techniques for involving administrative and work-level managers in strategic planning itself.

The processes of implementation are therefore many and varied. They are of great use in translating strategy into objective reality. They are, however, described in other books on management, administrative behavior, finance, industrial relations, organization design, and organizational behavior. Our mission in this book is to explain the first two processes which occur at the strategic level in organizations—strategy formulation and policy formulation.

Strategic Management: Strategy, Policy, and Implementation

We are now in a position to view the entire process of strategic management, the process by which decision making (strategy and policy formulation) is coupled with implementation (translating perceived decisions into real organizational alignment). The following model of the strategic management process has been most influenced by the work of the Harvard strategy group,[4] and many years of working with their method both in the classroom and in consulting with private and government organizations. It has also been influenced by the works of Thompson,[5] Parsons,[6] and Selznick.[7]

This process of management does not, of course, include the work of administrators at the middle levels of management. That is left to other books in management theory. It does include, however, the managerial work performed at the strategic level. Steps 1–4 are the decision-making responsibilities and work functions of strategists, whereas steps 5 and 6 are their implementation responsibilities.

1. The initial force for the first approximation strategy comes from a desire to satisfy forces in the environment of the organization. Strategists perceive either an opportunity or a threat in terms of product utility or product cost to a given product market.
2. In new, growing organizations, the perception is more often one of opportunity for improved utility or for lower cost. In mature organizations, the perception is often one of (a) a threat to existing products (consumers demand a service or product that more nearly satisfies their qualitative utility needs), (b) a threat to costs (the product or service is too costly), or (c) an opportunity to use existing resources to provide another product to a different market.

3. The opportunity or threat may *originate* (a) outside the organization (resource suppliers see the product or service itself as deficient in utility or cost); calling for a product/market-alignment decision, or (b) inside the organization. Inside, often some internal strength (TI) may be applied to opportunities for *other* market segments (e.g., the Hewlett-Packard example), or to lower the cost of existing products and services (e.g., the Boston Symphony Orchestra example). Or, some internal weakness (TI) may result in either lower-quality (less-utility) or higher-cost products.

4. Strategists react to these opportunities and threats by formulating product/market policies followed by and related internal resource policies, or vice versa. The network of policies in this strategy can be viewed as a structure of products, services and resources. It can also be viewed as the technical/economic system in the organization.

5. Once these have been formulated, the strategic-level group uses organization design and budgetary resource allocation, simultaneously, as implementation devices: (a) They create top administrative positions to elaborate the internal (TI.11, TI.21, TI.22) decisions necessary, and to test out the workability of decisions. (b) They create middle-level administrative positions to perform the same functions in geographic or functional parts of the organizations. (c) They create operating-level administrative positions to perform the same functions in still greater detail at the level where work is performed.

6. The function of resource allocation is to stimulate all kinds of adjustment and learning behavior at levels lower in the organization. This has been described as bargaining, consensus development, management by objectives, or program planning and budgeting. It can even be described, as one state senator later in this chapter describes it, as "knuckling under." This is not to say that there is an absence of conflict and confrontation, or even change in the alignment as implementation proceeds. It is simply to say that in organizations that are surviving and growing, strategists in fact use organization design and the allocation of budget funds to positions they have designed as their principal techniques of implementation.

Policy Formulation:
Trial-and-Error Learning

Of all fields of learning, that of strategy and policy, because it is action-oriented, depends most on practice and reality. Like law and medicine, it cannot rely solely on research and theoretical models. The following case histories of policy formulation in real organizations are therefore not simply examples or vignettes, designed to illustrate a theoretical point. They are absolutely necessary for a realistic understanding of the policy process. We shall look at specific cases in a business firm (Timex Corporation), a nonprofit organization (Boston Symphony) and a government organization (the Democratic party).

Timex Corporation

TRIAL AND ERROR   In the evolution of Timex Corporation,[8] we see a clear example of policy formulation by trial and error. The original strategy was composed of a network of consistent policies. Product policy called for an accurate, low-cost timepiece (TE). Manufacturing policy called for standardized manufacturing processes using pin-lever movements instead of jewels (TI.21). Capital-intensive machinery (TE.11) was to be used instead of the handcraft tools prevalent in the jeweled watch industry. Advertising (TI.21) was to utilize radio and printed media. Distribution was to be achieved by a corps of sales positions (TI.22) calling upon jewelry stores (TI.12).

Mr. Lemkuhl and a small group of executives who were doing the planning and administrative work (TI.12) delegated to the sales manager (TI.12) the task of further elaborating the distribution policy—working out the design of sales positions required, paying salespersons, motivating the jewelers with markups, etc.

Within three years it was found that jewelers would not accept the watches to be sold in their stores. They had learned another strategy, by responding to the rewards given them by the Swiss watch industry, and by other American makers.

Since policy formulation requires some strategy as a base from which to judge problems and make decisions, we can see how Timex changed to a distribution policy that fit the overall strategy. Drugstores, which had never at that time sold watches, were substituted for jewelry stores. In one sense, this appears to be accidental. In another, it is clearly part of a larger logical scheme.

ORGANIZATIONAL LEARNING   Just as persons learn "one thing at a time," but also develop personalities that link the many experiences into a set of abilities and beliefs, so organizations learn a comprehensive strategy over long periods of time.

Given the various policies in the strategy, Timex slowly worked out the details of operations. At the end of eight years, one factory

119

and a small sales force were in fact selling watches in the United States market. Ten years later, factories, advertising techniques, standardized production machinery, and specialized salespersons were cooperating to sell 7 million watches. Twenty years later, 17,000 employees, 9 manufacturing plants (located from Texas to Germany), and 250,000 retail stores were cooperating in a highly coordinated fashion to design, make, and distribute Timex watches.

Over this period of time, the *whole organization*—customers, strategists, middle-level managers, and employees—learned the comprehensive strategy. Two hundred and fifty thousand retail store managers had learned that watches belong in a drugstore. They also learned how to display them, how to bill the corporation for commissions, and how to converse with customers about watches as well as aspirin.

Strategic Attitudes, Beliefs, and Abilities: Other Organizations

In their landmark study of 85 organizations in electronics, book publishing, hospital care, and food processing, Miles and Snow[9] found that organizations do indeed move to formulate policies that solve the product/market problem (TE), the engineering problem (TI.11, TI.21), and the administrative problem (TI.12, TI.22). They found that organizations that could not somehow achieve a logical relationship between these policies were less effective than those which could.

In terms of organizational learning, they also found that the strategists in an organization tend to learn certain modes of behavior analogous to the many other attitudes, beliefs, and abilities developed by human beings. Specifically, they learn whether they will be more successful by pursuing one policy area (for example, looking for new product/markets, TE) or another (spending their time concentrating on operating processes, TI.21). They found four types of strategic orientation:

1. Defenders have learned that they are expert in certain product market (TE). They put their efforts on making policies to improve efficiency of their existing internal resources (TI).
2. Prospectors have learned that they are good at searching for outside opportunities (TE). They put their efforts on continuously searching outside the firm for opportunities.
3. Reactors have not learned strategic behavior. Though strategists may see in the environment opportunities or threats to existing strategies, they are unable to respond with policy formulation.

120

4. Analyzers have learned both. They take a product market where they are expert, and pay some attention to policies to improve the efficiency of internal resources. At the same time, they search for new products and formulate product/market policies.

Another important description of the beliefs, attitudes, and abilities that entire organizations learn over their lifetime is made by Miller and Friesen.[10] They studied 81 cases in business organizations which had been written either in Fortune magazine or by contributors to the Harvard Clearing House of cases. They identified six organizational "archetypes" very much as psychologists would identify personality types. Their research emphasizes that the environment an organization must live in (e.g., "moderately challenging" versus "very challenging") has a great deal to do with how strategists and administrators view the world, and how they cope with it. It turns out that a successful organizational personality is adaptive, dominant, a "giant under fire," an "entrepreneurial conglomerate," or an "innovator." Those organizations which are failures include "the impulsive firm," the "stagnant bureaucracy," and "the aftermath."

The Experience or Learning Curve

Not only do case studies provide empirical evidence that trial-and-error learning can cause organizations to survive and grow. We also have such evidence from quantitative research.

A number of researchers in marketing and finance have discovered that organizations with the longest learning experience with a product can probably produce a higher quality product at a lower cost to the constituency. The Boston Consulting Group has shown that the company with long experience will probably receive the greatest reward (revenues) from the public when compared to its competitors.[11] The Strategic Planning Institute has confirmed this in their studies.[12] The institute has also devised a way to measure product quality, and has shown that quality will indeed generate a higher market share and a higher return on investment to stockholders. A high market share in relation to competitors has been found to be caused by three things: (1) economies of scale (TI.11), which mean lower costs; (2) the experience curve (organizational learning of the comprehensive strategy); and (3) sufficient resources to keep its quality (TE) high and its internal resources (TI) in good working condition.

121

Trial and Error in The Boston Symphony

We can define a mature organization as one that has pursued a successful strategy in the past, but that, for any of a variety of reasons, now has a strategy that is rendered obsolete ("out-of-alignment" with present conditions). The Boston Symphony Orchestra case (Appendix) is a clear example of trial-and-error policy formulation in a mature industry.

The alignment (sequence) pattern used by Symphony strategists was to diagnose the problem in two ways: first, qualitative characteristics of service rendered (music repertoire) fit the tastes (utility needs) of only a small constituency, those individuals who wanted performance from year-to-year of the great classics of serious symphonic music. This was the product/market alignment problem, or, as organization theorists would say, the "domain" problem. To solve that problem, they engaged in a creative search for types of music available, preferences of different age groups, prices of tickets which various groups could afford, and desirability of offering free concerts on the Esplanade. The last would in turn attract resource suppliers such as business corporations and government. Over the years, they had experimented with the Boston Pops, which turned out to render a different repertoire to another constituency. They presented the Tanglewood Festival in the summer, combining other services (open-air enjoyment in the foothills) with the inherent utility in the music itself. In these moves, the strategists were reasoning from ends to means—adjusting means such as capital equipment (TI.11, the Tanglewood property, Symphony Hall in downtown Boston), and operating schedules (TI.21, the schedule of rehearsals, physical movement of musicians) to the ends.

At other times they reversed this process. Originally, the Symphony played only one program a week to a Saturday-night audience in Symphony Hall, a physical overhead resource (TI.11), seating 2600 people. Its work design (TI.22) specified that a fixed number of skilled musicians would play on Saturday nights. There were 106 players: 66 on strings, 16 on woodwinds, 15 on brass, 5 on percussion, and 2 on harps. Four hours of rehearsal were required for each hour of finished music played to live audiences.

Over the 50-year period starting at the beginning of the century, strategists made many changes to adjust the *ends* (market segments) to the *means* (the structure of overhead resources). They did this because musicians' salaries were going up, and the cost of maintaining Symphony Hall was increasing. Since cost of these two overhead resources originally had to be spread over 2600 tickets, each member of the audience market had to pay 1/2600 of cost of these resources. Further, other resource suppliers (wealthy third-party contributors) found it more and more difficult to make up the difference between the total cost of the orchestra and the revenues from customer constituencies.

The strategists first moved to two performances a week in Symphony Hall, thus spreading the overhead resource cost over 5200 tickets. Today, the orchestra rehearses two core programs, one for Friday night and one for Saturday night. The rehearsals themselves are treated as audience performances. Each week the orchestra repeats these core programs to matinee and evening audiences on Tuesdays and Thursdays. On Wednesdays they repeat the same programs to other market constituencies in New York and Providence. Overall, the overhead resource costs are spread over 12,000 persons instead of 2600. The cost of the service to the constituency can be reduced considerably. In this case the strategists actually created markets (ends) to fit the resources (means).

Logical Incrementalism

MUDDLING WITH A PURPOSE IN BUSINESS   Both the Timex Watch and Boston Symphony cases show that even organizations that are successful in relating to their environments cannot "mastermind" a *comprehensive and real* task strategy—real products, real fixed resources, and real processes. Strategists may and do envision a comprehensive visionary strategy, but it must be adjusted by increments. "Increment" in this case has three meanings. First, it means a part of the total. Timex channels of distribution policy (drugstores instead of jewelers) was a part of the comprehensive product/market, manufacturing, and selling strategy. It involved fitting the structure of retail outlets to the structure of manufacturing plants and the structure of basic human needs of the consuming constituency. Second, "incremental" means a "small" change rather than a sweeping change in the whole customer-company system. Third, it has a meaning in relation to time. Timex' change to drugstores was gradual, one of a long-term series of changes, rather than a sudden and traumatic change throughout the company.

Organizations that are able to keep comprehensive balance between products, markets, fixed structures, and operating processes —that can reconcile, balance, or optimize each of these with the other objectives (low cost utility and standard of living for society) are engaging in a process that Quinn has called "logical incrementalism."[13] Quinn studied in-depth case histories of ten major

123

corporations that faced important and unexpected changes in either the needs of their customers, the appropriateness of their internal structures, or the appropriateness of their internal processes. Success in these organizations was a result of strategists' ability to keep an ultimate product/market/utility orientation (thus providing strategic and long-term sense of purpose), to see the relationships between this orientation and the organization's internal structures and processes, and to make incremental adjustments between the three as unpredictable changes occurred. These unpredictable changes (Quinn called them "precipitating events") would have rendered the strategic system out of date had strategists not intervened.

Similar findings have been reported by Wrapp, who used the term "muddling with a purpose" to describe the behavior of strategists who could keep in mind the ultimate value goals of the organization while making incremental adjustments when (1) facts are not available to forecast detailed policies and (2) when political or social factors in the organization prevent any one "master plan" from being invoked from the top.[14] The *strategist's role* (which Wrapp calls a "good top manager") in this process is different from the *administrator's role*. Like Schumpeter's entrepreneur, the strategist or top manager is able to visualize ultimate goals and the balance between them, and to move the organization through time by learning and evolution.

MUDDLING WITH A PURPOSE IN GOVERNMENT   Recalling the concept of "government entrepreneurial organizations" from an earlier chapter, we see that *in fact* certain government officials act as strategists and top managers, almost as their counterparts in business do.

Henry M. Jackson, a powerful and influential member of the Senate, summarized this viewpoint in his statement to the Democratic Platform Committee in June 1972.[15] He started with an analysis of changes in means of satisfying the needs of human constituencies over a long time span. He pointed to the fact that since 1890 the nation has changed at a rate unexceeded by any other social transformation in history:

Powerful new tools applying the discoveries in the sciences were put to work for improving the health, wealth, comfort, convenience, and security of Americans . . . the world's highest standard of living was achieved in a very short period of time. . . . America has become an urbanized, automated, high technology society with publicly institutionalized values in social

124

security, labor relations, civil rights, public education, and public health that only a short while ago were considered utopian and radical.

The senator then pointedly referred to the Democratic party as a visualizer of ultimate needs and values of constituencies, and a conceptualizer of strategic *service programs* to satisfy these needs:

> The translation of these values and fundamental human aspirations *into public institutions* has been the work of the Democratic party. . . . [Its] leaders recognized and initiated the first public programs—
> To fulfill the desire of older Americans for social and economic security;
> To enable every child to have equal opportunity for a quality education;
> To provide quality medical care as a human right;
> To manage the economy for full employment, rather than to manage employment to stabilize the economy.

Jackson made explicit the role of strategic goals as ideals to be pursued over 82 years by leading strategists, who at the same time must engage in incremental policymaking every four years when the party draws up its platform. Though these year-to-year platforms may look to some as disjointed policymaking, or "political policymaking" without regard to comprehensive goals, they in fact are not. They are logical increments within a more holistic and strategic framework:

> [In this long process of goal pursuit] three insights are of overriding importance. First, our best party platforms have focused on goals and have been written in the language of idealists. Second, they have been developed in a spirit of tolerance and respect for the views of others. Third, they have been implemented with drive and vigor but with a realistic appreciation of the fact that compromise is the cement that binds lasting democracies together.

The use of the verb "to implement" refers to (1) creating government agencies and (2) action by those agencies to further elaborate the structures and processes necessary to produce a given service to the public.

Finally, Jackson pointed to beliefs of some groups in society— beliefs that might impede the long-term goal of productivity in social security, education, medical care, and industrial production and

125

employment. He calls these "cliches" or "fads" and says they have shorter durations than the basic needs of security, health, productive employment, etc. He holds that they are "simplistic and they divert attention from the real problems facing the country. Worse, they are out of step with the real needs and the aspirations of the great majority of American People."

Among the fads he cited are:

Private profit can justify all economic growth. His response: growth is good if it promotes the right ultimate human needs. It is bad if it contributes to private profits but not to human needs of other groups.

Population growth must be stopped. His response: High population is valuable in society. Birth rates are only slightly higher than those required for population stability.

Major energy programs should be stopped because of their impact on the environment. His response: Our nation needs energy for the benefit of mankind. The Alaska pipeline, offshore drilling, tanker ports, strip mining, and nuclear reactors cannot all be stopped, unless someone can advance serious alternatives.

America is too fat and too affluent. We must convert immediately to a no-growth economy. His response: There are 26 million people living below the poverty line, and 5½ million able-bodied Americans unemployed. To halt growth is not a tenable solution.

Having made the point that strategic behavior (strategy formulation) is a matter of long-term evolution, he then proceeded to show two things. First, policy formulation at this convention, at one point (1972) in the evolutionary process, is a matter of tailoring the decisions of 1972 to the social conditions in 1972, but it is also a matter of placing these incremental policies in line with the comprehensive goals of the party. Second, strategists at the convention have the function of making tradeoffs between conflicting values:

If our party is serious about leading and governing this nation, it must also be serious about the realism of its pronouncements on the environment, technology and the economy. It must propose a *package* of workable, technically and economically sound measures for protection of the environment, in the context of full employment, continuing economic growth and continuing improvement in the material welfare of the American people.

My recommendation is that the Democratic Party focus on writing a platform that rejects the temptation to simplify, to be

126

all things to all people, and to incorporate the fashionable cliches and points of view of noisy interest groups. This is a more difficult platform to write. It may be difficult to explain. But if done well, it can be an honest guide to the future.

Strategy Formulation: Global Objectives

At some point in the evolution of an organization, strategists often define some overarching, compact statement of goals that encompasses its output to society, its internal resource commitments, and its internal process aims. Such statements are highly abstract, defining ultimate ends broadly but implying thousands of policy decisions that align. Though they may sound somewhat like meaningless public relations statements to one not steeped in the process of strategic diagnosis, to the strategists who *are* so steeped they mean the same thing for the behavior of an entire organization that paradigms mean for the behavior of a scientist in a professional discipline. They define what the behavior of people in the organization is all about, just as a scientific paradigm defines to a new economist or psychologist what the profession is all about. They tell strategists what to pay attention to and what problems to formulate just as they tell a sociologist or accountant the types of problems to study and what variables are important. They function as decision-making rules to guide detailed behavior (TE, TI) just as the science paradigm contains a methodology to guide detailed behavior (experiments). Some would say that these are philosophies of the organization, or great assumptions from which all workers in the profession (whether strategic profession or scientific profession) must start their problem solving.

In the world of business, this has been phrased by Peter Drucker as the necessity for answering the question, "What business are we in?" Drucker holds that to survive and grow, the strategist must convert product goals into the *basic human needs* that are being served. The goal must be articulated in a broad abstract statement in order to do two things: (1) to keep the strategic mind clear by narrowing its field of perception in a complex world that might otherwise cause decision overload (future shock) and aimlessness when making more detailed alignment decisions, and (2) to explain to the public the vast complexity of the modern organization.

Drucker's example was well known in the 1960s. The Chesapeake and Ohio Railroad was one of the few successful railroads in the United States. While others were suffering because their internal

127

resources (vast networks of expensive tracks sprawled across the nation) were becoming obsolete in the new society (the age of interstate highways and jet aircraft), Chesapeake had a central focus for its business. It did not try to perpetuate existing passenger or freight traffic, frittering its resources away trying to satisfy all passenger segments and all freight segments of a bygone age. Other railroads behaved like this. They answered the philosophical problem by arriving at the conclusion, "We are in the business of operating a railroad." Chesapeake strategists did not. They diagnosed the philosophical problem and answered, "We are in the coal business." By this they meant that their ultimate survival and growth depended on an endless and complex stream of decisions about internal structures and processes, all of which should be aimed at the transportation of a vital natural resource, coal, from the fields in West Virginia, Pennsylvania, and Kentucky, to the ocean transshipment point at Hampton Roads, Virginia. According to Drucker, this paradigm enabled Chesapeake to avoid the aimless behavior that drove most railroads in the nation bankrupt.

It is true that sometimes these philosophies may not be real in the sense that strategists do not know how to connect the abstract statement to the vast network of real policies summarized. The statement may be only "official," blithely put out for emotional appeal to the public. Or it may be a "myth," believed in by strategists because they are myopic, prisoners of a culture that has trained them to believe in a strategy that fit bygone years, not today's or tomorrow's society.

It is also true, however, that strategists who *are* steeped in strategic diagnosis and policy formulation *are* able to develop holistic strategic vision and formulate today's network of specific policies in view of some super-philosophy or paradigm.

In Business

When Hewlett and Packard began, its strategists visualized electronic control processes applied to telescopes. They quickly moved to apply these to the nearest markets at hand: bowling alleys and motion pictures. Quite early in the anthropological development of the company they found that they were confused by the great number of options they had. They found that they would have to limit their own decision making, to stop thinking about such a myriad of possibilities, and stop draining their limited resources and energies in all directions. They arrived at a simple abstract guide for their own behavior and the behavior of others who worked in

128

Hewlett-Packard Corporation. (It was also a guide for the behavior of the public and potential customers.) They made a fundamental statement: "We will concentrate our energies and resources on electronic instruments." This has guided the behavior of the organization for 40 years, into medical instruments, scientific calculators, and pocket calculators, and a host of other products for a variety of constituencies.

Union Camp Corporation of Wayne, New Jersey, conceptualizes one of its corporate goals as "to be a major producer of paper, paperboard and packaging products." Connecting this goal to consuming constituencies, Union Camp then proceeds to clarify:

> Our corrugated containers are used to package every conceivable product from pianos to peanuts. Virtually everything the consumer uses, appliances, furniture, automobiles, food, clothing, is shipped at some point in a corrugated box. Consumers bring their food home in Union Camp grocery bags. Our heavy duty multiwall bags carry fertilizer, cement, charcoal and chemicals to both home and industry. Children learn to read from books printed on Union Camp white papers. Reams of our paper are helping computers produce answers to questions in homes and industry. Business transactions are recorded on our bond paper. When human beings look at their mail it probably came in an envelope made from our paper.

In this example, the complexity of products and the magnitude of different constituencies served is enormous. Yet to the strategists of the corporation, this is a guide to what their organization is in this complex society; it will guide day-to-day policy-formulation behavior of strategists, employees, and customers.

Avionics Research Products of Los Angeles began as a producer of flight trainers that enabled pilot trainees to simulate the flying of an aircraft while sitting in a machine on the ground. Over its 45-year history, it gradually applied its internal production experience to related products. For example, it recently introduced the Holter Electrocardiograph, an instrument that for the first time enables a doctor to attach the ECG machine to an ambulatory patient. The patient may work, play, eat, exercise, or simply rest while his or her heart action is recorded. Previous machines were fixed in the laboratory. Only brief samples of the patient's heart action (50 to 100 heart beats) were provided. The medical doctor might miss important abnormalities in cardiovascular diagnosis because heart activity could not be recorded across the entire range of human activity.

In making the decision to create this product/market domain and develop the complex alignment of internal resources required, strategists in the parent company used a theme they had conceptualized over the years:

> We specialize in using our particular experience and skills in certain areas: in bio-medical electronics, aerospace training systems, hydraulic products and plastics products. Our philosophy is to create, manufacture, sell and service unique products of the highest quality. We are heavily committed to research and development of more useful products for tomorrow.

In this statement can be seen the influence of a stream of individual alignment policies over the years. The areas contained in the statement originated this way: The aerospace-training area resulted from the original product, training machines to simulate flying. The hydraulic products came about because the original product (flight-training machines) contained 30 to 40 small hydraulic servomechanisms. These mechanisms were necessary to convert the pilot's hand and foot movements into movements of the machine. The internal resources of Avionics, from buildings and equipment to the organization of the manufacturing plant and the skills of workers on the production line, were *learned resources* that could be applied to an array of other hydraulic servomechanisms used in industry. The arm of a textile-mill machine could be moved in the same way as the rudder of an airplane.

In Government

The same type of paradigm is often used by government strategists for precisely the same reasons they are used in business. If one examines Senator Jackson's earlier statements, one sees two things: first, the long-term strategy itself reduced to a succinct and abstract philosophy that, to the senator, was an important guide for formulating a stream of policies to be made over the years; second, the specific incremental policies the senator saw as necessary at one time (1972) to be consistent with that strategy.

Whether or not these paradigms are formulated a priori (masterminded in advance of action), or a posteriori (like common law, discovered by the judge after the action has taken place) is not important at this point. They are formulated by a combination of both methods. What is important is that strategists do arrive at such paradigms and that they do serve as guidelines for policy formulation.

A second example from government illustrates the behavior of strategists clearly. On its 25th anniversary, the Department of Health, Education, and Welfare published a 32-page statement that summarizes at an intermediate level of abstraction the entire strategic alignment of the department: a logical model of all services produced, all market segments served, and the type and quantity of internal resources devoted to each service/market.[16] Starting with the fact that the department has 145,000 employees across the nation, produces over 350 identifiable services to as many constituencies, and spends $170 billion a year, Secretary Califano, asks what *is* the HEW?

Califano begins at the highest level of abstraction, though he points out that his statement is a result of 25 years during which "social needs of the people of the nation have been translated by the Executive branch and the Congress into concrete programs designed to ensure these needs." In the most general terms, "The Department of Health, Education and Welfare is engaged in the noblest work of a civilized society: helping people to help themselves and taking care of those who are unable to take care of themselves."

At this point, one might ask, "Is this not some vague philosophical idea that even Califano doesn't realize in his own mind? Is it not simply a public relations phrase designed to sound good? What is the department doing, that we can empirically see or touch, at 10 o'clock in the morning, if it is 'helping people to help themselves'? Will strategists in the various programs get any real guidance from this?"

The answer lies in the rest of the 32 pages. The next level of abstraction divides the book into three parts:

1. Programs for Protecting the Health of Americans
2. Programs Striving for Equality and Excellence in Education
3. Programs to Ensure Dignity and Peace of Mind Through Human Services

At the next lower level of abstraction, the first of these programs is described in one-third of the book. This section begins: "The Department's mission in the field of health can be stated simply: *to protect and advance* the health of the American people. Carrying out that mission, however, requires a complex and diverse set of interrelated activities that include . . ."

At this point in the document Califano proceeds to break down the entire range of health services and the markets they serve. It also indicates the types of manpower specialists who do the operating work to produce the services (TI.22: medical scientists, food inspectors, dentists, nurses) and the organization structure required

131

(TI.12: Public Health Service, National Institutes of Health, Alcohol, Drug Abuse, and Mental Health Administration, etc.).

Space does not permit a further discussion of this document. But anyone who analyzes it sees that the beginning paradigm is more than a cliche and gives meaning and specificity to the overarching theme. Anyone familiar with the controversies that have raged over the years regarding (1) helping people to help themselves (versus helping people in ways that make them more dependent on the helper) and (2) producing health services that only protect health (versus those that *advance* health) will know that Califano's carefully worded supergoals do indeed guide policy formulating behavior. To keep out of public criticisms that have been learned in the past, "help themselves" and "protect" and "advance" are matters not to be taken lightly.

Large-Scale Implementation of Learned Strategies

One pattern of strategy implementation deserves attention because we may be approaching the year 2000 with a different kind of geographic growth of large organizations—one in which strategies already learned can be replicated on a scale never before realized. They can be replicated in all of their complexity, in ever-larger geographic areas, in a shorter period of time than it took to learn them. Over the 25 years that the HEW strategy developed to the point just presented, and over the 28 years it took Sears, Roebuck to develop its retail strategy (1929–48), there were an enormous number of small adjustment cycles: the strategists would conceptualize a broad alignment plan; there would be trial-and-error learning of individual policies; adjustments would be made to discover the right policy to fit with all the others.

But HEW is in a different position in 1980 than it was in 1953, a position similar to that of Sears in 1950. Both organizations had by this time acquired a learned strategy—a vast network of products, markets, internal structures, and internal processes. The network of policies in Sears could be and were replicated by much larger volume and geographic expansion from 1950 to 1980. Such quick implementation of a comprehensive strategy is also illustrated by hotel chains and franchises (Holiday Inns, Hilton), automotive repair firms (Midas Muffler Corporation, with over 300 branches), retail stores (Radio Shack has 7000 outlet, opened 250 in 1979), food stores (7-11 Stores has 6500 branches and opens 25 per year), fast-food chains (in 1977 McDonald's added three stores in Sweden selling 15,000 hamburgers a day to its chain of several thousand in

132

the United States), and hospital chains (Hospital Corporation of America has 104 branches and is constructing 10 per year).

Strategy implementation on this scale, by which HEW aligns 7000 to 8000 children's day-care centers through geographic branches (states, cities), or McDonald's aligns several thousand restaurants through geographic branching, has some similarity to the expansion phenomenon in the Soviet Union. There, it is common practice to align an entire industry—the electronics industry, the agricultural equipment industry, etc., to nationwide product/ markets.

The purpose of presenting the following case history is to show (1) that after Sears learned a comprehensive strategy it grew from 1950 to 1980 by replicating that strategy, (2) that though the enormously complicated network of policies is difficult to grasp, strategists can logically and specifically visualize its parts, and (3) that in spite of difficulties in implementation, the strategy did in fact become a reality. In 1980 Sears branches do in fact approximate the comprehensive model.

Sears, Roebuck

As Sears approaches the 1980s, it is the world's largest merchandiser: $15 billion in sales and 400,000 employees. There are 862 Sears stores and another 1534 catalogue sales offices across the country selling everything from clothing to steel fenceposts. Twenty-three million people carry the Sears credit card, and an estimated additional 70 million support the organization by at least one purchase each year.

Over the past 30 years (1950–80), the growth of Sears was accomplished by means of a comprehensive strategy, including policies on product/markets (TE), internal overhead structures (TI.1) and internal operating process designs (TI.2). The organization had, in effect, a learned formula that could be replicated with much greater certainty and in much more concrete detail than it could have been in the developmental stage. The essential features are reproduced (and slightly altered for brevity) here:

TE: Product/markets. Sears has three classes of stores, each of which has a different configuration of products for sale:

A *Stores* (e.g., St. Louis) handle a large variety of products from refrigerators to women's clothing. They have complete automotive repair and parts departments.

B Stores (e.g., Jackson, Mississippi) handle a narrower line of products than A stores.

C Stores (e.g., Freeland, Washington) are mail-order stores in which one or two persons work to help customers select merchandise from the catalogue, help them with order forms, and provide them service to pay for the merchandise.

TI.11: Fixed-Resource Structures. Buildings, department floor space, nursery plant-growing and fertilizer space, automotive repair garages.

A resources, for major metropolitan stores, require buildings much larger and more specialized. They require large parking areas, expensive selling equipment, and large inventory and storage space.

B resources, for smaller city stores, because they are for a different market, have different building and equipment requirements.

C resources, for mail-order stores, require no inventory space, and no specialized space or equipment.

TI.12: Organization Design.

Each of the three stores has a different configuration of *administrative positions*, to match the complexity of product lines and fixed resources. In St. Louis staff specialists are necessary to control inventory and pay and supervise employees. General managers of departments and of the whole store are required to coordinate the many specialists in the operating work design. No such configuration is required in Freeland.

Each of the three stores has a different *information and control system*. Sales records, purchase records, and inventory control must be matched to the product/market. Freeland requires no inventory records since no inventory is carried. It is all ordered from a warehouse. St. Louis requires extensive computerized sales, purchase, and inventory records.

Each has a different *reward and motivation system*. Pay structures, as well as employee quality-of-life matters vary from St. Louis to Freeland. The pay system in St. Louis is much more complex if it is to pay different specializations with some sense of equity. In Freeland, there is only one classification. Big, impersonal St. Louis requires different quality-of-life considerations than Freeland, where the mail-order salesperson is in direct contact with all customers in the local community.

134

TI.21: Physical-Process Design.

The day-to-day flow of materials and services is different in the three stores. The traffic pattern design for the parking lot in St. Louis differs markedly from the simple traffic in Freeland.

TI.22: Work-Process Design.

Work and job design in problems in St. Louis differ from those in Freeland. Job enrichment in St. Louis may mean giving the salesperson feedback on the relevance of his or her job to other jobs in the store. Job enrichment in Freeland may mean only that the salesperson is intimately involved with the customer and all facets of the small store's operation. Hiring, training, paying, and "treatment" of Mary, a highly specialized buyer of women's dresses in St. Louis requires a different process than the same functions for Jack, a generalist who covers all items in the catalogue in Freeland.

The Department of Health, Education, and Welfare

Previously it has been shown that, strategically, many state and local government agencies should be viewed as *parts* of federal industries. They do not have freedom to determine their strategic alignments. At least in one respect they are geographic (administrative) branches of the federal industry. They take the strategy worked out in Washington and elaborate the details to be accomplished at the work level in their geographic territories. The following case history will show that HEW, like Sears, Roebuck, is indeed able to replicate a learned strategy over vast geographic territories in a relatively short time.

In examining the programs and organization charts of the State of Washington Department of Health and Social Services, or the State Department of Education, one finds a striking similarity between the programs offered by the state and those specified at the federal level.[17] These structural charts are a reflection of the *real* strategy at the state level. They show which programs have been allocated money, and what departments have been established to carry out *work* to produce different service outputs.

The similarity is not accidental. In order for a state to get federal money, it must discharge the responsibility for strategic alignment demanded by its resource supplier, the federal government. Another way of saying this is that federal entrepreneurs have power over state legislatures and executives. They are in the same relationship to "general managers" of state governments that staff executives are to regional managers in private industry.

Following is a list of 23 programs in the social (welfare) group of services that are performed in the state of Washington. Each has been strategically specified by the federal government.[17] Each must be performed for the state to receive matching grants of federal funds. There would be an equally extensive list of services in the health and education industries. For each of these services there is a very specifically described group of persons who are eligible. Thus we have both the *service* and the *market segment*. This is the same way General Motors would specify the characteristics of an automobile (Chevrolet) and the type of persons (market segment) who are potential customers in that market segment.

Child Protective Services
Child Foster Care
Services to Children in Own Home
Adoption Services
Health Support Services
Support Services
Family Planning
Information and Referral
Homemaker Services
Child Day Care
Sheltered Workshops
Adult Day Care
Adult Protective Services
Chore Services
Juvenile Parole Services
Placement Services
Juvenile Delinquency Prevention
Developmental Disabilities Case Services
Developmental Disabilities Home Aid Services
Developmental Disabilities Centers
Alcoholism Services
Developmental Disabilities Group Homes
Congregate Care Facilities

According to this list, HEW in Washington is a conglomerate producing three broad product lines: one in the health industry, one in the education industry, and one in the social services (welfare) industry. So diverse is this conglomerate that the welfare "division" produces 23 types of care for 23 constituencies. This is equivalent to saying that within the GM Chevrolet Division, there are 23 different automobiles (Impala, Chevette, Nova, etc.).

HEW has other similarities to GM, Sears, DuPont, and American Telephone and Telegraph. It carries out its three broad missions by expanding its geographical offices. It now has 10 regional offices, each of which has an organization structure that includes departments and positions to match the line of services. The geographic organization is further elaborated by the states. Washington State has six regional welfare offices (Seattle, Spokane, etc.) Each region in the state is further split into local branches (15 in the Spokane region, 10 in the Seattle region).

So dependent are states and cities on resources from federal programs that Missouri State Senator Webster feels it is difficult to respond to local citizens who want taxes cut. He says that it is difficult to cut back programs without turning down federal money, much of which must be matched locally. "Lots of people holler and scream about it, but in the end the legislature often knuckles under."[18]

The vast proportion of work in these programs is done by the cities, by the 3000 counties in the United States, or by the 26,140 special-purpose (sewer, water, drainage, or transportation) districts at the local level. These local governments today maintain large staffs to represent them in Washington, in order to find out what the federal strategy is and then to devise programs that will conform to it. They also "knuckle under" to their superiors at the state headquarters who receive funds from Washington, D.C.

Large-Scale Strategy Realignment

Now that we have seen comprehensive alignments implemented on a large scale, we must also see that these massive alignments get out of date. In this section we will see what happened to Sears, Roebuck strategy after 1980. A quite different picture emerges. We will then look at learning cycles as they were found to operate in a large corporation (Volkswagen) and in government (the United States in Vietnam).

Sears, Roebuck in the 1980s

We have seen that by policy formulation a smaller mature organization, the Boston Symphony, was able to realign its product (type of music repertoire) with quality demands of its market constituencies (segments of the population that like different types of music). It was also able to align the cost of the product to the public

137

by utilizing its physical plant (Symphony Hall) more effectively. This same phenomenon, in which strategists attempt to change the behavior of external constituencies as well as internal-resource designers and work-level operators, can be observed in very large mature organizations.

In 1979, Sears, Roebuck strategists found that its product strategy, which had been pursued since 1965 was out of line with the needs of its market domains, segments of the population that expected a certain utility and cost from the corporation. In the words of Sears' Chairman, Edward Telling, the problem centered primarily on the larger full-line stores. The evidence for the problem was that the share of retailing dollars customers were paying to Sears in a certain market (say, Cleveland or New Orleans) began to level off, or even slightly to decline. Customers were diverting their dollar support to Sears competitors of two types: general merchandise chains such as K-Mart Corporation or Target Stores, which offered a similar department-store range of products at *lower prices*; or specialty merchandise chains such as Herman's World of Sporting Goods or Handy Dan Hardware Stores, which offered *variety* in one product line that a full-line department store such as Sears could not match.

During the 1970s, Sears had tried two successive strategies that did not align in other respects. It first tried to up-scale its product line (and all of the TI resources necessary to align with it) to fashion-oriented department store items, for more affluent customers, with a corresponding increase in pricing (cost of utility to the customer). Though 60 percent of its old product mix was in hardgoods merchandise (from refrigerators to carpentry tools), the new strategy was to bring in higher-priced fashion apparel. Customers had not learned to "see" Sears as a fashion house. Also, the overhead structure of buildings (the layout of the stores) did not fit this new product/market.

At this point, Sears tried another strategy: it designed a mix of low-priced apparel departments (budget shops), redesigned the physical layout of stores (TI.11), and trained persons for positions in these departments (TI.12). It shut down the departments selling high-fashion (and higher-priced) Johnny Miller apparel. It changed its policy on national advertising of this image. It also slashed prices on all merchandise throughout the store, to compete with K-Mart on the one hand and specialty shops such as Herman's World of Sporting Goods on the other. This latter policy, of course, meant that the organization could not maintain long-term fiscal balance (T3) if it sold high-cost fashion items at such low prices.

As of 1980, after making policies that seemed disjointed, strategists have found what they believe will restore comprehensive balance. They conceptualize the overall strategy as one that appeals to one target market: the middle-class, homeowning family. As Mr. Moran, executive vice-president for merchandising, puts it,

> We are not a Bloomingdale's or Marshall Field. Sears has connotations of a barn or farm to some people. But Sears is a store that was built for, and helped create, an American middle class, a homeowning, car-owning Middle America with all the things that are bad or good—or that more sophisticated folks might look down their noses at. But that's what we are—an organization designed to serve these people.[19]

This overarching theme is now being elaborated. Buildings, financing, advertising, parking lots, department layouts, organization design (department head positions), and work design (salesperson positions, pay scales) are all being aligned with a broad line of staple goods that are geared to *functional quality* and *price*, rather than to novelty and fashion.

Learning Cycles

So far we have depicted a process by which comprehensive alignments oscillate between small increments of learning that are not consciously preplanned (e.g., the Boston Symphony, Timex Corporation) and comprehensive logically planned systems that are then implemented. The last Sears example shows an attempt to plan logically a major turnaround strategy. All of the cases in Quinn's book (e.g., Control Data, Chrysler, IBM) show such major turnaround realignments.[20]

There is another kind of learning and adjustment that some organizations go through. Mintzberg studied the history of several organizations over decades.[21] He found that organizations are somewhat analogous to human beings as they pass through stages of their lives and their careers. Sometimes there are periods when the organization indeed plans comprehensive realignments ("global change periods") as Sears. At still other times ("piecemeal change periods") a subnetwork of policies, but not the complete alignment, is changed. In between these periods of change some organizations, like the Supreme Court, as reported in a previous chapter, experienced periods of tranquility with little change ("continuity") or were ambivalent about trying anything new at all (periods of "flux"). There were even periods when strategists simply could not face making strategic decisions (periods of "limbo").

The German automobile company, Volkswagenwerk, exhibited these learning and development periods from 1920 to 1974. After World War II, the company was in a state of flux, since its environment had been so severely disrupted. Shortly thereafter, a global or comprehensive strategy emerged when Heinrich Nordhoff, former Opel executive, conceptualized a global objective and proceeded to implement it. The concept was the *Volkswagen* ("peoples' car"). Part of this strategy (TE), had been inherited from the war years of Porsche. The rest (TI) Nordhoff and his strategic team conceptualized and implemented. For nine years there was continuity, but in the tenth a minor (incremental) learning occurred: it involved increased advertising in the United States and design of the first significantly new model, the 1500. After this, four more years of continuity were followed by a period of flux or groping. There was an "anxious and disjointed search for new models." [22] Then four years of global change again: a new product strategy (the new Audi, the dropping of the "bug," other acquisitions) had to be accompanied by a host of internal resource changes, from advertising policy to capital expenditure policy.

Mintzberg also traced similar stages in the learning cycle of one government industry: the war industry. The United States foreign policy and military organizations proceeded through the development process in fits, starts, and comprehensive alignments.

Disjointed Strategies:
Stagnating, Declining Organizations

At the beginning of this chapter it was pointed out that this book is addressed to a study of organizations that are passing through survival and growth stages. After studying the case histories in this chapter, however, one can easily see that strategic *non*alignment is a key factor that causes organizations to pass into stages of stagnation, decline, or death.

In the Timex Corporation, the original strategy conceptualized by Lemkuhl was based on providing a highly accurate, low-price timepiece to millions of persons who formerly bought higher-priced jeweled watches. The latter had been manufactured by Swiss and American companies and sold through jewelry stores. To align the resources of the company, he visualized a manufacturing process (TI.21) that used highly mechanized production lines to produce a pin-lever (rather than a jeweled) watch (TE) in a different type of physical plant (TI.11). In the marketing area, he assumed the distribution process (TI.21) would be through normal channels. Some

140

9000 jewelry stores in the United States were the only institutions that sold watches in the 1940s. Drugstores and supermarkets had never sold watches. Yet the whole strategy depended on getting some kind of retail outlet to sell a cheap watch that did not bring in additional repair service (as jeweled watches did). The logic of the whole strategy would not work without this type of outlet. When jewelers refused to handle the watch (they had learned to sell watches as jewelry, not as cheaper instant sales for very low prices), Timex strategists responded by changing the *policy* (TI.21) to fit the *strategy* (TE/TI). They not only discovered how to sell and advertise watches through drugstores and supermarkets, but they were the "teachers" who got 250,000 stores to learn to sell watches. It took eight years to develop the entire new distribution system.

What would have happened had Timex refused to adapt to realities? What if they had not realigned the distribution policy to fit the whole strategy? Suppose that Timex strategists had simply stuck to their original distribution policy. It would have been a disjointed policy, because it did not logically relate to the manufacturing policy (mass production) or the product/market policy (cheap watches for millions of persons). Had Timex not found an institution that would act in ways that aligned with other policies, growth would have ceased.

Under its original strategy, the Boston Symphony offered classical symphonies once each week (Saturday night) to a wealthy constituency in Boston (TE). Other policies aligned with this. The needed capital to build and maintain Symphony Hall (TI.11) was contributed by wealthy donors. Musicians' salaries in those days were low (TI.22).

But social conditions in the environment around the orchestra changed drastically over the years. Musicians' organized into labor unions (CI) and salaries increased markedly (TI.22). Composers wrote more and different types of modern music (TE). Conductors themselves began to specialize in certain types of music rather than act as generalists (CI). Worse still, there sat Symphony Hall, an enormously expensive building in Boston. It sat vacant seven afternoons a week and six nights a week. Finally, expenses became so great that wealthy donors could not support the musicians and the building.

Symphony strategists *realigned* service-output policies (more diverse repertoires of modern music) and constituencies (low-income, diverse ethnic audiences). They also realigned capital-utilization policies, not only playing in Symphony Hall on Saturday night but repeating core programs at both matinee and evening performances on Tuesday, Thursday and Friday. They repeated the core programs in New York and Providence. All of this produced lower-cost tickets (TE.1) to thousands of people. The policy on capital funds was changed (TI.11). In addition to wealthy donors, the Symphony raised money from (1) larger audiences at lower prices, (2) the United States government, (3) the Ford Foundation, and (4) business corporations rather than prominent individuals.

All of these changes logically related or aligned with one another in a comprehensive strategic change. What would have happened had the strategists been myopic, continuing what they had been doing in the old alignment? According to Lanham Deal, General Manager of the Seattle Symphony, who has studied the case, "The Boston orchestra, like most others in the nation, simply could not have survived had it not made these changes. There would be no Boston orchestra today had not their Trustees made such decisions. There have been instances here and abroad when symphony orchestras did not keep up with the times and they *did* die." [23]

Arnold Toynbee's theory of history, discussed in Chapter 1, has a great deal of relevance for what would have happened in these instances. He performed massive research into the life cycles of the world's great civilizations and found that each civilization proceeds through stages of birth, growth, breakdown, and disintegration. The most important cause of breakdown and disintegration is strikingly similar to what Deal envisioned. Strategists simply lose the will and self-determination to face the complex process of realignment, and to have new strategic visions. The alignment gets out of date. Constituencies then secede from the system. The organization dies from lack of resource support.

In this chapter we have looked at comprehensive alignment and strategic management as they occur in organizations that survive and grow. We have seen that survival and growth are accomplished by fitting the resources of the organization to the needs and demands of consumers and resource suppliers. This is an interactive process that occurs between constituencies who want and need the outputs of productive organizations and the strategists, administrators, and work-level people inside organizations who shape a comprehensive alignment.

In the following chapter we will see the next series of events in an organization's life cycle. As we saw in Chapter 1, organizations are not only held responsible for effective task performance. They must also answer to society for their cultural performance. As task alignments begin to be put into place cultural demands arise.

142

Strategists must cope with these forces along with their attention to task performance.

Notes

1. Alfred D. Chandler, *Strategy and Structure*, MIT Press, 1962, p. 52–113.
2. A. C. Cooper and Dan Schendel, "Strategic Responses to Technological Threats," *Business Horizons*, February 1976, pp. 31–40.
3. Peter Lorange and Richard F. Vancil, *Strategic Planning Systems*, Prentice-Hall, 1977.
4. This literature is summarized in Chapter 4.
5. James D. Thompson, *Organizations in Action*, McGraw-Hill, 1967.
6. Talcott Parsons, *The Structure and Process in Modern Society*, The Free Press, 1960.
7. Philip Selznick, *Leadership in Administration*, Harper and Row, 1957; *T.V.A. and The Grass Roots*, University of California Press, 1949.
8. *Times Corporation*, Appendix.
9. R. E. Miles and Charles C. Snow, *Organizational Strategy, Structure and Process*, McGraw-Hill, 1978.
10. Danny Miller and P. H. Friesen, "Archtypes of Strategy Formulation," *Management Science* 24:9 (May 1978): 921–33.
11. G. B. Allan and John Hammond, *A Note on the Boston Consulting Group Concept of Competitive Analysis and Corporate Strategy*, Harvard Business School, 9-175, June 1976; Boston Consulting Group, *Perspectives on Experience*, 1972.
12. R. D. Buzzell, "Product Quality"; Signey Schoeffler, "Market Position," *Pimsletter on Business Strategy*, Nos. 3 and 4.
13. James Brian Quinn, *Strategic Change: Logical Incrementalism*, Dow-Jones-Irwin, 1980.
14. H. Edward Wrapp, "Good Managers Don't Make Policy Decisions," *Harvard Business Review* 45:5 (September 1967): 91–99.
15. Senator Henry M. Jackson, Statement to the Democratic National Convention Platform Committee, June 1972.
16. *This is H.E.W.*, United States Government Printing Office, 1978.
17. *Federal Industries*, (case file) Appendix.
18. *New York Times*, November 28, 1978.
19. *Business Week*, January 8, 1979.
20. Quinn, *Strategic Change*.
21. Henry Mintzberg, "Patterns in Strategy Formulation," *Management Science*, 24:9 (May 1978): 934–48.
22. Henry Mintzberg, "Patterns in Strategy Formulation," *Management Science*, 24:9 (May 1978): 934–48.
23. Interview with Lanham Deal, General Manager, Seattle Symphony Orchestra, May, 1975.

PART III

CONFLICT:
POTENTIAL BREAKDOWN
IN ALIGNMENTS

CHAPTERS 6–9 will show that as organizations begin, over time, to engineer their task alignments into practice, the products and services and the internal alignments they create have negative consequences on the values (self-interests) of diverse groups in the cultural environment (CE) and inside the organization (CI). One or more of these groups (the opposition groups) then take action. They try to get strategists to change the task alignment to a certain *other* product/market, or a certain *other* structure of capital equipment or physical operating process, which would have positive consequences (benefits) to its members.

A close analysis of case histories shows that as the conflict situation unfolds, and as strategists react and begin to search for alternate policies, still other groups are affected, each desiring a different end value and a different policy as a means to satisfy their ends. Somewhat oddly, it is found that some groups benefit by the present policy. It serves their best interests, even though it puts them in conflict with other groups. Still other groups raise a third or fourth alternative policy, because of the end they seek.

Thus we have a situation like this:

1. In stages 1–2 of organization development, strategists have formulated a task alignment to satisfy a network of task constituencies: consumers and resource suppliers—Task Constituency 1, Task Constituency 2, Task Constituency 3, etc. (TC1, TC2, TC3).
2. But in stage 3 of organization development, one or more cultural interest groups are affected negatively. These are the opposition cultural constituencies (OCC1, OCC2, etc.).
3. Other groups become part of the problem, either because they raise their own self-interest, or because policy formulators, as they search for a new alternative policy, discover which groups have a stake in what the policy should be. All of these groups together are pluralistic cultural constituencies (PCC1, PCC2, PCC3, etc.). Some favor the existing policy, but for a different self-interest than the task constituencies. Some raise an entirely different policy, because they like neither the existing policy nor the one that satisfies the OCCs.
4. The net result of all of this is that policy formulators are presented with several policy alternatives each of which have different value outcomes for cultural constituencies (C1, C2, C3, etc.)

Chapters 6–9 will further explain the cultural conflict which ensues. Chapter 6 shows how external interest groups arise and how government agencies frequently act as formal representatives

146

(leaders) of these groups. It shows that interest groups voice their expectations and demands in terms of themes that cannot be precisely defined or measured and that are not subject to being proved "right" or "wrong." Finally, it shows that interest groups interact with strategists in a process of political or social heuristics. That is, they *focus* the conflict problem in a certain way: they enunciate their themes, each using a chain of logic to connect *means* (the "right" policy from their viewpoint) to *ends* (their ultimate self-interests, human needs).

Chapter 7 further explains the external conflict problem, in which groups in society dispute task alignments. They demand that strategists realign products, markets, or internal resources to achieve a wide variety of cultural themes. Their demand themes include such values as equality, justice, clean air, or balance in the natural ecosystem. These demands are so numerous that we cannot catalog them as we have task performance demands, or as we will the demands of internal employees. Case histories, however, will not only show a great variety of such themes, they will show with reasonable clarity what "equality" or "ecosystem balance" mean to specific constituencies.

In Chapters 8 and 9 we will turn to the *internal* conflict problem, in which persons inside the firm dispute task alignments. They demand that strategists realign products, markets, or internal resources to achieve certain universal needs of persons who spend their lives working inside organizations. They use themes like "quality of work life" or "employee satisfaction" or "fair wages" to make their demands.

Chapter 8 describes certain deep-seated needs of all managers (CI.1), strategists, administrators and work level supervisors. These will be discussed as the demand for status quo (CI.11). It also describes a deep-seated need of middle managers or administrators, the need to suboptimize (CI.12).

Chapter 9 will show how task alignments conflict with the needs of workers at the operating level of organizations (CI.2). This is a subject that has received much attention in the field of organizational behavior. More specifically, we shall look at the demand for remuneration and job security (CI.21), and the demand for intangible satisfaction (CI.22). The latter has been covered in the literature under the general themes "improvement in the quality of work life," "job satisfaction," "morale," "commitment," and "alienation."

As case histories are presented to give more in-depth meaning to these various needs and demands, we need some organized way to view, for each category of internal participants (all managers, middle managers, employees), the wealth of demands that come up over the organization's life cycle. The most practical way is to present them just as they arise, in a heuristic fashion. Therefore, case histories in these chapters will be presented according to those which arise as objections.

1. To product or service alignments (demanding that the product or service, TE, be changed).
2. To structural alignments (TI.1), either to the structure of physical buildings and equipment (TI.11), or to the organization structure (TI.12).
3. To the operating alignments (TI.2), either to the work processes involved, or to the work design (reward systems, job descriptions, and roles).

CHAPTER 6

The Cultural
Conflict Problem

Cultural Alignment as Stage 3
in Organization Evolution

Stage 1

In case history after case history, we find that organizations go through a stage of inception or birth, during which product/market alignment is *the* problem attacked by strategists in their attempt to satisfy the needs of those consumers, clients, and resource suppliers who are directly involved with success on the task performance dimension. Strategic leaders, whether they be leaders in business or in government put almost all of their time, attention, and effort on a product or service alignment that appeals to their constituencies.

For example, in Chapter 2 we saw that Bill Kemsley and Jim Kern at first put all of their efforts and attention into one service to one constituency: they decided that the constituency was a group of persons who wanted to pursue hiking and that the first service output was advice to congressmen on how to write tax laws that would benefit hikers. Bill Hewlett and David Packard at first put all of their attention and effort on one service to one constituency: they decided that the constituency was composed of astronomers in observatories such as the one at Mt. Hamilton, and that their first product output would be an electronic control device that would move telescopes. The same was true of strategists at 7-11 Food Stores, Inc., or strategists in the Health Resources Administration, as they decided to concentrate on a certain kind of hospital service mix to be delivered to citizens with certain health problems.

Stage 2

After the inception stage, strategists turn their attention and efforts to *elaborating* the product alignment and internal resource alignment into a comprehensive task alignment. They put almost all of their efforts into elaboration, refinement, and "working out the specifics" of internal resources as they align in a logical way necessary to achieve the product or service goal. They experiment by trial and error, adjust their original strategic vision, and otherwise commit their attention and energies to task alignment. The Sears, Roebuck strategists in Chapter 4 focused enormous amounts of time, energy, and commitment on shaping not only the product lines to be offered, but also the complex network of buildings, human organization structures, operating process designs, and work designs so that they fit together in a comprehensive logic. The Boston Symphony strategists thought mainly of the kind of symphony hall and concert schedule that would offer listeners the type of music they wanted but at a cost that satisfied them. Timex Corporation strategists gave central attention to discovering how to get the watches sold through drugstores when jewelers turned them down.

Over the life span of an organization, there are some powerful reasons why strategists and policy formulators give sequential priority to task alignment (pleasing consumers, clients, and direct resource suppliers) in Stages 1 and 2 rather than to cultural alignment (pleasing cultural constituencies).

Chapter 1 has shown two of the reasons. There is the matter of complexity and overload of the mind. No human being, strategist or not, can attend to "everything at once." Aligning the product or service to the market, and then engaging in the slow evolutionary process of comprehensive resource alignment, is simply an enormous intellectual feat. There is also the matter of ultimate social expectation. As Hewlett-Packard Corporation becomes successful, acting out its strategic task alignment, the public holds the corporation primarily responsible for manufacture and sale of electronic equipment, not for creating natural history museums.

A third reason could not be thoroughly understood until this point—until we have an understanding of the complexity and duration of the task alignment process. It is a matter of the learned frame of reference, or viewpoint of top management strategists, living in, and dealing with the problem of task alignment throughout their careers. All professions have a frame of reference. It is a deliberate aim of law and medical schools to inculcate in students "the legal point of view" and "the medical point of view," as well as to teach them day-to-day skills. In science, advanced students absorb the paradigms and history of their discipline, and the kinds of problems it undertakes in the world. In both cases, the frame of reference is learned, absorbed sometimes by sheer experience over a long period of learning.

So it is with strategists in productive organizations. As we read case histories of the Boston Symphony, the Timex Watch Corporation, and the Community Health Center program in HEW, we might put ourselves in the shoes of a policymaker within one of these organizations. The Symphony specialist spends most of his or her time and career working out problems of audiences and music. The Timex specialist spends a career working out problems of time piece construction and customer need for watches. The Health Service Administration specialist spends a career working out problems of what kind of health center will serve the local community. In each case, this long process of successive problem-solving experiences generates a focus or frame of reference.

In each case, living in the organization serves the same purpose for strategists that living in a hospital serves for the medical student in residency. It focuses attention on the primary problems of the specialist. This is an additional factor that causes organizations to move through an evolutionary cycle in which task alignments take sequential priority over cultural alignments.

A final factor in this sequence is the most obvious of all. Until the strategists in Seattle City Light Company (to be discussed later) decided to align its internal resources by building a hydroelectric dam (thus aligning capital equipment with the market demand for kilowatts), there was no cultural constituency that objected to the fact that the dam would flood a valley with valuable trees and wildlife in it. Prior to this time, the Sierra Club, one of the constituencies that invoked the demand for ecological preservation, paid no attention to Seattle City Light Company. But once the company began to act out its capital equipment alignment by building the dam, the Sierra Club *became* a cultural constituency. Thus, the number of constituencies in an organization's cultural environment is actually a result of actions in the task alignment stage of development. Cultural alignment problems therefore *follow* task alignment actions. In the language of organization theory, managers first enact (formulate) the task domain. As this is acted out in reality, there is a chain reaction effect. The task domain creates the cultural domain.

All of these factors together help to shape one characteristic of the *managerial mind*[1]—the task accomplishment attitude. It remains for another set of experiences, the trial-and-error experience of

151

cultural conflict, to shape another characteristic—the cultural responsibility attitude.

Stage 3

It is sometime during stage 2 in the evolution of organizations that stage 3, the cultural conflict stage, emerges. This is the time at which the kinds of conflicts described in the Introduction to Part III begin to be activated. There is, of course, no instantaneous point of time that delineates task alignment (stages 1 and 2) from cultural conflict (stage 3). In some organizations cultural conflict may appear fairly soon after the task alignment is put into effect. For others, such conflict may appear only after years of seemingly tranquil behavior on the part of the many segments of our cultural environment.

In any event, strategists in all organizations must sooner or later face the fact that product, service and resource alignments do in fact have impact on groups that emphasize cultural demands rather than task demands. The rest of this chapter will concentrate on the nature of these groups (how they are formed and how they function) and the nature of their demands (the fact that demands express value themes).

Cultural Constituencies and Their Leaders

Productive organizations satisfy the particular needs of a particular constituency of consumers and clients. Timex Corporation produces watches that satisfy the needs of people wanting to tell time. Roosevelt Hospital produces a surgical operation, an appendectomy, to satisfy the needs of persons wanting to protect their health. All productive organizations together are expected to fulfill the responsibility for task performance in society: to produce a higher standard of living, to achieve freedom from poverty, and to protect man from the hardships of living as primitive man, buffeted by the forces of raw nature.

But productive organizations are not the only species that evolve to satisfy the demand for the social welfare. "The population" consists of an enormous network of other organizations each of which specializes in *some other value or need for some group other than the task constituencies of a particular company or hospital.** These groups may be unemployed, and demand jobs and meaningful work. Or they may demand a range of intangible values: equality, justice, beauty, or ecological preservation.

*Task constituencies, it will be remembered, are the product/market constituencies and the resource supplying constituencies.

It is the purpose of this section to show how interest groups arise and evolve and how government agencies arise to care for the cultural demands of different groups in society. We shall see that the leaders of these groups function very much as do strategists in productive organizations. They articulate the cultural needs of human beings. In the words of one eminent political scientist, interest groups feed information on what they want and need through interest groups to government officials. The latter, cognizant of these needs decide what is possible and feasible in the way of satisfying these needs and feed their decisions back to the people in the form of laws.[2]

Interest Groups: Informal and Formal

The simplest form of interest group is a loosely defined group of persons whose number is indefinite, whose leaders are spontaneously recognized, who have a vaguely recognized but somewhat unclear demand theme, and who have little or no task alignment (equipment, funds, specialized workers, analytical work procedures).

A group demonstrating in Chicago for women's rights, or in Cleveland for more jobs, without prior organization, would be examples. If not the grapevine, then the press, in the form of a newspaper reporter may be the nearest thing they have to a leader. The press as leader can, after all, "sense" important issues affecting numbers of people. It can also perform the first function of an organization, to provide an information system (part of TI.12, organization design) to announce meeting places and dates. These groups present their demands simply by calling attention to their cause, and the fact that "there is public sentiment on this issue."

The transition from informal to formal status comes about inevitably if the theme being expressed is important enough to a large enough number of people. Further, as another political scientist points out, history from Jacksonian Democracy to the present day shows that those interest groups which are better able to secure access to policy makers and to have impact, have leaders who (1) articulate some clear and relatively specific value goal or policy alternative, (2) are collectively more self-conscious of that goal, and (3) are better organized than amorphous groups.[3]

Observe a seven-month old organization named CURE, which originated with local people in rural Washington State. It has confronted strategists of the Washington Power Supply System, an electric utility seeking to build nuclear power plants. It selected the name CURE (Communities United for Responsible Energy) to symbolize its demand theme. It has volunteer members contributing personal funds. A vice-president, Mike Owens, specializes in writing newsletters, circulating a formal petition to be presented to county commissions, and giving interviews to newspapers. For presenting its demands, CURE depends on information to news media and to the county commissioners who have power and authority over policymaking, as they help determine the capital equipment (TI.11) in the task alignment of a productive organization — the Washington Power System.[4]

In evolutionary terms, a more advanced formal interest group is the Grey Panthers, founded by Maggie Kuhn. She articulated its purpose as militant, to counteract what she saw as a myth: the myth that gentle, contented older people do not engage in public action. Today the organization is a national one, with local chapters across the country. Kay Lee, a member of the Seattle chapter, expresses both the function of the organization for one human being, as well as its demand theme:

> Age comes to you quietly. You want to debate the point when someone refers to you as a senior, then you suddenly think, "hell, they've got their point." The mysterious process and products of growing old are serious. A lot of what the Grey Panthers is doing has to do with economics. That's what politics are all about.[5]

The Chapter 1 description of the American Hiking Society represents an interest group developed one degree closer to formality. Kemsley started with a vague strategic goal, "the interests of hikers." He then ensured that there was a board of directors. Jim Kern was recruited to spend effort and time focused on the goal. These were acts of organization design (TI.12). By-laws, subgoals, and a step-by-step program (TI.21) were elaborated.

As interest groups become more mature they attract more of a following and become more organized. Greenpeace, an international organization opposed to the killing of sea mammals, purchased a fully equipped ecology vessel for research and analysis (its own capital equipment, TI.11). It turned its attention to the joint policy of the Scottish and Norwegian governments, which would allow hunters to take 900 female seals and their pups, and 4000 moulted pups each year for the next four years. It presented its demands to the governments by sending its vessel, the *Greenpeace Warrior*, to intercept the Norwegian vessel *Kvitingen*, and to land a party of its members on the seal island, North Rona.[6]

154

Greenpeace, as a cultural constituency, thus operated in a dual capacity. It conveyed its objections to the product alignment (whale, fish, and seal products) of a Norwegian fishing company physically. It sent its own boat to interfere with the company's work processes aboard ship. It also tried to influence governments to pass laws that would change the product alignment of the Norwegian company, as well as other companies in the whale–seal–sea lion products industry.

No discussion of formal interest groups would be complete without mention of lobbying. For our purposes, lobbying is simply the operation of formal interest groups that are highly organized to influence government policymakers. They do more sophisticated scientific analysis. They have more specialized manpower to present their demands to those in authority or power. Their leaders perform the same functions as leaders of all organizations: they formulate goals and organize resources.

These organizations range all the way from the Chamber of Commerce of the United States to the National Consumers League, the National Organization of Women, the American Association of University Professors, and the National Association for the Advancement of Colored People.

Government Leaders' Impact on Task Alignments

The following examples will show how the actions of government leaders result in laws that in turn change the task alignments worked out by strategists in productive organizations. In the first example strategists in the education industry (i.e., school boards and superintendents) must alter their product lines in response to federal law. In the second strategists in companies that manufacture medical devices must alter their strategy. The third shows how manufacturing industries might change their production lines (their TI.21 alignments) as a result of government agency research.

SCHOOL SYSTEM ALIGNMENTS   In 1966 some congressmen became interested in the fact that many human lives are lost on the highways. They eventually were instrumental in passing the National Highway Safety Act of 1966. This act provided for a coordinated national safety program through financial assistance to each state. It provided also for federal budget funds to be paid to states that complied with the program.

The congressmen who articulated this broad demand theme ("human safety on the highways") had the assistance of staff person-

155

nel who further analyzed, specified, and articulated the theme. In the final law, Standard 303, for example, specified that each state should have a motorcycle safety program; Standard 304 required that every high school student should have opportunity to enroll in a course in safe driving; and Standard 314 required that each state develop a program on safety of pedestrians.

It took several years for general managers at various levels in the federal education industry to change their alignments, but they in fact did. The superintendent of public instruction in the state of Washington, acting as general manager of one of 50 geographic branches in the school system, had, by 1977, arranged for offering these services to new constituencies. And the general managers of 300 work-level branches (TI.22: the boards and superintendents in local districts) were actually offering programs whose curriculum included motorcycle and pedestrian safety. They were attended by 68,000 students in the ultimate constituency.[7]

MEDICAL EQUIPMENT COMPANY ALIGNMENTS   Until recent years, the federal government had regulated food and drug products, but it had never regulated "medical devices," as contrasted with drugs. Strategists in companies that produced such things as x-ray machines, pacemakers (electronic devices implanted into the heart), and interuterine contraceptive devices were free to decide on their product/market strategies. However, public uproar developed in 1968 regarding danger to health from x-ray machines. The Radiation Control Act was passed that year. In 1971 a great deal of public concern was reported in the press regarding dangers to health caused by pacemakers and interuterine devices. It took the Department of Health, Education, and Welfare six months, using intricate and scientific policy analysis, to elaborate the broad theme, "health protection when using medical devices." It published "Medical Devices: A Legislative Plan." The report was transmitted to Congress, which eventually passed the Medical Devices Act of 1976. After that date, all strategists in private corporations producing these products must design their product/market alignments to comply with design features specified by the Food and Drug Administration.[8]

ALIGNMENTS OF ALL MANUFACTURERS   Another example can be taken from a different dominant responsibility, the demand for employee satisfaction in work organizations. Though this (CI) responsibility will be discussed in Chapter 6, the example shows clearly the function of government leaders. In the 1960s, concern arose from

156

many quarters about the effects of assembly-line work on workers' mental health and satisfaction. This theme was first articulated by psychologists and behavioral scientists and it made human-interest stories for the press. Congress held hearings on the matter. Eventually, we find the secretary of Health, Education, and Welfare appointing a task force of ten persons from the fields of anthropology, political science, philosophy, labor relations, social services, and drug use studies.

This was an act of value elaboration by organization design. In essence, the secretary said to himself, "Out of all of the problems in the broad area of human health, human education, and human welfare, there is a group of people out there who have problems caused by the way they work in factories and offices." He thus *elaborated* from the broader theme, "health, education, and welfare of all Americans" into "quality of work life." The task force that eventually reported back to the secretary, found that the broad "HEW" theme had been elaborated within HEW into 300 themes, each guiding a separate program of the department, each specifying a particular value (education of the handicapped, provision of day-care centers to working mothers) directed toward specific group of people in society.

Given this value specification, the HEW, on the recommendation of the task force, contracted with the W. E. Upjohn Institute, a nonprofit research organization with the broad ethic of human health, to elaborate the theme even more specifically. Upjohn proceeded to arrange for the analysis of the problem through science: in this case, through assembling a team of 34 specialists. These were behavioral scientists who were interested in, and had skills in, the behavioral sciences as they applied to *work organizations* (as contrasted to those scientists interested in child development, family relations, or development of political attitudes). The resulting study, predicting in great detail the effects of work on human beings, implied that the principal solution to the problem is job enrichment and job enlargement, and that all organizations in the United States (private, government, nonprofit) should consider carrying out these forms of job design.[9] The HEW secretary then sent the research report to the Senate Subcommittee on Employment, Manpower, and Poverty (notice the broad value theme), which reported to the Senate Committee on Labor and Public Welfare (notice the still broader value theme).

As with formal interest-group leaders, government officials act as both elaborators of specific programs (leaders make history) and interpreters of public sentiments (history makes leaders). In this case, the secretary of HEW led in making history, in his acts of *value specification*. He formulated the theme of "health" or "welfare" in terms of the subtheme "quality of life on production lines." He used budget allocation and organization to elaborate the theme. It was only then, after the problem theme had been formulated, that analysis could begin on the factual elements in the problem (what job enrichment can or cannot do) to help solve the factual problem (redesign jobs).

Interest Group Demands:
A Decision-Making View

This section will discuss three characteristics of interest group demands that are of great importance in strategic decision-making. Unless we understand these characteristics at this point, it would be difficult to later understand, in Part IV, how decision-makers' minds work when they formulate policies and strategies.

From a decision-making view, the demands of interest groups are *themes*. Themes are a particular kind of intellectual inputs to the human mind. They are different from, and must be treated differently than, facts and quantitative data.

A second characteristic is that the demand of an interest group expresses a *group heuristic*. The group's own internal decision processes have created a certain kind of means-end logic. They have conceptualized both some *end* to be achieved (e.g., clean air for the population) and a *means* to achieve it (a certain policy that should be adopted by a manufacturing company to achieve that goal). Behavioral scientists would say that this is an intra-group heuristic because it represents the group's internal logical position.

Finally, policy makers can view all demands that are being made by all constituencies as a process of *political heuristics* or *cultural heuristics*. The somewhat random sequence of demands can neither be predicted nor controlled by the strategist. Various themes seem to pop up first here and then there. Each one has an impact on the strategic mind, forcing the decision-maker to jump from one focus of the problem to another. This temporary changing of focus back and forth from one theme to another has the effect of making the strategist view each theme as an end in itself, that is, an ultimate value to be achieved. Political heuristic processes are similar to what political scientists call pluralism (i.e., an intellectual interaction of ideas), what behavioral scientists call intergroup relations, and what organization theorists call inter-organization relations.

158

Themes to be Used in Clinical Judgments

One characteristic of demands made by constituencies, whether they be demands for task accomplishment or cultural accomplishment, and whether they be for effectiveness in the outside world or for efficiency inside the organization, is that they are not subject to a *generally acceptable definition*. They are used by different persons with different cognitive outlooks and different emotional needs to *mean* different things. This attribute of goals will have profound effects on how general managers and policymakers must cope with them in their decision processes, and how they use science and analysis as aids after these goals are somehow established. Some examples from practical affairs and from scholarly attempts to define them will show why this is true. We shall see that in each case the ethic comes to the policymaker in the form of what Opler has called a theme.[10] Policymakers use these themes for discussion (to uncover outcomes of a given strategy or policy), for clinical analysis (to diagnose outputs to various constituencies and to choose policies), and for leadership (to gain cooperation of other parties).

For policy formulation, there are two important characteristics of a theme. First, it expresses a deep-seated value or "end" desired by a group, which may be acted out in a variety of behaviors or actions. "The term is derived from literary usage, where in the course of a great novel, the same basic motif may appear in a number of different contexts or episodes."[11] Thus, a demand (theme) for ecological balance in nature may be acted out by attacking the technological process and capital alignment policies of a number of corporations in the utility business which call for construction of nuclear power plants. It may be used to attack the product/market alignment of a timber company that sells redwood paneling to homeowners. It may be used to stop sale of leaded gasoline, or to prevent a state highway department from building bridges near lakes. Second, a theme is *not* subject to scientific analysis. It cannot be defined precisely. It cannot be measured in feet or kilowatts. And it certainly cannot be proved "true" or "false," "right" or "wrong."

THE LOG EXPORT PROBLEM   Diagnosis of the Log Export Case shows that in deciding what to do about "the log export problem" many groups have different meanings for the theme "economic development."[12] General managers of large multipurpose lumber companies, small specialized lumber companies, and industry associations representing a network of companies, must somehow decide whether to export logs to Japan. Policymakers in government or labor unions, representing one or the other constituency, must also decide what position to take. Independent sawmill operators, who purchase their logs from public lands, employees in these mills, and the American Plywood Association, argued against exports because log prices were rising due to Japanese purchases, thus raising their costs and their prices. Many small mills were forced out of business, thus laying off several thousand workers. To the sawmill operators, economic development meant keeping their productive organizations going. To their workers, it meant keeping their jobs. Both opposed export of logs by Weyerhauser Corporation. But even if one equates employment with economic development, there are different themes of employment. The longshoremen at the ports of Seattle and Portland argued *for* exports by Weyerhauser (it meant employment for them) but the woodworkers' union argued *against* exports by the corporation (they would get fewer jobs because increased price of finished homes would depress the housing industry). The AFL-CIO, representing a general labor constituency, charged that the United States is allowing free international trade to divert jobs to overseas. Further confusion was injected if one compares the National Association of Homebuilders' position with that of the Japanese Log Importers Association. The former pointed out a deep concern over ever-increasing log exports since it violated the demand for low cost utility. Exports had the effect of pushing the price of homes to American families to "unprecedented levels." The Japanese Association pointed out that the clear white finish of Western Hemlock provided esthetic beauty for Japanese homeowners. Exports denied these people their need for utility. A final theme was injected by parties interested in free trade, fearful that if the United States curtailed export of logs, Japan might retaliate through quotas or tariffs placed on our other exports. According to this argument, "economic development" means that the gross national product, employment, and income of the United States would be negatively affected by any prohibition of log exports.

The Sierra Club and the Friends of the Earth used the theme "preserve our natural environment" to stress the fact that the United States is cutting timber faster than it can be grown, and is thereby destroying forests and wilderness. They said that Weyerhauser Corporation should not align log products with the Japanese market.

Out of this confusion in themes, the policymaker should recognize that there are simply many constituencies here, and that each constituency is using meaningful, yet somewhat ill-defined clinical logic to express the general themes "economic development," "shelter for human beings," and "natural environment."

160

HISTORY OF PHILOSOPHY AND SOCIAL SCIENCES   Any attempt by scholastic philosophy or modern science to define these terms so that they have general acceptance and applicability to all cases—from the log export problem to the New York City financial crisis—is bound to fail.

That is exactly what the history of philosophy and social sciences shows. The following examples are not intended to say that themes from philosophy and social sciences are irrelevant in policy decisions. Our discussion already has made powerful use of some. They do show, however, that these ideas must be taken as ethical themes of *one group* of people. They are ethical themes in the sense that they express one group's belief about what is right and wrong, or about what policymakers *should* do. They are not precise definitions to be invoked as true or false, right or wrong, in an *action situation*. Part IV will show that the *policy ethic* is a different matter. It requires reconciling conflicting themes.

In the history of philosophy, many attempts have been made to build a systematic, logical theory of right and wrong, starting with some end that is good and building successively, through deduction, more specific rules for behavior. Though these ideas have intrinsic meaning as themes, they have never been widely accepted. This was the problem in the Middle Ages, when both philosophy and religion were finally criticized for debating, "how many angels can dance on the head of a pin." Even two great religions, Judaism and Christianity, though accepting as their ultimate ends the same values (love of God and the individual, justice among men), disagree on the *weight* to be placed on each in deciding upon specific courses of action. Christianity places love first and justice second. Judaism reverses the weights: "Do justly, love thy neighbor, and walk humbly with thy God."

Such a situation continues in scholastic philosophy. As of the time this book is written, one of the leading authorities on justice (measured by the impact he has had on fellow philosophers) is Harvard's John Rawls.

> The critical reaction to Rawls' A *Theory of Justice*,[13] in the six years since its publication, has been quite extraordinary. We now have two full-length studies, a book of critical essays, and scores of published papers and reviews, and there must now be several hundred pieces in all.[14]

In spite of the power and usefulness of Rawls' concept of what justice *is*, as a *defined* concept, other specialists on justice cannot even agree precisely on what Rawls means by the concept, much less

161

on whether the concept is correct or incorrect, true or false, right or wrong. Similar results are to be found in both religion and psychology in attempts to define *love* or *individual worth*, or to specify what kinds of actions embody these themes.

In modern organization theory, a lot has been written on what constitutes *organizational effectiveness*.[15] Generally, social scientists have tended to define one goal. The choice of a goal is determined by the individual social scientist's own value theme and research interests. One overview of research revealed that there are at least 19 meanings of effectiveness, but that the most frequently used were productivity, satisfaction of employees, profit, and loss of talent (measured by employee turnover and absenteeism). More recently, some researchers, using multivariate techniques, have tried to include many goals, instead of one. This approach turns out, because of the limitations of science to handle such matters, to involve only a few of the complex demands made on the organization. One study uses three goals: productivity, flexibility, and absence of intraorganizational strain. General Electric Company and Peter Drucker have both postulated a list of somewhat similar goals: market standing, innovation, productivity, physical and financial resources, profitability, manager performance and development, worker performance and attitude, and public responsibility.

CONCLUSIONS   The final conclusions to be drawn from diagnosis of case histories, from history of philosophy, and from modern social science is that themes are rich and divergent; they are situational (depend somewhat on the action situation); and they differ from one time to another and from one culture to another. They are instruments for expressing deep and meaningful underlying human needs, whether for a philosopher, a social scientist, a lumber mill operator, or the executive secretary of the National Homebuilders Association.

Themes are and must be the variables, or outcome factors, that determine policy decisions. Because they cannot be defined by science and philosophy, the policymaker's decision making (literally, the operation of the human brain) must be more like that used by medical doctors ("clinical reasoning"), law judges ("rendering judgments"), historians, and anthropologists, than it is like that used by scientists. Scientists are indispensable for policy analysis. But policy analysis cannot take place without prior problem focusing.

Group Heuristics

Herbert Simon has provided us with a valuable insight into the mental processes used by one person (or a group with the same goal) to *focus* and *structure* a problem. He has called this "heuristic problem solving." It starts with what John Dewey called a "problematic situation"—some goal the person wants to achieve. Simon gives the following example: Suppose you are camping in the woods. You decide you need a table. Note the meaning of the word "decide" here. It is an act of intuition, will, want, or value—not an act of scientific analysis. It simply means that, as of that time, you want a table. You then focus attention on this as the center of your thought. The next step is to search around in your memory or experience for some way to get the table. You notice that there are trees around and that you have an axe. At this point, you switch your attention and focus of the problem, to some subproblem you can solve. You start constructing alternative ways to fell the tree, thinking about how the tree will fall, how to swing the axe, etc. The new problem focus (felling the tree) becomes a thing in itself, to be thought about and solved.

The analogy to policy formulation is as follows. One interest group has its own heuristic logic. It has an end goal, or demand theme. To achieve this, the group identifies a specific policy in the task alignment that is a subproblem in reaching this goal, for example, a product that is being sold or a production process that is being used. The group then focuses, or "homes in" on that policy and demands that it be changed. This is the case when only one constituency is involved.

Political Heuristics

Now compare this to *political heuristics*, a situation in which there are many constituencies, each with its demand theme. There is a complex set of themes, each with its own logic chain. Each implies, somewhere in the chain of logic, that the alignment policy is good or bad. This can be illustrated again from the Log Export Case. In that case, strategists in large timber companies such as Weyerhauser had decided to export logs to Japan, supplying low-cost, quality materials to people who needed homes. Senator Packwood, representing needs of the owners of small timber mills in Oregon (who did not own their own forests, and had to purchase logs on the open market) introduced a bill into the United States Senate to limit export of logs. He thus became a potential policymaker on product markets for the entire log industry of the United States. Both the business policymaker for a company, and a United States senator who must vote as a manager of the industry, must somehow make up their minds.

163

In doing so, they must listen to, and understand, various chains of logic involved. Here is a chain of logic used by the small timber companies and the workers in small companies.

"*If* we export logs, *then* prices of logs will go up, *then* only large plywood mills can afford to purchase them, *then* the small lumber mills will be unable to buy them, *then* the small operators will have costs larger than revenues, *then* small operators will go out of business, *then* workers lose their jobs, *then* their families will not have a decent 'standard of living' (houses to keep them warm, food to keep them healthy, etc.)." This represents one chain of logic tied to ethical themes. In scientific terms, each theme is an independent variable causing the next dependent variable in the chain. The themes in the middle of the chain are also intervening variables.

The Sierra Club, with an ultimate theme of natural resource preservation, used another chain of logic. "*If* we export logs, *then* the timber companies sell larger volume, *then* the larger demand raises prices, *then* timber companies will cut more logs to increase revenues, *then* we will deplete our natural forests, *then* people who gain satisfaction from beauty in nature will suffer, *then* timber companies will upset the ecosystem which will in turn affect deer, beavers, and other natural wildlife. . . ."

An earlier example has already been given. Strategists in the Department of Health, Education and Welfare who initiated the quality-of-work-life study used this logic (highly simplified here): Health of the national society is partly a function of health of one constituency, workers in factories and offices. Health of this constituency is determined by feelings of satisfaction and well being. These feelings are in turn a function of relief from routine, and the degree of self-control experienced by employees. Self-control is a function of the participation one has in determining the characteristics of one's work.

Notes

1. For other characteristics, see Charles E. Summer, et. al., *The Managerial Mind*, Richard D. Irwin, 1977.

2. This function of leadership is well known in political science. See Gabriel Almond and G. B. Powell, *Comparative Politics*, Little, Brown, 1966, Chapter 4; Charles E. Lindblom, *The Policy-Making Process*, Prentice-Hall, 1968, Chapter 12.

3. S. P. Huntington, "The Democratic Distemper," *The Public Interest* 41 (Fall 1975): 9–38.

4. Cultural Constituencies (Case File), Appendix.

5. *Seattle Times*, September 25, 1978.

6. Associated Press, August 13, 1978.

7. The Education Industry (Case File), Appendix.

8. Kenneth McNeil and E. Minihan, "Medical Technology Regulation," *Administrative Science Quarterly* 22:3 (September 1977): 475.

9. *Work in America*, U. S. Government Printing Office, 1973.

10. Morris E. Opler, "Themes as Dynamic Forces in Culture," *American Journal of Sociology*, November 1945, pp. 198–206.

11. Ralph Linton, "An Anthropological View of Economic Life," in *Goals of Economic Life*, edited by Dudley Ward, Harper and Row, 1953.

12. The Log Export Problem, Appendix.

13. John Rawls, *A Theory of Justice*, Harvard University Press, 1971.

14. David Miller, review of *Understanding Rawls*, by Robert Wolff, *Political Theory* 5:4 (November 1977): 541–44.

15. For a review of this literature, see R. M. Steers, "Problems in the Measure of Organizational Effectiveness," *Administrative Science Quarterly* 20:4 (December 1975): 546; S. Lee Spray (ed.), *Organizational Effectiveness*, Kent State University, Comparative Administrative Institute, 1976; E. Yuchtman and Stanley Seashore, "A System Resource Approach to Organizational Effectiveness," *American Sociological Review* 32 (1967): 891–903; Bertram Gross, *Organizations and Their Managing*, The Free Press, 1968, pp. 42, 273–75; Hal Pickle and F. Friedlander, "Seven Societal Criteria of Organizational Success," *Personnel Psychology* 20 (1957): 165–78; Bruce Kirchoff, "Organizational Effectiveness Measurement and Policy Research," *Academy of Management Review* 2:3 (July 1977): 346–55; and J. L. Price, *Organizational Effectiveness*, Richard D. Irwin, 1968.

CHAPTER 7

External Challenges

THIS CHAPTER will present highly condensed versions of case histories in which some group in the external cultural environment (CE) disputes the task alignment (TE/TI) that has been made to satisfy constituencies in the task environment (TE.1). Finding that such alignments have a negative impact on their own needs, they demand that they be changed.

The number of cultural constituencies in society is so great, and the *diversity* of their demand themes so broad, that we cannot list them exhaustively as we do in connection with task themes (Chapters 3–5) or cultural efficiency themes (Chapters 8–9). Nevertheless, case histories will show a variety of these themes. For example:

The demand for freedom and autonomy (CE.1).
The demand for justice (CE.2). This general theme has a number of variations. For example:
    CE.21. Align products and resources for the greatest good for the greatest number of people.
    CE.22. Align products and resources for those with greatest need in society.
    CE.23. Align products and resources to reward those who make the greatest contribution to society.
    CE.24. Align products and resources to treat each person as an "origin" (similar to the demand for equality).
The demand for equality (CE.3).
The demand for physical health (CE.4).
The demand for aesthetic beauty (CE.5); for example, in one case wilderness areas, and nature itself, are defined as beauty.

166

The demand for ecological balance (CE.6); for example, the value of nature and ecology will be seen to mean many different things to different people.

Numbers have been placed on these examples only to show that policymakers, when they diagnose value themes, must treat them in the same way as all other organization goals. They are not intended as a complete classification of cultural values in society. In fact, case histories will show a number of themes besides those in this list of examples.

This chapter is organized in the same way that such demands come to policymakers. That is,

1. Demand for product or service realignment. Objections may arise over the product or service that has been decided on. Either it may injure human health (CE.3), or the *mix* of services may violate one of the principles of justice (CE.21, the demand for highest use, or, the demand that product mix be designed for the greatest good for the greatest number of people in society).
2. Demand for structural realignment, either for redesign of the capital structure (it may for example violate the principle of freedom in society), or for redesign of the organization structure (it may for example violate the autonomy and freedom of sub-units).
3. Demand for operating process realignment (it may for example pollute the atmosphere and endanger human health, or, it may violate the principle of sexual or racial equality).

Bear in mind that, once the conflict is precipitated, it is not only a matter of conflict between one constituency, demanding one value and one set of policymakers representing task constituency themes. As the conflict unfolds, strategists are confronted with several groups that may disagree. For example, in one case history, when a black man demands equality, and that he be admitted to law or medical school on the basis of equality (CE.3), there does in fact arise another group, led by a white man, demanding another principle of justice.[1]

This is what was meant in Chapter 6 by the "process of political or cultural 'heuristics.'" Diverse groups in society in fact have different end values. Their chain of logic also differs as to the means to achieve these. One chain of logic uses the principle of equality (CE.3) whereas another uses the principle of justice (CE.2).

One final instruction must be given as preface to this chapter. Most case histories cited here will be long, clinical cases giving a complete history of the situation. They show how human beings have deeper emotional meanings for the themes mentioned so tersely above. For example, to a black woman with low income what is the meaning of "a kilowatt of electricity"?[2] What does it mean in terms of ultimate values? It turns out that it means human health— getting a child dressed in a warm room before school in the morning. What is the "demand for equality" to a black man who wants a law or medical school education? What is the "demand for justice" to a white man who has been rejected from medical school partly because black men were admitted under another principle of justice?

These things can only be understood in the real, down-to-earth context of living situations. Although our case histories are highly abstracted, and go part way toward imparting a true understanding, they are not a substitute, as Part IV will show, for *value-theme diagnosis*, a vital step in strategy and policy formulation. In this process, the typical *things* (the technological side of the world in terms of products, markets and resources) are diagnosed in terms of the deep values they represent to human beings.

Demand for Product/Service Realignment

In this section we will look at case histories in which the product or service being offered is the initial focus of the problem. On closer diagnosis, however, the problem quickly becomes one in which a variety of other value/market constituencies are affected. What started out to be a simple policy question of "what product do we produce for the greatest utility to the greatest number of people?" (TE), quickly becomes a comprehensive strategic alignment problem, affecting not only task resource suppliers who want the organization to serve the TE constituency, but also the entire range of internal resource policies (TI) and a network of constituencies in the cultural environment (CE).

Realignment: The Lawnmower Industry

The following case may be approached from the view of policymakers in a company manufacturing and selling lawnmowers, say, Toro Manufacturing Company. In this case, the focal organization would be Toro. Or, it may be approached from the viewpoint of policymakers in the United States Product Safety Commission or the United States Council on Wage and Price Stability. In these cases, the focal organization to be managed is the entire lawnmower industry.

In 1975, the state-of-art technology for power lawnmowers had been adopted by managers of most companies in the lawnmower industry.[3] Product lines (TE) were designed to satisfy needs of two constituencies: those who want walk-behind mowers and those who want riding mowers. A comprehensive task alignment had been worked out that supplied this utility at lowest cost to consumers (TE) by use of sophisticated capital equipment (TI.11), a specialized departmental structure within each company (TI.12), a mass-production process using standardized parts (TI.21) and a certain work design and pay system for employees at the work level (TI.22). Several million users were satisfied because of the quality of the product (it cut grass efficiently) and the price ($110 average for bottom of line walk-behind mower and $515 average for riding mowers). Evidence for consumer satisfaction was the total number of users (several million) and the increase in users (increasing at about 300,000 mowers a year).

During the same year, top managers in the Product Safety Commission, already concerned about the general theme "product safety," became concerned about the bodily injury caused by accidents to people using lawnmowers. The commission views its role as formulating product/market policy for the entire industry, consisting of some 80 manufacturers. It contracted with a private research group, Consumers' Union (CU) to do policy analysis (factual research as contrasted with value formulation) regarding such injuries. CU discovered that 198,000 injuries occur annually, ranging from those doing minor harm to those causing major injury. It also recommended standards for product manufacture: "deadman controls" to stop mower blades when the operator's hand leaves the handle, noise mufflers, improved brakes, protectors from hot metal burns, shields to reduce injury from blade-thrown objects, and electrical circuitry to prevent electric shock.

Responding to the theme "human safety," the industry contracted with the Stanford Research Institute, which switched the focus of the industry strategists. Whereas they had previously focused on the *present* alignment to maximize utility at least cost for several million users, they now focused on a *realignment* (TE, TI) required to maximize safety for the potential 198,000 accident victims. The research showed:

1. That the cost to several million users in the total task constituency would be increased by $44 in cheaper models that sold primarily to younger persons just starting households.
2. That 82 percent of total industry sales is in walk-behind mowers, and that prices of these would increase 34 percent on the average, due to more expensive manufacturing equipment (TI.11) and change in production processes (TI.21, TI.22).

3. That 18 percent of total sales is in riding mowers, and that prices of these would increase 15 percent on the average for the same reasons.
4. That total consumer expenditures for lawnmowers would increase by $367 million per year.
5. That 15 to 20 manufacturers of lawnmowers would be forced to stop manufacture, thus affecting constituencies who need employment (CI).
6. That the change in product, internal structures, and internal processes would probably provide safety to 198,000 people.

In the weeks that followed, other events occurred:

1. The Council on Wage and Price Stability, representing a broad constituency with the theme "cost of living" (CE) requested that the Product Safety Commission not implement the new standards "unless an alternative can be found that will give the consumer of lawnmowers benefits that will at least equal the added $367 million per year of costs they will incur" (you may notice that this is asking either the industry or the commission to find some alternative policy that satisfies the Pareto Optimum).
2. A leading investment analysis company that advises persons and pension fund managers on which industries are good investments (TE, resource suppliers) took note of the developments, especially the fact that total industry sales to constituencies might decrease as much as 20 percent. Investors were advised to be wary of the loss of the support of lawnmower purchasers.

Clearly, this case shows the large number of costs and benefits that accrue both to *task constituencies* (customers, resource suppliers) and to *cultural constituencies* (groups interested in the cost of living, safety and health, or employment of all citizens):

Group	Demand theme
Several million homeowners	High-quality, low-cost machines
198,000 potentially injured persons	Human safety and health
All citizens using lawnmowers	Standard of living: stop inflation
15 to 20 business owners	Right to engage in productive enterprise
Investors in lawnmower companies	Equitable returns
Employees in 15 to 20 lawnmower companies	Economic development: demand for employment

170

Demand for Equality:
Peoples Bank and Liberty Bank

In early 1978, the Peoples National Bank, which operates a branch bank on the campus of the University of Washington, was approached by two organizations, the Physicians' Planning Service (PPS) and the National Association of Residents and Interns (NARI). Both groups are leaders of a constituency of students enrolled in medical and dental schools. They articulate the needs of students and get other organizations to formulate action programs that satisfy these needs. PPS and NARI articulate as one goal the alleviation of financial problems faced by medical and dental students who incur high costs in their education. They approached Peoples Bank and negotiated a special service line for such students: free checking accounts, special availability of VISA credit cards, and specialized counseling on federal loans to medical students.

The bank viewed the product/market as an opportunity for service to a certain market: it provided utility (TE), helped the cause of medical education (CE), created good will among a group that might, after graduation, be valued loan and deposit customers. Also, statistics show that medical students are better risks for repaying loans than other groups. This protected the safety of depositors' (resource suppliers') money.

In the same year, *The University Daily*, a newspaper that has feature articles representing diverse groups, published an article saying that the medical student service, "has angered other graduate students who say they are being discriminated against . . . they feel they should be afforded the same privileges." A political science student, for example, said, "These benefits should be extended to all graduate students." Responding to the article, the principal bank executive in charge of marketing (whose duties include recommending service/markets) said that the bank strategists would indeed follow the problem, and that if there appeared to be deep concern among enough students the bank would review the policy for possible change.

A similar product conflict occurs in the banking industry between certain task responsibilities (TE, TI) seen by strategists and the theme "redlining" as enunciated by minority groups and their leaders. A particularly interesting case concerns the Liberty Bank.[4] The bank is owned and operated by black minority persons who formulate its strategy. It is located in the central area of Seattle, Washington, an area populated largely by blacks. The bank, like all

171

other banks, has two large customer constituencies: depositors (who supply funds for safekeeping) and borrowers (who need loans for homes and businesses). In order to execute high-quality deposit services (TE, to depositors), the bank's strategists believe that one of their highest responsibilities is for safety of people's money. In order to ensure safety, they have defined the borrower/product market as persons who have good risk characteristics: (1) all borrowers must have held their present jobs for one year, (2) all must be residents of the banking area for one year, (3) all must have records of repaying prior credit or have cosigners who have such records, (4) all persons who wish debt-consolidation loans must have property collateral equal to 65 percent of the loan.

Recently, Bernice Moreland, President of the Central Seattle Community Council Federation (CSCCF), an organization that represents the welfare (various diverse needs) of citizens of the central area, told Donn Swanson, the bank's loan officer and vice-president, that the CSCCF was requesting central area minority businesses to withdraw accounts from Liberty because Mrs. Louie Ogilvie had been denied a loan for $900 to improve her home. She said that Mr. and Mrs. Ogilvie had equity of more than $2000 in their home and owned their automobile outright. A bank spokesman said that he could not discuss publicly the individual case, but that the loan did not, in the bank's judgment, meet the product/market that had been defined by the bank. Clearly, the bank had one set of product/market standards and the CSCCF had another standard: that of "equality" to a constituency of persons wanting bank loans.

Demand for Highest Use: Mount Rainier National Park

One profound conflict between needs of various groups in society can be expressed as the demand for "highest use" of an organization's resources. Broadly put, the theme sounds like this: "Each organization should devote its scarce resources (TE.3) to producing that product (TE) which is of highest use to society; that is, a product that satisfies the most essential needs of the greatest number of people."

This theme is one way of demanding "justice" or "equity" based on:

1. How "strongly" a group needs the utility in the product. Hungry people may need food strongly, affluent people may need an electric can opener less strongly, according to the theme. Econo-

172

mists call this strength of need "marginal utility." Psychologists using expectancy theory borrow the term "valence" from physics to indicate how strongly one values something. In Chapter 3, this notion was expressed as "the most essential" services.

2. How many people are involved. It is one thing if millions of people have no food while some have electric can openers. It is another if very few people are hungry while millions have electric can openers.

The central question for product policymakers then becomes, "Which configuration of product-output policies will satisfy the most essential needs of the greatest number of people." The decision rule becomes: "Adopt those product lines which yield the highest utility for the greatest number and drop those lines with low utility for the fewest number."

Two case histories will be cited here, one from government and one from business. Both show how the (TE) alignment has benefits to some constituencies and costs to others, and that the benefits and costs should, in the ethics of some constituencies, be weighted by (1) the valence of the need and (2) the number of people involved.

In 1975, John Rutter, regional director of the National Park Service, had just made a long-range strategic decision: a *comprehensive master plan* for Mount Rainier National Park.[5] He had forwarded this decision to his superior in the federal government, Gary Everhardt, director of the National Park Service. Lengthy staff investigations and a number of hearings had been held regarding the future of the park, its mission in society, and the operations that would be required to serve the public. By "comprehensive master plan," the Park Service strategists (Rutter and his staff analysts), meant that it included *all* services (TE) to be rendered by the park, all structural resources needed (TI.11, roads, buildings, campgrounds, sanitary facilities), and all operating processes required (TI.2). In short, it was a comprehensive task alignment as described in Chapter 4. The plan had been drawn up by a task force of nine experts in the NPS staff. It contained 197 pages of data and analysis, and required 18 months of study. Among other recommendations, 210,700 acres, 90 percent of the park's total acreage, would be set aside as a wilderness. This would require that the internal (TI) resources of the park be adjusted: no roads, no maintained trails, and no hostels would be allowed.

The staff further specified the market: it projected that there would be "1500 wilderness users a day" and that the wilderness area would provide "a unique experience for the backpacker, providing

173

unspoiled primeval beauty and escape from stress-inducing urban centers."

Other recommendations dealt with the remaining 10 percent of the park:

1. Limit the number of people who can come to the park in automobiles by simply refusing to build new parking lots, and by closing "5 miles of Mowich Lake Road, 5 miles of Carbon River Road, and 8 miles of the Puyallup River Road" (TI.11).
2. Limit the number of people who eat and stay overnight at the park's only hotel by simply refusing to enlarge it (TI.11).
3. Limit the number of people who come in by automobile to camp by simply closing 62 campsites that are near parking areas.

Each of these recommendations defines a service/market. Regarding these markets, the report acknowledged that 90 percent of the present 1.6 million people who come to the park each year come only for a day trip, and that 70 percent or 1.2 million "view the features of the Park from within or near automobiles. There were 69,788 hikers last year and 23,945 wilderness type backpackers."

During the course of the hearings on the plan, 3 public agencies, 14 private organizations, and 520 individual persons acted as leaders of a constituency that demanded highest use. They objected to the service alignment that had been formulated by the National Park Service strategists. The United States Department of Transportation, the State of Washington Department of Outdoor Recreation, and the Federal Bureau of Recreation had views similar to those of the *Seattle Times:* "Unfortunately, most people are not rugged outdoor types. They must get to Mt. Rainier by convenient vehicular transportation."

The chief engineer of Mountain Safety Research, Inc., put it this way: "Washington already has over 1 million acres which are classified as wilderness. It is the feeling of the vast majority of people who use the Park as short hikers, picknickers, or day visitors that we have plenty of wilderness. What we need now is a 'park.'"

Kenneth Johnson, speaking on behalf of older persons, said: "Older persons cannot run, hike, or backpack. They, too, would like to experience some of the beauties of the areas being closed."

Libby Mills spoke in behalf of working people who do not have free time to take long backpack hikes of several days' duration: "I urge you not to close the roads you are going to close. Closure will mean that only those people who have more than 24 hours for hiking will be able to see those beautiful areas."

Analysis of the figures in the case shows that the recommendations would decrease the utility (ecology, beauty, health, solitude) gained by somewhere near 1 million persons while increasing the utility gained by approximately 100,000 hikers and backpackers.

After the strategic alignment had been received by Everhardt in the National Park Service headquarters, it began its two-year series of reviews in the service, and in the higher headquarters, the Department of the Interior. Before it was finally adopted as part of the nationwide strategy of the Park Service, Larry Penberthy, president of Mountain Safety Research, Inc., representing constituencies who would be denied access to the park by certain roads and campgrounds that would be closed, contacted the newspapers and threatened to sue in court to prevent the restrictions imposed in the master plan. The *Seattle Times* published an editorial saying, "We hope that Mount Rainier Park can retain a suitable balance between concern for ecological values and a reasonable degree of access by that large majority of park visitors who are incapable of backpacking to remote viewpoints on the mountain."

Responding to these pressures, Russell Dickenson, who had by that time replaced Rutter as general manager (director) of the Park Service in the Northwest, changed the strategy. He recommended to federal headquarters that the roads at Round Pass and Mowich Lake remain open, to ensure greater public access. This behavior, as we will see in Part IV, is a case of "muddling with a cultural purpose," very much like the "muddling with a task purpose" observed in Chapter 4.

Diagnosing Other Intangible Values: Mount Rainier National Park

In the course of realigning the service/market, policymakers in the National Park Service learned from experience how to diagnose tangible policies like the *service* itself or the group of human beings which constitute the *market* in terms of some profound value themes. For example:

The demand for equity (a) defined as the greatest good for the greatest number, (b) defined as "to each according to need," (e.g., old people need to get to the park).

The demand for beauty defined by some groups as "unspoiled primeval beauty."

The demand for physical health defined as freedom from automobile noise and exhaust fumes.

The demand for mental health defined as "solitude and escape from stress-inducing urban centers."

The demand for ecological balance defined as preservation of 700 species of vascular plants, including virgin forests; preservation of the species Rocky Mountain Elk.

Demand for Highest Use:
The Dog Food Industry

In June 1978, the vice-president of a large San Francisco corporation, attending a seminar at Pajaro Dunes, California, raised a problem that he had been presented with as he attended community planning sessions with various groups in the Bay Area.[6] These sessions had been set up to provide citizens with the opportunity to give their opinions to corporate and government officials—opinions about how to make their communities, and society in general, a better place in which to live.

The vice-president said that he had heard a similar demand theme from several diverse groups: labor-union leaders representing such working groups as window washers and longshoremen, minority-group leaders in the poorer areas of San Francisco, and informal spokesmen for tenants in low-income housing projects.

The theme raised by the leaders of all three groups boiled down, he said, to criticisms of "the affluent society," which produces too many products for high-income groups while ignoring the need for quality useful products at low cost for poverty-level groups. At one of the meetings, the leader representing black people in poor neighborhoods raised an example. He said that recently social workers in San Francisco had found a number of cases in which elderly persons with extremely low incomes were buying dog food to eat because they knew it was nutritious and sanitary, and because it cost only 30¢ a can. He also said that "the system" in society concentrates on producing dog food for the wealthy while ignoring low-cost, serviceable products for the poor.

After these meetings, the vice-president collected some data on his own. He found:

That there are 25 million persons who own dogs in the United States.
This task constituency of the dog food industry spends $2 billion a year on dog food.
That high-priced dog food (canned meat) accounts for $680 million in sales each year, dry dog food accounts for $930 million, dog snack-treats account for $90 million, and diet dog food (for overweight dogs) has just been introduced into the market.

176

That "le Dog," a retail store at 230 East 59th Street in New York City, has a product alignment that includes satin wedding coats for dogs, custom made gold lame coats for walking dogs after dark, jewelled necklaces, patent leather coats for the dog with matching handbag for the owner, a "sleep shop," featuring bedding for dogs, etc.

At the same time, the vice-president found what he called "a dilemma." His statistics on poverty from the United States Bureau of Census showed that there are 10.3 million households in the United States that have a total income of less than $4000 a year, well below the poverty level.

During the community meetings, there were dog owners who spoke up to say that animals are living creatures who are also part of nature, that they deserve care and affection. There were other persons who said that it was their free choice as to what they spent their money for, whether it be meat to eat, beer to drink, or dog food to feed their pets; and that in a free society nobody has a right to legislate what products are produced. Finally, the vice-president himself used this last theme to stress the free enterprise theme: It is the right of businesses to sell, within reason, whatever free people want to spend their money for.

In summary, there were, as usual, many themes in the final problem:

Inequity for poor persons, where "equity" is based on "each according to their need."

Freedom of dog owners to pursue their own beliefs about kindness to animals.

Freedom of all citizens to spend their incomes (whether big or small) on what means most to them.

Freedom of business firms to offer whatever products people want.

Part IV will have to deal with this kind of policy situation. What does one do when confronted with such conflicting value demands?

Demand for Structural Realignment

The cases we have looked at show cultural objections to the product or service policy (TE) contained in the comprehensive strategic alignment. We shall now look at some cases where it is not the product, but policies on capital equipment (TI.11) or organization design (TI.12) which produce unfavorable effects on cultural constituencies. As with the previous case, though decisions may *originate* with these two policies, they quickly involve a wide variety of other demand themes.

Efficient Capital Equipment versus Cultural Values: Seattle City Light Company

The case to be presented here is a classic example of conflict between the economic quality of life in society and the cultural quality of life in society. It shows that investment in capital equipment of a high technology nature, the state-of-art equipment, is a powerful satisfier of human beings in the task environment. The term "state-of-art equipment" means two things. First, the quality of the capital itself is of advantage to society. In this case, a hydroelectric dam with turbine generators produces electricity much more efficiently (without waste) than turbine generators run by steam, which must in turn be produced by burning oil or coal. Second, the *cost* of a given technology, in terms of product to the final consumer may be an advantage to society. The cost of mining coal, or drilling for (or importing) oil is greater than hydroelectric generation which relies on gravity flow of water. These two factors have important impacts on the standard of living in society.

At the same time, however, a hydroelectric dam has costs to society in terms of intangible values. Here is a highly abstracted version of the factors, both technological and cultural, as they entered into a decision by strategists in Seattle City Light Company (SLC), the nation's second largest electric utility company owned by a city government.[7]

During the 1950s, SLC was in the process of installing generators at a hydroelectric dam on the Skagit River, north of Seattle, on the Canadian border. At that time, strategists forecasted that in about 20 years homeowners and industries in Seattle would grow to the point where they needed an additional supply of electric power. They installed generators large enough eventually to raise the dam by 121 feet.

By 1967, economic development and population of the area had reached the point where SLC policymakers decided to apply to the Federal Power Commission for a permit to raise the dam. Over the 12 years to 1979, numerous interest groups voiced either their support for, or their opposition to, the type of capital technology alignment SLC chose. No firm decision has been made by government authorities.

178

Groups supporting the dam included the SLC strategists, acting on behalf of consumers and industries in the area, as well as farmers in the Skagit valley, and others:

SLC pointed out that the increased height of the dam would produce 35,000 kilowatts of "firm electricity," enough to serve a city of 50,000 people. Statistics showed that the average household burns 13,800 khr per year, therefore it would serve 22,100 households.

The peaking capacity (as contrasted with firm electricity), which could meet emergencies, such as the New York City overload blackout, would be 244,000 kilowatts, enough to meet the emergency demand of 150 hospitals the size of Seattle's largest.

If oil-fired generators were used, it would require 1,200,000 barrels of oil per year, at a cost of $12 million, compared to less than $3 million per year, for use of waterpower.

Water is a renewable resource from melting snow. Oil and coal are nonrenewable, taking millions of years to form in nature. Further, water power does not pollute the atmosphere whereas coal and oil produce smoke.

Celia Adams, a black woman in Seattle, pointed to the inexpensive electricity the city has historically provided by waterpower. She said that she was much more interested in keeping herself and her children warm at low cost. She said that those who want to preserve trees in the valley that would be flooded are more affluent people who have all of the electricity they want. They care more about trees that few people will ever see than they do about cheap electricity for her family.

Farmers in the lower Skagit valley have repeatedly been subjected to floods. The last one, in 1975, destroyed 18,000 head of livestock. Many small dairy farmers were wiped out. They favor the dam because it will be a source of flood control when heavy snows are melting in the mountains.

A variety of groups, however, were opposed to the SLC policy on the type of capital technology to be employed:

The Sierra Club, representing 150,000 people, stated, "We oppose the dam for the same reason that we have always opposed dams in the Grand Canyon. The permanent destruction of these unique and beautiful places, which are part of our national heritage, cannot be compensated for by the electricity."

The United States Forest Service stated that the unique stand of western red cedar trees, many of them over 30 feet in diameter and perhaps 1000 years old, would be killed. These trees grow in the 3600 acres of land that would be flooded in the valley.

The Washington State Department of Ecology pointed out that SLC had focused its attention on "the production of electric power as its first objective, with concern for the environment decidedly a second objective."

As with other cases, this one, if analyzed carefully, contains many demand themes from diverse groups. They range all the way from the concern of a black woman for low cost electricity as a means to health of her children, to the desire for unique and beautiful areas of natural ecology, to the use of oil as a scarce natural resource.

Efficient Capital Equipment versus Cultural Values: The Urban Transit Industry

In 1978 strategists in city-government transportation departments faced a problem of trying to comply with the demand for low-cost, state-of-art technology (TI.3) on the one hand, and equal access of handicapped persons to buses on the other. Steven Roberts, of the *New York Times* Washington bureau, acts as an informal leader of all of these city transportation companies by summarizing the problem, focusing on the difficulty faced by strategists who must cope with both issues.[8]

A number of congressmen representing a constituency of handicapped persons, passed the Rehabilitation Act of 1973, prohibiting discrimination against the handicapped. By 1978, 28 federal agencies were writing regulations to implement the law. These will require companies, public agencies, and institutions to "spend billions of dollars to comply. The Department of HEW estimates that its client groups alone, such as hospitals and school systems, will spend $2.8 billion each year to meet the regulations."

Spokesmen for 12 associations representing the nation's 30 million handicapped persons have successfully convinced Secretary of Transportation Adams that the solution to discrimination in city-owned buslines is the Transbus, a special vehicle with very low floor levels 22 inches off the ground. Floors could be lowered hydraulically and hydraulic ramps that can be lowered to bring wheelchairs aboard would be carried on board the bus. By issuing an order (in May 1977) to all cities that receive federal money, making the Transbus standard equipment for all systems, Adams thus decided the capital equipment alignment for the city transportation industry throughout the nation.

180

Three major companies, AM General, General Motors, and Grumman Flexible, produced prototypes of the Transbus. General Motors estimated that it would cost $40 million to retool its assembly lines and that the cost of the bus to city governments would be 15 percent higher than its Advanced Design Bus, a high-floor vehicle designed for handicapped persons before Adams issued his Transbus regulation, and one now used by Long Beach, California; Brockton, Massachusetts; and other cities.

The American Public Transit Association (APTA), whose members are city-government officials who specialize in bus transportation, objects strongly to the Transbus, because it would cost bus riders, or citizen taxpayers, too much money. It notes that the cost to New York, Chicago, Philadelphia, and other cities would be $1.8 billion higher than other systems city strategists are working out. One such system is Dial-a-Ride. According to APTA, Dial-a-Ride would make the public transportation system totally accessible to all handicapped persons, who would then not have to get themselves to a bus stop. Further, Dial-a-Ride would be more comfortable in bad weather, and would not require redesign of the entire fleet for an expensive vehicle that may not be used by enough handicapped persons to make the project worthwhile. In the words of Mr. Stokes, APTA executive secretary, "The imposition of any program which would imply the use of scarce federal resources, for a bus we believe is a non-solution in the first place, borders on the ridiculous."

At the same time, the House Public Works Committee, representing this kind of reasoning, and focusing on the enormous cost of the new equipment, adopted a resolution which would require Adams to stop the conversion to Transbus, and reevaluate his regulation requiring its use. At this point, lobbying organizations representing the cities, the handicapped, and General Motors (which says it cannot produce a bus cities will not buy) are prepared to try to influence individual congressmen if the resolution comes to a vote of the House.

According to Roberts, "The fight to save the Transbus is a showdown, a precedent-setting confrontation." Many handicapped leaders say that civil rights (equality of access to buses on the part of handicapped persons) "should not carry a price tag." James Raggio, an attorney representing disabled groups, argues that a special service such as Dial-a-Ride, even though it would prevent handicapped persons from having to travel to a bus stop and wait there for the bus in bad weather, would "carry with it a stigma, a mark of inferiority. Separate transit services, like separate schools, can never be truly equal."

Thus, strategists for the bus company owned by Chicago or New

Orleans face a problem. To what extent shall they lobby for a policy to adopt Transbus, a policy to adopt Dial-a-Ride (using a lesser number of special smaller vehicles at less cost), or some other equipment policy as yet undeveloped? Members of Congress, when they vote on the Public Works Committee resolution, face the same question, except that they become, at that point, strategists who are aligning the capital structure of the entire national bus industry. Should the resolution come to vote, the judgment of the secretary of transportation will carry considerable weight. As policymaker for the bus industry, what capital policy would *he* arrive at?

In summary, this case presents a conflict between profound values:

Low-cost utility (bus tickets) for millions of nonhandicapped riders.
Equality of access to the same equipment used by millions of non-handicapped riders for 30 million handicapped riders.
Cost of capital equipment to be borne by citizens of cities in subsidizing Transbus, or, by citizens of the United States who pay income taxes if Transbus should be subsidized by federal grants to cities.

Effective Organization Design versus Other Values: Morgan New York State Corporation

The following is a case in industrial organization. Strategists in the Federal Reserve Board actually plan the organization structure of banks in the nation. They may decide how many banks are to be part of the total industry, where they are located, and whether a number of banks (separate decentralized organizations) may merge into one larger bank (one centralized organization). In making these decisions, they are faced with conflicts between the efficiency of centralized design versus the freedom of individuals to start banks, and the motivation of bankers within the organization. The New York State Banking Commission performs these same functions for the State of New York. Although this case takes place a number of years ago, it is still a prototype of the classic problem in industrial organization.[9] Any policymaker who plans organization design by merging one or more previously independent, decentralized units into one centralized unit faces the same basic value conflicts.

In 1964 the presidents of banks in Rochester, Buffalo, Syracuse, New York City, Albany, Oneida, Utica, and Binghamton proposed that their eight banks be merged into one bank. They had done a large amount of research on what their customers wanted in the way of services, and showed that one bank could offer higher-quality services at lower cost. Hearings were held by the New York State Banking Commission (which approved the merger because of its advantages to the economy and standard of living in New York State) and the Federal Reserve Board (which denied the merger because of its disadvantages to the free economic system). During the hearings, the value themes emerged clearly. These are summarized here:

Mr. Wilson, president of Xerox Corporation, with headquarters then in Rochester, testified that his corporation needed the expert advice of international economists as it did business all over the world. If the merger were allowed, the larger bank could afford a foreign department composed of 20 or 30 persons, each specialized by area: Japan, the Common Market countries, the Middle East, and Africa. Without the merger, the Rochester Bank could afford to hire only three persons in the foreign area, "generalists" because they would have to cover the entire world. Not only would the *quality* of advice be better with the merger, but the *cost* of advice would be less. The salaries of the 30 "specialists" would be spread over a number of other corporations using time sharing, rather than paid for by the limited number of clients of one bank in Rochester.

W. V. Daugherty, president of a company in Oneida, made two points. His company had grown large, and the bank in Oneida could not make loans to any one customer as large as his company required. Second, when his company needed working capital, he had to negotiate with several banks to form a consortium to make the loan. These negotiations were long and expensive, and sometimes the joint partners in the consortium could not agree to lend the money. Under the merger, he would have access to one large bank that could make a decision quickly.

The president of Syracuse University testified that his university would receive better advice from the trust department of the larger bank, which would be able to afford experts on university administration. The present Syracuse bank trust personnel must serve (1) persons with inherited wealth, (2) corporate pension plan managers, and (3) university and museum officials who must manage their endowments. Since universities are a very special problem (unlike the other two clients) the larger bank's increased specialization would increase the quality of advice.

The president of one of the smaller banks testified that each of the eight banks must purchase its own expensive electronic computer and hire a staff of experts on the hardware and software of computer systems. With a merger, only one computer system and one department of programmers would be necessary.

The governor of New York testified that the population, nature of businesses, and geographic distribution of economic activity in the state was changing. A merged bank would be able to provide private individuals and businesses throughout the state more modern and less costly services than eight smaller banks.

The state banking superintendent testified that the merger would "contribute to the kind of expanding economy which is so essential to the welfare of the state and the country."

Congressman O'Brien of Albany testified that the new company would assist his district in coping with serious unemployment because its larger capital and staff services could attract new industry to the region.

The mayor of Binghamton stated that large urban rehabilitation projects for housing, as well as the financing of public schools, would be aided by both the advice of the larger bank, and the funds it would be able to loan to his city.

Congressman Celler, chairman of the Judiciary Committee in the United States Congress, testified: (1) That the number of banks in the United States had shrunk from 15,000 to 13,000 at that time, due to mergers. In fact, the eight banks concerned in this merger were the result, over their combined histories, of the merger of 56 small independent banks. (2) That the spirit of initiative, and the "learning by hard knocks" of many officials in the eight smaller banks, kept alive the involvement of many human beings in the problems of the country. If the merger were allowed, the top officials of the centralized bank would do all the thinking and problem solving, simply conveying instructions on interest rates and other policies to the branches. This would help destroy the free spirit of enterprise that had made our industrial system one of the best in the world. (3) That the potential power of the new bank, controlling 11 percent of the banking assets in New York, would be dangerous for any new banks that might want to begin business, thus further damaging the potential free enterprise spirit in the nation.

In short, policymakers in the banks of the country, as well as in various state and federal agencies, must judge conflicts between the most effective organization structure for meeting a wide spectrum of

184

themes having to do with effective task performance (TE) and the most effective structure for contributing to initiative and free enterprise spirit in our culture (CE). The New York State Banking Commission weighted the former more heavily in its policy decision. The Federal Reserve Board weighted the latter more heavily in its decision.

Effective Organization Structure versus Other Values: Roget, S.A.

The same conflict described above occurs when strategists for a given company plan the internal organization design of the company. In a complex case history of Roget, S.A., one of the largest chemical companies in Belgium,[10] the organization-design problem is whether to establish a centralized organization in Belgium to manufacture and sell XL-4, a paper-making chemical, to the worldwide market or whether to establish a decentralized organization in Sweden, whereby the Swedish subsidiary company (AB Thorsten) would make and sell its own XL-4 in Sweden.

The Swedish management had taken a product (XL-4) that is manufactured in Belgium for worldwide sale to food companies, had done three years of research and development with paper companies in Sweden, and found how to apply the same chemical to paper converting by changing slightly the processes used by paper manufacturers. Finance staff members in Sweden had done complex analysis (discounted cash flow investment analysis) to prove that a plant could be built in Sweden, and that large paper corporations in Sweden would receive a new product that would lower the cost of paper to their customers.

Finance staff members in the parent company in Brussels did their own analysis using the same method (discounted cash flow). They proved that the chemical application discovered in Sweden could be manufactured in Belgium for worldwide sales at a lower cost. It could then be offered to customers throughout the world at a lower price, thus winning in competition with large paper chemicals companies in Germany. The reason for lower cost was that the Belgian company already had a plant with excess capacity which could produce the chemical in very large quantities. In other words, the same factor as in the proposed bank merger dominated Belgian strategists' decision: the most effective organization design (TI.12) for supplying world wide customers is to locate the XL-4 operation in Belgium. Just as a centralized computer system, or a centralized trust department, spread over many customers, would provide

185

cheaper banking services in the merger case, so a centralized Belgian XL-4 department, serving the whole world, would provide cheaper chemical products.

At this point, the same objections to centralized design were raised as in the bank merger case. Swedish law requires that all subsidiaries of foreign corporations have at least one Swedish director to insure that the contributions of corporations to *Swedish culture* are emphasized. The Swedish director raised two issues. First, like Congressman Celler, he said that the headquarters managers in Sweden had spent an enormous amount of their time, energies, and initiative developing this chemical into a viable product for the paper industry. They had been the ones who exercised free enterprise initiative, not the managers in Belgium. The organization structure of Roget, S.A. should be decentralized, so that when a subsidiary management discovered a product they would be able to carry through with it. Otherwise their initiative and enterprising spirit would be killed. Second, like the governor of New York, the Swedish director said that employment and income of Sweden depended on having a healthy industry. Thorsten should be allowed to establish the plant in Sweden to fulfill its cultural obligations for (1) employment of citizens, (2) economic development of businesses, and (3) contribution to the gross national product of Sweden.

Since the Swedish director threatened to resign, and to complain to the Swedish government, strategists in Brussels reconsidered their organization design. Though a *centralized* XL-4 manufacturing and selling organization located in Belgium would be most effective for worldwide customers (task constituencies), a *decentralized* organization would be more effective from the standpoint of cultural constituencies' demands in Sweden. As of the time the case was written, they had not resolved this conflict between task effectiveness and cultural effectiveness.

Demand for Operating-Process Realignment

Every organization includes in its task alignment certain operating processes (TI.21) that are required in order to produce a product or a service. These may include a production line that produces automobiles, a flow of chemicals from one piece of equipment to another to produce gasoline, or a set of operations that freeze food, wrap it in plastic, and transport it into a refrigerated warehouse. These are manufacturing operations. They are tangible and easy to see.

But service organizations also have operating processes. A social work agency has a certain kind of work each counselor performs (for example, family counseling as opposed to individual psychiatric interviews) and a workflow system that specifies the steps required in the process (for example, steps necessary to arrange for foster parents to adopt a child). The United States Coast Guard has a system for detecting fog on a rocky point. When fog reaches a certain density, there is a procedure to turning on the lamp and rotating prisms in a lighthouse. The United States Department of Labor has a complex set of operations necessary to find jobs for unemployed persons: procedures for interviewing, for displaying job openings on computers for interviewers, and for summarizing the number of jobs that are filled in the same day they are received as openings. The West Virginia Department of Welfare has just realigned its procedures for determining which individuals are eligible to receive welfare checks.[11]

Such a rationalization of work to be done is a necessity if the organization is to achieve its primary goal for its task constituency. It is also a necessity to prevent waste of manpower and other resources. It is enforced, as we saw in Part II, by task constituencies. In the hospital industry, Congress specified in 1972 that all states dispensing Medicare and Medicaid must set up Professional Standards Review Organizations (PSROs) in order to ensure that medical care delivered to patients is of acceptable quality, and that it is accomplished within costs acceptable to HEW (which must budget the money), and to Congress (which must answer to taxpayers when making the federal budget). The PSRO is a complex group of procedures by which local physicians review and evaluate services. It is intended that such procedures will reduce unnecessary surgery and x-rays, decrease the length of hospitalization for many conditions such as appendectomies, and discourage unnecessary prescribing of drugs. The Minnesota PSRO, for example, has not only judged the quality of care received by patients, but has also devised criteria for diagnosis and treatment of a variety of illnesses. At Bethesda Lutheran Hospital in St. Paul, the PSRO procedure has lowered the average hospital stay from nine to seven days.[12]

Thus, in devising standard operating processes and procedures, policymakers are frequently responding to demands in the task environment, designing a process that is required to produce low-cost utility to customers and clients. But these processes often generate multiple effects on different *cultural* constituencies, the same kind of multiple effect we saw in connection with structural alignments. First, some group is adversely affected and objects to the alignment on the basis of its particular demand theme. It demands a change to some other process. As the situation unfolds, other groups are brought into the picture, some of whom benefit from the present policy and some of whom incur costs from it.

In this section, we will first briefly review a familiar type of process-alignment conflict, one in which the process being used has negative effects on certain groups that focus on the intangible quality of life in the community. These groups object to a process that produces pollution, urban congestion, or depletion of natural resources. But they are not the only ones affected. Other groups then assert their self-interests. They fear that should policymakers focus on environmental factors exclusively, they will suffer adverse consequences.

After a summary of one such case, this section will have two case histories from service-producing organizations that are less familiar. In the Teachers Insurance and Annuity Association, conflict occurs between the internal mathematical (actuarial) process used by this insurance company and the demand for equality for women. In the University of Washington Law School, conflict occurs between the internal standards and processes used to admit students to the school and the demand for equality for minority persons who want a law school education. These cases are important to show the true nature of conflicts between task performance and cultural effectiveness. They also demonstrate how to diagnose process conflicts.

Process Alignment
Versus Cultural Values:
Manufacturing Companies

American Smelting and Refining Company (ASARCO) has been producing copper at its Tacoma, Washington, facility since 1915.[13] The plant produces 144,000 tons of pure copper each year for sale to a wide variety of industrial and consumer products companies. Producing 7 percent of the copper in the nation, the plant is significant, for example, in the further production of electric wiring for households, telephone equipment, cookwear, alloys for metallic money, automobile ignition systems, electronic computers, household appliances, and a host of other products. It is the only smelter in the United States capable of removing copper from difficult ores containing quantities of gold, silver, and arsenic.

To smelt and refine the copper, 400,000 tons of ore flow into the plant annually. The state-of-art operating process is as follows:

1. Smelting begins in a giant roaster where powdered ore is heated in air to drive off volatile materials. The substance flowing out of

188

the roaster is calcine, a fine mixture of copper sulfides and impurities.

2. The preheated calcine enters a reverberatory furnace, a large rectangular furnace heated from the top, where it is melted at 2700°F. The substance flowing out the bottom of the furnace is heavy, copper-bearing matte.

3. The matte is transferred to a cylindrical converter furnace where silica is added and extremely hot air is injected. The air and silica cause the remaining iron and sulfur (each of which has a high affinity to combine with oxygen) to be driven off as a gas or to become part of the relatively lighter slag material. In weight, 70 percent of the nonvolatile materials from the original ore end up as slag. The output of this converter is known as "blister" copper. It is 98 percent pure.

4. The blister copper is fed into large casting machines that produce rectangular sheets about a yard square and 3 inches thick, each weighing 500 pounds. These sheets are called anodes.

5. The anodes are suspended in giant electrolytic refining tanks in a solution of sulfuric acid and copper sulfate. The tank has electric cathodes through which an electric current is passed. Copper ions from the solution are deposited on the cathodes as pure metallic copper (99 percent). Impurities fall to the bottom. The anodes must remain in the tank under electrolysis for 28 days. The pure copper output from this process is the cathode.

6. Cathodes are melted down in casting furnaces into wirebars, 40 inches long and 5 inches square, weighing 265 pounds.

7. Shipping operations are a network of storage procedures, internal material-handling procedures, and loading procedures.

The output from the smelter is sold in competition with highly efficient producers in Japan and Germany. In fact, Arthur D. Little, Inc., an independent research agency employed by the federal government concluded that if any American company should exceed the current cost for smelting copper in existing smelters (7–10¢ per pound), it would probably lose a significant portion of its sales. Customers would switch to more efficient (lesser-cost) producers. Tacoma currently produces just under 10¢ per pound.

The case history shows an eight-year series of events between the Puget Sound Air Pollution Control Agency (PSAPA) and policymakers of the ASARCO smelter, during which many groups made demands about what the operating process ought to be. Some demanded that the process be changed drastically. Others opposed the drastic changes and insisted that it be modified slightly.

PSAPA was established in 1967, when the Federal Clean Air Act required all states to establish and enforce air quality standards or face the loss of federal funds. It is governed by a nine-person board representing cities and counties. It employs a staff of 47 and a budget of approximately $1 million per year, 34 percent of which is paid by cities, 26 percent by the state, and 40 percent by federal grants.

In the spring of 1968 and again in 1970, PSAPA adopted regulations governing the amount of sulfur dioxide (SO_2) that could be emitted into the atmosphere, since this gas can cause respiratory health problems. Its regulations were more stringent than federal guidelines. Among them was a requirement that 90 percent of the sulfur entering the plant in the ore must be captured and prevented from escaping as sulfur dioxide in the atmosphere. Two steps in the ASARCO operating process alignment (steps 1 and 3) liberate sulfur dioxide.

Since ASARCO was at that time recovering only 17 percent of the sulfur in its ore, it responded by asking for three years in which to act. During the three years policymakers changed the plant's operating processes by installing a 200-ton-per-day plant to convert SO_2 to liquid. This new alignment plant, costing $18 million, recovered 51 percent of the sulfur entering the plant. The company also hired four trained meteorologists and purchased $100,000 in weather forecasting equipment to predict weather conditions under which the atmospheric standards would be violated.

As of this time PSAPA is insisting that the 90 percent recovery rule be observed. ASARCO policymakers say they cannot meet this standard, since it would be impossible to do so without pushing copper smelting costs above the 10¢ level. It would require a completely new technology, costing $89 million. This would be in addition to the $20 million ASARCO has spent on pollution control devices at Tacoma in the past 8 years. Further, they assert that they have met the *federal* air-pollution guidelines with the realigned liquid SO_2 plant, if not the local PSAPA 90 percent guidelines.

During the eight-year negotiation between the two parties, other interest groups voiced their opinions:

1. *Demand for employment and standard of living:* labor leaders noted that over 1000 persons are employed in the smelter. Any threat to this employment would invoke a serious hardship. Dock workers focused on the fact that 24 ships each year call at the Port of Tacoma to service the smelter.
2. *Demand for economic development:* a number of small business leaders came forward to point out that the payroll of the smelter is

$16 million a year. Loss of this amount of support for grocery stores, local automobile mechanics, and restaurants, as well as for employees working in these establishments, would be "crippling." Further, the smelter purchases $6 million worth supplies each year in Tacoma, from businesses selling everything from stationery to pumping machinery. The Burlington Northern Railroad, itself having financial difficulties, receives approximately $1 million in revenues from the smelter each year.

2. *Demand for urban renewal:* some groups called attention to the fact that downtown Tacoma is in serious need of urban renewal. Taxes paid to the city by the smelter amount to $1.2 million a year.

Process Alignment Versus Demand for Equality and Equity: The Insurance Industry

The following case history is a classic example of conflict between a process alignment that achieves maximum utility benefit to the client task constituency yet conflicts with the demand for equality by women, and the demand for equity by other constituencies.[14] It is classic for three reasons. First, because it relies on mathematics to *prove* the task performance advantages to all clients, we can see the dispassionate results of science as an indicator of task-performance benefits. Second, because it involves a service output and a "paperwork process," instead of a product output and a "manufacturing process," it calls attention to the fact that process efficiency is as important in government bureaus, nonprofit agencies, and service firms as it is in manufacturing businesses. Third, because of the mathematical proof in the case, it shows that a value called "equality" is difficult if not impossible to achieve, and that it conflicts with various meanings of "equity." Finally, it shows leaders in government acting as policymakers for the insurance industry, each representing a different constituency with a different demand theme.

Teachers Insurance and Annuity Association (TIAA) is the fifteenth largest insurance company in the United States. A nonprofit mutual company, it has assets of $2.7 billion, and provides pension plans for 350,000 persons who are teaching at 2600 colleges and universities. It pays benefits currently to half a million retired persons.

One of the service outputs of TIAA is a retirement pension that, for the individual person, has certain characteristics. The person pays a certain amount per month during working years, and the university or college contributes an equal amount. TIAA takes this

191

stream of payments (say, $90,000) and invests it in stocks and bonds over 20 or 30 years, as the payments come in. Dividends and interest from this investment (say, $210,000) are added to the total fund the person owns when he or she reaches retirement age of 65 (now $300,000). TIAA then gives total security to the person by guaranteeing that he or she will receive a certain amount per year so long as he or she lives.

In order to provide this service (TE), TIAA, like all other insurance companies in the United States and Europe, employs a process alignment (TI.21) that achieves the effect of spreading risks. This process is based on actuarial statistics. The process works like this: *If TIAA could predict that all human beings will die when they are 75,* it would simply divide the $300,000 by 10 years and come out with payments of $30,000 per year. But a host of factors determine when a person will die. Some die before the average, others later. TIAA uses mortality statistics from the United States Public Health Service and its own actuarial department to predict when human beings *do* die. These statistics show how many die at 67 years old, how many at 70, how many at 75, etc. Present statistics show that the average male college professor will die when he is 82 years old, whereas the average female professor will die when she is 86 years old.

In order to provide total security of payments until death, the company uses those who die early to subsidize those who die late. If a man dies at 80, the funds from the extra two years are used to pay a pension to the man who lives two years longer than expected, until 84. The same is true in the case of a woman. If a woman dies at 84, the funds left over are used to pay the pension of a woman that lives until 88. Because of equal contributions during the work years of life, the entire insurance industry asserts that this is the *only* way a company can offer this type of total security policy, one that guarantees maximum and certain payments until death. Without it, the company would go bankrupt, and thus jeopardize the security of the entire client constituency. Actuarial statistics are also the most accurate, objective, and "real" way, since the statistics are direct measures of reality. They show when people do die, not when someone else guesses that they will die, or when someone else would like them to die.

The fact that women live four years longer than men, until 86 years of age instead of to 82, means that two persons, one male and one female, who join TIAA at the same time, at the same age, and who make equal payments until 65, will have the same retirement fund at the date of their retirement ($300,000). However, to guaran-

EXHIBIT 7-1

	Men	Women
Accumulated fund at retirement	$300,000	$300,000
Maximum account can pay each year	31,110	28,560
Total paid out by TIAA to person who lives exactly the expected number of years	528,870	599,760

tee payments until death, TIAA pays women for 21 years but men for 17 years. A woman, therefore, gets less each year but a *greater total* amount over her retirement years. The larger total is caused by the fact that the $300,000 is invested at compound interest over 21 years instead of 17 years. In Exhibit 7-1, the $300,000 is hypothetical for two persons joining in the same year. The other figures are actual. They are based on TIAA actuaries' prediction of compound interest on a person's account as the balance declines while retirement benefits are being paid out. This state-of-art technology has been used by the insurance industry for over 150 years. It was developed originally by Scottish mathematicians at the University of Edinburgh.

However, in 1977, the National Organization of Women (NOW) and the American Nurses Association (ANA) objected to the fact that TIAA did not give equal monthly payments to women after retirement. Here is a summary of the constituencies that became involved over the period 1977–79, together with their demand themes.

Congress represented rights of women in the Equal Rights Act. In classic strategy-structure fashion, it assigned the general goal of equal opportunity for jobs to the Equal Employment Opportunity Commission with the expectation that EEOC would further elaborate specific rules. The EEOC wrote rules that told insurance companies to stop writing policies with unequal annual payments after retirement. It was on the basis of these rules that NOW and ANA objected.

Congress passed the Equal Pay Act of 1963, formulating the general goal of equal pay for women. It assigned responsibility for elaborating specific rules to the wage and hour administrator in the Department of Labor. In elaborating the goal the wage and hour administrator's rules *do* allow insurance companies to use the TIAA method.

193

Congress included in the Equal Pay Act an educational amendment (Title X) delegating the responsibility for elaborating the goal for schools and colleges to the secretary of health, education, and welfare. This official, noting the conflicting rules, recommended that the president somehow get the agencies all to agree on the same rules. As of this time, the president has appointed the Equal Opportunity Coordinating Council (EOCC) to do this. The secretary of labor is its chairman.

Various newspaper articles have carried complaints from men, should the insurance industry be required to combine all people into one actuarial group. In effect, the main theme is, "It is not our fault that we die four years sooner, so we should not be required to subsidize women. Furthermore, they already collect more total funds after retirement than men."

The financial vice-president of a large midwestern university, representing the state's taxpayers, says that the solution is not simply to equalize things by having universities contribute more to retirement payments before retirement. The taxpayer revolt shows that states cannot go on forever increasing spending.

The same officer at a private university, representing students or fund donors, says that in order to equalize retirement benefits for all it would cost this one university about $3 million per year, or $60 million over 20 years. He says it would be impossible for the 20,000 students in the university to pay enough tuition or for alumni gift donors to give enough to make up the difference.

Should the federal government attempt somehow to make up the difference in the actuarial balance, citizens in general may pay (if, through inflation, the difference is paid for by printing more money) or federal income taxpayers may pay (if the funds were obtained by raising taxes).

Process Alignment Versus Equality and Equity: The University of Washington Law School

The following case is one that presents a dilemma often called "reverse discrimination." Though it covers process alignment by policymakers in a law school, it is in some respects identical to other cases that have been tried in the courts in 1977, 1978, and 1979. Some of these other cases are: [15]

Policymakers in the University of California Medical School at Davis struggle to resolve the conflict between the demand to admit students who will be the most competent doctors and the

194

demand to admit a certain quota of minority applicants (*Regents of the University of California* v. *Allan Bakke*).

Policymakers in the United States Department of Commerce offices in Los Angeles and Pittsburgh must reconcile these demands:

The demand to select the most competent firm to construct school buildings, highways, water reservoirs, and other public works projects: the demand for task efficiency.

The demand to follow the Public Works Act of 1977, which requires that 10 percent of all public-works-project contracts be awarded to firms owned by minority persons: the demand for equity based on need.

The demand by white owners of six small business-contracting firms in Los Angeles that they be given equal opportunity to obtain contracts without reference to race: the demand for equity based on ability to contribute.

Policymakers in the Kaiser Aluminum and Chemical Company plant in Gramercy, Louisiana, must reconcile these demands:

The demand by minority persons, represented by rules formulated to meet EEOC regulations, to hire 50 percent of all new trainees for electrician positions from minority groups: the demand for equity based on need.

The demand by Brian Weber, a white applicant for a job, that he had more experience and seniority in electrical work, but was turned down under the 50 percent rule: the demand for equity based on experience.

The demand by Kaiser customers that competent electricians be employed, with lowest training costs, in order to produce high-quality, low-cost products in the plant: the demand for task effectiveness.

The last resort for policymakers in these cases is, of course, the United States Supreme Court. In this capacity, it will be determining the internal process alignment of all educational institutions, all manufacturing companies, and all government contracting agencies in the nation. It is significant that lower courts, the United States District Courts, and the United States Courts of Appeals, have resolved these cases in different ways. For example, lower courts in California have ruled that a flat quota of 10 percent for contracts to minority-owned firms is unconstitutional because it discriminates on the basis of race against small businesses owned by white persons. At the same time, the lower courts in Pennsylvania have ruled that the 10 percent rule is constitutional because it protects the equal opportunity of minorities.

Against this background, it is worthwhile to diagnose one of the first cases of this type. It shows the original purpose of the admissions process alignment (TI.21) in the University of Washington Law School, which was to discharge the responsibility for high-quality service in its task-performance responsibility (TE). As time went on, this ideal process alignment ("ideal" in the sense that it was judged best for task constituencies) was changed in order to satisfy another demand: the demand for equal opportunity for minorities who want to enter the law school (a CE demand). This was the opposing group. But as the realignment (the new TI.21) was instituted to accommodate this demand, still another group arose to insist that the original admissions process was the correct one. The case is entirely too complex to cover in detail.[16] Only the essential elements can be presented.

Prior to 1970, the University of Washington Law School saw its output to society as serving two constituencies. One was the task constituency (TE)—the "customer," persons in society who need legal advice on buying a home, getting a divorce, or dealing with the aftermath of an automobile accident. The other was the citizenry in general, which is dependent on competent lawyers to act out a certain behavior necessary to preserve the common law system. This was a cultural constituency (CE).

Policymakers in the school explain the latter as follows:

> One of the ultimate goals of the law school is to turn out graduates who can help keep the system of English common law operating in a way that is highly regarded, respected by citizens, and obeyed. This common law is a delicate and beautiful thing. It is part of the apparatus in society that enables us to provide a government based on relative freedom and democracy.

> The graduate must be able to perform a certain series of mental processes if he is to act as a lawyer, or judge. He or she must be able through research to *discover* the law by inductively generalizing from a number of case histories. When one finds a series of cases that are similar to the one at hand, one must find the *principle of law* in these and apply that principle to the present case. Judgments in each of the parade of cases become part of the law of the land. It is only by having lawyers do this difficult research, and doing it with competence and excellence, that common law will survive. And if common law does not survive, the people are the losers. The alternative is having a country ruled only by legislative laws, in which the elite, the legislature, masterminds all law "from above." This is

196

very different from having lawyers and judges discover the law from the various practices which arise "from below."

Services to these two constituencies, then, are the ultimate goals of a law school. It attempts to "manufacture" law students who then go out and provide (1) service to direct clients and (2) service to all citizens by maintaining the common law system. The first of these is a product/service constituency (TE). The second is a cultural constituency (CE).

The law school, like any organization, must have an internal task alignment: buildings and equipment (TI.11), an organizational structure of persons divided by specialization (TI.12, groups of professors who teach international law, or philosophy of law, for example), work processes (TI.21, such as admissions procedures and grading procedures) and work design (TI.22, assignment of individual professors to courses).

One policy in the task alignment of the school was the admissions process. It was designed to ensure that students would be able to achieve the TE goals of the school. Too complex to describe fully, it consisted of a series of steps by which a committee received applications, ranked them against special test standards worked out by the Educational Testing Service and against certain academic performance standards (grade-point averages), judged the prior experience of candidates as indicated by reference letters, and made a final decision based on these three sources. Each candidate took a LSAT (Law School Admissions Test). This was designed to measure a person's ability to perform the difficult research referred to earlier. Most students scored in range of 400 to 700 on this test, with the norm or median at 500.

In order to comply with growing sentiment in society that minorities should be given equal opportunity, and with government regulations emerging to emphasize this demand theme, policymakers in the school realigned their admissions process. They made a new policy on admissions procedures. In effect it tended to assign all minority applicants who scored below the median to a special group. This group was given priority over a number of white applicants who scored higher than 500.

One of these white students, Marco DeFunis, sued the university. His test score was 613. The admissions committee, acting under the new realignment, admitted 36 minority students who had less than 500 test scores, and who had lower grades in prior college work than DeFunis. He demanded equality of treatment without regard to race.

197

Since the DeFunis case, policymakers in a wide variety of educational, manufacturing, and service organizations, as well as policymakers in the courts, have been experimenting with various hiring and admissions processes. In doing so, they are constantly attempting to reconcile two or three of these important value themes:

The demand for task effectiveness (TE). Customers and clients of the organization have a right to quality products and services.

The demand for equality (CE). Minority persons have a right to learn and develop. They have a right to be hired as readily as any other human being or to enroll in educational programs as readily.

The demand for equity based on competence: *Justice* requires that persons be hired or admitted on the basis of their contribution to the task to be done.

The demand for equity based on "original position." Justice requires that all persons should be regarded as human beings and treated as origins. To treat a person as an origin, it is necessary to "back up time" and view him or her as having started out as equal, taking into consideration the person's situational opportunity for bettering him- or herself.

The Courts as Policymakers

With the exception of the last, case histories in this book have made it appear that Congress is the agency that established broad cultural goals and that executive agencies often simply elaborate these goals. Congress passed the Equal Employment Act, the Equal Pay Act, the act that created the Environmental Protection Agency and gave it the broad goal of ensuring clean air. Congress also assigned to agencies created by these acts the work of elaborating broad goals into greater detail by issuing rules and procedures, their own work-process alignments to accomplish the broad goals. In the past, the role of courts was "to *restrict* the executive and legislative branches in what they could do." In recent years, the role has as often been to "extend the role of what the government could do, even when the government did not want to do it."[17]

At this point we should take note of the courts as final goal-setters, formulators of broad goals (and sometimes detailed rules) about what policymakers can or cannot do. This is an important development that has taken place in the past 15 years. Courts have indeed been proactive in setting cultural goals, as contrasted with the traditional legal paradigm that they are *reactive*, only *interpreting*

198

the laws of Congress (which was to be the proactive goal-setter in response to public opinion).

In May 1977, at the very time when courts were trying the cases mentioned in the previous sections, the Gallup poll reported that 83 percent of all people in the United States believed that reverse discrimination should not be used in hiring or in determining admission to colleges and universities. Even 64 percent of all nonwhite persons believed that "ability, as determined by test scores, should be the main consideration for hiring persons for jobs or admitting persons to college, rather than preferential treatment for minorities, as a means of making up for past discrimination."[18]

Similar statistics for public opinion exist in the case of busing schoolchildren. Nonwhite parents are themselves in disagreement as to whether or not they want their children bused. In September 1978, mandatory busing in Los Angeles, which had been mandated by the California Supreme Court, was halted by the United States District Court of Appeals. Justices in that court decided that the potential damage to all children in the mandatory busing plan was greater than potential damage to racially isolated children. In the same year, a black woman in Atlanta, herself one of the original heroes of the civil rights movement at the University of Alabama, sued to prevent her child from being bused because she believed that it damaged the child's natural development. Even with such evidence, the Supreme Court, by the *Swann, Keyes,* and *Milliken* decisions, decided that policymakers in city school systems "*must* move children around to distant schools against the will of their parents."[19]

In 1973, the Supreme Court ruled in *Roe* and *Doe* that all state abortion laws were unconstitutional. It decided that all state legislatures must realign work processes in the hospital industry to treat each third of a woman's pregnancy period according to different standards.

The Environmental Protection Agency "did not wish to issue rules preserving pure air in areas without pollution or to impose drastic transportation controls. . . . This did not seem to the EPA what Congress intended; but under court order, it was required to do both."

"In these, as in other cases, government is required to do what the Congress did not order it to do and may well oppose, what the executive does not feel it wise to do, and most important, what it does not know how to do. How *does* one create that . . . community in Boston so that vandalism repair costs may be brought down to what the authority can afford?"[20]

199

The purpose in citing these cases is not to criticize the court system. It is solely to point out that the third branch of government is active in cultural policy formulation as are the other two branches, which have so far been given more prominence in the case histories cited in this book.

Notes

1. "University of Washington Law School," Appendix.
2. "The High Ross Dam," Appendix.
3. "Cultural Demands on Product or Service Alignment" (Case File), Appendix.
4. "The Liberty Bank," Appendix.
5. "Mount Rainier National Park (National Park Service)," Appendix.
6. "Cultural Demands on Product or Service Alignment" (Case File), Appendix.
7. "The High Ross Dam," Appendix.
8. "Cultural Demands for Capital Equipment Alignment" (Case File), Appendix.
9. "Lincoln Rochester Trust Company," Appendix.
10. "AB Thorsten (A-C, R)," Appendix.
11. "Cultural Demands for Operating Process Alignment" (Case File), Appendix.
12. "Cultural Demands for Operating Process Alignment" (Case File), Appendix.
13. "American Smelting and Refining Company," Appendix.
14. "Teachers Insurance and Annuity Association," Appendix.
15. "Cultural Demands for Operating Process Alignment" (Case File), Appendix.
16. "University of Washington Law School," Appendix.
17. Nathan Glaser, "Towards an Imperial Judiciary?" *The Public Interest* 41 (Fall 1975): 104–23.
18. *New York Times*, May 1, 1977.
19. Nathan Glaser, "Towards an Imperial Judiciary?," *op. cit.*, p. 109.
20. *Idem.*

CHAPTER 8

Internal Challenges: Behavior of Managers

The Concept of Cultural Efficiency

In Chapter 1 we saw that one of the four principal demands made on all productive organizations and their general managers is the demand for cultural efficiency. This demand is made by *internal* members of the organization rather than *external* constituencies. It covers a range of subdemands that reflect the self-interests of different classes of members, just as the demand for cultural effectiveness covered a range of subdemands reflecting the self-interests of different groups outside the organization.

The organization as a whole, and general managers who plan its strategy, depend on internal members for several reasons. They are resource suppliers, exchanging their efforts and work for both tangible rewards (self-interest in terms of remuneration) and intangible rewards (self-interest in terms of basic needs and quality of work life). Further, strategists and policymakers depend on internal members because, as organizations grow in size, only specialists are in a position to know enough specific facts to elaborate the strategy into detailed operational actions. Finally, internal members have types of power and influence that can be used to resist any task alignment with which they might disagree.

Chapters 8 and 9 taken together have two purposes. First, they will establish the concept of cultural efficiency as a goal of organizations and a responsibility of strategists and policymakers. These goals and responsibilities are assigned by internal employees of the organization. Second, they will present an analysis of subdemands made by a set of different constituencies inside the organization. A wealth of research from the fields of political science, sociology, and social

201

psychology has yielded powerful demands made by groups inside most large organizations. This research also shows us deep reasons for employees to make these demands. Further, it enables us to predict results of such demands in terms of the kinds of decision these groups make. For example, they make suboptimizing decisions, which serve the interests of a part of the organization rather than the whole. They also make decisions that emphasize (put great weight upon) keeping the whole strategic alignment the way it is, making small policy decisions that are similar to the existing task alignment, rather than making major strategic decisions that would substantially alter the comprehensive task alignment. Finally, they sometimes make decisions that put higher weight on their own needs than on the needs of external task constituencies.

These demands are facts of life. They are not "bad" per se. In fact, we shall see that they are as normal as the self-interests of any other constituencies. For example, suppose internal employees form a labor union that (1) defines employment qualifications for hiring and (2) protects security of older employees by a seniority system that specifies how people are to be promoted. Suppose further that one external cultural constituency is a set of minority persons who want jobs and employment, and a guarantee of promotion up the ladder if hired. The qualification system prevents minorities from being given preference in hiring new employees. Yet minority constituents need to be hired so that they can learn and develop skills. The seniority system means that older employees would for some years have priority in promotions, preventing newly hired minority persons from learning and developing even higher level job skills. What we have here is a clash of self-interests. It is important to recognize that both are indeed "right," from the viewpoint of the parties themselves.

Internal Constituencies

As we examine internal constituencies, it soon becomes evident that there are several different value-markets inside the organization, based on decision-making level and demand theme at each level.

For our purposes, there are three major internal constituencies: general managers, middle managers, and work-level (operating level) employees. This trichotomy is similar to the distinction made by Parsons among the institutional level, the managerial level, and the technical level.[1] It is also similar to the distinction made by Katz and Kahn among three leadership roles: the policy-formulation role (formulating broad alignments), the interpolation-of-structure role (piecing out the incompleteness of strategy, and elaborating, clarifying, and improvising), and the administrative role (taking the alignment and putting it into active operation).[2] Both Katz and Kahn and Mintzberg,[3] have given us a more detailed description of how managers behave in these roles.

Finally, these three levels are similar to the distinction made by Vancil and Lorange among the chief-executive level, the division-manager level, and the functional-department-manager level.[4] These authors, discussing strategic planning in large divisionalized companies, show that a functional department manager has one function in common with work-level operators in smaller and simpler companies. Such a manager contributes detail to higher-level decisions, but he or she also puts such decisions into active operation at the work level.

Needs and Self-Interests of Managers

In this chapter we will analyze the needs, motivations, and demands of managers (CI.1) as contrasted with those of employees at the work level (CI.2). It turns out that for strategic purposes, there are really two managerial motivations, each held by a different internal constituency:

1. *The demand for status quo* (CI.11) is often made by all managers, that is, by both general managers (strategists), and middle managers (administrators). The *behavior* that results from this need is sometimes called "inflexibility," "resistance to change," or "rigidity."
2. *The demand for suboptimization* (CI.12) is one that is often made by middle managers. It is both a social and intellectual need, generated by one's position level in the decision-making hierarchy. The *behavior* generated by this need is sometimes called "parochialism" or "local rationality" (as contrasted with "cosmopolitan rationality").

Managers as a class (including general managers and middle managers) demand small changes or no changes in the existing alignments. Underlying such a demand is a deeper motive: the need for stability and security. This same motive has been widely discussed in the literature as a need to avoid uncertainty. This is a *reactive* or reactionary demand. It is activated in situations where there is an outside stimulus to change (such as a demand by clients and customers for task realignment). Managers react by resisting

203

such change. Or they react by making small incremental policy decisions that are similar to the strategic alignment they have learned in the past, rather than by making major changes in the strategic alignment. Both of these behaviors are manifestations of the demand for status quo.

The second managerial constituency of importance consists only of middle-level managers, the group of division or department heads who perform the function of elaborating, specifying, and filling in the pieces of broad strategic alignments after they have been enacted by general managers. We have already seen examples in previous chapters of how such managers take a broad product/service/market goal and work out intricate internal task alignments. The Sears, Roebuck case, as well as the health maintenance organization and Nursing Home cases, showed how vital the middle-level alignment function is.

Stated in simplest terms, such managers have a strong need to *suboptimize*—to place higher weight, in their decisions, on the welfare and performance of their part of the organization than on the welfare and performance of the whole organization. This is a proactive need because it is activated by a desire to change alignments. We shall see that in behavioral terms, managers act out this need in a wide variety of behaviors, from empire building to simply trying to create excellent technical operations in their own departments.

All Managers: Demand for Status Quo

Existing task alignments are extremely complex. They develop slowly. Managers who spend their lives working with alignments learn a routine that itself is a source of security. But security is a complex thing. There are different kinds of security depending on what kind of stimulus threatens a manager and what aspect of the manager's person or self is being threatened. For a real understanding of managerial demands we need to look at three types of insecurity that are aroused when external groups demand task realignment. These three types of insecurity are given in Exhibit 8-1.

COGNITIVE SECURITY   One of the most powerful needs of middle managers is intellectual or cognitive stability. In Chapter 4, we saw that the task alignment of Sears, Roebuck, for instance, was enormously complex. It consisted of a broad strategy in the form of

EXHIBIT 8-1

Type of insecurity	Type of stimuli	Aspect of the manager's self or person that is being threatened
Cognitive (intellectual) insecurity	Information overload or information deficiency	Cognitive processes: ability to think clearly
Social (interpersonal or intergroup) security	Unexpected actions of other persons or groups	Emotional processes: ability to maintain peace and tranquility
Political (formal status and power) insecurity	Actions of other persons or groups that are perceived to take away status or power	Tangible and intangible possessions: property, job rights, status and importance, income

products policies, markets policies, capital-allocations policies, and an organization design specifying divisions and departments. This broad strategy was then elaborated into thousands of more detailed decisions on capital equipment allocations, further organization specializations, operating processes, and work roles.

The complexity is overpowering, to the point where the human brain must simplify the focus of problems and the search for alternatives. Most managers would experience "future shock" or "decision overload" if they were to try to figure out the whole alignment. Furthermore, they know that the task environment "out there" is always changing, and that they cannot predict that if they build a certain Sears, Roebuck store today to sell one product line six years from now, customers will have the same tastes. These two factors, complexity and uncertainty, cause them to do what most people would do under similar circumstances. They rely on what they know—on what, over the years, the learning curve has taught them by logical incrementalism. This in turn means that new changes in policy will be met with resistance.

For those familiar with the literature of cognitive decision making, the behavior of middle managers under such circumstances can be explained in different ways as treated by different authors. Herbert Simon, first in *Administrative Behavior*[5] and later in *The New Science of Management Decision*,[6] called this satisficing behavior and heuristic behavior. Managers are faced with complexity of two types. First, any decision they take has a myriad of possible alternative actions, too numerous even to list. Second, each of these alternatives in turn has a myriad of outcomes that are different from those of all other alternatives. What does the normal person do? He or she *satisfices* (rather than try to list all of these alternatives and then try to maximize his or her goal). And to satisfice means to simplify the problem into a few, more or less obvious alternatives and a few more or less obvious outcomes.

But which alternatives and outcomes are "more or less obvious"? Here the notion of *heuristics* comes in. Faced with a problem containing many unknowns, one does what one can, with an emphasis on *can*. Recalling Simon's concept of heuristics from Chapter 5, this means falling back on past experience, learned in a thousand different ways by coping with problems in the past. Faced with the need for a table while camping in the woods, one notes that there are trees, and that one has an axe. The deep meaning of past experience can be understood by asking the kind of question we seldom ask. *How* did the person know what an axe is, and how it operates? *How* could one begin to think about alternative ways the tree could fall—to picture them in one's mind? Answers to these seldom asked questions throw some glimmer of meaning onto the concept of cognitive security. They also throw light on why Sears managers might resist the realignment described in Chapter 4. Put yourself in an advertising position, or a retail-store-manager position. For seven years you have been gearing your job to advertising and selling Johnny Miller apparel. You work in a physical store layout (TI.11) that gives certain space to such merchandise, displays it in a certain way. The salespersons' work roles (TI.22) have been relating to customers day-in and day-out in a certain way, emphasizing fashion trends and higher-priced clothing. Dealing with the advertising agency in New York, you have worked out national television and newspaper copy, all geared to such merchandise. Suddenly, your whole life style must change. You would, in the future, walk through a different physical space (TI.11), one that reflects low-cost budget shops. Salespersons would have to talk with customers about different things than higher prices and high fashion. All of the television programs and newspaper presentations would be obsolete. Artwork would have to be redesigned. Artists' work roles (TI.22) would have to change. Wording of advertising must be completely revised. Copywriters' work roles will change. Even a quick summary such as this gives some indication of the magnitude of cognitive change, the degree to which managers must change their ways of thinking in order to respond to change initiated in the outside marketplace.

Cyert and March give an explanation of this kind of behavior in large organizations.[7] They show that managers usually make only small, incremental policy decisions, covering one part of the organization at a time. They seldom make broad strategic decisions to try to change the whole network alignment at once.

Allison explains the same basic motivation (cognitive security) but emphasizes a different, observable kind of behavior that results from it. In a detailed history of the Cuban missile crisis, he shows that if quick changes in strategy are made, middle managers in the chain of command cannot understand or act out new orders which are strange compared to existing rules and procedures (i.e., existing alignments).[8] Instead, they perceive the new alignment in terms of existing rules. This explanation of bureaucratic behavior (acting out existing rules rather than behaving according to changing needs of external constituencies) is quite different from the one often heard. In Allison's terms, the behavior occurs because it is the only thing a human mind can do when confronted with entirely new information. It would be as if you were sitting in the woods but had never seen a table, a tree, or an axe. Anthropologists have noticed the same kind of shock when persons in primitive societies are suddenly brought full-force into contact with modern industrial civilization.

There are other explanations for the demand for status quo alignment besides those used by organization theorists (Cyert and March) and political theorists (Allison). Two psychologists, Irving Janis and Leon Mann, present powerful evidence that whenever managers consider a policy alternative that creates reasons both to accept and reject the policy, or when the alternative creates unknown outcomes, these managers experience severe stress. As cases cited in previous chapters show, these two characteristics, conflicting outcomes and uncertain outcomes, are hallmarks of all strategy and policy decisions. Janis and Mann further show that managers in practical situations react to such stress by two kinds of behavior. They hesitate to make the new decision, and they vacillate rather than commit themselves.[9]

SOCIAL (INTERPERSONAL) INSECURITY A second type of insecurity managers face results from the fact that as external constituencies demand more rapid change in product/market alignments, this tends to create more upset, uncertainty and anxiety among the managers *inside* the organization who must cooperate to change alignments. Here we are talking not about uncertainty regarding the technical or "thing" side of life, but uncertainty about the human side of life. Endlessly and rapidly confronting other human beings, each of whom has his or her own learning curve and past experience, and his or her own ideas about what the new alignment should be, can become a source of acute anxiety. This motivation, in turn, produces the same results we have noted in the case of cognitive anxiety. It causes managers either to demand the status quo alignment (or small changes to it) or to demand law and order. The latter is an already familiar bureaucratic behavior: managers fall back on existing policies, procedures, and alignments, rather than face the painful process of trying to work out new alignments.

It took years for the strategists in charge of the sales force in Timex Corporation (Chapters 3 and 4) to develop salespersons throughout the world to deal with 250,000 drugstore retailers. These retailers had in turn learned their part of the task alignment as it fit with the 17,000 employees in manufacturing plants who had already learned their part. Yet each facet of the alignment depends on the other, and anyone who tries to change one part must face a host of other persons who are accustomed to doing things differently. Had Timex sales executives wanted to make still another change back to jewelry stores instead of drugstores, they would not only have had to confront the entire habitual behavior of district managers, state managers, and drugstore managers, they also would have had to try to change the type of watch manufactured, the kind of research and development activities necessary to produce jeweled watches instead of pin-lever watches, and the kind of financing required to buy new machinery to produce the jeweled watches.

This kind of demand is well known in most social science disciplines. Classical political philosophers were constantly concerned by the question of why free men would subject themselves to the rules, leadership decisions, and the reward-punishment structures of the modern state. Locke answered this question clearly. He postulated that man, without these three things would exist in a state of acute anxiety. Consequently, man demands (1) a known, stable, and relatively unchanging set of policies or laws (in the case of organizations, task alignments); (2) a known and relatively stable set of people who make decisions (managers); and (3) a power, in the form of rewards and punishments, to make the decisions stick. The last is needed, Locke said, because even after judges have rendered their decisions the parties to confrontation *still* may persist in disagreeing.[10]

Social psychologists have reached the same conclusion. Bennis and Shepard give detailed descriptions of what human beings do to one another when they must face each other endlessly over a period of several weeks.[11] Sociologists have found that even when it means that the customer or client is harmed by such actions, managers frequently "go by the rule book" rather than change their customary policies and procedures to fit outside demands.[12]

In a well-known study of the Scottish electronics industry, Burns and Stalker found that customer demands were changing rapidly. They were changing from a demand for older types of radios, to newer types of radio and television sets that could be produced only by radical changes in research and development, manufacturing and sales. Firms that survived were indeed run by what these authors called organic organizations, in which members in various parts were forced to abandon their routines and interact rapidly. In firms that declined or went bankrupt, managers refused to engage in such behavior. However, a very serious level of anxiety was found in the surviving firms. It was great enough for the authors to believe that managers have a fundamental and profound crisis to face when outside constituencies force rapid change. They must face the fact that their whole way of life is in a state of uncertain confusion. And they must decide whether or not their careers at work are worth the kind of interpersonal confrontation required.[13]

Finally, in a recent best-selling book, Alvin Toffler characterizes the kind of behavior described in the successful electronics companies as ad-hocracy rather than bureaucracy. He argues that this kind of behavior is indeed one source of acute stress, a stress he calls future shock.[14]

SOCIAL SECURITY AND GROUPTHINK   If we single out the general manager group from the larger constituency of all managers, this constituency has been shown to have a particular behavior pattern caused by the deeper need for social security. The term given to this behavior by Irving Janis is "groupthink." Conflicting demands such as we have seen in the responsibility matrix give people a high feeling of risk attendant in strategy formulation and policy making. Strategists must find some way for dealing with such anxiety.

From an array of case histories in public policymaking, including decision making by groups surrounding military leaders, a British prime minister, and three presidents of the United States, Janis concludes that under certain conditions, when teams of policymakers work together intensely on a particular decision, they avoid being harsh on one another's ideas, adopt a soft line of criticism, avoid bickering, and perform a variety of other activities in order to gain social support from each other.[15] Janis later applied this concept to business administration, showing how a large pharmaceutical company's board of directors, faced with a product/market decision as to whether to launch a certain drug for customers, engaged in the same kind of social support activity. Members of the board did this to avoid confronting one another and to avoid paying the price of social

209

insecurity when faced with clear and conflicting costs and benefits to various constituencies.[16]

If we look carefully at Janis' line of reasoning, we see that social security affects the policy process in two ways: (1) a principal source of insecurity is the conflict between constituencies inside and outside the organization. The policy situation itself is thus the root of the demand for social security. But this situation is in turn a *cause* of (2) another round of social security seeking *within* the policymaking group. Both of these factors together mean that the demand for the status quo, as it is caused by the need for social security, is, in our terms, an important subcategory of task alignment–cultural efficiency conflicts. It is a principal reason why the self-interests of external task constituencies, customers, and clients, may well at times be sacrificed in favor of the self-interest of the policymaking group.

POLITICAL INSECURITY Motivations centering on protecting the manager's own status, power, prestige, and income are so well known that little more need be said to explain them. In essence, when managers put such weight on these self-interests, they may make policy decisions that put less weight on low-cost utility to clients and customers, or payoffs to funds suppliers such as stockholders and taxpayers. Policies made under such conditions therefore yield high cultural-efficiency benefits to managers (CI.1) but lower task-effectiveness benefits to external task constituencies (TE), or to external cultural constituencies (CE).

Such behavior, protecting power and status, stems from *political insecurity* as contrasted with behavior that protects one's need for *interpersonal security*. The latter is anxiety caused by face-to-face interaction with other people on a personal basis. The former is caused by a threatened change in formal, impersonal status and power symbols.

These motivations are so widespread that they figure prominently in research done in almost all social science disciplines: in political science (Rourke[17]), sociology (Thompson[18]), organization theory (Cyert and March[19]), economics (Williamson,[20] Downes[21]) and psychology (Blake and Mouton[22]).

Downes describes the executive who is a "climber," one who weights his or her own personal advancement in the company so highly that it overrides factors such as the cost of making products for the consumer, or the amount of funds that have to be supplied by taxpayers. This is a proactive form of political aggrandizement. On the other hand, the "conserver" acts out the same motive in his or her day-to-day policymaking decisions but in a reactive or passive way. He or she is more concerned with *protecting* whatever salary, rank, and position he or she already has than with acquiring more of such perquisites.

Thompson clearly realizes that this kind of behavior is damaging to the interests of external constituencies when he labels it "bureau-pathology." By this term he means that the good of the organization as a whole (as contrasted with the good of an individual manager), as well as the good of clients who depend on the organization for low-cost utility products, tailored to their needs, is ignored in favor of the manager's personal interests.

Cyert and March show the clash between personal interests of managers and the interests of external constituencies by use of the concept "organizational slack." In brief terms, policymaking works like this. First, policy decisions are made by political coalitions of managers who bargain with each other. In bargaining, managers make side payments to one another in the form of budget money, perquisites, and personal things an individual might want. The coalition can survive and be viable only if the total of payments made to individuals is adequate to keep them in the organization and functioning as policymakers. If the organization were focusing solely on external task goals (lowest possible prices for the best possible services), there would be no "organizational slack." Slack would be zero. But managers do *not* focus solely on the good of task constituencies. In fact, at times they may even focus solely on their self-interests. When companies go through favorable times in the marketplace, with resource suppliers furnishing a large pie to split, "it makes only slightly more sense to say that the goal of a business organization is to maximize profit than to say that its goal is to maximize the salary of Sam Smith (an internal employee)."[23] On the other hand, when the company faces unfavorable times in the marketplace, with resource suppliers cutting their support rather than expanding it, stored-up slack enables coalition members to pay each other off to keep the political coalition alive.

Middle Managers:
Parochialism and the Need to Suboptimize

Middle managers in an organization specialize in planning, elaborating, and operating *one part* of the comprehensive strategy. For example, in Shoe Corporation of Illinois,[24] product/market alignment (TE) specifies that the company will design, manufacture, and sell lower-priced women's shoes. In order to do this, the organization structure (TI.12) must be arranged so that there is a manager of research and styling who specializes in keeping up with fashions in Paris, Rome, and New York and in being thoroughly familiar with the technical facets of shoe design (lasts, widths, leather and plastics materials specifications, etc.). The manager of manufacturing, on the other hand, devotes most of his or her time, energies, and interests to the kind of machinery necessary to manufacture shoes, the labor skills required on production lines, the relationships with a labor union in collective bargaining, the kind of scheduling between sub-departments that results in the right amount of finished inventory, and like matters. The manager of sales devotes his or her work life to far different matters, matters of advertising copy, relationships with retail store managers, the best methods of sales compensation (salary versus bonus), consumer motivation analysis, etc.

This kind of technical specialization, when practiced day after day over a career produces excellent results in terms of task performance (TE). Each person becomes an expert in one field. Each learns a different orientation toward what is and is not important in the world. The customer would no more want the manufacturing manager to design shoes for aesthetic quality than he or she would want the advertising manager to decide on the type of machinery that will produce shoes at the lowest cost!

Not only is one middle manager's technical *knowledge* (task frame of reference) different from another's, his or her constant living with one type of specialty produces profound differences in other attitudinal orientations. Lawrence and Lorsch have clearly shown us, for example, that a manager of research and development develops different attitudes toward time (don't worry about time, pursue your job deliberately and methodically) than a sales manager does (time is of the essence in getting the job done). A manufacturing manager develops different attitudes toward relationships with other people (somewhat formal and matter-of-fact) than the sales manager does (more relaxed and informal relationships are the important ones).[25]

If one takes *both* the technical (intellectual) differences and the attitudinal differences in frames of reference which different careers breed in middle managers 8 hours a day, 5 days a week, we see what Lawrence and Lorsch called simply a state of significant *differentiation* in the way one manager will make a policy for the company and the way another will make it.

Such differentiation is a double-edged sword. On the one hand it makes for excellence in the parts of the organization: excellent styling of shoes based on real knowledge of fashions in Rome and Paris, excellent manufacturing of shoes based on real knowledge of

212

machinery and of production scheduling techniques. On the other hand, middle managers develop what John Dewey called a *trained incapacity* to see either the needs of other parts of the organization, or the needs of the whole organization as it must integrate operations for the good of the customer. Later case histories will show that many times a middle manager will make a policy decision based on excellence in his or her part of the organization with the result that the interests of some other part is damaged. Benefits to the manufacturing department may indeed result in costs to the research department, to the customer, or to both.

This same phenomenon has been discussed in sociology in terms of the goals professionals pursue (i.e., the self-interests of a doctor in a hospital) versus the goals managers pursue (i.e., those of the administrator or director of the hospital). It has also been discussed in terms of line versus staff. Line executives specialize in trying to relate the organization unit to its outside world whereas staff executives most often specialize in one facet of the unit's operations.

From the viewpoint of the integration, coordination, and performance of the whole organization, this kind of behavior has been called a variety of names, depending on which academic discipline the person studying the phenomenon is from. Systems analysts have called it suboptimization, denoting the fact that it tends to optimize the good of the part rather than optimizing the good of the whole. Sociologists have called it parochialism, local rationality as contrasted with cosmopolitan rationality, or bifurcation of goals. In the language of some business and government officials, the middle manager has a "departmental bias" or a "provincial viewpoint."

Task Alignment Versus Self-Interests of Managers

Conflict between the ideal task alignment for external constituencies (TE.1–TI.2) and the ideal cultural alignment for internal managers (CI.1) appears in many contexts. Case histories in the following sections will not only give a more realistic understanding of the theoretical demands presented earlier but they will also show that conflicts arise over *specific* policies: product/market policies (TE), capital investment decisions (TI.11), organization designs (TI.12) and operating process policies (TI.21).

Nature and Importance of Policy Diagnosis

As with conflicts between task alignment and cultural effectiveness, the conflict between managers' needs and task-constituency needs can only be understood by clinical diagnosis. This is true for two reasons. First, though the conflict *originates* with one specific policy area (products, capital investment, or operating processes) it is soon seen that the whole comprehensive alignment is affected. Thus, the conflict in Shoe Corporation of Illinois *arises* because the manager of styling wishes to change the operating processes (TI.21) used to style ladies shoes in his department (from copying Paris styles to creating original styles). This would also change the product/market alignment (TE) by forcing the company to compete in custom-styled, high-priced shoes sold in luxury stores instead of adhering to the present alignment, which is to produce lower-priced women's shoes sold through chain shoe stores throughout the nation. It would also force the company to change the manufacturing organization structure (the job description of the manufacturing manager, (TI.12), the operating processes in manufacturing (different inventory control systems, TI.21) and the organization structure in the sales department (the job duties of the advertising manager, TE.12).

The second reason policymakers must use clinical diagnosis is that in any one situation a different *set* of managerial demands may be operating. The models discussed earlier are valuable in *suggesting* (serving as a checklist for discovering) the root needs and demands of managers, but they can by no means be applied to a specific company or government agency as a stereotyped and mechanistic formula. In Shoe Corporation, for example, it happens that the manager of styling's need to suboptimize (CI.12) is a factor in the situation. But as the problem unfolds, the manager of manufacturing acts out a need for status quo (CI.11). Frequent changes in style would so disrupt his operations that success in his career seems threatened. Uncertainty, plus the complexity of the manufacturing process necessary to produce shoes, he believes, would result in shoes of lower quality, higher cost, or both.

This case points up the fact that a variety of managerial demands and needs may be operating in any one case.

Conflict Over Product/Market Alignment

Conflicts between the product or service alignment that serves changing needs of external customers and resource suppliers (TE) and the cultural alignment that serves the needs of managers (CI.1) occurs in private firms, nonprofit institutions, and government agencies. Here we shall review cases in the Chandler studies (Sears, Roebuck; DuPont; and others), the Quinn studies (General Mills,

General Motors, Xerox, and others), the Family Service Association of America, and a federal savings and loan association.

THE CHANDLER STUDIES: SEARS, ROEBUCK AND DUPONT   One of the most important findings by Chandler in his massive research into almost 100 companies was that when changes occur in the task environment (such as changes in population, in needs of consumers, or in new technical innovations to serve the consumer) there is a significant delay between the formulation of a new product/market alignment (TE) to meet the needs of society and the making of specific internal resource policies (TI) necessary to operationalize a new alignment. Chandler found that executives were unaware of the need for realignment. They were so involved in the day-to-day execution of the existing alignment, and their education and training were so strongly influencing them to maintain the status quo that they had neither the perception nor the ability to change things. Furthermore, executives were acutely aware of threats to their power and status. Most important, it was their psychological inse-curity, their fear of the unknown, that caused DuPont and Sears, Roebuck to stick with current strategies to the point where the survival of the companies was threatened.[26]

THE SWISS WATCH INDUSTRY   One of the most complete case histories showing the results of the demand for status quo is that of the Swiss Watch Industry compiled at Harvard Business School.[27] At the time when worldwide consumer demands were turning to highly accu-rate, mass-produced low-cost *pin-lever* watches, and even more highly accurate, mass-produced *electronic* watches, the Swiss indus-try was organized in a massive cartel composed of separate com-panies tied together by an elaborate internal technology and contract (political) agreements. These companies provided the capital equip-ment (TI.11), organization structure (TI.12), and work-level jobs (TI.22) necessary to execute the strategy. There were 486 companies with plants and machinery making jeweled mechanical watches, 17 companies with plants producing ebauches (plates, bridges, pinions), and approximately 500 companies specializing in balance wheels, hairsprings, and the production of jewels. These last com-panies were joined into a trust that planned their alignment. The 486 jeweled-watch makers were also joined in a trust that planned their alignment. At the top, the Swiss Watch Chamber functioned as headquarters, and had over the years worked out the alignment for the whole industry.

The case history of this organization covers a 40-year period. Due to excellence in its product strategy (excellence in the consumers'

215

eyes) and a corresponding excellence in gradually developing and learning a complex internal alignment among all of these companies, the industry captured 99 percent of the United States market for imported watches. Twenty years later, it had lost 20 percent of this market to Timex, Seiko, and other companies that had achieved new and modern alignments. Evidence suggests that it will lose more due to the entry of such electronics firms as Texas Instruments. In spite of the handwriting on the wall regarding changing population, watch wearing, technology, and cost considerations, the enormously complex and rigid nature of the cartel's present alignment and the corresponding inability of its managers to cope with equally complex change in technology and society meant that these managers were powerless to meet the challenges of change.

In spite of such reverses, the Swiss industry is making changes, trying to cope incrementally to overcome the inertia generated by present alignments. Whether or not over the next 40 years the industry will be able to realign sufficiently to gain world leadership depends on the strategic ability of its leaders. Chandler's research shows that even great corporations such as Sears, Roebuck, DuPont, Exxon, and General Motors have, at crucial times in their histories, faced crises of institutional lag. Each, at some period, came close to losing their position as leader in excellence of task performance. Each has so far been able to turn the company around, realigning the whole strategy.

THE QUINN STUDIES: GENERAL MILLS, INC. Ten recent case histories by Quinn suggest that the problem of achieving change in comprehensive alignment indeed involves difficulties in perceiving, sensing, and acting on new external developments, but that some companies have been successful in making such changes. For example, the history of General Mills, Inc., from 1965 to 1977 shows that a logical strategy coupled with incremental policymaking can change a company that, since 1886, had relied primarily on milling flour for consumers. The company changed to supply consumers with a wide range of products that match the society of the 1980s.[28] Similar changes in alignments in the face of an already learned alignment are recorded in complete case histories of: Exxon Corporation (facing the North Sea oil developments and an age of energy shortage), General Motors (facing changing demands for smaller and more fuel efficient automobiles), Control Data Corporation, Chrysler Corporation, Pilkington Brothers, Ltd., Xerox Corporation, KMS Industries, and German Power Devices, Inc.[29]

216

FAMILY SERVICE ASSOCIATION OF AMERICA   The same kinds of conflict can be found in nonprofit organizations as in business corporations. A history of the Family Service Association of America shows that this organization is one of the largest nongovernmental social work agencies in the nation.[30] It began as the Travelers Aid Society, with a service alignment designed to provide emergency money to a certain constituency: the newly arrived immigrant who was traveling through railroad terminals. Over a 30-year period, it changed this alignment to the point where it was, in the 1960s, a federation of local agencies (e.g., the Jewish Family Service of Los Angeles, the Catholic Family Service of Boston) that provided a certain type of counseling. For those unfamiliar with client counseling, this service is a type of client relationship somewhere between nondirective psychiatric interviews practiced by psychiatrists and the more therapy-oriented relationships advocated by Carl Rogers.[31] The constituency, however, was defined as the *family as a group*, not one human being, and not another group of persons than the family as perceived in the 1960s: mother, father, children, and a legal marriage contract.

As society changed approaching the 1970s, the FSAA found that its service/market was threatened by a number of developments. New demand groups that had needs arose in society. More unwed persons lived together as "families." More children were born out of wedlock. More couples demanded an adoption service—there was one constituency wanting to place infants and another wanting to adopt infants. Still another constituency arose: the government and the Ford Foundation, resource suppliers who wanted poverty-level persons to receive social services, seemed to avoid giving to FSAA because its product/market alignment in most cities seemed to include middle-class persons rather than poverty-level persons. The strategists in the Community Chest of Cincinnati objected to another facet of the alignment: with scarce funds, it seemed that the operating-process alignment (TI.21, the social counseling interview methods) was very costly. Whereas one social worker could handle only 8 or 10 families at a time, and the agency could only serve 300 to 400 families a year, other agencies touched thousands of people instead of hundreds. The Boy Scouts, for example, with different services and different processes, could help 40,000 boys.

Faced with these changing demands, the heads of the agencies in the FSAA federation met for two weeks of strategic planning at Arden House, near Tuxedo, New York. Repeatedly, it was reported that agencies had a difficult time explaining to the government, the

217

Ford Foundation, and city United Fund agencies why their services deserved more resources. The most important difficulties were:

1. Every time FSAA managers appeared before resource suppliers, they devoted most of their time to explaining the value of client counseling. This was the present service output. FSAA personnel were trained in counseling. It occupied most of their working hours. Like Chandler's executives who "simply were not *aware* of other strategies," they could not spend equal time discussing day-care centers for children in poverty.
2. To FSAA managers who held values about traditional family life, it was difficult to appreciate services that fit needs of other constituencies: (a) Adoption services "did not seem the correct thing to do." "Our work is devoted to keeping families together, not encouraging mothers to split from their children and put them up for adoption." (b) Services for couples living together but not married were something foreign. "We do not know how to deal with so many temporary situations."

These events are not unusual. They are normal reactions of managers who have spent their work lives pursuing one strategic alignment. They do, however, have implications for survival, growth and decline of the organization. Demands by resource suppliers, the federal government, the Ford Foundation and the United Community Appeal, demands for keeping service/markets in line with needs of the population, must be regarded as signals of change.

CALIFORNIA FEDERAL SAVINGS AND LOAN ASSOCIATION California Federal Savings and Loan Association provides a final example of the conflict between service alignment and the needs of internal managers.[32] In the mid-1970s, the president of CFS&L became concerned about why two constituencies, persons who put money in savings accounts and persons who borrow money for home mortgages, select a given savings and loan association. A research study showed that, in addition to low-cost utility in the form of interest rates to homeowners and high-return utility in the form of interest rates paid to savings depositors, certain things governed whether a customer would select CFS&L over a competitor. One of these was the amount of time it took to (1) park an automobile and get into the building and (2) wait while loans or savings passbooks were being processed by bank personnel.

In order to appeal to customers, strategists instituted these realignments:

218

The work processes of both loan officers and new account officers in all branches were to be changed. This represented a process change (TI.21).

But to find out which changes to make, a headquarters staff manager was appointed to do research on customer demands and design processes that would meet them. This represented an organization-design change (TI.12).

The headquarters staff manager for planning indeed found out the basic needs of customers. He proposed procedures to provide these needs. However, the case shows a variety of reactions by branch managers. Some focused on the need for status security of the branch manager: "In our business, the local manager must not be hamstrung by procedures. We must be free to treat customers differently, each in a personal way"; "headquarters must not interfere with the branch manager's position as head of his branch." Others concentrated on cognitive security: "Monetary transactions are matters which must be extremely accurate. We have a system now that everyone knows and understands. If we make changes, there will undoubtedly be mistakes. And a mistake in a customer's passbook will be serious. We must stick with a system that is known and reliable."

Conflict over Capital Alignment

The responsibility for efficient allocation of capital (TI.11) often conflicts with the responsibility for satisfaction of managers (CI.1). Here we shall see this conflict as it operates in a large chemical company, the pharmaceutical industry in Iceland, the commercial banking industry, the airline industry (Air France, Britannia Airways), and the secondary school system.

A LARGE CHEMICAL COMPANY   In Chapter 7 we discussed Roget, S.A. in terms of conflict between organization structure and cultural effectiveness. This case history also shows a more fundamental conflict between capital alignment and the needs of top managers and middle managers.

Recalling that the Swedish middle managers had developed a new product, XL-4, and that they wished to build a plant in Sweden to produce this chemical for the Swedish market, one can easily see that it was the capital alignment that was at the root of the organizational problem. The case clearly demonstrates the need for suboptimization by middle managers in one part of the company as contrasted with the need for optimization by top managers of the whole company.

219

One of the costs that was projected was the cost of the plant, using modern financial-analysis techniques (discounted cash flow of incremental future returns). The plant would cost 700,000 Swedish Krona. The sales forecast over seven years was for 2500 tons of XL-4. The 700,000 Krona would, therefore, enter into the per-ton cost of the product. After figuring all fixed costs (depreciation) and variable costs (labor, materials) the entire project over seven years would result in a net cash flow after tax of 246,000 Krona.

General managers and middle managers in Sweden were enthusiastic about producing XL-4. All felt that they had worked long and hard on the technical development of the product with the pulp customers (TE), the internal manufacturing processes necessary to build and operate the plant (TI.21), and the financial work processes that would have to be accomplished to manage the plant (TI.21). They felt that the project would benefit Sweden's gross national product and its reputation as an industrial nation.

Meanwhile in Belgium, middle managers in manufacturing and finance were also concerned with XL-4. A plant already existed to produce the chemical, but the product had not before been sold to pulp manufacturers. Though the case shows a complex relationship between many managers in Sweden and Belgium, the heart of the technical and financial conflict emerges as follows. Belgian headquarters did its own discounted cash flow to predict what would happen if Belgium manufactured 2500 tons of XL-4 for export to Sweden from Belgium. Because excess capacity in the Belgian plant could be used, the per-ton cost of making the product would be lower. In fact, the net cash flow after tax would be, after converting Belgian Francs to Krona, 263,000 Krona. Belgium could export 2500 tons to Sweden for 17,000 Krona less than Sweden could manufacture the product.

This pinpoints the crux of the suboptimization dilemma. On the one hand, M. Juvet, president of the parent company in Belgium, wanted to decentralize decisions to the subsidiaries in order to bolster the initiative and morale of subsidiary middle managers. He knew they had worked well. They had created a new product market and worked through all internal alignments by their own initiative and hard work. On the other hand, the whole company would be better off, and the customer would receive a lower-cost chemical, if the product were manufactured in Belgium. Capital efficiency accounted for the difference between the cost to produce in Sweden and the cost to produce in Belgium. Juvet also had to consider the morale of Belgian middle managers. They knew that the product could be produced more cheaply in their own plants. As of the end of

220

the case, Juvet and the general managers in Belgium still have not been able to reach a decision under these conflicting conditions.

Though this happens to be a multinational company, wherein personal motives surface more visibly (because middle managers in subsidiaries can often speak up against headquarters), the same phenomenon exists in all domestic companies. As Peter Drucker has said, the whole is not simply the sum of the parts. Strategic balance often requires that some part of the alignment be harmed in order to promote the good of the whole. Ansoff has made such a concept central to all strategic planning by use of his term "synergy." A synergistic relationship existed between the Belgian and Swedish parts of the whole company: if strategists put together the manufacturing capacity in Belgium with the market demand in both Sweden and Belgium, they come out with a cash flow that is greater than either could accomplish alone.[33]

THE PHARMACEUTICAL INDUSTRY IN ICELAND   A similar dilemma faced the minister of health, justice, and ecclesiastical affairs in the government of Iceland.[34] In this long case history, the minister functioned as one of the general managers of the pharmaceutical industry. The problem was this: because there were seven manufacturers of ethical drugs, each trying to manufacture tranquilizers (e.g., Librium) and intravenous solutions for hospitals, there was a duplication of capital equipment (production-line machinery) for producing needs of a country with a population of 200,000. This meant that the consumer had to pay a price for pharmaceuticals high enough to enable seven different companies to buy the same expensive machines to produce the same products. In the case of certain drugs, if all seven companies were merged into one, output for the entire constituency (200,000 people) could be produced with one production line using virtually the same machinery as used by any one of the seven. Such a merger (which had been proposed by hospital and health-care constituencies), would enable consumers in Iceland to get drugs at a considerably lower cost. Further, if all companies merged, drugs could be produced that were out of the question in an industry splintered into seven companies. One large company could afford to buy the advanced technology.

As the policy situation unfolded in Iceland, a variety of self-interests of managers surfaced. Individual company managers (viewed from the industry level, these were "middle managers") resisted industry-wide optimization because they could see only their own present alignments. They feared the new and unknown results of a new alignment. And they saw that the new align-

221

ment would have adverse effects on their status and their money income.

THE COMMERCIAL BANKING INDUSTRY   We now turn to the history of domestic corporations. General managers of seven New York State banks reasoned exactly the same as the Icelandic minister. They proposed that their banks merge into one: the Morgan New York State Corporation.[35] Outside customers of the banks testified that the service output would be higher quality and lower cost if the banks were allowed to merge. The reasoning of these customers and the data they used to support their themes were described in Chapter 7.

Most of the added efficiency of the merged bank would be due to investment in capital resources—either machinery such as a central computer system, or fixed manpower departments such as a larger and more specialized foreign department or a larger and more specialized trust department.

Although accountants and economists do not usually classify manpower as a fixed cost, the case history shows that for strategic planning purposes the departments are fixed resources in the same sense that a computer is.

Oddly enough, it was not the bankers themselves who stressed the value of managers' personal motives. It was the chairman of the Anti-Trust Committee of the United States Congress. He testified that the seven banks in question were themselves the result of 110 mergers over their history (these mergers had taken place for the same reasons: increased task efficiency and increased service to customers). On the other hand, the merger would have serious effects on middle managers. Here are the essential details of this argument.

The presidents of the independent banks would in effect change roles in a particular and vital way. At present, they are strategists and policymakers who must cope with all of the complexity of comprehensive alignment. In this role, they deal with the outside world, exercise initiative in making internal alignments, and otherwise learn and develop into persons of leadership. They are involved with and committed to relating banks to society. They have an interest in society "out there."

In the merged system, persons who are presently bank presidents would become middle managers (branch managers) of the Morgan New York State Corporation. It would be the headquarters general managers who would learn and develop both cognitive information (interest rates, business cycles, cultural responsibilities) and atti-

222

tudes (initiative, freedom, responsibility). Branch managers would in a sense be underdeveloped persons, with neither the knowledge nor the attitudes necessary to serve society. Though the bank may be more effective in the short run for its customers, in the long run society would lose the talents of the corporate staffs in seven independent banks. In short, Congressman Cellar used the needs of individual managers to oppose the capital alignment advocated by other parties. In the end, the Federal Reserve Board agreed. It acknowledged that capital alignments as described by bankers would benefit present customers. But it gave greater weight to the motivations of future middle managers in its final decision. The merger was denied.

THE HOSPITAL INDUSTRY   A final case showing how capital alignment clashes with the needs of managers comes from the hospital industry.[36] The case describes a current method that has been developed by the United States government for aligning capital across the nation in order to serve three task constituencies. The alignment is designed to (1) lower costs to patients who pay their own bills, (2) lower costs to insurance companies that supply resources to hospitals to treat patients, and (3) lower costs to taxpayers who supply resources to pay hospital bills under Medicare, Medicaid, and similar public programs.

The central capital alignment problem is this: hospital buildings cost a great deal of money. If hospital buildings are too numerous, with unnecessary numbers of beds, then their cost per patient is higher than necessary. Likewise, hospital equipment is costly. An x-ray machine known as a tomographic scanner costs $800,000. If all hospitals in a given area try to buy tomographic scanners, medical costs to task constituencies will be unnecessarily high, especially if each scanner is unused much of the time.

Originally, in the early 1940s, philanthropic organizations in cities tried to form what was in effect a cartel to keep capital equipment costs low. They banded hospitals together in loose alliances to try to decide which hospital in the city would buy a certain piece of equipment. But this arrangement failed for the same reasons many other voluntary arrangements fail: the self-interests of individual hospital managers outweighed the low-cost utility needs of task constituencies. "Self interest of participating hospitals took precedence whenever an opportunity for institutional aggrandizement presented itself. Not only were hospitals *themselves* given to self-serving activity but certain sponsoring groups, particularly prideful communities and religious, fraternal and labor organizations, very

223

often chose to go their own way."[37] These general managers often perceived that it was more *convenient*, "to have our own equipment." There is also evidence that modern equipment was a status symbol for doctors and managers.

In 1969 Mary Fletcher Hospital in Burlington, Vermont, purchased a $300,000 generator for radiation treatments. De Goesbriand Hospital, also in Burlington, soon bought the same machine even though the Mary Fletcher generator was idle half the time. Sometime later, Mary Fletcher spent another $300,000 for electronic heart monitoring devices. De Goesbriand followed by purchasing the same equipment, only to find, in the words of one physician, "that it is idle most of the time, just gathering dust." William Cowles, a civic leader in Burlington, predicted that if the hospitals did not merge with each other soon to stop such duplication, "Mary Fletcher would have run De Goesbriand right into the ground."[38] The hospitals did indeed merge, for reasons similar to those advanced in the Morgan New York State Corporation case above. But many hospitals throughout the nation continued to fail to formulate the most efficient capital alignment. Consequently, first the state governments and later the federal government began to engage in capital-alignment planning.

In 1964, New York passed a law requiring that a certificate of need be filed before any hospital could construct new buildings. Such a certificate mandated efficient capital alignment (TI.11) in the state. California and Connecticut followed in 1968 and 1969. In 1968 the American Hospital Association endorsed this type of alignment planning. By 1973, 23 states had passed legislation forcing such alignments. From 1974 to 1979 the federal government moved into the capital-alignment planning. Laws were passed requiring all hospitals in the United States to file certificates of need before they could construct new hospital buildings and buy hospital equipment. First a law was passed that required hospitals to file certificates for any expansion over $100,000. A later act extended this requirement from hospitals to ambulatory-care facilities, in-patient clinics, intermediate care facilities, and other institutions. In 1974 the secretary of HEW elaborated the organization structure (TI.12) necessary to do such planning at lower levels. States were required to set up regional health-planning districts, with each district planning the number of hospital beds required, the number of doctors and nurses needed, and the kind of equipment allocations that would result in least cost to resource-supplying constituencies. In 1977 still other regulations were published in the Federal Register. Here are some of the capital alignment guidelines now specified:

224

The number of hospital beds in any area should not exceed 4 per 1000 persons. Occupancy rates should not fall below 80 percent (i.e., 80 percent of beds must be in use or no new construction will be allowed).

There should be no new obstetrics departments established unless each hospital in the area is delivering at least 2000 babies per year (for areas over 100,000 population) or 500 babies per year (for areas less than 100,000 population).

Individual hospitals in the area must be performing at least 200 open-heart surgeries per year; otherwise no new open-heart surgery departments will be allowed.

No hospital can purchase a computerized axial tomographic scanner unless the existing machines in the area are being used for at least 4000 diagnostic procedures per year.

Strategists in HEW estimate that the regulation on number of hospital beds alone will save private patients, insurance companies, and taxpayers over $2 billion a year in maintenance costs for unused beds and $80,000 in construction costs for each bed.

In addition to the self-interests of local hospital managers cited previously, there is evidence that under this capital alignment program there will still be a clash of managers' needs and the needs of task constituencies. In Seattle, four major hospitals applied to install computerized axial tomographic scanners in 1979: Children's Orthopedic, Harborview, Swedish, and Providence Hospitals. Only two were approved. Interviews with doctors and middle managers from the two unsuccessful hospitals showed they would still weight highly the needs of managers in the local hospital.

> Our hospital really needed that equipment. It is good for neither the doctor nor the patient to have to send all of our patients to Harborview. Further, we are going to have a diffi-cult time attracting the best young doctors (to *our hospital*) if we do not have all of the most advanced medical equipment. Can you blame competent young doctors if they want to work on such equipment?

AIR FRANCE, BRITANNIA AIRWAYS   Air France is a *national industry*, similar to the Post Office or the Social Security Administration in the United States. These industries differ from the *federal industries* such as health care in the United States. Whereas in the latter strategic planning is done at the top level of government with states and cities doing the operating work, national industries are self-contained. Both the strategic planning (e.g., setting policies for the

225

airline) and the operating work (operating the airline) are done in the same organization.

For many years, Air France has had a capital alignment (TE.11) that weighted the needs of managers for prestige (CI.1) greater than the low cost utility needs of passengers and taxpayers (TE). In 1974 Air France's board of directors noted that the Caravelle, built in France, was 19 years old and behind the state-of-art technology for commercial airlines. Its passenger cabin seemed cramped and uncomfortable compared to the Boeing 737 and McDonald Douglas DC-9, which the board proposed as replacements. Its gasoline consumption was so inefficient that its cost of transporting passengers was considerably higher than that of other available aircraft. The finance minister of France, M. Fourcade, stressing the prestige of flying French-built aircraft, threatened to dismiss the board if members persisted in trying to purchase American airplanes. He said that government policymakers for the airline industry are committed to purchasing either French or European planes. By 1978, Gilbert Petrol, director general of Air France, concluded that Air France was in a worse position than its European rivals because it was forced to fly older and less economic aircraft. The supersonic Concorde is likewise a very high-prestige airplane. But its fuel consumption is among the most inefficient in the industry. Each Concorde flew only 3 hours and 16 minutes a day in 1976, with a passenger load of only 61 percent of capacity. As a result, Air France had to price the tickets on Concorde routes 20 percent higher than first-class tickets on other aircraft on the same routes. Petrol believes that in the end, the aircraft will be viable, but that it will have to be utilized 7½ hours a day and carry a load equal to 65 percent of capacity.

Britannia Airways is also a national industry. It had for many years operated under a policy that required it to buy aircraft from countries which favored British exports. This meant that at times strategists purchased not the most economical airplane for passengers or taxpayers but the most political airplane for foreign-trade strategists. In 1978 Britannia was freed from such restrictions. It immediately proceeded to rationalize its capital alignment. Company strategists had formulated its product/market as "carrying charter passengers from 22 airfields in the U.K. to vacation destinations in Spain, Italy, Greece and the Canary Islands." They explained the capital alignment this way:

> The most economic airplane for our average route, 1080 miles, is the Boeing 757, modified to seat 230 passengers rather than the 175 passenger equipment normally used on longer haul

routes. The vacationing passenger had rather be seated 230 to a plane, and pay less money (thus adding more funds for vacation spending) than to have the plane constructed to seat 175 passengers.[39]

THE SECONDARY SCHOOL SYSTEM   As this book goes to press, there are indications that the same type of conflicts faced in the Air France case are also faced in the secondary education systems of the United States and some European countries. The difference lies simply in the fact that in one case the capital involved is a fleet of expensive airplanes whereas in the other the capital involved is a network of expensive school buildings, libraries and other educational equipment. Strategists at the highest levels in school systems are caught between two opposing forces. On one hand government revenues are scarce resources. On the other hand taxpayers demand that strategists allocate capital efficiently, without undue waste. Strategists react by closing small, less capital intensive schools (those which cannot take advantage of economies of "scale" or "mass production") and sending students to the larger, more efficient schools where fixed cost can be spread over large student bodies.

England is a case in point. There, strategic alignment policies are formulated by the Secretary of State for Education and Science, aided by such bodies as the Plowden Committee. Over the ten years from 1968–1978, 2,000 schools in England and Wales were closed. The reason: the Plowden Committee had set a minimum size in order that a school would be able to afford the library, specialized teachers, and diversified courses necessary to fit children for life in modern society. Since the primary school population of England and Wales is expected to fall from 4.6 million to 3.4 million from 1978 to 1986, more closures are planned. However, there are still 2017 schools that operate with fewer than 50 pupils. There are 2827 with 50 to 100 pupils. In September 1978, the heads of these schools (i.e., the middle managers in the total school system) met at St. Andrew's and St. John's School in Waterloo (itself threatened with closure) to protest further closures. Mr. Rhodes Boyson spoke for them: "The small village school, even the school with only one classroom and one teacher, can and in most cases does offer an excellent grounding for children drawn from the same locality."[40]

CITY AND COUNTY GOVERNMENTS[41]   Throughout the 1970s, there has been a significant movement in cities and counties to align capital so that duplicating and overlapping services might be eliminated, thus lowering the cost of government. These moves by strategists in local

227

government have ranged from small incremental changes, through full merger of city and county governments, to the partitioning of government into what has become known as the "two-tier" government.

Smaller incremental changes include proposals in Seattle, Washington, to merge city and county computer operations so that only one expensive computer need be purchased and maintained; the proposed merger in Fresno, California, of 54 fire and water districts into a more efficient organization that could afford the latest state-of-art technology; and the merger of the health departments of Salt Lake City and Salt Lake County, Utah, into one unit. Policymakers in three small towns in Massachusetts (Goshen, Williamsburg, and Chesterfield) found that they could not afford to operate three ambulance services. "It now costs $1,600 for a Motorola radio for each ambulance. No wonder we are running a deficit."

Mergers of whole cities and counties have run into severe criticism from middle managers who prefer to keep things the way they are. Indianapolis, Indiana, and Miami-Dade County, Florida, have been leaders in moving toward such mergers. After an enormous amount of work by a Commission for City-County Merger, the merger of the city of Portland, Oregon with Multnomah County was defeated in 1974. Strategists in the village of Catskill, New York, and the Catskill Township found that a merger would eliminate overlapping services, and cut tax bills on a $10,000 house in the village from $264 to $131, yet maintain the existing level of services. The merger was opposed by many who lived in the township. By adding such services as police protection (which township citizens had never had), the merger would increase their tax bills $27 per year.

The two-tier system of government, under which cities jointly plan which unit will spend money for large-capital facilities, has been developed to the greatest degree in Toronto, Ontario. There, city agencies deal with police, fire, and other functions. Regional government deals with public transportation, growth planning, and land-use planning. Such planning has been considered sporadically by the Puget Sound Council of Governments over a period of ten years. As reported by the *Seattle Times*, "Such proposals often are opposed by local officials who fear that local decision-making, and their own power, would be diminished by the presence of a regional agency."

Conflicts over Organization Design

It has been necessary in previous sections to describe case histories in some detail in order to demonstrate the importance of diagnosis and to show that diagnosis of each situation produces a different set of managerial demands. Space does not permit such detail in this and the next sections, which deal with organization-design conflicts (TI.12) and work-process conflicts (TI.21). The succinct and somewhat mechanistic way of abstracting the cases should not cloud the fact that each case history requires diagnosis to find out which demands of managers are activated in each company or agency.

WESTERN OFFICE EQUIPMENT COMPANY   Western Office Equipment Company, with headquarters in Salt Lake City, Utah, manufactures and sells desks, steel shelving, bookcases, and file cabinets.[42] Its product/market alignment (TE) specifies customer constituencies as (1) those office managers who want a medium-priced line of equipment as contrasted with either luxury or cheap-grade equipment, and (2) a geographic market composed of four cities: Salt Lake City, Vancouver, San Francisco, and Los Angeles. The organization design (TI.12) necessary to elaborate the product strategy consists of four branch headquarters. Each branch manager plans selling activities and oversees the work of salespersons.

The policy problem originates when company strategists determine the size of the sales force to be used in each city. The president appoints a new manager of planning at headquarters, who uses a quantitative technique known as marginal analysis to determine the exact number of sales persons in each location that will yield the greatest amount of revenues with the lowest commitment of scarce resources. This has implications for pricing the product to the consumer (TE). By lowering costs of the sales force, the firm can lower prices in competition with other firms. The resulting organization structure requires that changes be made as shown in Exhibit 8-2.

The case shows rather sophisticated economic techniques used to arrive at these numbers. For the total company, sales will be

EXHIBIT 8-2

City	Present number of salesmen	Proposed number of salesmen
Salt Lake City	4	2
Los Angeles	1	5
San Francisco	6	4
Vancouver	4	3
Total company	15	14

increased from $3.8 million to $4.1 million by reducing the sales force from 15 to 14 persons. In other words, more customers can be supplied with more furniture by one less salesman. The case also shows the human dynamics between headquarters and branch managers. From Exhibit 8-2 we can see that different managers are affected rather drastically. The manager in San Francisco is upset when he finds that the most efficient organization structure would mean decreasing his sales force from 6 to 4. Worse still, the most efficient allocation would deliberately lower total sales volume in San Francisco from $1.5 million to $1.3 million in order to increase total company sales volume to $4.1 million.

Here is a classic case of the demand for suboptimization. The San Francisco manager cannot understand the reasoning behind the move. He is emotionally opposed to it, especially since he believes he has a new training program for salespersons that would benefit the company.

A closer look at the proposed changes also shows why, in meetings between the president and branch managers, only one manager, the one in Los Angeles, was enthusiastic about supporting the strategy.

METROCENTER, OHIO POLICE DEPARTMENT   The mayor and police commissioner of Metrocenter, Ohio, become concerned because traffic accident rates in the city are higher than in other cities.[43] An opinion poll of the task constituency (TE, citizens demanding high-quality police work to ensure safety) showed that 72 percent of citizens believe that the rates of injury and death due to automobile accidents are higher than in neighboring cities. In order to comply with this demand for service/market alignment, the chief of police establishes a Department of Police Administration and brings in Captain Mullaney (a specialist in operating planning) to analyze statistics by census areas in the city. Mullaney pinpoints problem areas and makes recommendations for redistributing policemen among precincts. The branch organization structure consists of seven precincts, each headed by a captain. Each precinct is in turn divided into patrol squads headed by a sergeant.

The case describes in detail the actions and statements by strategists at the top (the mayor, Commissioner Allen, Captain Mullaney) and middle managers (precinct captains, particularly the most outspoken manager, Captain Terenzio).

The demand for suboptimization is clear at the precinct level. As the situation wears on, Captain Mullaney begins to feel a great deal of social anxiety caused by constant confrontation of fellow officers. Finally, Commissioner Allen is affected by the uncertainty of the whole situation. He postpones any new policy decision because there are so many conflicting demands in the situation.

NATIONAL BANK OF SAN FRANCISCO National Bank of San Francisco is, like the office equipment company and the police department, organized according to (1) general managers who plan strategy, (2) specialist headquarters managers who plan strategy in areas such as loan policy or depositor policies, and (3) branch managers who elaborate the strategy in greater detail in their geographic areas.[44] Conflict occurs when the president, feeling competitive pressures from other banks that provide low-cost services to depositors, seeks to lower the cost of manpower and the cost of equipment in branches. He appoints a planning committee composed of loan officers from branches and the headquarters specialist on personnel and equipment.

The behavior of committee members is reported in detail. They avoid addressing the question of expensive furnishings in the branch because they do not want to threaten the status of their bosses, the branch managers. They agree, however, that changes must be made in job descriptions of branch personnel in order to enable the bank to achieve the same level of service (the output of loans and services to depositors) with less manpower.

When the committee reports to a meeting of all managers (the president and branch managers) behavior very similar to that of the sales managers and police precinct captains occurs. Accustomed in the past to making decisions on personnel and equipment at the branch level, these managers neither understand nor emotionally accept the proposed changes.

In the end, the president and vice-president for planning both show signs of indecision. Confronted by a great amount of logical reasoning by the committee, and an equally great amount of logical reasoning by branch managers, they postpone making a decision and call for "further study."

Conflicts over Operating Processes

A number of case histories show that decisions about the actual operating processes to be used at the work level (TI.21) bring forth the same kinds of conflict described in connection with product, capital, and organization-design policies. In each case, the dispute *originates* as a question about work operations but has ramifications for the self-interests of external resource suppliers (customers, clients, stockholders) or external cultural constituencies.

In Seaboard Chemical Company, Cleveland headquarters proposes a change in the physical operations for storing expensive valves and heat exchangers in the Houston plant, which produces sulphuric acid. Corrosion engineers from Cleveland have a different frame of reference than the Houston plant manager. Engineers and middle managers both seek to invoke solutions that have been used in the past. Further, each seeks to optimize one part of the company rather than the company as a whole.[45]

In British Commercial Investments, the clash is not between specialists from headquarters and middle managers down the line. It is between the president of the London-based conglomerate and the general manager of Harrogate Asphalt Products Company, a subsidiary. One can easily see the cognitive security needs of the General Manager as he is confronted with new and unknown changes, changes that his own past experience and learning do not equip him to face. As the problem escalates, one can also see that both the president and the general manager seek to protect their prerogatives of power.[46]

In Mercury Stores, Inc., a large supermarket chain, behavior of managers is virtually identical with that observed in cases already cited. There is one interesting difference in the policy situation, however. Headquarters strategists in the area of public relations are interested in changing certain operations at the store level for the benefit of outside cultural constituencies rather than outside task constituencies. Proposals are made to increase the civic activities of personnel within the stores as contrasted with their product/market activities. In the end, the conflict process is similar. Branch managers do not cognitively understand the new internal cultural alignment being proposed. They also view it as a threat to their autonomy.[47]

Notes

1. Talcott Parsons, *Structure and Process in Modern Society*, the Free Press, 1960.

2. Daniel Katz and Robert Kahn, *The Social Psychology of Organizations*, John Wiley, 1978, Chapter 16.

3. Henry Mintzberg, *The Nature of Managerial Work*, Harper & Row, 1973, pp. 109–13.

4. Richard F. Vancil and Peter Lorange, "Strategic Planning in Diversified Companies," *Harvard Business Review* 53:1 (January 1975): 81–90; Reprinted in Lorange and Vancil, *Strategic Planning Systems*, Prentice-Hall, 1977.

5. The Free Press, 1976, pp. 38–41, Chapter V.

6. Prentice-Hall, 1977, Chapter 2.

7. Richard M. Cyert and James March, *A Behavioral Theory of the Firm*, Prentice-Hall, 1963, Chapter 6.

8. Graham Allison, *Essence of Decision*, Little, Brown, 1971, pp. 102–31.

9. *Decision Making*, Macmillan, 1977, pp. 46–49, Chapter 5.

10. For an abstract, see Charles E. Summer et al., *The Managerial Mind*, Richard D. Irwin, 1977, pp. 226–27.

11. "A Theory of Group Development," *Human Relations* 9:4 (1965): 415–57.

12. For a summary of the Merton, Gouldner and Selznick studies, see James G. March and Herbert Simon, *Organizations*, John Wiley, 1959, pp. 36–47.

13. Tom Burns and G. M. Stalker, *The Management of Innovation*, 2nd ed., Tavistock, 1961, preface.

14. Alvin Toffler, *Future Shock*, Random House, 1970, Chapter 7.

15. *Decision Making*, Macmillan, 1977, pp. 46–49, Chapter 5.

16. Irving Janis and D. Krause, *Group Dynamics: Groupthink*, McGraw-Hill, 1973.

17. Francis E. Rourke, *Bureaucratic Power and National Politics*, Little, Brown, 1972, pp. 260–61.

18. Victor Thompson, *Modern Organization*, Knopf, 1961.

19. Richard M. Cyert and James March, *A Behavioral Theory of the Firm*, Prentice-Hall, 1963.

20. Oliver E. Williamson, "Managerial Discretion and Business Behavior," *American Economic Review* 53 (1963): 1032–57.

21. Anthony Downes, *Inside Bureaucracy*, Little, Brown, 1967, pp. 84–85, Chapter 9.

22. Robert Blake and Jane Mouton, *The Managerial Grid*, Gulf Publishing Company, 1964.

23. Richard M. Cyert and James March, *A Behavioral Theory of the Firm*, Prentice-Hall, 1963, 3: p. 30.

24. Shoe Corporation of Illinois (Appendix).

25. Paul Lawrence and Jay Lorsch, *Organization and Environment*, Richard D. Irwin, 1967, Chapter 2.

26. Alfred D. Chandler, *Strategy and Structure*, MIT Press, 1962, pp. 14–17.

27. *The Watch Industries in Switzerland, Japan and the United States* (Appendix).

28. General Mills, Inc. (Appendix).

29. James B. Quinn, *Strategic Change: Logical Incrementalism*, Little, Brown, 1980.

30. Family Service Association of America (case file), Appendix.

31. Carl Rogers, *Client-Centered Therapy*, Houghton Mifflin, 1951.

32. California Federal Savings and Loan Association, Appendix.

33. H. Igor Ansoff, *Corporate Strategy*, McGraw-Hill, 1965, pp. 75–103.

34. The Pharmaceutical Industry in Iceland, Appendix.

35. Lincoln Rochester Trust Company, Appendix.

36. Capital Alignment in the Hospital Industry (case file), Appendix.

37. Clark Havighurst, "Regulation of Health Facilities by Certificate of Need," *Virginia Law Review* 59:7 (October 1973): 1143–1232.

38. Capital Alignment in the Hospital Industry (case file), Appendix.

39. *New York Times*, September 18, 1977, Sec. 3, p. 1.

40. Capital Alignment in Government Industries (case file), Appendix.

41. Capital Alignment in Government Industries (case file), Appendix.

42. Western Office Equipment Company, Appendix.

43. Metrocenter, Ohio Police Department, Appendix.

44. National Bank of San Francisco, Appendix.

45. Seaboard Chemical Company, Appendix

46. British Commercial Investments, Appendix.

47. Mercury Stores, inc., Appendix.

CHAPTER 9

Internal Challenges: Behavior of Employees

JUST AS MANAGERS have self-interests about various task alignments so do employees at the work (operating) level. Employees have means to enforce their needs and demands because of the exchange relationship that exists between employees and the organization.

First explained by Barnard[1] and later by March and Simon,[2] the exchange mechanism works like this: Employees first make a decision whether to join an organization and remain in it. They do this by judging the total inducements the organization gives them to satisfy their needs and the total costs they incur by performing in the organization. This is the decision to participate. Once employed, they make a second decision, the *decision to produce*. Employees do not have to be productive just because they join the organization and remain physically present on the job. There are various ways, both formal and informal, employees can object to, avoid, fight about, or even sabotage the product alignment (TE, products and services to be produced), the capital alignment (TI.11, the efficient use of machinery), the work-process alignment (TI.21, production processes, procedures), or the work-design alignment (TI.22). Furthermore, employees need not be *proactive* in opposing alignments. They may simply be apathetic and unimaginative in helping to elaborate the best way to produce products or to do their jobs.

This is, of course, another way of explaining resource dependency, discussed in Chapter 1. The corporation or government agency depends on employees to execute task alignments. Whether or not they execute such alignments depends on how they calculate the benefits they get (the inducements provided) and the costs they incur (the contributions of time and effort that task alignments require).

234

In order to understand employee demands, we shall classify them into two main groups: the demand for remuneration and job security (CI.21) and the demand for intangible rewards and quality of work life (CI.22). We shall first look at these needs as they have been explained in paradigms of various social sciences. This will provide more understanding of what the demands are and how they arise from human nature and human organizations. It will also provide understanding of the actions that result from such demands.

But in a field which studies policy behavior, one needs more than theoretical models from social sciences. The remainder of the chapter will contain case histories that show how people act out these demands in a wide variety of organizations in business and government.

Demand for Remuneration and Job Security (CI.21)

The history of labor relations in industrial societies shows that workers are deeply and profoundly dependent on corporations and agencies for their economic standard of living and for security of jobs to earn incomes. Anyone who has read the history of the labor movement must be impressed by the degree to which these dependencies have shaped the very lives of workers. Karl Marx put this dependency, and the resulting conflict between task alignment and cultural efficiency, in boldest terms. Task alignments were indeed producing a stream of income to corporations. In fact, corporations were so successful in supplying utility to their customers (TE), by means of efficient machines (TI.11), specialized mass-production processes (TI.21), and specialized low-wage jobs on the production line (TI.22), that there was a gap between revenues from production and costs of production.

Conflict Between Worker and Organization: Private Sector

Conflict over this gap was the original explanation of the conflict between task alignment and internal cultural alignment, more specifically, between task performance (TE/TI) and cultural efficiency (CI).

According to Adam Smith's capitalistic explanation, this gap was called profit. It belonged to owners because they supplied resources in the form of money savings to buy machinery and tools (TI.11). Smith also recognized that owners performed the function of comprehensive task alignment: they had a vision of a network of external

235

constituencies, products, and internal resources, and of how these fit together. They also performed the incremental learning process by slow policy formulation over time, as explained in Chapter 4. Smith's pin factory, which he used to illustrate the tremendous task performance potential of industrial England, stressed the learning curve as a means to gradually improve capital machinery (TI.11) and processes (TI.21). Like Chandler explaining the rise and success of DuPont 150 years later, or the Boston Consulting Group explaining the success of corporations today, Smith saw that great industries are not built overnight. They are built by interaction between entrepreneurial vision and incremental policymaking as the industry *learns* how to execute the vast and intricate network of operations we have called comprehensive alignment.

But earlier capitalist writers concentrated on private property of the strategists, and their supplying of monetary capital to purchase the physical capital. It was left to later economists, Marshall[3] and Schumpeter,[4] to stress the second reason why profit belonged to the comprehensive strategists. It was not only the money they supplied but their strategic vision and incremental policymaking. Marshall and Schumpeter would probably agree that the descriptions in Chapters 3–5 are accurate in showing the tremendous importance of strategy formulation and policy formulation to the corporation, and to society's standard of living.

Marx reasoned from a different paradigm. The gap between revenues and costs of production belong not to external funds suppliers or strategic leaders, but to internal workers. It is they, who, in the last analysis, create the value or utility in the product or service.

Some of the case histories to be cited show that this conflict still persists in modern society, at least when measured by the *behavior* of workers. Collective bargaining at the plant, company, or industry level is frequently aimed at how much of the "total pie" workers shall get and how secure their jobs shall be. In the United States, unit bargaining within a specific plant, company, or industry has been the pattern pursued by major unions to this day. In Europe, the trend has been more toward *political unionism* as contrasted with *company bargaining* unionism. But the behavioral aims are in many respects similar. Instead of bargaining between a specific union and a specific company over pay and security, workers join large, nationwide unions of "workers in general." They hope to elect governments that will then pass laws ensuring higher pay and better security. In the United States, pressure on management to comply with demands is direct between the two parties. In Europe, it is often brought about through a third party, the government.

Conflict Between Worker and Consumer:
Private Sector

Neither the capitalists nor the Marxists worried very much about the responsibility for low cost utility to the consumer or customer. The former believed that the unseen hand of competition would force profits if not to zero then to a very modest amount. Marx, interested in the worker, wanted whatever gap or surplus remained to be reserved for the worker.

It remained for someone later in the Industrial Revolution to become concerned about the consumer. This someone turned out to be the trust-busting members of Congress who created the Federal Trade Commission. They saw that the comprehensive task alignment that builds great corporations can also be used to monopolize vital goods to the consumer, resulting in higher prices and less utility.

Even in modern books on industrial organization, one of which is authored by a prominent official in the Federal Trade Commission,[5] it is the excellence of the comprehensive task alignment, its internal efficiency and its external effectiveness with the consumer, that makes it possible for a very efficient company later to become a monopoly that can take advantage of the consumer.

Conflict Between Employees and Other Constituencies:
Government Sector

We turn now to the conflict between internal workers in government organizations and the consumer (those who depend on low-cost, high-quality service outputs) and the outside resource suppliers (the taxpayer or higher government agencies that supply budgets to lower-level agencies). The bureaucracy theories discussed earlier have been supported by considerable empirical research showing how often internal workers in a government agency might have a conflict of interests with these other constituencies. And the social psychology theories dealing with quality of work life (to be discussed later) are supported by research showing that the most efficient work processes and work roles (TI.21, TI.22) for the consumer or taxpayer are often not the alignments that give most intangible rewards to internal employees.

But we have no models from economics such as Smith, Marx, and antitrust philosophy to highlight the fact that internal demands for remuneration and job security by employees conflict with the demands of external clients and taxpayers. The nearest model we have is the one put forth by the Founding Fathers of the nation. Both the

237

Declaration of Independence and the Constitution contain articles that leave little doubt that it was the levying of taxes by the British government, and the subsequent spending of taxes in ways that did not benefit taxpayers, that helped cause the revolt of the colonists. The brief discussion in Chapter 3 of the taxpayer revolt in both states and national societies, as well as the case histories to be presented later, show that conflict of this type existed in 1976 very much as it did in 1776. If workers in private companies have a demand for remuneration and job security there is no magic reason why workers in government agencies are different. If this demand conflicts with interests of consumers and stockholders in private industry, there is no magic reason why it does not conflict with the interests of government agency clients and taxpayers.

Demand for Intangible Satisfaction and Quality of Work Life (CI.22)

The demand for remuneration and job security is in advanced industrial societies only one of the two principal demands made on policymakers by internal employees. The other is the demand for intangible satisfaction and a high quality of work life (CI.22). In this section we will look at the historical development of this demand and some of the paradigms from behavioral sciences that explain what it is and how it operates. Finally, we will look at a principle of psychology that is well known to social scientists but is seldom described from the policymaker's viewpoint: the principle of individual differences.

Historical Development: Evolution from Physical Needs to Intangible Needs

Contrary to popular belief, the capitalistic economists of the eighteenth and nineteenth centuries were well aware of the human suffering, both physical and mental, that could be caused by industrial production processes (TI.21) and job designs (TI.22) that were beneficial to external constituencies. In other words, they saw the conflicts of interest among society (which benefited by a greater gross national product), consumers (who benefited by highly efficient coal mining processes), stockholders (who likewise benefited by such processes), and workers who suffered physical deprivations (by working in the coal mines or the industrial factories). Both Adam Smith and Alfred Marshall saw these conflicts as clearly as Marx. They simply put higher weight on needs of external constituencies.

In the early labor union movement in the United States and

238

Europe, labor leaders likewise saw the conflict between efficient production for society and the quality of work life for employees. Yet with some exceptions, such as coal mining, chimney sweeping and industries using child labor, neither economists nor labor leaders focused their time and energies on the mental, psychological needs of workers. Instead, they focused on policies that would improve the physical needs of workers: wages, hours of work, vacations, and, later, such things as lighting and safety conditions in factories.

This focus was caused by development of the whole of culture. We now know that when physical needs such as food and shelter are not satisfied, or when security and safety needs are not satisfied, human beings will spend most of their waking hours attempting to satisfy those needs. It is only after such needs are satisfied that people turn to such higher-order needs as love and friendship, self-confidence and respect, and self-actualization.

It is not surprising, therefore, that attention to mental satisfaction occurs in leading Western societies after they have already developed a system of capital (TI.11), organization (TI.12), process (TI.21), and work roles (TI.22) sufficient to put most people into a state of relative affluence, or at least above the poverty standard.

This is exactly what has happened, most notably in the United States, Sweden, and Britain. As development occurred slightly later in other countries (e.g., in Germany there was the problem of recovery after World War II), it has happened in exactly the same way in all Western industrial countries. In Russia, the present alignment system must be viewed as a massive experiment. As that country becomes more and more affluent after the long recovery from World War II, social science would predict that focus on intangible satisfactions will occur inevitably, in one way or another.

In the United States, there was some early attention to mental satisfactions by psychologists (such as Mary Parker Follett at the turn of the century),[6] and small-group sociologists (such as the Western Electric researchers in the 1930s).[7] But the great leap in understanding and publicizing intangible quality of work life began in the 1950s, just as United States society in fact was able to recover from World War II and begin a spectacular increase in applying high technology to the production of the highest standard of living ever experienced.

The Psychological Contract:
An Exchange Relationship

To highlight the amount of effort employees give to the task alignment (i.e., to contribute to the interests of other consti-

EXHIBIT 9-1

Exchange Relationship Between Employees and the Organization

Nature of task alignment (TI.21 and TI.22)	Response of Employees
1. Coercive. Alignment is worked out for constituencies other than workers and forced on employees.	1. Alienation. Employees like neither the mission (TE) nor the internal alignment (TI), and will perform aggressive acts against these if they can.
2. Task alignment worked out for benefit of external constituencies. Organization pays monetary rewards for its execution.	2. Calculative. "I will do just a fair day's work for a fair day's pay. No more, no less."
3. Task alignment worked out so it appeals to needs of employees. They like the mission (TE) and the internal work processes (TI).	3. Active involvement. Employees not only will help elaborate the details of the alignment but will feel that it is a "good" one.

tuencies), a psychologist,[8] drawing on the work of a sociologist,[9] presents the exchange relationship shown in Exhibit 9-1. In the left column, we see the task processes and job designs as they are viewed by the employee. In the right column, we see the kind of motivation and behavior the employee will give in return.

Another picture of the exchange relationship between employees and the organization has been presented by Barnard and Simon.[10] According to this version, employees have a "zone of acceptance" or a "zone of indifference" within which they will simply accept and carry out their part of the alignment. They develop this over months or years of living in the organization. If the alignment has in effect "been good to the employee," giving sufficient monetary and intangible rewards, the zone of acceptance will broaden. Employees will carry out the alignments as they are fashioned by policymakers. On the other hand, the costs (in terms of effort and work) of the alignment may be high enough, or the benefits (in terms of total satisfaction the alignment work brings) low enough, that the employee's zone of acceptance is narrowed. This explanation yields the same prediction as that of Schein: the greater the rewards a task alignment might bring the greater the chance that the employee will perform the alignment. The less the alignment satisfies human needs, the lower the probability that employees will contribute their part of the alignment.

240

Content of Employee Demands

The literature in organizational behavior generated from 1950 to 1970 is enormous. We can do no more than give the barest outline of demands originating from persons who work at the operating level.

One of the early contributions was made by the Institute of Social Research at the University of Michigan. The concepts stressed were employee needs for freedom and autonomy which, if satisfied by the supervisor's participative leadership style, would result in higher worker morale. Research was carried out in such diverse settings as a large insurance company and a railroad labor gang.[11]

This was followed by studies focusing on leadership style, originally conducted at Ohio State University,[12] and now conducted at the University of Washington. The Michigan tradition was followed in that people-oriented leaders produced higher satisfaction. One interesting development was the addition of the contingency theory of leadership by Fiedler.[13] According to this research, satisfaction of employees depends on what kinds of task-process alignment (TI.21) and work roles (TI.22) are required to produce the final product (TE). If the task alignment has been worked out clearly, and if it must be, say, a mass-production alignment, employees not only do not resent mechanistic procedures, but they will tend to carry them out. On the other hand, if the task alignment is an unknown or new process, which policymakers themselves cannot formulate clearly, then employees will not accept and carry out policymakers' orders.

One school of psychology that has had profound effects on policymaking in business and government is that based on clinical psychology. This school also views human emotional needs as the primary determinant of whether or not workers will support the task alignment, and whether or not they will work together to carry out that alignment. Founded upon the work of Abraham Maslow,[14] this was the school of thought used by Argyris to develop a theory of conflict between workers and the interests of other constituencies.[15] It was used by McGregor to develop a theory of conflict between policymakers who use "Theory X leadership" and workers who would prefer "Theory Y leadership."[16] It was used by Herzberg to develop the theory that employees will join the task alignment and stay on the job to fulfill their physical and security needs, but that they will not *actively* support the task alignment unless it offers them something more, that is, higher-order psychological satisfactions, particularly satisfaction from making or adjusting the task alignment by their own free thought and will.[17]

Essentially, Maslow predicted that all human beings have five needs: physical, security, social (love and friendship), self (respect and esteem), and, finally, self-actualization (a state of doing what one is most fully capable of, helped along by both the right amount of support and the right amount of freedom to act). In the long process of personality growth from infancy to maturity, each person strives to climb the ladder from low-order needs to the highest order, each stage bringing forth new forces that control behavior, each prior stage being forgotten and put aside as its need is satisfied.

Another clinical school of thought that has influenced business and government extensively is the organization development (OD) school. Arising principally in the 1960s, this paradigm views human beings in organization primarily as individuals submerged in face-to-face groups and having above all a social need to trust other persons in the organization. This trust is in turn needed so that employees can jointly work out task alignments to satisfy their needs whatever they may be. It may be that employees in the group need security and protection built into task alignments. Or they may need alignments that satisfy their need for freedom and self-respect. By stressing consensual decision making, which hinges on relationships of mutual respect and trust, the OD school, therefore, stresses team building as the primary way policymakers get workers to develop and accept the task alignment.

Another theory of importance that arose in the 1960s was one stressing the need of individuals to achieve. This theory, developed by McClelland,[18] holds that all individuals have within them the capacity to achieve tasks in their external environments but that some have received the kind of help necessary to act out this need, whereas others have not. Those who can act out the need are likely to support task alignments that provide them with three things: someone (e.g., a policymaker) must *expect* the worker to accomplish the task; someone must, during task performance, give broad and helpful guidance (as contrasted with detailed instructions); and someone must give feedback on how well the person is doing. The implication is that task-alignment processes that provide these things will be supported by workers. Those which do not will not.

The concept of feedback is also used by the behavioral school of thought to predict whether or not employees will carry out task alignments. This school neither assumes that man is emotional (as the conative school assumes) nor that man is rational (as the cognitive school assumes). Man is simply conditioned by the rewards and punishments that the task alignment metes out day in and day out. Conditioning is thus a matter of habit. Since employees tend to repeat actions that give them satisfaction (thus learning a habit) and drop actions that give them negative results, this school of thought predicts that workers will support only those task alignments which are positively reinforcing.[19]

A final paradigm of worker motivation has been put forth by cognitive psychologists. These psychologists tend to arrive at their theories through experimental research as contrasted with clinical research. This research suggests that man's behavior is not primarily caused by emotions but by thought, intellect, or reason. The expectancy school recognizes that the *end value* people seek may be a need such as security or love, but that the important determinant of behavior is the *thought process* people use to reason through alternative actions. According to this research, workers have many alternative actions they can carry out in their personal lives and during their work hours. They look at those alternatives and predict which action will probably give them the most satisfaction. One cannot think clearly (estimate probabilities of payoffs) unless there is high probability that if they choose a certain alternative then they will get a certain reward. Therefore, the implication for policymakers is to establish clear alignments, which tell people what they can expect. Further, policymakers must ensure that alignments are relatively *stable* over time. Nothing impedes the ability to think and reason so much as inconsistency, an alignment that is so unclear or so changing that it leaves the person undecided as to what to do. Stated in terms of expectancy theory, such a person simply will not be "aroused to exert effort."

A similar cognitive view of man is used in the goal-setting school. Most prominently put forth by Locke,[20] this view is that employees respond more favorably to task alignments when (1) specific goals are enunciated rather than generalized and (2) higher goals rather than lower goals are set (if the goal is accepted and attainable). Such things as freedom to participate, reward reinforcements, praise, and feedback of results have no effect on employee motivation unless it affects their goals.

The purposes of presenting this brief overview of employee motivation are to show the seriousness of the demand for cultural efficiency in comprehensive alignment decisions and to show that demands by internal employees, like demands by external cultural constituencies, are very complex. They vary greatly depending on the particular individual, the particular organization, and the particular employee group.

Principle of Individual Differences

One principle of human behavior universally known and accepted among psychologists is of particular importance to strategists and policymakers. It is the principle of individual differences. Simply stated, its message is that a human being is a very rich and complex phenomenon—in reality, infinitely variable. No two persons are alike in their motivations. They certainly are not alike in the behaviors caused by deeper motivations.

In academic psychology we have what seems to be a paradox here. On the one hand, psychologists know and accept this principle. Yet on the other hand they violate the principle by attributing to all people in general certain motivations and behaviors. Simply formulating a principle of human motivation they imply that all human beings are alike.

In this respect, they are obeying the true spirit of the natural sciences, most highly developed in physics and astronomy. Great scientists know that science itself would be destroyed were it not for an intuitive belief on the part of scientists that there is a natural order of things. "Order" means general recurrence of the same phenomena without divergent phenomena and without individual differences. Yet in the words of Whitehead, "Nothing ever really recurs in exact detail. No two days are alike, no two winters. . . . Mankind expects broad recurrences, but accepts (divergent) details as emanating from the inscrutable womb of things beyond the ken of rationality."[21] In Sullivan's words,

> Kepler's deepest conviction was that nature is essentially mathematical. All his scientific life was devoted to an endeavor to discover nature's hidden mathematical harmonies. Galileo, also, had no doubt that mathematics is the one true key to natural phenomena. It was this persuasion that gave these men their criterion for selection amongst the total elements of their experience.[22]

Finally, in Einstein's words: "I believe with Schopenhauer that one of the strongest motives that lead men to art and science is escape from everyday life with its painful crudity and hopeless dreariness, from the fetters of one's own ever shifting desires."[23]

This characteristic of science, ignoring the richness and divergence of real phenomena while instinctively looking only for generalities does not mean that social science principles of human behavior are worthless to policymakers. These principles help one to look for causes and effects in the behavior of employees. It does mean, however, that policymakers have to deal with the real world of different people in any given situation. The policymaker cannot simply assume that this motivation or that behavior is present in all companies or government agencies.

Early political philosophers recognized this because they were most interested in government of the population. They were constantly bothered by the question, "Why would free human beings subject themeselves to, and actually form out of their own free will, governments?" John Locke gives us the answer. It is that human beings have different interests and arrive at different decisions. A human being needs rules because he or she knows that others will not arrive at the same decisions.

> There wants an established, settled, known law . . . for though the law of nature be plain and intelligible to all rational creatures, yet men, being biased by their interest, are not apt to allow of it as a law binding to them in particular cases. . . . Passion and revenge is very apt to carry one too far, with negligence and unconcernedness for the other person's interests.

Here, Locke is simply stating in political language, the principle of individual differences.

External Alignment Versus Self-Interest of Employees

Throughout this chapter we will review case histories[24] in which the demands of employees conflict with the demands of external task constituencies and external cultural constituencies. This is another way of saying that the responsibility for cultural efficiency (CI) often conflicts with the responsibilities for task effectiveness (TE) and the responsibility for cultural effectiveness (CE).

Such conflicts do not occur simply as abstract political or ideological disputes. They occur in the context of real task alignments. They involve disputes over the best product/market alignment, the best alignment from the viewpoint of outside resource suppliers, the best capital alignment or the best work process and job design alignment. Each of these will be examined separately.

Conflict among Consumers, Resource Suppliers, and Employees

Chapter 3 showed how strategists and policymakers align products and services to satisfy demands of consumers and clients and of

245

external resource suppliers. But the ideal alignment for these constituencies often turns out to conflict with demands of employees.

In October 1977, the American Telephone and Telegraph Company was faced with such conflicting demands. On the one hand, the company was under pressure from customers (TE) to keep the cost of telephone calls low. It was also under pressure from the United States government to keep both the price of telephone calls and the wages of labor low, in order to keep from contributing to inflation in society (CE). Negotiations with the Communications Workers of America, representing 700,000 telephone company employees across the country, revealed that workers and their leaders had their own needs and demands (CI.21). With the United States Council on Wages and Prices monitoring the negotiations, the union made its first wage demand. This appeared to be unacceptable to the company, which would have had to raise consumer prices to meet the demand, and to the government, which would have had to witness higher inflation in society. In the end, the agreement increased wages by 8.3 percent the first year and 7.7 percent each of the two following years. Counting fringe benefits, it increased compensation by 31 percent over the three-year period. By government estimate, this would in turn cause a 6 percent increase in the cost of a telephone call, to be paid by the American public.

Though this conflict was resolved in favor of internal employees, others can work in favor of the consumer, the resource supplier, or both. In early 1971, the Hamilton Watch Company was facing a crisis in its comprehensive alignment. Imported watches from Japan, and a domestic competitor, Timex, were driving the prices of watches down. This of course benefited the consumer (TE). At the same time, a general slowdown in the economy meant less sales of watches. Faced with these realities, 1200 members of the Watchworkers Union not only gave up their previous demands for wage increases but accepted a 10 percent pay *decrease*. According to Ralph Frey, union president, "It was the toughest decision in my career. If we continued to demand increased salaries, it would cause the company to go into bankruptcy." The final meeting of the union, which approved the cut was, according to Frey, "One of the roughest meetings the Union has ever held in its 28 year history." Only after the union hired a certified public accountant to examine both the price of watches to consumers (thus verifying the self-interest of consumers) and the company cost records did it clearly see the conflict of interest. Having seen this, the only solution was to sacrifice the interests of employees in favor of the interests of consumers.

Reference was made in Chapter 4 to what has become known as the taxpayer revolt in government. After the passage of Proposition 13 in California, by which taxpayers forced the state to drop non-essential services in its total service alignment, the general movement spread from the state level to both the city and national levels. From a range of statements by both citizen leaders and government leaders, taxpayers seem to be enunciating two themes. First, they believe that the product/service alignment (TE) is not the most effective for citizen consumers. Either nonessential services should be curtailed, or there should be a prioritizing of services according to which produce the greatest utility to society. Second, they believe that the internal resource alignment (TI) may be inefficient. Either there are too many workers (TI.22) or existing work processes (TI.21) are inefficient.

At the state level, a public opinion poll by an independent agency revealed, "There is a strong belief that government is inefficient in its use of taxes. This belief is apparently stronger even than the simple desire to reduce their property taxes."

The revolt spread rapidly to other states. In 1978, 12 state legislatures passed laws that limited taxes, government spending, or both. Such bills were defeated in four state legislatures. A national poll by the *New York Times* and CBS News showed that the rest of the country is as interested in tax reductions as the people of California. By a margin of 51 percent to 24 percent, respondents outside California said they favored government taxing or spending restrictions.

By early 1979, 23 state legislatures had also passed resolutions calling for an unprecedented action. They demanded that a convention be called by the federal government to insert into the Constitution a provision that would limit taxes or government spending, or both.

Citizen actions demonstrate the nature of consumer and resource-supplier demands. But the subsequent reactions of government employees demonstrate the nature of internal employee demands. The two together show that these demands conflict.

One official in the Coalition of American Employees (CAPE) described the above events as, "An avalanche of bills, resolutions, recommendations and amendments which could drastically affect the future incomes of the members of our unions" (the coalition is made up of five public service unions). Jerry Worf, president of the American Federation of State, County and Municipal Employees (AFSCME), announced that he would mobilize a widespread alliance to fight the spread of government tax or spending restrictions. At its

247

national meeting, the AFSCME resolved to stop such initiatives which kill members' jobs. Since AFSCME is the largest AFL-CIO union in the nation, one can assume that the interests of internal employees will be clearly represented.

Speaking in Denver in July of the same year, Rev. Jesse Jackson, a prominent civil rights leader, warned that society is heading toward a confrontation between public employees and the public. "Public workers are demanding increased wages and, too often, decreased production. There is a cold war heating up between the public that pays for and receives services and the public workers who are paid and deliver services."

Turning now to a more specific government service, the providing of airport services for the traveling public, we see a similar conflict of interests. Policymakers for London Airport Authority faced these conflicting responsibilities in August 1978 at the height of the tourist season. On one side were 150,000 travelers waiting in Gatwick, Heathrow and Luton airports. On the other were traffic controllers manning the airport towers. Their demands included both greater remuneration for each employee and a greater number of employees to monitor the tower. As it turned out, the clash of interests was settled by increasing the pay of traffic controllers. Such an increase will be paid by the British government and, ultimately, the taxpayer.

Occasionally this kind of conflict is presented in ways that arouse unusual public reaction. In August 1977, 362 firefighters in the Dayton, Ohio, Fire Department were negotiating a contract with the city. City officials cited United States Bureau of Census figures showing that Dayton's firefighters were paid $15,320 per year whereas those in cities of comparable size were paid less: Des Moines ($12,082), Corpus Christi ($9,816), and Virginia Beach ($13,200). Reaching no agreement, the union decided to respond only to fires that threatened lives. During the ensuing week, 30 families were left homeless because of lack of firefighting service. The strike was settled with a 6.2 percent raise for firefighters in the first year, and other raises in subsequent years.

A similar situation occurred in 1978 in Anderson, Indiana. While firefighters refused to respond, a city block, containing a number of business establishments and the office of the county prosecutor, burned. Meanwhile, firefighters in a nearby city had voted at an emergency meeting to honor the strike, and not cross picket lines. According to the fire chief from this city, "For this reason we were delayed by the picket lines in responding. Had they not given us permission, we'd still be standing there watching the block burn."

Another case of this type involves the strike by municipal ambulance drivers in London in 1979. City policymakers were responding to a demand by the national government that wage increases be held to 5 percent in order to prevent further inflation (CE). At the same time, 2300 ambulance drivers were demanding a 69 percent increase in wages. During the negotiations, William Dunn, president of the union, drew heavy public criticism when he stated, "If it means lives lost, that is how it must be."

A final case involves British Leyland Ltd., largest automotive manufacturer in the United Kingdom. Lord Robens, former Minister of Labor and Member of Parliament, summed up the case for increased productivity on the part of autoworkers. He referred to the fact that Toyota, a Japanese company, could produce 2.3 million vehicles utilizing 43,000 employees. British Leyland, on the other hand, produced 1.9 million vehicles utilizing 170,000 employees. He further noted that Britain had lost 23.9 million man-days in strikes during the year. Germany, on the other hand, had lost 66,000 man-days, and even in its worst recent year had only lost 14.8 million man-days. Lord Robens reflected the needs and demands of consumers when he said, "Is it any wonder that the Japanese can supply people with low priced cars while Britain cannot?"

Conflict between External Cultural Constituencies and Employees

In some of the case histories just presented, there was in addition to the conflict between task effectiveness (TE) and cultural efficiency (CI), an additional conflict between cultural effectiveness (CE) and cultural efficiency (CI). For example, American Telephone and Telegraph policymakers were under pressure from the leaders in government who represent such constituencies as elderly persons whose pensions would be jeopardized by inflation, or persons who hold savings accounts that would be eroded by inflation. These are external *cultural* constituencies (CE). They are different from external *task* constituencies such as consumers of products and resource-supplying stockholders or taxpayers. The case histories that follow report additional conflicts of this type.

In the United States, labor unions throughout the 1960s and 1970s have been less active in demanding significant wage increases than in some European countries. This was not always true. In the 1930s, and again in the immediate postwar 1950s, labor unions ran squarely into conflict with guidelines of government. This appears again to be a problem area in the 1980s.

The United States Steel Corporation case is one demonstrating a conflict between union and government in the 1960s.[25] From 1940

249

onward, the company had responded to demands of workers with a succession of union contracts that increased employment costs by 8 percent annually, a fairly large increase measured by inflation rates then existing. In 1959, a prolonged strike for higher wages was settled by the company, which provided for a much lower increase.

By 1962, however, the Council of Economic Advisors (to the president of the United States) had become concerned again about the inflationary effects of either price or wage increases. It issued guidelines that focused on increases in *productivity*. In effect, no labor union was supposed to ask for a greater increase in wages than the increase in productivity that had been achieved since the last bargaining and contract period. In making these recommendations, the United States government, representing the constituencies that would be harmed by inflation, in effect said to the workers, "Your wage demands may conflict with those in society hurt by *cost push inflation*, therefore, do not demand any more wages than you provide in increased productivity." In the same way, the government said to stockholders, "Your demand for profits and dividends may conflict with those hurt by *demand pull inflation*, therefore, do not raise prices any more than you provide through equal increases in productivity of capital."

History shows that the voluntary guidelines issued by governments in the United States, Canada, and Britain, from those issued in 1962 right up to those issued in 1979 and 1980, have not been accepted by labor unions for any sustained period of time. In Canada, Finance Minister MacDonald stated in 1975 that voluntary guidelines simply had not worked. New governmental formal controls were instituted that year, preventing 4.3 million persons in Canada's 10-million-member labor force from raising wages more than 8 percent in the year, 8 percent in the following year, and 6 percent in the third year. By this act, the government acknowledged the conflict between demands of workers and inflation constituencies.

In the United States in 1978, we saw a similar conflict between employees in the Postal Service and the public. Unions representing the 554,000 postal workers demanded a wage increase that would, by estimate of the president, have resulted in a 14 percent increase in the first year. Such an increase would have had, in the president's opinion, been greater than society can afford in terms of inflation. In 1979 an identical conflict was highly publicized when the president of the AFL-CIO rejected new guidelines adopted by the president. This conflict reduced to simple terms was one between the government, which said, "You must not get more than 7 percent in wage

250

increases," and the union, which said, "We will get more than 7 percent wage increases."

Nowhere has the conflict between employees and inflation constituencies been so pronounced as in Great Britain. Throughout 1978 and 1979, the British government was determined to slow inflation through use of a 5 percent pay-increase guideline. So determined, in fact, that the prime minister's very continuance in office seemed to hinge on whether or not the 5 percent guideline would be observed. In September 1978, the chancellor of the exchequer warned that England could avoid inflation greater than 10 percent only if all workers observed the 5 percent guidelines. The prime minister addressed the Transport Union: "What I cannot tolerate is wage demands which are in excess of the guidelines and which add to the total costs and prices of the products produced in Britain. Were I to approve these, I could not in all honesty pretend that I am going to keep down inflation."

Shortly thereafter, the general secretary of the National Union of Public Employees, representing 693,000 workers in government, warned the prime minister: "If you are not prepared to depart from your rigid pay policy, it may lead to a major confrontation in the public sector." In answer, the prime minister addressed the Trade Union Congress: "Until we can reach a consensus the Government must state their views in terms of what is most likely to keep inflation under control. We have done so. You know our views. We do not intend to depart from them."

A final case, Hitachi Ltd. of Japan, shows conflict between worker demands and another external cultural constituency, persons seeking employment in the electrical industry. It is a conflict between existing internal workers in the electrical industry and external job seekers. In early 1977, Hitachi strategists were considering various nations throughout the world as alternatives for locating a plant to produce color television sets for sale to consumers and tubes to be sold to other manufacturers. They were solving the well-known comprehensive-task-alignment problem, making policies about product/ markets (TE) and capital alignment (TI.11). One of the alternatives was Washington New Town, a medium-sized town in England.

As negotiations proceeded to acquire 14 acres in this town, labor unions in England waged what the *London Times* referred to as a long campaign to oppose the plant. The union campaign stated clearly the needs of existing workers: if Hitachi locates a plant in Britain, workers in existing plants may have to be laid off. Whole plants might close due to competition with Hitachi, especially if Hitachi should produce sets that are cheaper for the consumer.

251

In December of that year, Hitachi indeed obeyed these demands. The minister of industry told Parliament: "Hitachi officials have told me that they would not wish to establish a manufacturing facility in the U.K. unless the climate were more favorable. They feel that even if they secured government approval of the plant they could not expect normal operation of the project in the U.K." Here we have a three-way conflict. Internal worker demands conflicted not only with job-seeking workers outside the existing companies (CE), but also with consumers who might benefit by the possibility of lower-priced television sets (TE).

Conflicts over Capital Alignment (TI.11)

History shows that whenever corporations introduce new capital technology that increases quality of the product or decreases cost of the product, and that at the same time decreases the amount of labor necessary to produce the product, the result is a conflict between external constituencies (consumers, resource suppliers or both) and internal employees. In economists' terms, when new innovations in capital convert a production process from labor-intensive to capital-intensive, conflict of interests is generated.

Histories of industries such as electronic computers, pocket and desk calculators, color television sets, solid-state watches, tape recorders, artificial leather articles, and synthetic-fiber clothing suggest that the interests of stockholders predominate in the earliest phase of the product's life cycle but the balance swings in favor of consumers in the mature and declining phases. For example, when color television sets and individual desk/pocket computers entered the market because of new capital technology, prices were very high in the beginning. They later decreased significantly because of (1) the learning curve (costs come down as problems are solved), (2) increased volume of sales (which spread the capital cost of initial technology), and (3) varying degrees of competition as other firms either duplicate the technology (if not protected by patent) or find close substitutes (if protected by patent).

This kind of conflict comes to public attention when policymakers, responding to needs of external constituencies, try to align capital by introducing some new technology but organized labor, responding to needs of internal employees, prevents its adoption. Such has been the case in the newspaper industry during two successive waves of technological innovation from 1940 to 1980. The first innovation involved elimination of the costly linotype process, by which machines funnelled melted lead into type trays in response to an

252

operator's selections as he or she sat at a typewriter-like keyboard. The second involved replacing an intervening technology with photographic processes. In both cases, many newspapers, for example the *New York Times*, the *New York Daily News*, and the *New York Herald Tribune*, were forced to maintain the old technology long after they could have lowered the cost of newspapers by efficient use of new machinery.

The classic example given in history-of-the-labor-movement textbooks is that of the railroad industry. At union insistence, the Atlantic Coast Line Railroad maintained firemen on locomotives some 15 years after labor-intensive, coal-burning locomotives were replaced by lower-cost, capital-intensive diesel locomotives. The firemen's previous duty, shoveling coal into the boiler, completely disappeared when there was no longer any coal to shovel.

A notable settlement of this kind of dispute occurred between the International Longshoremen's and Warehousemen's Union (ILWU) and the Pacific Maritime Association in 1960.[26] Ocean-shipping technology was undergoing a profound change. From World War II liberty ships, loaded piece-by-piece by cargo slings and longshoremen gangs, the industry wanted to move to mass crane handling of standardized containers. Though today's huge container ships cost $50 million, with another $50 million of equipment on board, they move international cargo at a fraction of the cost required by smaller ships and hand labor. In short, the ocean terminal business was moving from labor-intensive to capital-intensive technology.

In the end, the ILWU agreed to allow shipowners and stevedoring contractors to be "freed of restrictions on the introduction of labor-saving devices, relieved of the use of unnecessary men, and assured of free flow of cargo or quick ship turnaround." The employers agreed to give the union: 1. $5 million a year for five and one-half years; 2. $3 million to be used for early retirement and death benefits; and 3. $2 million to be used to make up the difference if workers' wages fell below what they would have made had they been employed a full 35 hours a week. When this contract expired in 1960 the association negotiated a similar set of rules to ensure self-interests of longshoremen. The contribution to the workers' fund was increased to $6.9 million a year.

Two extensive case histories in the airline industry also show the clash between external and internal interests. In the early 1960s, introduction of new jet airplanes, which carried up to three times more passengers than older aircraft and cut flying time between New York and Chicago in half, meant that one jet could replace three and a half conventional older craft in meeting airline schedules. Every new jet on every airline meant about 24 fewer airline crew members, principally fewer pilots.[27] In a long series of negotiations with Eastern, Continental, United, and TWA, the Airline Pilots Association secured the right for pilots to take over the third seat in the cockpit, acting as flight engineers. This corresponded with the practice of using older piston-type aircraft. There were two pilots in the cockpit plus the flight engineer. The Flight Engineers International Association demanded that flight engineers, not pilots, fill the third seat in the cockpit.

Caught between these two unions, policymakers in Eastern, American, and Pan American airlines were forced to carry *four* persons in the cockpit: three pilots and a flight engineer. TWA also maintained four-person crews and granted a guarantee that pilots would also be able to obtain flight-engineer certificates.

The most recent of these conflicts occurred in the late 1970s and involved Wein Air Alaska, an airline linking Seattle with various points in Alaska. This was a dispute over another aircraft, the Boeing 737. The Federal Aviation Administration and the manufacturer showed evidence that 70 airlines around the world fly the 737 with a two-person crew while three, Wein, Western, and United, fly it with a three-person crew. They also provided statistics showing that the accident rate in 737's with three-person crews was higher than the accident rate with two-person crews. As this book is being written, a presidential fact-finding board is attempting to settle a strike by Wein pilots, now in its 22nd month, who demand that three pilots be used in the cockpit.

Work Processes and Work Design
versus Quality of Work Life

Earlier in this chapter a brief overview of research in organizational behavior showed that work-level employees have a broad range of intangible needs, which they seek in everyday work life. We shall now review case histories that show that the operating processes (TI.21) and work-design structures (TI.22) that are most efficient for task performance often conflict with the intangible needs of employees (CI.22).

THE HARVARD BUSINESS SCHOOL CASES   The most extensive collection of cases demonstrating this conflict has been accumulated over the past 30 years at the Harvard Business School. These cases were originally written for use in the Administrative Practices course and may be found in various editions of *The Administrator*.[29] Later, emphasis shifted to an analysis of organizational behavior. Cases reflecting this shift may be found in *Managing Group and Intergroup Relations*,[29] *Motivation and Control in Organizations*,[30] and *Organizational Behavior and Administration*.[31]

No short review of this vast collection can provide a real understanding of the conflicts that constantly recur between task efficiency and worker satisfaction. Because of the richness of differences between tasks themselves and between individual human beings, each case requires separate diagnosis if one is to achieve such understanding. Nevertheless, some of these cases are classic and enduring. Like great precedent setting law cases such as *Dartmouth College* v *Woodward*, the essence of the conflict reappears in different time settings whether they be in 1950 or 1980. We can but mention the essence of one or two of these cases.

In the National Elevator Company, the firm's product/market alignment is the sale and servicing of elevators for residential and commercial customers.[32] Servicing is one of the vital alignments from the customer's viewpoint. If elevators break down or become unsafe, the effect on the customer is severe. The company is organized by regions in order to provide this service. Maintenance and repair workers in the midwest region are located in different cities. Efficiency of the work schedule depends on having the right number of workers in the right city at the right time. This means that policymakers must engage in manpower planning (aligning the right number of workers), selection (hiring workers with the right specialized skill), and training (developing experienced and skilled repairmen).

As the case unfolds, union officials tell a high company official, Thorkelson, that a 35-year-old repairman named George Gleason has good reason for wanting a transfer from his base city, Indianapolis, to Dayton. Gleason is apparently highly experienced. The union officials say that Gleason is not able to get his supervisor, Mankos, to heed his need for transfer. They also say that the union has discovered over the years that the company puts so much stress on efficient manpower planning that it does not take into account the personal lives of workers such as Gleason.

Close diagnosis of the case shows that this indeed is true. The way communications flow up and down the chain of command about the Gleason situation shows that efficient repair of elevators pressures managers to put the right number of repairmen at the right place to serve the customer. This pressure runs squarely counter to the personal needs of Gleason, and, probably, of other repairmen throughout the system. Finally, the case shows that if managers want to integrate the two demands, there is a cost in efficiency to this course of action, too. Either there must be some slack in efficiency (i.e., slightly overstaff the workforce to provide room for personal transfers) or the managers must spend long hours listening to and diagnosing personal needs (as contrasted with customer needs), or both. If policymakers are to reach the optimum solution, some trade-off between short-run task efficiency and employee satisfaction is necessary.

Another classic case is Ontario Manufacturing Company.[33] The case concerns the relationships betwen Robert Lewis, a 19-year-old worker, his supervisor, Eric Hamer, and the company's manpower rule system. Lewis works in the packaging department, which must package products for customers on a rather tight time schedule. He is shown to have a real need to get time off from work to pick his tomato crop before a heavy frost destroys it. Close diagnosis shows that the tomato crop is indeed important to Lewis. It is related to his real interest in this activity, his sense of achievement in working at several jobs at once, and his need for freedom and autonomy to initiate his own work life. As the case unfolds, Lewis violates the manpower rule system by leaving the plant without permission. Communications between managers trying to cope with his request (i.e., get him time off) show that (1) managers are under pressure to keep the packaging plant running on schedule, (2) they might have solved the Lewis case by finding a replacement had the managers put higher weight on Lewis' personal needs, but (3) such solution would have meant still some loss of efficiency: managers cannot listen to all employee needs all of the time and find custom-made solutions without providing additional time and effort for this activity.

SAAB AUTOMOBILE ENGINE ASSEMBLY DEPARTMENT   A case history dealing with worker reactions in Sweden shows a variety of conflicts between job design and needs of employees.[34] At the same time that assembly-line technology in the Saab Company was becoming more and more specialized and repetitive, thus requiring fewer skills and less discretion, young people entering the work force had more education, more skills, and a greater demand for meaningful work. The company need for production-line skills was one thing, but the supply of workers was another. A survey under government auspices showed that only 4 percent of students graduating from high school were willing to take a job in a task alignment of this type. In fact, the Saab/Scania Division became heavily dependent on foreign workers. Fifty-eight percent of all workers were from less affluent nations.

Given this state of affairs, the company endeavored to use autonomous work-group design. Under this design a small group of workers assembled an engine with considerable autonomy in planning their own work. This contrasted with mass-production technology where more workers on a production line had very little discretion over what they did and when.

Close analysis of this case reveals two kinds of conflicts, which policymakers faced as they used the new work design. First, there is strong circumstantial evidence that productivity in terms of man-hours per engine decreased. This fact was never proven by industrial engineering. It was thought that time-and-motion study engineers would have caused the true spirit of the program to be jeopardized in the eyes of workers. But enough evidence exists that we may be quite certain that there was some loss of productivity. The conclusion is further strengthened by the fact that Volvo, another Swedish company with experience in autonomous work group design, decided not to use this design in a plant it hoped to establish in the United States.

Second, there was the problem of individual differences. The autonomous design was installed on the theory that all human beings want and need autonomy, discretion, a variety of tasks, and a high degree of team interaction as they make decisions. What the case shows is that this is only partially true. Although some workers in Sweden, and some visiting workers from Detroit did indeed have these wants, others did not. In fact, they reacted negatively. For them the new work design (1) gave them responsibility they did not seek, (2) made them dependent on the group rather than on themselves as individuals, (3) made them work harder than they wished, and (4) lowered their status. These two problems—the clash between efficiency and satisfaction and the clash between *any* work system and certain individuals—highlight the kinds of conflict policymakers must accept and deal with.

WORK DESIGN FOR MEDICAL DOCTORS: PSRO   Conflict between the demand for task performance (as seen by outside constituencies) and the intangible needs of medical doctors treating individual patients has a striking similarity to this same kind of conflict as it exists between outsiders and production workers in factories. In simplest terms, the conflict appears as follows.[35]

On the one hand, there is evidence that external constituencies are demanding either higher-quality work or lower-cost work by doctors, or both. The number of malpractice suits in which patients assert that doctors have performed poor-quality work has risen

257

sharply. At the same time, resource suppliers in the role of insurance companies or the federal government have demanded that the cost of doctors' work be controlled. There have been advertisements by insurance companies in national magazines showing a patient getting up from the operating table, shouting, "What! Seven hundred dollars for *this!*"

The federal government has responded in classic strategic sequence. First, in 1972 it passed Public Law 92-603, the so-called Bennett Amendment to the Social Security Act. The goal of this act was to monitor services paid for by Medicare, Medicaid, and maternal and child health programs to make sure that the services are medically necessary, meet professional standards, and are provided in the most economical medically appropriate site of treatment. Second, the act specified an organization structure (TI.12) to implement the strategic goal. Over 100 local professional standards review organizations have been set up across the nation to monitor what an individual doctor does with a given patient and to compare his or her work with that judged by other doctors to be correct. To elaborate this structure, the secretary of HEW established the Bureau of Quality Assurance and directed that within 18 months the country should be divided into geographic areas, each with its own PSRO. Two years after the law was passed the federal register published the final organization structure: 203 PSROs covering the nation.

An early leader at the local level was a PSRO in Minnesota. There, Dr. Gilbertson, of Bethesda Lutheran Hospital, points to the benefits of work monitoring. The average hospital stay has decreased from nine days to seven days. The occupancy rate of the hospital has decreased from 87 percent to 71 percent of capacity. He explains that he must often take his turn at reviewing performance. For example, he has the charts of two patients on his desk; one had had a total knee replacement and the other minor surgery for a female disorder. A preliminary review shows that each patient has already been in the hospital long enough so that most similar patients would have been discharged. The attending physicians are seeking to keep the patients in the hospital but Dr. Gilbertson recommends otherwise.

In Colorado, the PSRO estimates that reduced hospitalization in the state will result in a saving of somewhere between $3 million and $9 million in every 18-month period.

This work design and monitoring program has not been without its effect on the individual doctor's need for freedom, autonomy, and self-actualization. When the Colorado PSRO attempted to require physicians to submit each plan to admit nonemergency patients to the hospital, Dr. Chessun, of the Presbyterian Medical Center put it

258

this way. "To me this is interference with the doctor's right to put patients in the hospital. I don't think doctors in this hospital or any other will tolerate it." Dr. Edward Hyman, a Louisiana physician joins other doctors in fearing that the government is about to seize control of the practice of medicine: "Rape, even if presented as motherhood, becomes rape again."

The American Medical Association has tried to work with HEW to implement the PSRO strategy, but some of its officials have talked about ultimate repeal of the law. According to Senator Wallace Bennett, sponsor of the legislation, two other organizations, the Council of Medical Staffs and the American Association of Physicians and Surgeons have vigorously worked to have the PSRO law repealed.

At the present time, seven years after the initial law was passed, the controversy still persists. The Oversight and Investigations Subcommittee of the House Interstate and Foreign Commerce Committee has just issued a report concluding that state licensing agencies, medical societies, and PSRO's are failing to control the work of doctors. "We are appalled at the amount of evidence of incompetent as well as unnecessary surgery being performed in the United States today." Subcommittee research showed that there are 2 million unnecessary surgeries performed each year. This has resulted in an excess cost to patients or taxpayers of $4 billion in one year and in the deaths of more than 10,000 people. The subcommittee specifically referred to the excess number of tonsillectomies and hysterectomies currently performed. It said that unnecessary operations could be reduced if the federal government would set up a program of mandatory second opinions to confirm the need for elective surgery performed under Medicare and Medicaid. Dr. James Sammons, executive vice- president of the American Medical Association responded, "The subcommittee has applied limited, early results from a few studies to the nation as a whole without justification."

Work Processes and Design
Versus Remuneration and Job Security

We will now look at some case histories in which conflict appears to arise because the ideal alignment from the standpoint of task efficiency conflicts with workers' demands for remuneration and job security.[36] In a number of these cases, close diagnosis reveals that it is a combination of material needs (remuneration and job security) and intangible needs (autonomy, freedom, self-actualization) that stirs worker opposition to the alignment. Thus, it is the whole

259

worker, with a complex set of material and intangible needs, who reacts, not a human being who is either economic or self-actualizing.

Some social science researchers have indeed categorized workers as motivated by jobs and pay. Others have categorized them as motivated by need for social friendship, self-esteem, and autonomy. Some economists have held that workers, like all other humans, have an insatiable demand for products, services, and components of the standard of living. Some psychologists have held that material needs cease to operate when a certain level of affluence is attained. Neither is entirely correct in every situation. The following cases show that when policymakers align work processes and job designs any or all of these demands may be actuated.

NATIONAL MOTOR PARTS COMPANY   The case history of the National Motor Parts Company is a modern example of a classic conflict between the responsibility for efficient job design and the demand for job security and remuneration.[37] National Motor Parts Company is one of the five largest manufacturers of basic automotive parts in the nation. Pressure from customers (TE, the automobile manufacturers) forces policymakers to design production-line positions (TI.22) in a way that reduces manpower costs. This pressure is exerted in two ways. First, the automobile manufacturers' *product* has changed over the years to meet innovations in the type of automobiles driven by motorists. This means that the parts they order from NMP also change. NMP's technology and machinery have also changed because of new inventions. For example, William Sullivan performed a job on the production line known as "the lock-pin-assembly job." In this job, Sullivan used one large automatic screw machine to produce a tiny metal lock pin that in turn fitted into an automatic transmission. The job had been designed 10 years previously when Ford and Chevrolet transmissions were different from those today. Further, a new type of automatic screw machine had been developed within the last five years and installed in the NMP plant. Because of these changes, a careful statistical analysis showed that the worker in this job position (Sullivan) was actually idle 4 hours per shift. This was confirmed not only by industrial engineers but by informal comments of fellow workers, who resented the fact that they worked a whole day while Sullivan did not: "If your study doesn't pick up that soft touch Sullivan's got, you'd better toss the whole thing down the drain."

The crux of the task alignment problem was that because of changes in technology and materials, the person with the lock-pin-assembly job can actually operate two of the newer type of machines.

This was the new job design that Martin, the supervisor of industrial engineering, proposed.

The rest of the case shows behavioral reactions well known since the time Frederick Taylor first proposed his scientific management. Not only did Sullivan object, but John Andrews, the shop steward, and Ed Lillian, president of the union, demanded that the plant manager, Donald Leach, stop trying to make Sullivan the victim of a "speedup." Leach said:

Ford and Chevrolet will not continue to buy from us unless we can maintain an efficient operation. New processes mean that Sullivan can produce 2880 lock pins per day instead of the present 1440, simply by working during what is now idle time. We owe it to everyone concerned to change to the new standard.

Andrews, the shop steward, responded, "The Company is violating the fairness and equity clauses in the labor contract."

Sullivan's grievance was filed, and quickly became a *cause celebre* in the town in which the plant is located. The local newspaper urged caution, because a similar dispute over job design had ended in a 6-month strike in a nearby town.

SAFEWAY STORES   Time-and-motion study is regarded as somewhat unimportant in the modern business-school curriculum. It is thought to be out-of-date compared to modern operations research and systems analysis. This should not obscure the fact that methods very similar to the original Taylor-Galbraith system are prevalent throughout the United States and Europe today. As this book goes to press, Safeway Stores, the largest supermarket chain in the United States, is faced with a replica of the classic conflict. Policymakers in the company have recently been concerned about several trends in the environment that together have put them in a profit squeeze, thus under pressure from stockholders (TE.21). On one hand, there has been a strong demand by consumers that prices of food are too high in a period of inflation (TE). On the other, the demand of farmers for higher prices from the supermarkets has been aired by the farmers' march on the Federal Capitol in Washington (TE.22).

Responding to these forces for lowering costs, policymakers used a combination of time studies and an analysis of worker capabilities to reduce labor costs in warehouses. Specifically, they analyzed a job in which the worker loads cartons of food onto pallets. These pallets are then picked up by a fork-lift truck and loaded onto trucks for delivery to retail stores. It was a change in technology that precipitated the

261

conflict. The company installed a computer-based system that determines how many pallets can be loaded in a certain period of time. First, a computer sheet tells the worker what food cartons (both by number and type) are needed in a specific truck going to a specific store. It also shows the length of time required to "pull" this composite order. The warehouseman is expected to achieve a daily quota based on these figures.

Reactions from workers such as Tony Silva, a 50-year-old man who has been a warehouseman for Safeway for eight years, have been negative. The reaction of nine local teamster's unions in Northern California has been more forceful. The unions called their 2500 members to a walkout that lasted 15 weeks.

SOCIAL SECURITY ADMINISTRATION   In 1975 the House Ways and Means Committee became concerned about the cost of operating various government agencies. Most members of the committee were on record as believing that scarce resources prevent the government from engaging in some needed services and that one way to provide additional services is to obtain the most efficiency from resources in all operations. As part of its general data collection, the committee directed the General Accounting Office (GAO) to study the utilization of manpower in the Social Security Administration offices that pay out Medicare funds to a constituency of persons in need of medical care.

The GAO proceeded to collect data on the amount of work done by personnel in the SSA offices versus the amount of work done by personnel in four private companies that do similar work for the government. It then compared the salaries paid by these organizations. The research showed that the average federal SSA employee processes 2500 claims per year. The average employee in Travelers Insurance Company processes 3900 claims, in Mutual of Omaha 4200 claims, in Blue Cross of Maryland 5700, and in Blue Cross of Chicago 6600.

At the same time, an average worker in the SSA received $21,600 in wages and fringe benefits per year whereas an average worker in Blue Cross of Chicago received $18,600. Corresponding salaries in other organizations were: Blue Cross of Maryland, $17,300; Travelers Insurance, $13,800; Mutual of Omaha, $13,700.

The combination of number of employees required plus cost of each employee resulted in a total cost to the government of $12.39 for each claim processed for one Medicare patient. The corresponding average cost for the other four organizations was $6.45. The general conclusion in the report was that government workers in the SSA get paid more but do less work.

In this case the United States Congress has used the same method for assessing manpower alignment (number and cost of personnel) as many private corporations. The approach is similar to time-and-motion study in that it uses research to arrive at a standard manpower alignment such as $6.45. It then compares actual results ($12.39) to this standard to test whether the alignment is efficient or inefficient.

NEW YORK STATE: PRODUCTIVITY STRATEGY AND PRODUCTIVITY BARGAINING One extensive case history shows the behavior of both strategists (in the New York State Legislature) and workers (Civil Service Employees Association with 133,000 members) as they conflict over the kind and amount of work that should be accomplished in state government jobs.[38] The case covers a period of years in the 1970s. Strategists were worried about scarce resources available to the state and the fact that the most output must be gained from what limited resources were available. About that time, the *Public Administration Review* had devoted a special issue to productivity in government. The public was depicted as upset by its increasing tax load and by inefficiencies in government. "Budget crunches" were seen as continuing, if not increasing, at every level of government.

The case first shows a combination of strategic behavior and incremental behavior by the state and the union. The state stressed the broad goal of productivity. Incremental bargaining enabled both parties to arrive at more specific policies. Both state and union agreed on "the need for cooperative efforts to increase productivity." A joint committee was established to study and seek agreement on matters such as charging tardiness against leave time, raising the work week from 37.5 hours to 40 hours, granting flexible working hours and building job enrichment into formerly routine jobs. A contract was signed whereby both parties would hire a consultant to develop output standards for state jobs that could be measured.

In the long series of negotiations described, it is clear that the state was compromising some of its demands for productivity to accommodate workers' job security, pay, and intangible needs. At the same time, responding to public pressure, the union was compromising some of its former demands that job standards *not* be created.

As the case concludes, the author who wrote it believes that the long, arduous process of (1) broad strategic goals supplemented by (2) persistent and time-consuming negotiations did indeed result in a workable strategy. He held the case up as a model of how logic (broad goals) and bargaining (working out details) could solve the thorny question of productivity. The reader is also left with the impression that mutual compromise had indeed solved the problem.

But the case has a surprise ending. Between the time it was written and the time it was published another event occurred. An editor's note on the first page reads: "A few months after Dr. Balk made this study, the matter of mutual investigation of productivity factors by employees and the New York State management was abruptly dropped at the suggestion of the Civil Service Employees Association. This demonstrates how threatening and loaded with uncertainty productivity issues can be for employees."

THE FEDERAL GOVERNMENT: MERIT RATING   Reacting to the same kinds of pressure from the public that have already been mentioned, the United States Congress passed what the president called "the most sweeping reform of the Civil Service System since it was created nearly 100 years ago." The goal of the Civil Service Reform Act of 1978, according to the president, was to "put incentives and rewards back into the federal employment system comprising 2.8 million civilian workers. Our nation was built on a system of rewards and incentives. 'You get what you pay for' is a part of the American folk wisdom. Civil Service reform will help taxpayers get what they have been paying for." In the words of the Civil Service commissioner, the law will provide "the right balance between the freedom necessary to serve the public's needs and the oversight required to protect the system's integrity."

Space does not permit a full description of the new system. Among other things it creates an Office of Personnel Management to elaborate and implement a merit-rating plan. It provides for 9000 top managers who will be "held accountable for success of their programs, for goal-setting and for achievement." This Senior Executive Service will be managed through a system of incentive pay awards based on appraisals. The performance of all other employees up through grades GS-15 will likewise be appraised annually. Based on these appraisals, a system of merit salary adjustments will replace what the chairman of the Civil Service Commission called habitual and automatic salary increases.

Negative reactions by employees and their representatives was immediate. Frederick Thayer used Douglas McGregor's paradigm, which distinguished between managers who empathize with employee needs ("Theory Y Managers") and those who emphasize only work efficiency ("Theory X Managers"), to convey employee needs. He called the new law "the president's management 'reforms,'" and called the new law's provisions, "Theory X Triumphant." Lawrence

264

Howard, himself a minority person, stressed that a majority of the federal work force (80 percent) is comprised of women and minorities and yet the bill was presented to the Senate "virtually without mentioning minorities, women, or the handicapped." He pointed out that there can be no real increase in productivity unless it is accomplished in a certain way—by the majority's opportunity (i.e., that of the 80 percent of federal employees who are minorities) to serve the public.[39]

In addressing such a controversial issue as this it is necessary to reiterate a point made at other places in Chapter 8 and in this chapter. The point to be made here is not that one side (the president, Congress, and the Civil Service commissioner) is right and the other side (the workers and their representatives) wrong. The Civil Service Reform Act is simply a case history showing that strategists and policymakers often decide on task alignments because of constituencies' demands for effective and efficient task performance. In the evolutionary history of organizations, these alignments then affect the needs and demands of cultural constituencies. This brings forth a conflict that must be dealt with by policymakers: the conflict between task performance and cultural performance.

Before leaving the subject of merit ratings in government, we should note that the type of reform undertaken by the federal government, is also being widely applied by state and local governments. In 1976, a 29-member advisory council to the governor of the State of Washington completed a 19-month study that was presented to the legislature. It recommended linking pay to job performance, the creation of better work standards, and the establishment of career training programs. In 1979, the City Council of Seattle voted 8 to 1 to amend the city's charter in a way that would discard the existing personnel system and substitute a system based on merit pay and merit promotions. Michael Waske, business manager of a union representing 1500 city employees, said, "This is a direct affront to the bargaining units. It is a real sad day. This ordinance will bring politics into the personnel system and make city employees servants of the City Council."

It should be recognized, too, that incentive pay systems do not always end in conflict. In 1973, police in Orange, California, bargained with city officials regarding a merit appraisal and pay system to improve law enforcement. Both sides agreed that policemen would get merit pay bonuses if the combined number of rapes, robberies, burglaries, and auto thefts dropped below certain standard levels. Over the next few years, all of these crimes, especially burglaries, declined substantially—so substantially that police were eligible for the highest wage increases possible under the plan. At the same time, state auditors and researchers from a private foundation investigated the Orange system. They concluded that the improvement in levels of crime committed was a valid and real decrease in crime rather than the result of any manipulation of crime records.

FEDERAL GOVERNMENT: JOB DESIGN   Another conflict between task alignment and employee demands—this one centering on job design—has occurred in the federal government. Policymakers in the Civil Service Commission had designed jobs according to a time-honored procedure. First, they wrote job specifications according to the task to be accomplished. For example, if the Social Security Administration's service alignment called for paying claims to retired persons they analyzed what operations it took to pay claims and divided these into positions. One job was to interview persons who reach retirement age and help them fill out applications. Another was to process the filled-out application, setting up the necessary records and forwarding them to a distant city where someone in another job position placed the new retiree's name and pension amount on check-writing computer tapes. In the United States Forest Service, one job is to act as ranger in a certain national park and another is to act as observer in a fire-prevention tower in a certain area. Other positions in both the SSA and the Forest Service are as supervisors of groups of applications interviewers or forest rangers.

These positions or roles were drawn up without regard to a specific human being. They were further elaborated by writing job descriptions showing the specific duties and activities that any ranger or any interviewer should perform in order to accomplish the service output goal—service to people visiting national parks or to people seeking retirement payments. They were not drawn for John Jones as a person or for Mary Smith as a person.

The connection between the objective job description and human beings was accomplished by a next step. Job specifications were converted to person specifications by listing the skills, qualifications, experience, education, and other attributes that any person should have in order effectively to carry out the required activities to serve the clients. An inspector for the United States Bureau of Fisheries is required to be educated in biology and fisheries management, and have five years experience in lower positions in the bureau's fish hatcheries.

The next step in this kind of manpower planning is to select persons to fill the jobs or to train persons to fill them. This involves interviewing and appraising applicants' present skills, identifying

266

any gap between required skills and present skills, and providing training to fill the gap. Notice that all of these steps are aimed at the comprehensive task alignment. They are intended logically to connect the job design (TI.22) to the service/market alignment (TE).

The final step in the manpower-planning process is to attach a salary level to the job description. One way to have equity in salary is to pay people according to the amount they contribute. Very difficult jobs or jobs requiring long education pay more than easier jobs or less skilled jobs. Another is comparability. Jobs in one industry or agency should be equated with jobs in other agencies and industries. Thus, the government ends up with 15 grades in Civil Service, from GS-1 to GS-15.

All administrators know that this system does not work perfectly. Other factors enter in. The human being who fits into the neat square on the chart may not be square but round, or oval. Politics enters in when some person is selected for reasons other than the fact that their qualifications fit the job specification.

In early 1979, the Civil Service Commission published its first comprehensive and statistically reliable survey on "overgrading" in the federal government. For years many persons in government had known that there were times when a particular person's supervisor might arrive at the following conclusions:

1. Mr. Jones or Ms. Smith deserves a salary raise or a promotion (a variety of reasons may lie behind this conclusion). But
2. Ms. Smith or Mr. Jones cannot be given a salary raise or a promotion (a variety of reasons may lie behind this conclusion). Therefore
3. I should leave Jones or Smith in his or her present job but change his or her classification from GS-8 to GS-9.

The Civil Service Commission's survey showed that 11.5 percent of all federal workers have a rank and salary that is higher than the job duties call for. The cost to taxpayers of paying these 155,000 persons more than the job descriptions call for is $436 million a year. Alan K. Campbell, Civil Service commissioner, exercised his responsibility to external constituencies when he issued a bulletin to all federal departments asking them to focus attention on the grading problem and reduce the incidence of overgrading.

Employee representatives disagreed. Kenneth Blaylock, president of the American Federation of Government Employees, said, "The only reason the commission has brought these distortions to the public is to create the impression that the taxpayer is being ripped off."

NEW YORK CITY: PRODUCTIVITY MEASURES   Probably no other governmental unit has been under so much pressure for so long a time to bring its affairs into fiscal balance than New York City. Faced with declining revenues and increasing costs to the point of bankruptcy, both city strategists and workers have tried to invent new work processes and job designs that produce equal or more service with less manpower input. This has yielded results not accomplished by other governments in the United States.

Overall, Mayor Beame reported in 1977 that struggles over the past six years had resulted in the city's ability to maintain the same level of services in spite of the fact that 12,000 fewer employees were on the payroll. In 110 pages of agency-by-agency analysis, Beame cited performance statistics. Over 300 performance measures are now used by the agencies, from "number of elevator inspections in the Buildings Department" (97,000 this year compared to 78,000 last year) to "new cases of syphilis monitored by the Health Department" (6530 this year compared to 5044 last year). Performance targets were also set in other areas. There were 1119 trees pruned in the city's parks in one month when the target was 1239. The Marionette Children's Theatre produced 115 shows in one month when the target was 113. The Corrections Department washed 388,000 pounds of laundry in one month, 28,000 pounds above its goal.

All of these performance standards were not achieved without conflict. For example, workers in New York have for many years worked a 7-hour day (9 to 5 with one hour for lunch) instead of an 8-hour day. In the summer, city employees had worked a 6-hour day (9 to 4 with an hour for lunch). This custom was established 43 years ago when air conditioning did not exist.

In an effort to improve productivity, the mayor ordered all municipal employees to work 9 to 5 during the summer. The mayor estimated the value of the extra hour at $22 million annually. Victor Gotbaum, executive director of District 37 of the State, County, and Municipal Employees Union threatened to have employees leave work at 4 P.M. and to distribute several thousand leaflets depicting a clock set at 4 o'clock with the words, "The Hour is Ours." In the end, the union and the city agreed to submit the matter to arbitration. In the words of Dorothy Fidler, a worker in the Housing and Development Administration, "People do not think we are human beings."

In the Board of Education, policymakers sought to realign manpower by increasing the sizes of classes in order to reduce teacher manpower costs. From a present average of 32 pupils in elementary schools, 33 in junior high schools, and 34 in high schools, they

268

proposed class sizes in the range of 40 to 45 pupils. Albert Shanker, president of the United Federation of Teachers warned that the 57,000 teachers in the system would not accept such increases. Citing the decrease in quality of instruction as well as the possibility of increased incidence of violence in the classroom, he said that teachers simply cannot and will not cope with classes of the proposed size.

PENNSYLVANIA: STATE COLLEGE SYSTEM Conflicts over manpower planning and staffing of jobs erupts not only between policymakers and organized labor but also between policymakers and middle managers. The latter are motivated by factors discussed in Chapter 8, and also by their being closer to the work level, and thus in a better position to identify with workers.

In 1975 such a conflict arose between John C. Pittenger, Pennsylvania state secretary of education and Gilmore B. Seavers, president of Shippensburg State College. The commissioner was under pressure from the legislature, which was trying to align all state programs within the state's tax budget. He had also been urged by Governor Schapp to cut the total budget for all 13 state colleges by an amount equal to the system's deficit, $16.6 million a year.

With other policymakers in the commission, Pittenger took the total deficit and assigned targets to each of the thirteen colleges. Expenses at Shippensburg, they felt, should be reduced by $1.27 million a year. The state also issued guidelines for reducing manpower in the colleges. Each president was to cut persons from the payroll without changing the ratio of white males to minority persons. The impact of the cutbacks should be distributed among two groups, teachers and nonteachers, without favoring one or the other. Each president was to submit, by June 30, a list of employees to be laid off.

Twelve college presidents complied with these guidelines. Dr. Seavers did not, saying, "I have felt that it is wrong to lay off employees before studying seriously every other alternative." He therefore submitted to the commissioner budget cuts but no personnel layoffs.

On June 27, Jerome Ziegler, state commissioner for higher education, went from Harrisburg to Shippensburg. He handed Dr. Seavers a letter from Secretary Pittenger that said, "By this letter I hereby order you to deliver to my office by 5 P.M. Monday, June 30, 1975, Plan A containing the complete list of proposed employees to be retrenched at Shippensburg State College in accordance with the guidelines. If this list is not in my office at that time it is the Governor's intention to remove you from the office of President of Shippensburg State College as of 9 A.M. Tuesday, July 1, 1975." President Seavers chose Plan A, as the Presidents of twelve other colleges had done.

UNITED NATIONS: EUROPEAN HEADQUARTERS   Conflicts between task efficiency and cultural efficiency are not limited to cities, states, and nations. A conflict very similar to those already reported occurred in the Geneva headquarters of the United Nations.

The Geneva headquarters employs 10,000 persons in two categories, general staff, who make up to $600 a week plus allowances, and professional staff who make up to $1000 a week plus allowances. The total payroll of $500 million a year is provided by the General Assembly in New York, which in turn collects dues from member nations.

In 1975 a special General Assembly Committee had responded to demands by member nations that certain abuses be stopped in order to lower the cost of manpower. For example, a report by the United States Senate had said, "All too often the UN Organizations, headquartered in extravagant and luxurious surroundings, are ineffective, overstaffed with high paid officials uncertain of their purposes, and unduly repetitious of the activities of other organizations."

The General Assembly Committee ordered all employees to provide exact descriptions of their job purposes and duties, their salaries, and their dependent, nonresident, and language allowances. It further reported that it had evidence that the salaries were being paid to persons when they were absent from work without authorization. Finally, its investigating team reported after investigation that, "The hierarchy of salaries and pensions for the staff as a whole in too many cases is inversely proportional to the level of qualifications and responsibilities required." Notice the use of the term "required." UN policymakers were enunciating the task performance demand of resource suppliers (TE.21) and the fact that job designs (CI.22) should be logically related to ultimate service demands (TE.1).

Spokesmen for the unions that represent employees at the headquarters pointed out that they had in the past been successful in a strike that shut down most operations in Geneva. They expressed fear that the freeze on salaries, which the General Assembly had instituted until the special committee's work was finished, might last too long. Should this occur, they said, there could be another general strike.

270

Relations of Worker Demands
to Other Demands

In this chapter we have seen a wide range of workers' needs and of mechanisms by which workers translate these needs into demands. From the strategic point of view, these needs and demands are facts of life. They are to be taken in the same sense that consumers have needs (TE.1), stockholders and taxpayers have needs (TE.2), cultural constituencies have needs (CE), and managers in organizations have needs (CI.1).

Of course, all of this complexity presents a seemingly disorganized and insurmountable problem for policymakers. On the one hand, demands from various groups are not theoretical, as case histories in the last four chapters have shown. They are very real. On the other hand, it is abundantly clear that there are very few policymaking situations in which all demands can be satisfied. That would be Utopia. And Utopias do not exist in the real world of government and business.

Given such complexity, how can strategists and policymakers hope to make sense of their responsibilities and execute them in real situations? Parts II and III have at least shown a way to organize the demands into categories useful for decision-making purposes. These categories become factors or variables to be used in the problem-solving process. It remains to us in Part IV to suggest ways in which policymakers might further use these factors in strategic leadership.

Notes

1. Chester I. Barnard, *Functions of the Executive*, Harvard University Press, 1954, pp. 161–84.

2. James G. March and H. A. Simon, *Organizations*, Wiley, 1958, pp. 48–53, 84–94.

3. Alfred Marshall, *Principles of Economics*, Macmillan, 1952 edition, Chapter 8.

4. Joseph A. Schumpeter, *The Theory of Economic Development*, Oxford University Press, 1934, pp. 74–94; *History of Economic Analysis*, Oxford University Press, 1954, pp. 893–900.

5. F. M. Scherer, *Industrial Market Structure and Economic Performance*, Rand McNally, 1971.

6. Mary P. Follett, "Constructive Conflict," in *Dynamic Administration*, edited by H. Metcalf and L. Urwick, Harper, 1940, pp. 30–49.

7. F. J. Roethlisberger and W. Dickson, *Management and the Worker*, Harvard University Press, 1939.

8. Edgar H. Schein, *Organizational Psychology*, Prentice-Hall, 1970, pp. 50–55.

9. Amatai Etzioni, *A Comparative Analysis of Complex Organizations*, The Free Press, 1961.

10. Barnard, *Functions of the Executive*; Herbert A. Simon, *Administrative Behavior*, The Free Press, 1976.

11. For a summary of this tradition, see Lickert, Rensis, *New Patterns of Management*, McGraw-Hill, 1961; *The Human Organization*, McGraw-Hill, 1967.

12. R. M. Stogdill, *Handbook of Leadership*, The Free Press, 1974.

13. Fred E. Fiedler, *A Theory of Leadership Effectiveness*, McGraw-Hill, 1967.

14. Abraham Maslow, *Motivation and Personality*, Harper, 1954.

15. Chris Argyris, *Personality and Organization*, Harper, 1957.

16. Douglas McGregor, *The Human Side of Enterprise*, McGraw-Hill, 1960.

17. Frederick Herzberg et al., *The Motivation to Work*, Wiley, 1959.

18. David C. McClelland, *The Achieving Society*, Irvington, 1961.

19. F. Luthans and R. Kreitner, *Organizational Behavior Modification*, Scott, Foresman, 1975. This book summarizes for the layman the work of B. F. Skinner, author of the most important research studies in behavioral psychology.

20. E. A. Locke, "Toward a Theory of Task, Motivation and Incentives." *Organizational Behavior and Human Performance* 3 (1968): 157–59.

21. Alfred North Whitehead, *Science and the Modern World*, Mentor, 1948, pp. 4–5.

22. J. W. N. Sullivan, *The Limitations of Science*, Mentor, 1949, pp. 128–30.

23. Albert Einstein, *Essays in Science*, Philosophical Library, 1934.

24. Unless otherwise specified, cases from: Conflict Between Cultural Constituencies (case file), Appendix.

25. United States Steel Corporation, Appendix.

26. Harry Bridges and the ILUW, Appendix.

27. Trans World Airlines, Appendix.

28. J. D. Glover, R. M. Hower, and R. Tagiuri, *The Administrator*, Richard D. Irwin, 1973.

29. Jay W. Lorsch and Paul Lawrence, Richard D. Irwin, 1972.

30. G. W. Dalton and Paul Lawrence, Richard D. Irwin, 1971.

31. Paul Lawrence et al., Richard D. Irwin, 1976.

32. National Elevator Company, Appendix.

33. Ontario Manufacturing Company, Appendix.

34. SAAB Automobile Engine Assembly Department, Appendix.

35. Professional Standards Review Organizations (case file), Appendix.

36. Unless otherwise specified, these case histories are from Conflicts Between Work Processes and Job Security (case file), Appendix.

37. National Motor Parts Company, Appendix.

38. Walter L. Balk, "Decision Constructs and the Politics of Production," in *Productivity in Public Organizations*, edited by Marc Holzer, Kennikat Press, 1976, pp. 173–95.

39. F. C. Thayer, "The President's Management 'Reforms': Theory X Triumphant;" L. C. Howard, "Civil Service Reform: A Minority and Woman's Perspective;" *Public Administration Review* 38:4 (July 1978): 305–314.

PART IV

STRATEGIC LEADERSHIP

CHAPTER 10

Strategic Leadership Patterns

Strategic Leadership: A Summary

In Part II, this book described how organizations progress through the first two stages of their life cycles. It has drawn on experiences in retail stores, health care systems, banks, symphony orchestras, national park systems, electric utilities, law schools, and chemical companies to show that successful organizations grow because their primary missions (product outputs and resource allocations) are aligned with society, and to show that strategic decision making (policy formulation and strategy formulation) is a central factor that causes them to be aligned with society.

In Chapter 10 we will argue that the leadership pattern used by strategists in growing and developing organizations can serve as an ideal model for strategic leadership. A closer look at this leadership pattern will show that it produces a chain of five events, each of which "causes" or "builds on" the other:

1. Strategic decision making (strategy formulation and policy formulation) increases the *power* of the organization in society.
2. It increases the influence of the organization in society.
3. As a result of 1 and 2 it increases the freedom and autonomy of strategists—their discretion to make strategic decisions.
4. As a result of 1 and 2 it increases the communicational influence (charisma) of strategists: their coherence and their credibility as suppliers of needs of constituencies.
5. As a result of 1 and 2 it increases the strategic group's ability to use whatever power and authority it has to enforce imperfect alignments.

This chain of events in strategic leadership shows that the influence and power of the organization itself as well as of the strategic group, depends in the last analysis on strategic task alignment, the alignment of primary missions. It is this alignment which determines how well the three parties in the strategic system adjust to each other. If strategic leadership is successful in creating such an integration, the power and influence of both the organization and the strategic group will be increased. If it is not successful, the power and influence of the organization, and the discretion society allows to the strategic group to continue "leading" the organization, will decrease.

Chapter 10 will also show, however, that this ideal model breaks down in the period of conflict. The same cycle of five events that was so successful in the growth stage is set in reverse motion in the conflict and disintegration stages. The first cause is the same: strategies and policies get out of line with society, and, as a consequence, both the power and the legitimacy image of the organization deteriorates. These two factors set off a deterioration in the discretion society allows strategists in setting organization goals, in the credibility of strategists as they try to explain what they are doing, and in the strategists' own ability to use whatever authority and power they have.

Finally, in Chapter 10 we will look at the root causes of breakdown and the chain of other events that these set off to cause further breakdown. In summary, there are five defects in the strategic systems of developed organizations which themselves are the seeds of disintegration. These defects affect the cognitive (intellectual) ability of the strategic group to continue effective strategy and policy formulation. They also affect the emotional willingness of strategists to continue to cope with complexity and conflict. Strategists are either paralyzed and become inactive, or are thrown into active leadership patterns that *increase* rather than decrease conflict, and that *hasten* rather than retard, disintegration.

In Chapter 11 we will use causes of disintegration as the starting point to ask, "What can be done about it?" The breakdown of organizations, and its causes, is not a matter to be taken lightly. As Chapter 1 pointed out, this book will not take the position that all organizations either *should* or *can* live forever. Rather, those organizations which can, at the conflict stage, realign themselves with society, should continue to grow. Those which cannot should disintegrate. Furthermore, as Chapters 6–9 have shown, the strategic system is an enormously complex mixture of technological and human events. It may be presumptious even to inquire as to whether

276

leadership *can* fly in the face of natural forces of disintegration. Chapter 11 will, therefore, be speculative and tentative. It will simply suggest leadership patterns that might be able to cope with the larger and more complex organizations of tomorrow's industrial civilization.

Task Alignment as Power

The beginning of the chain of five leadership acts, or leadership events, is the comprehensive strategic task alignment. In successful organizations, formulating this alignment is in itself the central act of strategic leadership. It results in a certain pattern of organization that is aligned with the needs of society. This pattern is composed of (1) a set of outputs to society (TE, products, services, and programs) and (2) a set of internal resource competences (TI, capital, organization, operating processes, and work designs). These real (objective) alignments are created by the two decision processes described in Chapters 3–5, strategy formulation and policy formulation.

In viewing the task alignment as a source of power, it is convenient to start with the difference in power and influence. Power is the possession of current resources and the ability to continuously attract future resources to meet challenges in the future. Influence is the ability of an organization (1) to create in the minds of constituencies positive attitudes toward, beliefs in, and images of the organization's goals and (2) to gain from society the autonomy, discretion, and authority necessary to set goals in the future.

There are at least two powerful explanations from modern social sciences as to why an alignment, the kind discussed in Chapters 3–5, is a source of power: the exchange/historical explanation in this book, and the population/ecology explanation from sociology. Both of these are variations of what was called, in Chapter 1, the cultural anthropology viewpoint.

The Exchange/Historical Explanation

Exchange, already explained in Chapter 1, shows that organizations are open systems, that to survive they depend on the external world for resources, and that they cannot get this support without producing something of value for society. As the organization moves through its growth and development stage, growth is, in the last analysis, a stream of successful actions the organization takes to meet challenges in its outside world—the mastery of opportunities "out there" and the avoidance of threats "out there."

The process of meeting challenges is in turn an interactive series of events. In meeting each challenge, the organization acquires

277

distinctive competences of two types: *external* competences (TE, products and services of use to certain market or population segments) and *internal* competences (TI, resource configurations or patterns). As the *richness* (number, size, variety) of competences increases, the abilities of the organization to meet future challenges increase. The probability that the organization can and will meet future challenges increases. In this process, the organization also creates a distinctiveness, a specialization, or a variation for itself. It is unlike other organizations in the total strategic system. It has a specialized functional relationship, a niche or domain that relates it to the rest of society. Because of all of these things it has the power to exist, to survive, and to grow in society, and to achieve greater functional worth to society. In return, it receives the nourishment (resources) for survival and growth.

We saw how the Southland Company, originally operating a chain of ice service stations in Texas, met the challenge when General Electric developed electric refrigerators. It met the challenge by changing its output to society. It changed these ice stations into small 7-11 convenience stores. In doing so, the company had to learn a new set of internal competences. These competences in turn enabled the company to open still other stores, to expand to still other markets, and to attract $2.1 billion each year from outside resource suppliers.

We also saw how the United States Office of Education met one challenge, the fact that a large percentage of the United States population's skill in reading and writing is below that required to function effectively in today's society. The Office of Education had no previously learned competences in remedial reading programs for adults, though it did have a rich set of competences in high school education programs and elementary school programs. The global goal of the new service (TE, the Right to Read Program) was conceptualized as achieving a 90 percent literacy rate among adult citizens of the United States within nine years. First, a few local programs were established by an act of organization design (TI.12). They provided rich new specializations and competences (TI.11, TI.21, TI.22) inside the USOE. These competences in turn made possible the opening of 120 branches, to serve 120 new constituencies across the nation. Total performance of the Office of Education, including the successful meeting of this challenge, is a major factor in attracting budget funds from headquarters, the Department of Health, Education, and Welfare. As these funds are attracted, still more challenges can be met by the creative act of strategy formulation, similar to that done by Hewlett Packard and Bill Kemsley (Chapter 1).

278

The Population/Ecology Explanation[1]

A second explanation of how organizations gain power to survive and master environments stems from the biological evolution model first conceptualized in Darwin's *The Origin of Species* and later applied to social organizations by Herbert Spencer. In this social Darwinism model the whole process of evolution of organizations is comprised of three stages: variation, selection, and retention. Using this model, we can interpret the Timex Watch Corporation case (Chapter 5) as follows.

Timex, for whatever reason, *varies* from all other organizations in society in two respects. First, it is different in its product/markets, and second, it is different in its internal resource configuration. For example, the Timex watch (TE) had a metal case that was different from those of Swiss watches. It had a pin-lever mechanism to drive the hands instead of the Swiss jeweled-lever mechanism. Internally, (TI), Timex used mass-production lines whereas Swiss companies used hand-crafting at work stations. Timex distributed through drugstores whereas Swiss companies distributed through jewelry stores. These numerous variations, each suited to a certain environment, enable Timex to adapt to its environment rather than die. The greater the variations (the larger the number of products, and the richer the complexity of internal resources) the greater the chance Timex has to survive and grow in the technological and human system (ecological or population system) which we call society. In Chapter 1, one of the goals of this book was listed as explaining the behavior of three actors in the strategic arena or strategic system: the network of constituencies around an organization, the organization itself, and strategists (the central groups that integrate the other two).

In the language of the population ecology model, the strategic system becomes the ecological system. It is the Timex Corporation embedded in its total environment. Variation is both a state at any one time (Timex Corporation's distinctiveness in products, markets, and internal resources) and a process (Timex Corporation's continuous acts to maintain itself as a separate, specialized, distinctive species). This process of continuously meeting challenges can also be called *mutation*.

How is this process accomplished by Timex Corporation? It is accomplished in the same way that (as Charles Darwin showed) plant and animal species accomplished it. In the same way (as Herbert Spencer showed) that social groups accomplish it. In the same way (as modern sociologists show) that organizations accomplish it.

Selection is the process by which an organization senses the outside world and attends to opportunities and threats that are relevant to its own survival and growth. As Lemkuhl and the strategic group in Timex looked into the world, they were aware that Timex had a distinctive competence, a mechanism that served to clock time for artillery shells in World War II. But World War II was over in 1945, the environment around the company was changing, and Timex was in danger of becoming extinct. Lemkuhl and the strategic group scanned the environment and selected from it things like the former Waterbury Clock Company's cheap watch. They saw that watches manufactured by other companies, Swiss as well as American, were available only to limited segments of the population, that they were expensive, and that they were usually sold as jewelry. They had an idea: why not combine the existing competence in precision tooling and engineering with the new environment? Thus, variation became environmental scanning and forecasting, and a tentative hypothesis of how the corporation *might* select, out of millions of alternatives in a complex world, a match between itself and its external ecological system. These were acts of *strategy formulation:* a conceptual vision of a broad net- work of external product/markets related to a network of internal resources.

The long processes of adaptation and mutation, are a matter of time, of trial-and-error discovery, and sometimes accidental discovery. In this process the organization retains that which is really (objectively) workable and discards that which is not. This process, we have seen, is also called *policy formulation*. Timex's strategists were wrong in a part (a "piece" or "increment") of their strategy. The policy on distributing watches did not align with the environment. Specifically, strategists in jewelry stores (another species in the Timex environment) had *learned*, adapted, and mutated to their present place in the ecological system, too. They did not wish to give up the niche that they had learned to occupy. They refused to sell the cheap watch (it did not provide them as much in markup-margin resources, or fit the "image" that customers had learned to expect from a jewelry store). But Timex did what all mutating organisms (at least those which survive) do. It engaged in a balancing act between its present nature (its more or less stable strategy) and its new nature (a required change). Timex strategists formulated a new distribution policy, taking into account its present holistic strategy. In this process, it dropped or discarded an unworkable policy, distribution. This policy did not *align with* other policies in the master

280

strategy: the policies of low price, mass production, and mass advertising.

Before leaving the population/ecology explanation of organizational survival and growth, we should be aware of important similarities and differences between this theory and the theory of historical evolution in this book. Like the exchange/historical model, the population/ecology model predicts that organizations must go through successive mutation processes of variation, selection, and retention in order to survive. Both theories predict that the source of change can come from inside the organization (some defect is found in the present form of organization) or outside the organization (some pressure or force threatens survival). In both the organization can actually change its environment (migrate to new domains or niches). Beyond this, the population ecology theory tends to minimize the *proactive* "determination of one's own destiny" as the cause of adaptation. Or it assumes that the whole process is one of chance and random accident. This latter assumption leads some authors to the conclusion that organizations really have very little control over their environment.[2]

The position taken in this book is that such a view is caused because the population ecology model relies too heavily on the evolutionary process originally discovered in natural sciences as contrasted with social sciences. Evolution of plant and animal species is one thing but evolution of human organizations is another. The former are more subject to the vicissitudes of nature because their intellectual mechanisms are more restricted, and because their internal organic resources are determined more by nature than by acts of intellectual will. Chapters 3–5 seem to demonstrate the opposite in the case of productive organizations in business and government. Strategists do indeed have conceptual visions that are proactive. They do indeed set these visions into motion by deliberate acts of organization design, capital-equipment design, operating-process design, and work design. Thus, after *selection*, which is heavily influenced by acts of will and intellect, the next step is *retention* by trial and error. Policy formulation (retention) also involves deliberate acts of intellect and will. In both processes the role of the strategic group in determining the ultimate destiny of the organization is important.

For additional understanding of the metaphysical question of which comes first—the organization's existing competence and niche as it affects the environment or the environment as it affects the organization's competence—one should realize that even in

281

biological evolution, some writers have held that the anatomy and physiology of a plant or animal species

> is what it is because of the pattern of successful adaptation built into its genes. It is programmed to grow and develop in a highly specific way, and the program is transmitted from generation to generation in the genetic code. If we know enough, on the one hand, about its evolutionary history, we will be able to answer the deliberately naive questions: Why is it like it is? Why does it do what it does? It is like it is because of the history of its adaptational strategies. It does what it does because this behavior has paid off in the struggle for survival.[3]

According to this statement there is proactive behavior even in plants and animals, extremely crude by human standards but nevertheless a behavior that could be called learning. The fact that some authors use the term "adaptational strategies" is of particular significance to strategists in government agencies and business corporations.[4]

Translated into these terms, Timex Corporation's distinctive competences (the entire complex network of interrelated internal and external parts described in Chapter 5) make up a *pattern* or *form* built into the corporate genes at any one point of time. "Genes" in this case are the thousands of interrelated products, markets, manufacturing processes, advertising practices, retail store relationships, financing methods, and human work designs that have been learned by the corporation over time. The "genetic code program" is comprised of an equally complex system of formal and informal practices. Formal statements of policy, production-process flows, engineering diagrams, budget systems, dealer-relations policies, and reward systems, all become part of the code. Even a rule that employees get four weeks vacation each year is part of the code. Informal customs, developed as they have been over history, are part of the "common law code" as contrasted with the formal "legislative law code." These customs include the facts that the strategic group in Timex believed that borrowing from banks was not a proper way to finance the corporation and that the salespersons believed that retail store-owners should be treated with courtesy. Only when one puts together thousands of pieces of Timex's genetic code, its outward appearing formal rules *and* its hidden customs and practices, does the true nature and essence of the corporation emerge. In this sense, the objective or real strategy of the corporation, resulting from perceived strategies during strategy and policy formulation, is a genetic code. This is a highly important fact for strategists in Timex at

282

any one time. It means that what strategists in 1950 do is bound to put boundaries around what strategists in 1985 can do. If strategists in 1985 are to act responsibly in the interests of the organization and of society, they must not only have a sense of history, they must view the future as history. They must predict the future in some way regardless of whether this can be done with scientific accuracy.

Task Alignment as Influence: Legitimacy and Social Responsibility

Earlier in this chapter we saw that one form of influence is the ability of an organization to create in the minds of citizens in society positive attitudes, beliefs, and images about itself, its products, its markets, and its ways of internally carrying out its operations.

Sociologists have used the term *legitimacy* to denote a particular belief about an organization such as a police department or a manufacturing company. This is global or summary belief, a theme in the minds of human beings that "this company is good," or "that agency has a legitimate place in society," or "that aircraft manufacturing company has a legitimate right to continue its operations."

Another way to state this belief is in language very much in use by business executives and government officials today. The same themes can be expressed as "that insurance company is socially responsible" or "those nursing homes are carrying out their ethical responsibilities to society."

Of course, these, like many other themes discussed so far, have some relevance to strategists but they are entirely too general to bridge the gap between philosophy and practice. It must become possible to express the general concepts of social responsibility and legitimacy in a way that shows who is holding these beliefs and why.

One way to move closer to reality is to realize that the whole society around the organization (including internal employees acting in their roles as human beings and citizens, rather than in their roles as resources for production) is not composed simply of two big divisions, those who believe that the organization is legitimate and those who believe that it is not. Rather, the society is split into *zones*, containing subgroups, each of which believes and acts differently toward the organization. Each has a mental image of its own relationship to the organization.

The *zone of support* is composed of constituencies that actively support the organization through resources or political help. For example, the Boston Symphony Orchestra (Chapter 5) had task constituencies that were directly involved with its primary mission.

283

It had audiences that liked its repertoire, wealthy individuals who sought to support the Symphony, and the National Endowment for the Arts, a federal agency that sought to foster the arts for the population. It had players and conductors who wanted work, self-expression, and a means to earn a livelihood. As Chapter 6 pointed out, other groups in the cultural environment may arise that are not receiving direct functional benefits from the orchestra but that, for their own self interests, support the orchestra's work. For example, one group may be interested in developing Boston as a world commercial center, and may believe that a good orchestra will cause more electronics companies to move their headquarters and employees to Boston. Another may be interested in Boston as a place with low unemployment. The orchestra not only employs musicians, but electricians for lighting the hall, and ticket agencies to handle subscriptions. It generates employment in hotels because people regularly come from as far away as Canada and New Hampshire to hear an excellent orchestra.

The *zone of approval* contains a cluster of constituencies that, though not actively supporting the orchestra, nevertheless feel that the orchestra is good, that it is a legitimate part of the community, and that it should be supported if, say, a referendum were taken. These cultural constituencies range all the way from those which take pride in having excellent and successful organizations as part of their social system to those which have a nonspecific belief that the organization may some day "do them some good." An excellent example of such a constituency was found in a long case history describing the Seattle-Tacoma International Airport.[5] In a carefully designed public opinion poll, it was found that a sizable segment of the population in western Washington State takes pride in this airport, and believes that it is one of the "best-operated" airports in the United States. Somewhat surprising to airport strategists, this segment of people, who incidentally did not directly use the airport, were willing to vote more county tax money to subsidize the airport "should this become necessary."

The *zone of opposition* arises somewhere in stage 2 of organization development. It is composed of a network of constituencies described in Chapters 6–9. These constituencies have their now-familiar reasons for opposing the Boston Symphony Orchestra or the Seattle Airport. They can be broken down into external opposers (Chapters 6–7) and internal opposers (Chapters 8–9).

The *zone of indifference* is the large part of society that simply does not have the Symphony or the airport registered on its perception screen for taking actions. To these groups, the Symphony is

284

neither good nor bad. They have no functional or cognitive ties with it. Like organisms in a natural ecological system, which do not come into contact with each other except *very* indirectly, their theme would be something like "live and let live," or "I'm doing my thing and the Symphony is doing its thing."

From this list of publics, it can be seen that the first two have legitimacy images of an organization for various reasons. The important point is that these *sociological images grow out of and are derived from the task alignments* that are formed as the Boston Symphony mutates its services (repertoire of music), client constituencies (various groups who have different incomes and like different types of music), and internal resources (Symphony Hall, the Tanglewood Festival grounds, the Charles River Open Concert Shell, the quality of musicians and conductors hired, etc.). Task alignments are indeed a powerful act of influence—so powerful, in fact, that one prominent sociologist holds that organization growth and development depends on how well strategists can increase the functional significance of the organization to society.[6] This of course means somehow expanding the zone of support and the zone of approval, somehow narrowing the zone of opposition, and somehow converting parts of the zone of indifference into the zones of support and approval. In Chapter 11 we will speculate on some ways these things might be carried out.

Discretion, Autonomy, and Authority of the Strategic Group

In the beginning of this chapter we recognized an additional kind of influence: the ability of an organization to cause society to give it freedom to continue meeting challenges, and to continue innovating its products, services, constituencies, and resources. Though on first thought this may seem the same kind of influence as legitimacy, it is different in two important respects.

First, the belief in legitimacy is an attitude toward what the organization *is*, what its meaning in society has been and is *today*. Based on that performance, another attitude develops, a faith in the organization's ability to continue adjusting in the *future*, regardless of what specific goals may be envisioned. It is a nonspecific attitude that says, in effect, "We will delegate to you the right to formulate new visions, and engage in new experimental policy formulation, without even knowing what the content of these products or services might be." Thus, the National Endowment for the Arts, having seen the strategists in the Boston Symphony offer new music to new

285

audiences, having seen them include low-income groups as constituencies by lowering the price of subscription tickets, and having seen them do this by not wasting capital resources of Symphony Hall, gives the Symphony a nonrestricted grant to help develop itself in the future. The voters of King County, having seen the airport strategists solve its internal operating process problems (traffic congestion on access roads), secure better routes for citizens (by allocating its airspace for maximum numbers of landings and takeoffs), and decrease noise pollution for homeowners (by restrictive rules on which craft can use the airspace), delegate to the strategists in the future the right to make still other, but unknown changes.

This points up the second characteristic of discretionary influence as contrasted with legitimacy influence. It results in a right granted to the strategic group, rather than a legitimacy granted to the organization. Though few people in society can name the members of the strategic group in either the Boston Symphony or the Port of Seattle, most people realize that there is such a group and that it is a very important factor in what the organization will be in the future.

Charismatic Leadership Roles

The Concept of Charisma

The idea of charismatic leadership was first conceptualized by Rudoph Sohm in 1892. Sohm found that charisma was an important factor in the foundation and growth of religions. He postulated that all religions that succeed in growing from small groups into expanding "movements" do so because one or more leaders conceptualize for members what is thought to be the will of some divine being. He argued that these leaders themselves have a faith (strong belief) in their conceptual visions. Followers, in turn, have a faith (strong belief) in the ability of leaders to "see" the will of God and to elaborate it into religious customs and practices. Max Weber, early in this century, used the concept in his theory of authority in secular organizations. He was interested in how political and social organizations become organized, and the role leaders play in this kind of organization. Particularly, he wanted to answer the question, "Why do people obey the authority of leaders?" His famous answer was that there are three reasons. Sometimes it is because of traditional dignity and custom (as in the case of hereditary status and position). Sometimes it is because of official or legal status (as in the case of appointed officials). Finally, it is sometimes simply a faith (strong belief) in the ability of a leader to innovate or change things to a

286

situation that is *different from* the situation the followers find themselves in.

The theory of charisma has been criticized by some social scientists and praised by others.[7] Some critics have pointed out that the religious phenomena in Sohm's original concept (e.g., the relationship of disciples to a master, in which followers have a religious devotion to the leader) simply are not relevant to modern political or economic organizations. Others have pointed out that even if such concepts can be applied in this century to societies that are emerging from undeveloped nations with low educational levels to full-blown industrialized nations (e.g., Ghandi's leadership in India, Nkrumah's leadership in Ghana), they are not valid when applied to developed industrial nations in which the population is highly educated.

Social scientists who favor Weber's theory have shown that charisma is indeed relevant to developed nations, especially when there is a large amount of uncertainty in the minds of followers that is caused by complex and swiftly changing events. They show that the response of American citizens to Franklin D. Roosevelt's leadership in 1933, the response of British citizens to Winston Churchill's leadership in 1940, or the response of American citizens to John F. Kennedy's leadership in the 1960s all contained the characteristics of charisma.

This controversy provides an important lesson for those who use the theory of charisma for understanding leadership in any society or organization. On the one hand, charismatic leadership is situational. Whether it exists or can exist depends in part on the behavioral codes and practices in the culture under study. It is one thing to study charisma in a culture where people relate to leaders as disciples to a master and it is another thing where people relate to leaders as prime ministers or presidents. On the other hand, there seem to be certain common characteristics in the behavior of both leaders and followers, regardless of the situation. It is these common characteristics that are of use to strategists in modern business and government organizations.

First, leaders and followers find themselves in a strategic system that has a complex problem—complex enough that persons inside and outside the organization begin to feel that "things are out of control" or that "neither we nor our leaders can make sense out of this." In language of this book, the three actors in the strategic system are out of alignment. All concerned sense that the existing way of doing things, both technologies and human organization practices, will not solve the problem. This in turn causes feelings of

287

anxiety, distress, frustration, ambivalence. People are no longer able to make sense of the situation. They suffer an "identity vacuum" in terms of both what the system is and what their place in the system is. In modern organization-theory terms, there is a high degree of *uncertainty* in the minds of all. There is finally an inability of all concerned clearly to diagnose the problem (put it into a framework that can be understood) and certainly to formulate solutions.

Second, some leaders do diagnose the problem. They put it into terms they themselves can understand and that other parties can at least partly understand. As a result of this understanding, the leaders themselves have faith in (believe in) their formulation of the problem and their solution. In modern expectancy theory terms, this gives them the arousal or motivation to be persistent in trying to solve the problem, and to devote the large amount of energy necessary to try to put solutions into practice.

If we look at the behavior of strategists in Sears, Roebuck, HEW, or DuPont (Chapters 3–5), the complexity of the problem is evident. The persistence and energy required to engineer programs of that magnitude into practice must come from somewhere. The energy required of the commissioner of Education as he engaged in ten years of trial-and-error formulation came from faith in the global strategy (90 percent literacy rate in the United States in ten years, the vision of branch programs across the nation). The persistence of HEW officials, and of Dr. Gilbertson in Minneapolis (Chapter 3) in executing the PSRO program in hospitals, even in the face of working out many conflicting details, came from their faith in a global strategy for increasing the quality of patient care and, at the same time, conserving valuable capital resources of society.

Third, people who have faith in the leader's ability to see the complex problem, and to do something about it, confer charisma on the leaders. This occurs in two ways, depending on the stage of development of the organization. In the inception stage, there is simply faith in the vision itself, in the perceptions in strategists' minds. Global goals are appealing emotionally because they make some sense of the situation. The development stage is the crucial test of whether perceived visions will be built into *movements*, that is, into real institutions (with resources and services) that begin to solve real problems. Weber himself was well aware that charisma (faith) had to be substantiated by evidences of real performance. It had to be reinforced by evidence, in order to maintain the influence of the leaders. It is here that policy formulation comes in. In the histories reviewed in earlier chapters, it is evident that the original *inspiration* (*begeisterung*) provided by Hewlett and Packard or Bill

288

Kemsley in the inception stage of their organizations would have never attracted capital from bankers, or membership fees from hikers, had not the real policies of Hewlett Packard Corporation and the American Hiking Society materialized in real programs and paid off to constituencies in real terms.

Weber made it clear that throughout the growth and development stage it was not necessary that followers *agree* with leaders on all occasions, or even that they refrain from arguing with leaders. It is well known, for example, that Lenin, as founder and principal leader of the Bolshevik movement, encountered powerful disagreements among peers long before he had the official power to deal with them as a hierarchical "boss." What was required, however, was a coherent vision of what the problem was and what could be done about it, and an ability to articulate that vision in terms clear enough that both he and most followers could understand it.

Two final comments on the meaning of the term "charisma" may help us more fully to understand the motivation itself. First, in today's organizations of the type we are studying, it is partly an emotional feeling (faith in the leader personally) and partly a cognitive concept (belief in a global strategy the leader has formulated). Psychologists have always realized that there is a very narrow line between beliefs as acts of intellect (cognitive acts) and as acts of emotion (conative acts). Charisma is partly both. Second, it is a faith and belief held by *both* leaders and followers. In those situations where it has operated in practice, leaders were not simply "public relations types." They could not sustain the kind of behavior they did had they simply been trying to "fool" the public. Followers could not have rallied to the cause had they not sensed the commitment of leaders. Third, various words have been used to try to describe the *active* form of charisma. "Faith" and "belief" are inactive words. Some writers have used the word "enthusiasm" to denote the active arousal of "motivation to action." McClelland has pointed out that the nearest English translation of Weber's original word *Begeisterung* is "inspiration."[8] This, then, is what the psychology of expectancy would say causes arousal in both leaders and followers. Both become proactive workers for the cause. Both are activists. Both "arise to action."

Sources of Charisma: A Restatement

In terms of modern organizations such as this book studies, a restatement of charismatic leadership is necessary to show the leader's role in relation to followers. The central influence mechanism that runs throughout all the earlier discussion is a belief in the leader's ability to conceptualize the problem and to formulate solutions.

There is one view of "the problem" which we have not yet looked at and which can now be seen. "The problem" is one of opposed forces. On the one hand, actors in the policy arena need the certainty and security of the present order. They sense that history and tradition are the glue that holds the social order together, and that too much change (revolutionary chaos) is to be avoided if at all possible. Violent change may be necessary (and sometimes occurs) in stage 5. But in stage 3 there is what could be called a "hunger for stability." This motivation was stressed by the classical political philosophers, who were trying to explain why free people subjected themselves to the power and influence of new and emerging nations.[9] It is stressed by modern political scientists who are trying to explain why a group of proximate policymakers, none of whom have hierarchical power over the others, would form a coalition to support a certain policy alternative.[10] Opposing this desire is the equally strong need for change, what one author has called a "hunger for charisma."[11] There is, as Weber put it, a faith in leaders who will "repudiate the past."

The belief that leaders can maintain intact the functional or "good" parts of the old alignment stems from the organization's performance in the past. This has already been discussed as legitimacy. The belief that leaders can create new alignments, discarding the dysfunctional or "bad" parts of the old alignment, comes from the leaders' own behavior, their ability to formulate global alignments.

Communication of Strategy and Policy

The present section will argue that successful strategic alignments as described in Chapters 3–5 are in fact acts of influence. That is, these alignments, when communicated to other parties as global strategies, and when acted out in the reality of policy formulation, can generate in the minds of followers a faith in the ability of leaders and a belief that their strategies will solve crucial problems faced *by followers themselves*. In arguing this thesis, however, we can still recognize individual differences, and the fact that not all parties will share this faith. What the theories from social sciences and the case histories in this section do prove is that strategists who conceptualize effective global strategies, who communicate these to other parties, and who then engage in effective policy formulation, have a higher probability of influencing other parties, and of expanding the zone of organizational support, than leaders who do not act in these ways.

Communication is always a two-way process if it is successful in promoting mutual understanding. On the one hand, the sender of the message must have intellectual clarity in his or her own mind. Otherwise the message will be garbled in its original form. The sender must also have enough confidence in, belief in, and emotional commitment to the message that he or she can have the arousal motivation so necessary to attempt influencing others. On the other hand, the message must be stated in terms that mean something to the receiver. It must have intellectual content that is within the experience of the receiver, and it must have an emotional content that sufficiently arouses the receiver to devote enough energy to try to understand.

If one looks carefully at the global strategy statements of Hewlett Packard, Union Camp Corporation, Avionics Research Products, the Democratic party as conceptualized by Senator Jackson, or H.E.W. as it is explained by Robert Califano, one will see elements of effective communication.

There is other evidence that the acts of strategy and policy formulation themselves, and their communication to others influence behavior. Huntington, an eminent political scientist, while acknowledging that there is in the United States a "weakening of the coherence, purpose, and self-confidence of political leadership" and "a marked decline in the confidence of political leaders in themselves," nevertheless points to solid evidence that all organizations that have clear and specific goals, and that are deliberately and self-consciously organized, are better able to influence outsiders than are organizations that are more amorphous, less well organized and more diffuse in stating their goals.[12]

Sociologists who study sociocultural evolution of organizations have noted a similar relationship between clear strategic goals and the charismatic motivation of other parties. In organizations that are moving from loosely knit, amorphous social groupings (stage 1) into more structured institutions (stage 2), the group itself helps to develop a hierarchy of leadership as part of its distinctive competence to meet ecological challenges. "The group singles out persons who vary the customary practices in ways that appear more adaptive, and then the group elevates these persons to positions of authority."[13]

This finding is consistent with the charisma bestowed on Lenin as the Bolshevik party moved into full-scale institutional growth. One of the principal phenomena in Lenin's leadership, as well as in Churchill's, Roosevelt's, and Kennedy's, was an ability to conceptualize strategic plans that varied from the current practices of government, to have these appear [to other parties as] more

291

adaptive, and to influence other parties, which in turn elevates these persons to positions of authority.

These charismatic motivations in the follower group are similar to those expressed by middle managers (administrators) in case histories of Mobil Corporation,[14] IBM Corporation,[15] Roosevelt Hospital,[16] and Shoe Corporation of South Africa.[17] In all of these organizations, middle managers expressed thoughts similar to the following comment by P. J. Boglioli, manager of executive development for Mobil.

> He [the president] is an absolute wizard. He started out as a financial planner, but he has learned this business and its problems from stem to stern. When you add that kind of knowledge to a very sharp analytical mind, everybody in the company respects his decisions. You walk in his office with a complicated problem and he can cut through the confusion like nobody I have ever seen. We are very lucky to have him as president.

Evidence that clear goals, well articulated, in fact inspire external resource suppliers was reported in Chapter 3. Bank loan officers, as resource suppliers to corporations, are inspired by strategists who can present a coherent picture of company operations in the future. The United States government is equally inspired, since only those corporations which can satisfactorily spell out their strategies in terms understandable to the Securities and Exchange Commission are allowed to receive the right to issue stock to the public.

Another case history shows that persons at the administrative level (middle managers), if they become strategists on their own, can inspire their hierarchical "bosses" to follow their leadership.[18] In fact, this should be a crucial test of charisma since the bureaucracy higher up the chain of command actually had some reasons *not* to follow the leadership of their subordinates. In this case, the United States Navy Torpedo Station in Keyport, Washington, was a dying institution. It produced and tested what had, during World War II, been the Navy's most powerful weapon but was, in 1970, outdated by technologies of the nuclear age. Personnel at the base felt that they had many distinctive competences that should be of use to the navy. But they had witnessed a steady decline in resources (their budgets from Washington) because their strategic niche in the world was disappearing. These people also loved the region in which they lived and began to search for a more ecologically viable niche in the much larger bureaucracy, the United States Navy.

They instituted a strategic planning project that started by scanning the environment. The question asked at this point was, "What opportunities exist 'out there' for our distinctive competences?" Arriving eventually at 11 programs that might appeal to higher headquarters, together with the logic of how the complex of resources (human talents, physical terrain, etc.) aligned with the navy's global strategy, they presented their case both formally and informally up the navy's chain of command. The effort took considerable energy and persistence. There were times when the Keyport Station's out-of-date image in the minds of higher officials was an impediment. Various bureaus in Washington had the station catalogued in their memories as a certain species, one that fit the ecology of 40 years ago rather than the ecology of the last part of the twentieth century. Various other stations on the East Coast, each of which seemed more "modern" in nuclear technology, not only had the attention of higher headquarters but also put forth efforts themselves to mutate into a more important species in the naval establishment. Gradually, however, the strategic formulation envisioned by the Keyport group received both the political support and the resource (budget) support of higher headquarters officials. It was not hierarchical authority and power that swung the navy to support the strategy. It was the very careful "homework" done by strategists. This homework involved an orderly plan, composed of (1) a service goal (maintaining the navy's fleet of nuclear powered submarines) and (2) a set of internal physical resources and human talents that matched the service goal.

A final case will show that strategic leadership can also inspire employees inside the organization. This case history was written in the pharmaceutical industry in Iceland.[19] Strategists in the Department of Health, Justice, and Ecclesiastical Affairs were considering merging seven small pharmaceutical companies into one large company. Reasons for the merger included the fact that the seven were not the right species for the present society in Iceland and Iceland's place in the modern world (see Chapter 8). What was called for was a more varied and complex manufacturer of ethical drugs, one that had considerably richer competences than the existing companies.

In the course of writing this case, the author interviewed a number of younger pharmacists. Most of them were graduates of the Royal Danish School of Pharmacy in Copenhagen. All were work-level employees in the seven small companies. Mr. Axel Sigurdsson, immediate past president of the Icelandic Pharmacists' Association, indicated that he had recently changed jobs to one of the larger of the seven companies because,

293

Even though I was making more money at the other company, I came here because the company has a larger and more complex manufacturing operation. I can work on the making of complicated drugs, of great value in hospitals, and use the education I have. In the smaller company, I had to spend time on less complex activities that did not build my own competences as a pharmacist.

Regarding the possible merger of the seven companies into an even larger and more complex organization, Mr. Almar Grimsson, present president of the Pharmacists' Association, saw the advantage of the change to his own career development:

I prefer more complicated work because I feel I am accomplishing something. I can also see that the ethical drug industry in Iceland must be modernized to serve the people of Iceland, which it can do only if it has more advanced and specialized departments, the kind which you find in Denmark. The industry will never be able to serve our own population efficiently, or to export drugs and benefit the whole economy of Iceland, without extensive modernization of this type.

This statement shows two kinds of motivation that can be generated by strategic formulations that align with the social environment around the organization. First, there is the matter of personal competence. In building the competence of the organization, strategists were also building the career competences of operating-level employees. This has been called the "achievement motive" by McClelland and others.[20] It is considered by some authorities on organization development to be one of the most important inspirational motives in the work life of individuals.[21] Second, there is the matter of being a part of, or affiliated with, other human beings in an organization that itself has greater meaning in the larger society. Some call this esprit de corps. Psychologists today refer to it as the "affiliation motive."[22]

Further understanding of the relationship between strategic alignment and the affiliation motive can be had by considering the reverse of this motive: alienation. Sigurdsson and Grimssson were saying that they were *not part of* a company whose internal technology was ecologically modern. In the world production of pharmaceuticals, major products such as intravenous solutions and antibiotics are significant to a changing society. Companies such as Geigy in Switzerland and Lilly in the United States have niches in the world that fit modern society. The very small company that

Sigurdsson worked for was not rich enough in internal competences to produce products with high significance to society. In fact, it produced aspirin tablets, made on a single machine, and capsules filled by mixing powders. At the same time, the society in Iceland was changing and was importing all of its antibiotics.

What these two workers were saying, then, was that the new company would be more integrated with Icelandic society. It would produce something of significance for the people and for hospitals. It would perhaps be able to export some drugs, thus helping the country's economy. These things would to them be *involvement* (greater contribution) rather than *alienation* (gradually becoming out of date in contribution). By being able to use the complex education they learned in Denmark they would get a second benefit, over and above affiliation: achievement.

Initiative, Feasibility, Influence

Up to this point, we have seen that successful strategy formulation and policy formulation in stage 2 are themselves acts of power and influence. They *create* power and influence. They create legitimate power in the zone of support because they provide valuable outputs to task constituencies which cause the latter to respond by supplying resources in exchange. They create both legitimate and charismatic authority in the zone of support because these constituencies have faith and belief in the strategic alignment.

Strategy and policy formulation create legitimate and charismatic authority in the zone of approval, though to a lesser degree than in the zone of support. Because these constituencies have no direct functional (resource exchange) relationship with the organization, there is no power relationship here.

Strategic decision making creates a form of legitimate authority in the zone of indifference. Constituencies here are involved with the organization in no particular way. They acquiesce in the organization's activities, adopting a "live-and-let-live," indifferent attitude. They are saying, in effect, "You have freedom, discretion and legitimacy to proceed so long as you do not affect us one way or the other."

Source of Influence: Specialization

In Chapter 1 and later chapters we have pointed out that all organizations in fact have a group of influentials who specialize in trying to relate the total organization (its TI parts) to the social environment (TE, CE, CI). The "strategic level" is a fact of life in all

295

organizations beyond simple face-to-face social groups that have no technological outputs to the rest of the world. Strategic groups are a fact of life in small organizations that have tried to exist without "hierarchies," but that must somehow grapple with integrating a social system with a technological system. Research on small primitive societies in anthropology supports the existence of specialists.[23] Research on communes in the United States supports their existence.[24] Research on Kibbutz organizations in Israel supports their existence.[25] Even the New England town meetings of 1800 had to have agendas made up by some subgroup. What all of these small groups have found is that *pure* social relations "in a vacuum" are impossible. The world (i.e., a culture) is made up of both things and people, raw nature and raw humans, machine systems and human systems. Once this fact of complexity is recognized, it becomes impossible for any but the face-to-face group that assembles for friendship (that is, it consumes its own output and provides its own inputs) to exist without *some* mechanism for strategy formulation, however crude and informal that mechanism might be.

The same can be said for larger organizations. The existence of strategic groups was most forcefully put in Robert Michaels' "Iron Law of Oligarchy."[26] Michels studied socialist political parties in Germany to determine why such organizations as these, which, somewhat like Utopian communes, fervently wanted democracy, should end up by having de facto leadership groups—groups that seemed to formulate the strategy of the party. Were not such groups "elites," the very thing the socialist parties sought to avoid or eliminate? Michels found that the underlying causes for the existence of strategic groups included not only the fact that different persons have different abilities and ambitions, but the fact that it was impossible to keep every person equally informed of everything, no matter how much they tried. It was, as the ecological theories in this chapter have already predicted, impossible to exist unless certain persons specialized in monitoring the information flows from outside the organization while others specialized in other functions. Persons who end up at crucial points where information flows between the outside world and the inside world become "boundary spanners," "strategists," "proximate policymakers,"[10] or "institution-level managers."[6]

Influence of Initiative

What does this fact of life have to do with a more practical question, namely, what power does the strategic group really have to invoke its decisions? It means that, as Child has put it, the strategic group has the influence of initiative whereas other groups are "in a position of having to respond to such decisions."[27] There are two reasons for this. First, there is a probability that the strategic group knows more about the strategic fit than others. That is not because of heredity—the strategic group is not more intelligent than other groups; but because of environment—the group's day-to-day work activities generate specialized knowledge. Second, most rank-and-file constituencies are reluctant to take the initiative. Not only do they lack the knowledge possessed by the strategic group (they may make real mistakes or look ineffectual to their peers). They also lack the legitimacy (other peer parts of the system may resent one part assuming strategic initiative when in the past they have not been "expected" to do so).

In considering these assertions, we must be careful to remember the tentative and experimental posture of successful strategic groups in stage 2 of organization development. It is assumed that they have used policy formulation not only as a decision-making device (to discover alignments) but as a sociopolitical device (to pay attention to the humanistic demands of constituencies).

Feasibility Influence

Another way of viewing essentially the same kind of power is to shift from the notion of *initiative* to that of *feasibility*. The former comes from sociology whereas the latter comes from political science. Lindblom depicts the policymaking process in a democracy, or at least in democracies that stand the test of evolutionary survival, as composed of a ladder of influence.[28] At the bottom of the ladder are nonvoters (these would be in the zone of indifference). Proceeding upward, we find ordinary voters (those in the zone of mild support or opposition); politically active citizens (those in the zone of active support or opposition); lower-level interest group, public-opinion, and party leaders (middle-level managers); ordinary legislators and some administrators (higher in the middle level); legislative leaders, policymaking judges, (high-level administrators); congressional leaders, top administrators and supreme court justices (members of the strategic group); and president (most prominent coalition member in the strategic group).

Flowing up this ladder are communications that "constrain, instruct, command, permit, and otherwise bend" the strategists to the wishes of the next level below. These communications tell what is wanted. Flowing down the ladder are communications of what is

297

possible and feasible. Viewed in this way, the strategic group is making judgments on the pragmatic workability of the system, choosing policies and adjusting global strategies to balance the wants of constituencies.

Resource Power

A last form of power is well known. It is the possession of resources, or the ability to control the distribution of resources. These resources serve as either rewards or penalties to other groups. City councils and mayors have more impact on where budget funds are spent than ordinary citizens or department heads. The capital budget committee in General Motors has more impact on whether various divisions (Chevrolet, Pontiac, Oldsmobile, Buick, Cadillac) get large capital appropriations than any one division manager. The personnel committee in most organizations has more impact on what the wage rate is for one job classification than does any one employee, department head, or section head.

In our society, the control of money and budgets is the single most prevalent form of sanction or resource power. Indeed, the entire society of the Western World is based on the concept of private property precisely because the framers of governments believed that the control of resources is the most important cause of personal (or organizational) freedom. Though societies in Russia or Poland have decided that ownership of resources by private organizations in fact limited freedom, and therefore lodged ownership in the state, they have nevertheless substituted one group of strategists (bureaus, or commissariats) for another (private boards of directors) when it comes to allocating resources in society. In other words, both in the United States and in Russia there are still strategic groups that in fact have more impact on the allocation of resources than citizens, employees, or other organizational units.

By this time this universal existence of strategic groups should not be surprising. The reasons that these groups possess the ability to allocate resources are the same as the reasons that they have the initiative and feasibility influence. Namely, society cannot do without some partitioning of decision making and specialization. Even in Utopian organizations, such as communes, when the friendship group begins to engage in technological operations, such as growing crops or making furniture, some form of strategic specialization has always had to be devised.

Nonlegitimate Power

Earlier it was noted that successful strategic decision making in the growth and development stage generates *legitimate* power and authority of the organization, those forms of power and authority that are viewed positively by constituencies. Such decision making also generates charismatic authority of the strategic group.

We now come to what is undoubtedly one of the most controversial issues in all of organizational, governmental, and strategic theory: under what conditions do or should strategists utilize nonlegitimate power, power that is not acknowledged by the constituencies involved as "positive" or "right." To use terms more familiar in modern sociology and psychology, when do or should strategists use sanctions to dominate or coerce people rather than influence them to acknowledge legitimate forms of authority and power?

Here we will attempt to answer the descriptive question. When *do* strategists use nonlegitimate power? From society's point of view there is a very important difference in use of legitimate power and use of sanctions. The former indicates that large portions of society (in the zones of support, acceptance, and indifference) recognize both organizations and strategists as legitimate. The latter indicates that such legitimacy has been withdrawn.

In considering when such power is used, we must also realize that two things—initiative influence and resource sanctions—may be involved. The first is a form of "mind control," in which strategists define problems and solutions against the cognitive conclusions of other parties. The last is the more familiar "punishment by sanction," the withholding of rewards or the meting out of punishments.

In stage 2 of organization development, successful strategists *do* use nonlegitimate power in the zone of conflict after they have used their best efforts to align the organization with society. It is thus a residual power, used in a conflict zone that is relatively small and that is created because no alignment is ever perfect. The alignment can only approximately integrate the organization with the large network of constituencies. Why do they use it *then?* First, because they *have* it. They have enough sanctions and enough legitimate authority from the zones of support to do so. Second, there is an inevitable rule of justice, to be explained in Chapter 11, that is the only possible logic that matches the situation: the greatest good for the greatest number.

After the organization reaches stage 3, breakdown and conflict, there is no way to predict what strategists *do*. If anything, the argument later in this chapter suggests that they may attempt to

299

dominate constituencies but that this will not work in the long run. Here is the crux of the controversy: *Should* strategists use either mind control (initiative and feasibility) or resource control (sanctions) in the breakdown stage of organization development?

The answer to such a value-loaded question is best discussed not in global political terms, but in terms of the work expected of the strategic group. If we can somehow view this as a question of work responsibility rather than of godlike celestial responsibility, it will be more understandable. Briefly, the answer to the question is a qualified yes. But we must be very careful to specify under what conditions.

Self-Confidence: Professional Ethics

So far, each of the forms of power and influence we have discussed have been the result of an interaction between strategists and constituencies. In each, constituencies have had varying degrees of freedom either to confer on or deny to strategists their instruments of power and influence. They confer legitimate authority and charismatic authority partly because strategists influence them to do so and partly because they want to do so. They at least have some freedom to limit the boundaries of initiative power and feasibility power.

The next type of power we are about to examine comes not from society around the strategic group, but from within the strategic group itself, its own self-confidence and willingness to use all three of its powers (initiative, feasibility, and resource sanctions) to enforce strategic alignments. Because such a willingness is in the last analysis based on belief in one's own ethical righteousness, this form of power can be called "ethical power," "the ethics of professional practice," or "professional power."

In approaching the deliberate attempt to dominate any constituency in the zone of conflict, whether it be done by power over the human mind (initiative and feasibility influence) or by use of physical resources as sanctions (resource power), we must realize that this is an issue to be approached with caution. On the one hand we have seen that organizations cannot do without a strategic group. On the other, Lord Acton's famous words, "Power tends to corrupt and absolute power corrupts absolutely," sound a note of warning. So do the defense mechanisms by which any group develops "groupthink" (Chapter 8), the resignation of the president of the United States in 1975 (the Watergate scandal), the various maladaptive leader behaviors Toynbee found in advanced civilizations (to be discussed later), and the many findings of modern

300

behavioral sciences which show the dangers of authoritarian leadership.

Nevertheless, the model of strategy formulation we are examining has certain built-in mechanisms for preventing Lord Acton's corruptions. For one thing, social (ethical) responsibility is protected somewhat by the policy-formulation process, a trial-and-error, reality-facing stream of decisions during which constituencies not only act out their sanctions against the organization when their interests are not cared for, but a process in which the strategic group learns the diverse ethics of society. For another, each of the processes discussed in this chapter suggest that successful strategists use other means of power and influence first, before invoking sanctions against the restricted number of constituencies in the zone of conflict.

The following beliefs are the kind that help to define the overall relationship of strategists to other parties in the system. They are labeled "ethics" because they are beliefs about how the strategic group ought to view its place in the natural order.

Ethic 1: Law of the Situation

One of the conditions for the ethical use of power is that the strategic group must not have inherited an organization that has progressed from the breakdown stage into full disintegration. It must not have inherited from past strategists a disintegrated organization, one that is so out of alignment with the demands of constituencies that use of power to correct the situation would be ecologically unnatural. In such a case, use of power would not only be an attempt to dominate (rather than lead) human beings, it would be an attempt to mastermind *technologies* (products, markets, services, work designs) that simply do not fit the natural order, the balanced cultural system. Such domination and masterminding would increase progress toward disintegration rather than foster further growth and development. It would expand the zone of conflict at the expense of the zones of support, approval, and indifference.

Ethic 2: Responsibility for Future

It is because of the Law of the Situation that the second rule of strategic ethics can be stated as follows: *The strategic group is responsible to future generations in the strategic system—to the future organization, to future external constituencies, to future*

301

internal constituencies, and to future strategic groups. The fact that today's strategic decisions will affect tomorrow's integration or disintegration is the most powerful of all arguments for long-term horizon forecasting (however imperfect) and for strategic decision making. Disjointed policymaking with short-term horizons can damage the future strategic system's ability to cope. Those who cannot remember the past (do not have a sense of history), and who cannot use the past in coping in the future (cannot view the future as history) are doomed to lose control over their own destiny.

Ethic 3: Society and the Strategic Group

A second belief that strategists must have in order to wield their powers in a socially responsible manner is that society has (for good reason) a distrust of their role in society but at the same time has a deep and profound need for this role. Strategists must understand this often ambivalent feeling toward them if they are to make sense of their overall role in the natural order of things.

As McClelland puts it, most people in our own society, and probably most people in most societies throughout history, are suspicious of a person who wants power, even if that person should want it for sincere and altruistic reasons.[29] Successful strategists, like most socialized human beings, are conditioned to be suspicious of themselves. They do not want to be in the position of seeking power to exploit others. This is pronounced in a society that values freedom, democracy, and brotherly love, where brotherly love can be defined as helping other persons to be themselves, not to be something strategists want them to be. Furthermore, social suspicions of this type indeed have factual bases. The cliche that more crimes have been committed in the name of religion and truth than in the name of real brotherhood can be substantiated in history. Did not Pizarro annihilate the Indians of Peru in the name of God as well as in the name of gold? Did not Rev. Jim Jones lead several hundred men, women, and children of the People's Temple to suicide in the jungles of Guyana as recently as 1978? Did not Louis XIV, the Hapsburgs, the Romanovs, the Hohenzollerns, and Hitler wreck the social fabric of Europe?

Such social suspicions are hardly mitigated by research in contemporary psychology. One of today's definitive works on power is *The Authoritarian Personality.*[30] McClelland, a psychologist himself, notes that this book depicts persons with power motivations as "harsh, sadistic, fascist, Machiavellian, prejudiced, and neurotic." Further, works using this paradigm as a value theme also picture the

302

power relationship as one of "dominance and submission." These two terms are hardly descriptive science. They can as accurately be viewed as ethical concepts, with a strong "bad" (as contrasted with "good") connatation and with a strong "thou shalt not" as contrasted with "thou shalt" connotation.

The profession of medicine has the Hippocratic Oath to guide doctors in their relationships with their clients. This oath requires that the doctor "preserve human life above all." Such a belief defines the doctor's fundamental function in the universe. The profession of strategic leadership lacks such a generally accepted belief system. However, in suggesting such a system we must clearly recognize that ethical guidelines do not do away with the necessity for making judgments between conflicting values. "Human life above all" cannot be applied blindly. It becomes a sticky matter in wars, or when the parents of a person believe that the person has become a living vegetable and demand that the apparatus that has sustained breathing be turned off. Are strategists, as a profession, as concerned about their power relations in society as medical doctors? They ought to be.

Summarizing a third ethical condition for the social use of power, strategists must recognize their place in the order of things. They exist primarily because organizations have evolved their specialization (their species) to serve a function. Organizations desperately need strategists to do their part to keep the system in alignment. But sociey at the same time distrusts strategists, because strategists in the past have done as much to disintegrate organizations as they have to integrate them.

Ethic 4: Instruments of Power and Authority

Whether society, strategists, and psychologists like it or not, strategists in successful organizations (stage 2) in fact have two kinds of authority and three kinds of power. These are relationships of one group of human beings (strategists) to other human beings in the world (all other constituencies). It is important that strategists have a deep understanding of what these are, how they come about, and how they might be used for social good. It is equally important that strategists realize that these relationships can be used to destoy the very natural order that brought them into being.

Legitimate power and authority, and the discretion and autonomy of the strategic group, come into being through mutual adjustment. Strategists continuously cope to try to integrate the organization with society's needs. Legitimate authority can come

303

into being only through time. Charismatic authority is likewise a joint process, though much more informal and customary than the process of legitimation. In it, constituencies first have a faith in the conceptual power of strategists, and, later, either confirm or discard that faith.

Initiative and feasibility influence are different from legitimacy and charisma. For the same reason that "whoever has control of the agenda has control of the meeting," strategists in these relationships exercise a kind of "control over the mind." In harsh terms, they can be put to use at best as "information control" and at worst as "propaganda."

The use of sanctions leaves little room for a two-way process. The scales are tipped heavily in favor of strategists. Control over money, budgets, and machinery is the usual way sanctions are found in our society. When resources are used deliberately to secure compliance with strategies, without other forms of authority and influence, we can say without hesitation that this is domination. Domination should be used only after strategists have used their best efforts to achieve integration by other instruments of authority and power.

Ethic 5: Strategic Work Ethic

By far the most powerful, practical, and ethical thing strategists can do to fulfill their total responsibility to society is to focus on the *work* role of general managers. Since it can be a source of legitimate and charismatic authority, since it draws on initiative and feasibility power, and since it limits the need for sanctions, it has the best chance of achieving the ultimate end: the use of organizations as instruments in the service of society.

Strategic decision making—policy formulation and strategy formulation—is at the same time the most important work responsibility and the most important ethical responsibility of the strategic group. Unfortunately, it leaves us with one final dilemma, the same dilemma faced by judges, statesmen, lawyers, army generals, and medical doctors. The dilemma is this: how can general managers possibly reconcile conflicting ethics, either in strategy formulation (global, very long-term concepts) or in policy formulation (decisions involving shorter time horizons). This is a subject to which we must return in Chapter 11.

The Strategic Contract

Another way of viewing the notion of the strategic group and its relationships to society and to the natural order, is to use a concept

304

originally derived in political philosophy, the concept of *the social contract.* Jean Jacques Rousseau, like most of the great classical political philosophers, was puzzled over a central question, one that seemed to be a paradox. He saw that the population did not want increased government decision making because it limited freedom and autonomy. However, he also saw the population forming governments to regulate human affairs. Why, he asked, would people deliberately form governments if they do not want their freedom limited? The answer lies in a contract between the people (the population) and the government (the strategic group). From constituencies' points of view, each person in effect says, "I will identify myself in two roles. I am a free person, but I am also part of a larger whole. I will recognize your legitimate authority so long as you, the strategic group, act responsibly in maintaining the whole system, for I cannot exist alone. I am *both* an individual and a part of the system."

Stated in strategic terms, this philosophy translates into a contract betwen three parties: the organization (its products, services, resources), constituencies that cannot exist alone (task constituencies, cultural constituencies) and strategists (those who act responsibly to "give back" a viable alignment). In fact, none of the three actors can exist alone.

The highest responsibility in the contract calls for strategic alignment to maintain the health of the system, for no constituency can exist without "the system." In fact, the clauses in the contract would read very much like the ideas already presented in this chapter. A healthy system would be defined as one that is approximately aligned at any one time and one that is viable for future alignments.

Perhaps the most important clause would state the type of work expected of strategists. It would describe a very difficult, time-consuming job (Chapters 3–5, 11) involving endless attention to parts of the system (policy formulation) and attention to how all parts relate together (strategy formulation). The most important clause requiring constituencies to perform something would be the one about legitimate authority and power. Constituencies would agree to delegate legitimate authority and power to strategists if strategists observe their responsibilities in the contract. Another clause would state that constituencies will confer initiative and feasibility power only "if the strategic group agrees to use its best efforts to maintain long-term alignment."

Because society is not homogenous, but a network of constituencies with diverse interests, there would actually be a number of contracts, one set for constituencies in the zone of support, another

305

for those in the zone of acceptance, and still another for those in the zone of indifference. The contract in the zone of conflict, to be acceptable, would have to be based on some evidence that the strategic group is working to reduce, rather than increase, the negative balance of payments, and to restore ecological balance to the system.

Modern psychologists have used Rousseau's paradigm to explain the commitment of one constituency (internal employees) to the total system.[31] They have pointed out that both the organization and the employees have expectations of each other. The organization expects that a certain amount of a certain kind of work is to be done. The employee, on the other hand, expects a wide range of benefits, described in Chapter 9. The result of these two sets of expectations is a *psychological contract*. If the organization can succeed in providing its payments under the contract, the employees will acknowledge the authority of the strategic group. If not, legitimate authority will break down.

Breakdown in Alignments

By this time it is evident that the strategic task alignment is the force that has the most influence on the destiny of the organization. It affects not only the technological and economic performance of the organization but also its cultural performance. It determines whether the organization will be effective in the outside world and whether it will be efficient internally. It also determines whether the strategic group will have legitimate power and authority, charismatic authority, initiative power, or no power at all. In short, the strategic task alignment is a powerful independent variable. It affects a whole array of technical and human events that constitute social performance.

When something goes wrong with this alignment, strategists need to know three things. First, they need to know what kinds of conflict or breakdown are occurring, the symptoms of breakdown. Second, they need to know what causes the breakdowns. If they treat symptoms and not causes, the breakdown will continue. They particularly need to know what in their own leadership behavior can cause breakdown. Finally, they need to speculate, as we do in this book, about what guidelines they might use to improve leadership in the breakdown stage.

There are two types of breakdown, each of which has different symptoms. The first is a breakdown in task performance (T). Symptoms include problems and objections from task constituencies.

306

Customers, clients, taxpayers, stockholders, and higher budget officials simply begin to object that the quality of services rendered, or the cost of products and services, do not match the demands and needs of the primary constituency. Or there may be conflicts between task constituencies. Resource suppliers may complain that the product is being rendered at too low a price, or that they are not receiving enough for their tax money or their stock ownership. Clients and customers may complain that taxpayers and stockholders are not providing enough money to gear the quality and cost of the output to their own interests. The dollars simply stop coming in. In Chapter 3 we saw how this could happen to the railraod industry. Chapter 4 showed that it could happen to A&P Food Corporation. Chapter 5 showed it could happen to the Boston Symphony Orchestra or Sears, Roebuck. This breakdown in task performance can occur early or late in stage 2. In either case it shows that the organization is in trouble.

The second type of breakdown occurs in cultural performance (C). Constituencies outside the organization (Chapters 6–7) arise which are not directly involved as consumers or resource suppliers but which have other needs and self-interests that are adversely affected by the task alignment. They object to products or services, or to internal resources and processes on grounds that they negatively affect a wide range of cultural values. Symptoms include everything from adverse newspaper publicity, and informal interest-group action to formal sanctions: boycotts, pressure on resource suppliers, or lobbying in legislatures for laws that will curtail the legitimate authority and discretion of strategists. Constituencies inside the organization (Chapters 8–9) also arise. They begin to pay a somewhat ambivalent role. They are administrators and employees, deriving benefits from the task alignment. However, they object to internal alignments that violate their role as human beings or department heads. Symptoms include everything from informal foot-dragging and opposition cliques to formal sanctions: strikes and labor conflicts. In short, the zone of conflict begins to expand because the organization is attacked from within and without.

Causes of Breakdown

THE BREAKDOWN PROCESS   The causes of breakdown in strategic systems can best be understood by tracing a series of events or steps shown in Exhibit 10-1. This diagram depicts the dynamic operation of the strategic system in both growth and development (events

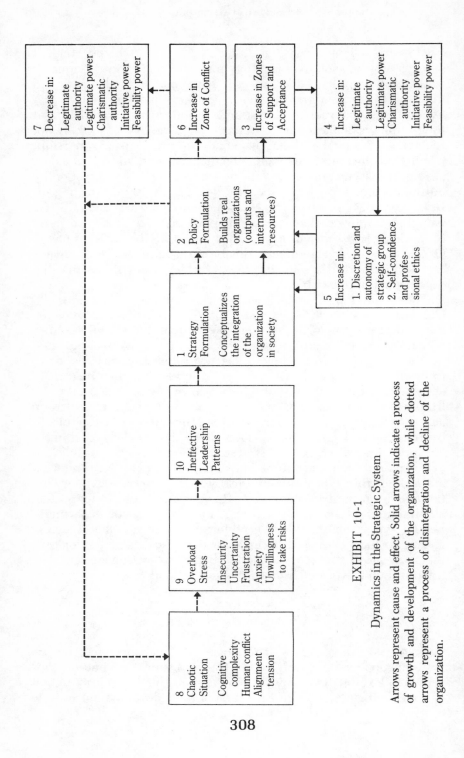

EXHIBIT 10-1

Dynamics in the Strategic System

Arrows represent cause and effect. Solid arrows indicate a process of growth and development of the organization, while dotted arrows represent a process of disintegration and decline of the organization.

1–5) and breakdown (events 6–9). Arrows on the diagram represent causes and effects.

Black arrows show the functional or adaptive forces in the system, those which are constructive. They are the ones that represent, in ecological terms, adaptive mutation: variation, selection, and retention. In terms used in Chapter 1, they result in the organization's developing more and more competences to meet successive challenges. In event 1 strategy formulation results in a broad concept of the organization as a species in society. Event 2, policy formulation, is a long trial-and-error learning process that converts the strategic concept into an organization: into products, services, and a set of internal resource competences. This results in event 3, the creation of zones of support and acceptance. In event 4 constituencies in these zones delegate legitimate authority and legitimate power (resources) to the organization, and that they delegate to the strategic group the right to use charismatic power, initiative power, feasibility power, and resource power. This leads to event 5, the autonomy and discretion possessed by the strategic group to continue doing what they were doing in the first place—strategy formulation and policy formulation.

Events 6–10 show breakdown and disintegration. These are dysfunctional or maladaptive events in the system, those which are destructive. The red arrows represent, in ecological terms, maladaptive mutation. They show that the organization selects the wrong attributes to adapt to its environment, retains these wrong elements, and begins to die. In terms used in Chapter 1, they mean that the organization loses its distinctive competence to serve society, and that the more competences it loses the greater the probability that it will disintegrate.

In event 6 the number of constituencies in the zone of conflict increases. As the organization gets out of alignment with its task constituencies, and as its task alignment causes an increasing number of opposing cultural constituencies to arise, there is a decline in the amount of authority and power delegated to the organization, and to the strategic group (7).

Events 8, 9, and 10 will be explained in the following sections. Briefly, what happens is this: Events 2, 3, and 6 result in a state of the strategic system, or a situation, that seems almost impossibly complex (event 8). This situation can be characterized as "complexity," "interconnectedness," "dynamic," and "turbulence." The situation is so complex that it is "unstructured."

Because of this situation, strategists' minds become overloaded. They experience anxiety, frustration, acute uncertainty, insecurity, and an unwillingness to take risks (event 9). Such stress in turn may produce ineffective leadership patterns (event 10). These leadership patterns in turn affect strategists' ability to formulate strategies and policies (events 1 and 2) that might correct the situation. If they fail to correct the balance in the situation, the organization moves through the cycle of red arrows again and again until full-scale disintegration sets in.

THE UNSTRUCTURED SYSTEM: CHAOTIC   Anyone who has studied Parts I and II of this book will now be aware of the enormous complexity of the system strategists find themselves in after organizations have moved through the long stage of growth and development. As one ploughs through the endless details involved in forecasting the demands of customers or clients (Chapter 3), in trying to shape products that match needs in market segments (Chapter 4), and in aligning the vast and intricate resource system (Chapter 5, capital structures, organization structures, technological operating processes, human work designs), it almost seems impossible to make sense out of the technological and economic sides of strategic decision making. But this is only the beginning. As one looks at the realities of cultural conflicts that develop in stage 3, one's confusion increases. The organization and its strategists seem to be attacked from the outside by an almost limitless array of constituencies, each with a different value demand (Chapters 6 and 7). They seem threatened from the inside by administrators and middle managers, who have their own human needs (Chapter 8) and by employees whose human welfare is adversely affected (Chapter 9). Each of these constituencies not only appeals to strategists on moral or ethical grounds (the humanistic needs of persons) but can wield real power (the power to cut off funds, or to engage in political activity).

It is the sheer magnitude of variables, and the difference in variables, that bring to mind such static concepts as interconnectedness, interdependence, and complexity and such dynamic words as turbulence, rate of change, and uncertainty. Because the social sciences do not customarily deal with the type of system we have here, we choose two terms to try to capture the nature of the mature system. Toynbee's word "enormity," though somewhat colorful, is intended here to denote static magnitude and difference. The word "chaos" or "chaotic" is intended as to indicate turbulence and rate of change. Both terms picture a system that has not been structured by paradigms in the social sciences. For example, in the "golden age of operations research," management scientists made sense out of certain systems by structuring them into *optimized systems*. Later, management scientists made sense out of systems by structuring them into *interactive or simulated systems.*[32]

It may be worthwhile to view the content of such a system as being enormous and chaotic in three respects. First, there is a chaotic intellectual (cognitive) complexity and variability. There are simply vast numbers of ideas, concepts, arguments, scientific findings, reports of experts, ethical claims, and moral judgments floating around in the system. Second, there is a chaotic *human* situation. Government officials, labor unions, workers, college professors, specialists in cost-benefit analysis, administrative department heads, philosophers specializing in human rights or justice, stockholders, taxpayers, and strategists themselves are each coping with their world, their needs, and their self-interests. Third, there is a chaos caused by the mutation process itself. The constant pull of forces for stability (retaining that which is workable) coupled with the constant pull of forces for change (searching for and selecting that which might be workable) create an *alignment tension* that cannot be ignored.

THE STRATEGIC GROUP: OVERLOAD AND STRESS   These are powerful situational forces, which play on the strategic group as it goes about its day-to-day decision making. Cognitive chaos creates intellectual insecurity, accompanied by high levels of anxiety and frustration. Chapter 8 referred to this as the "decision-overload" or "future shock" that any human being feels when placed in an ambiguous situation in which neither past experience nor scientific models can structure things enough for him or her to derive clear meaning. Psychologists have shown that even persons with a high tolerance of ambiguity can reach a point beyond which they cannot cope with additional stimuli. Chapter 8 also showed that chaotic levels of human conflict produce other kinds of insecurity: interpersonal or political insecurity. In summary, strategists are no different from other human beings. The very success of the modern government agency or business corporation, its growth and development, places them in situations that seem nearly untenable.

Although in Chapter 8 we cited social science principles and speculated about the feelings of executives in Timex Corporation and Sears, Roebuck, two other cases will help to underscore the phenomena we are talking about here.

The first comes from an interview in 1979 with a cabinet-level minister in the Canadian government. He states,

For many years, the Canadian civil service system made life easier for our cabinet ministers than for your [United States]

cabinet secretaries. We were respected for the jobs we performed to a degree higher than top executives in private corporations were respected. We were in general paid higher salaries. I think that our status in society was higher and as a result
we had a great deal of freedom. I recently recalled the word
deference from my college days. It seems important to me
today. It seems now that the population used to show us
deference. They respected our hard work in trying to picture
what would be best for Canada and for trying to work out laws
that made for a better Canada. Today things are different. I
would never have believed that the life of a minister could
become so frenzied and filled with trouble on all sides. You in
the United States may think I am only describing the Quebec
movement. I should tell you point blank that this is important
but only the beginning. Only if you could see the endless
stream of details that I have to face day in and day out you would
understand what I mean. I'm somewhat sorrowful about my
final conclusion. There's a good chance that within the next
year I will retire from public life forever. It is too much to take.
Too much to endure. Especially if you don't think you can do
much about it.[33]

A second case comes from an interview with a high-level officer of
Rainier Bank in Seattle.[34] This interview took place in late 1970,
approximately six months after marchers in the streets of Seattle had
broken windows in the bank building. The marchers had rallied
around two themes: the harmful effects of the Vietnam War and the
part the military-industrial complex had played in the war.

I am at a complete loss to understand the situation. For many
years the bank has been a respected institution. We were of
course trying to make a profit but I, and certainly most of my
fellow officers, have had a genuine love for this city and its
people. I often thought how attached to both I was, compared
to attachments I would have in a larger Eastern city where
people are less known to each other and where neither the
human population nor the natural setting would be as natural
to me. I personally do not know any high military officers and
I don't feel a part of the military-industrial complex. When
those windows were being broken, it was horrifying to me. I felt
like I was in another world. I didn't really believe it could be
happening.

At this point, the case writer asked, "What are you doing about
it?" There was a pause. The senior vice-president then responded, "I

don't know what you mean." The case writer answered: "I mean that
the bank had its windows broken, and that you are really upset about
it. I want to know what your position is, or what the bank's position
is, for the future." There was another longer pause. "Well, I still
don't fully understand your question. I don't understand it because
the situation is so confusing that I don't think there is anything we
can do about it."

In a number of case histories cited in Chapters 6–9 this same
phenomenon was observed. Strategists in the California Federal
Savings and Loan Association, Roget S.A., Western Office Equipment Company, Metrocenter Ohio Police Department, and
National Bank of San Francisco all, at the end of the case, showed
tendencies toward inaction. This is consistent with the reports of
public affairs analysts that it is becoming more difficult to attract
persons to run for political office. Social scientists have pointed out
the same trend.

THE STRATEGIC GROUP: LEADERSHIP PATTERNS   The argument in this
section is that strategists as a class are no different from other human
beings, at least when they find themselves in chaotic and conflicting
situations. Anyone—whether a worker, a high government official,
or a university professor—takes some action in this kind of situation
to defend his or her ability to think, to protect the very core of the
thought process from becoming paralyzed. Though some people
have put a "bad" connotation on the psychologists' term "defense
mechanism," psychologists themselves have seen that such mechanisms can either be adaptive or maladaptive. It depends on how the
person copes, what help he or she has, and whether the situation is
relatively tranquil or chaotic.

In the following ineffective leadership patterns, therefore, one
must not jump to the conclusion that they are necessarily caused by
some "authoritarian personality," a person that is, as McClelland
says, "harsh, sadistic, fascist, Machiavellian, prejudiced and
neurotic." Nor should one assume, as some sociologists have, that for
unknown reasons top executives simply have "a demand for control."[35] All persons, workers, administrators, and strategists do
indeed bring certain characteristics with them to the job, but
heredity is not the only cause of behavior. Environment can be a
powerful shaper of action and a powerful source of learning.

As the breakdown process enters its initial phases, one common
leadership pattern emerges. Toynbee calls this *resting on their oars*.
Strategists in successful organizations feel a pride in what has been
accomplished over the long years of policy formulation, and a com-

313

mitment to perpetuating existing products and services, and to serving existing constituencies. In pronounced cases, they have a feeling of *koros* (being "spoiled by success," or even "intoxicated by victory"). A number of case histories in this book show that strategists at least feel comfortable enough with the status quo that they become myopic to what is happening in the rest of the world. They also show that strategists can, as Toynbee suggested, put heavy emphasis on "idolizing" internal parts of the strategy—either the present organization structure, or the physical technology that has been so successful in the past. Toynbee found another kind of leadership pattern emerging in the time of breakdown;—caused partly by pride in the successful strategy and partly by the anxieties produced by the chaotic system. He saw leaders *putting new wine into old bottles*. This is a form of disjointed policymaking. Strategists *partially* give up the difficult job of strategy formulation, of trying to relate the parts of the system logically to outside challenges. Instead, they patch up pieces of the strategy, without trying to change other parts. An excellent example of this behavior was found in a school of business administration recently. The school of social work in the university had given the business school enough budget funds to pay the salary of a full professor. The reason was that society is changing. Both federal and state governments were demanding more persons trained in welfare program management. The school of social work recognized this and, rather than duplicate the organization structure of the business school (TI.12), it relied on the latter's distinctive competence. However, strategists in the business school, not recognizing the strategic problem, simply parceled out the budget money among existing faculty teaching existing courses, without giving attention to the new curriculum changes that would maximize training of persons for federal and state governments.[36]

When these first two kinds of ineffective behavior exist, things become slightly worse because the *causes* of the problem (changing environments, changing people inside the organization) have gone unrecognized. As the conflicts get worse and worse, strategists come under more and more stress. They begin to try first one leadership pattern and then another, none of which corrects the situation. If things become really bad, Toynbee sees them as *retreating to chance*. They adopt the attitude that the whole system was never made to be logically understood anyway, that nature is simply chaotic in its outward appearance, and that somehow must have some grand design. In practical application, this behavior comes out as disjointed policymaking. Strategists give up altogether trying logically to relate the parts. They make policies without taking into account the whole system. In political terms, they arrive at the conclusion that "whatever will get acceptance in a coalition is the *right* policy." To Toynbee, this was a serious malfunctioning in leadership. Nature may require a certain amount of randomness in policy formulation. But nature also gave human beings reasoning powers, conceptual skills that helped strategists build the society and the organization in its period of growth and development. To Toynbee, then, the retreat to nature was a deep and profound attitudinal change that comes over politicians, top business executives, judges, and other professionals who occupy strategic positions in society.

But as time goes on, and nature *fails* to solve the problem, strategists may try anything in their behavioral repertoires to try to make sense out of the system. If the retreat to nature fails, there is always the *retreat to science*. This, like idolization of certain technical processes or organization structures, and like the retreat to nature, at least relieves strategists' acute frustration by allowing them to abdicate responsibility for strategy formulation. The practical application of this attitude is something like "science must have the answer, therefore hire experts in cost-benefit analysis, operations research, psychology, or sociology, assign *them* the policy problem, and *they* will come up with answers."

But as Professor Simon points out in Chapter 4, science is not a profession that deliberately deals with *value themes* or undertakes to study and structure the type of global systems described in this book. Furthermore, scientists have their own way of escaping unstructured and chaotic situations. They formulate hypotheses covering micro parts of the system, then make sure that their experimental design keeps out the rest of the world, in order not to contaminate the part under study. They may even, as Einstein said, become scientists primarily to "escape from everyday life with its painful crudity and hopeless dreariness" and to escape from "the fetters of one's ever shifting desires."[37] This leadership pattern Toynbee also views as much more than a simple flight of fancy. Science is an important part of policy formulation but it leaves something missing: the kind of creative and conceptual model building strategists used to build the organization in the first place.

But scientists are not the only ones who avoid chaotic and unstructured situations by building models that provide structure and stability. One leadership pattern that has received a great deal of attention in modern behavioral sciences, Toynbee called *creating the universal state*. In modern terms, what happens is that the existing structures of organization (TE, products and markets; TI.11,

315

capital structures; TI.12, organization structures; TI.21, operating processes; and TI.22, work designs) become the strategists' model of the system. This is a structured equivalent to the scientists' hypothesis models, optimizing models, and simulation models. The leadership pattern, when this happens, has been described by different behavioral scientists in different terms. Strategists may become the sociologists' rigid bureaucrat, who dysfunctionally displaces in his or her own mind the real goals of the organization and assumes instead that the rule system is the goal. They may, to avoid the endless conflicts in Chapters 7–9, become McGregor's Theory X leaders, who assume that "the people" cannot help work out a strategy for the firm. They may adopt leader behavior found in a large literature on leadership: the "task-oriented pattern" rather than the "people-oriented pattern." They may indeed become "authoritarian personalities."

A final leadership pattern Toynbee labels *turning inward rather than outward*. Modern psychologists give us, in the concept of groupthink, a powerful explanation of this kind of leadership. It was explained in Chapter 8 and will not be repeated here.

This chapter has summarized various leadership roles that strategists play in relation to organizations and to society outside of organizations. It has shown that two kinds of work performed by strategists place them in positions of leadership. Strategy and policy formulation can generate not only legitimacy and social responsibility but also the very freedom and discretion strategists have to engage in their work. They can also generate charismatic authority, initiative influence and the power of professional ethics. However, the chapter also showed that as organizations grow and develop they become very complicated. This complication is most difficult for strategists to cope with. As a result of it, strategists may well fall into leadership patterns that reverse the course of growth and cause breakdown. If the causes of breakdown are not diagnosed and understood, breakdown may turn into full-scale disintegration. In Chapter 11 we will speculate about how such causes might be diagnosed and understood, and how strategists might make sense out of chaotic situations.

Notes

1. Howard E. Aldrich, *Organizations and Environments*, Prentice-Hall, 1979. Aldrich's work draws heavily on Donald Cambell, "Variation and Selective Retention in Socio-Cultural Evolution," *General Systems*, Vol. 16, pp. 69–85, 1969, and Amos Hawley, *Human Ecology*, Ronald Press, 1950.

2. Aldrich, (Footnote 1) concludes that although there are "some occasions" in which strategists can proactively determine the organization's future, there are in general severe limitations to strategic choice, and that "most organizations are not powerful enough to influence their environments." *Organizations and Environments*, p. 28.

3. Lionel Tiger and R. Rox, *The Imperial Animal*, Dell, 1971, p. 3.

4. Use of the term "strategies" in this context will be found in G. C. Williams, *Adaptation and Natural Selection*, Princeton University Press, 1966, as well as in Tiger and Rox, *Imperial Animal*.

5. Seattle-Tacoma International Airport (Appendix).

6. Parsons, Talcott, *op. cit.*, Chapter 1.

7. The explanation of charisma in this section draws heavily on Robert C. Tucker, "The Theory of Charismatic Leadership," *Daedalus* 97:3 (Summer 1968): 731–56.

8. D. C. McClelland, J. W. Atkinson, R. A. Clark, and E. L. Lowell, *The Achievement Motive*, Irvington, 1953.

9. John Locke, *Concerning Civil Government*, The Great Ideas, Encyclopaedia Brittanica, Vol. 35, pp. 53–54.

10. Charles Lindblom, *The Policy Making Process*, Prentice-Hall, 1968, pp. 34–35.

11. Tucker, "Theory of Charismatic Leadership," draws on oral remarks by E. H. Erickson, Tuxedo Conference on Leadership, October 1967. Erickson also referred to followers who experienced this kind of distress as feeling an "identity-vacuum."

12. Huntington, *op. cit.*, Chapter 6.

13. Karl Weick, *The Social Psychology of Organizing*, Addison-Wesley, 1979, p. 125.

14. Mobil Oil Corporation (Case File), Appendix.

15. IBM Corporation (Case File), Appendix.

16. Roosevelt Hospital (Case File), Appendix.

17. Shoe Corporation of South Africa, Ltd., (Case File) Appendix.

18. United States Navy Station, Keyport, (Case File) Appendix.

19. The Pharmaceutical Industry of Iceland, *op. cit.*, Chapter 8.

20. D. C. McClelland, J. W. Atkinson, R. A. Clark, and E. L. Lowell, *The Achievement Motive*, Irvington, 1953.

21. Noel Tichy, *Strategic Change Management*, West, 1980.

22. Stanley Schachter, *The Psychology of Affiliation*, Stanford University Press, 1959.

23. Margaret Mead (ed.), *Cultural Patterns and Technological Change*, New American Library, 1955.

24. "Bedrock" in J. W. Lorsch and P. R. Lawrence, *Managing Group and Intergroup Relations*, Irwin, 1972, pp. 66–92; A. C. Filley, *Organization Invention: A Study of Utopian Organizations*, Wisconsin Business Papers #3, 1973.

25. K. S. Fine, "Worker Participation in Israel," in Hunnius et al., *Worker's Control*, Random House, 1973.

26. Robert Michels, *Political Parties*, The Free Press, 1949.

27. John Child, "Organizational Structure, Environment and Performance: The Role of Strategic Choice," *Sociology* 6:1 (January 1972).

28. Charles Lindblom, *The Policy Making Process*, Prentice-Hall, 1968, pp. 34–35.

29. D. C. McClelland, J. W. Atkinson, R. A. Clark, and E. L. Lowell, *The Achievement Motive*, Irvington, 1953.

30. T. W. Adorno et al., *The Authoritarian Personality*, Harper, 1950.

31. E. H. Schein, *Organizational Psychology*, Prentice-Hall, 1970, pp. 12–13; H. Levinson et al., *Men, Management and Mental Health*, Harvard University Press, 1962.

32. J. R. Emshoff, "Experience-Generalized Decision Making," *Interfaces* 8:4 (August 1978): 40–48.

33. Canadian Ministry, (Case File) Appendix.

34. Rainier Bank, (Case File) Appendix.

35. J. G. March and H. A. Simon, summarizing the theories of Merton and Gouldner, *Organizations*, John Wiley, 1958, pp. 40–47.

36. Graduate School of Business Administration, (Case File) Appendix.

37. Albert Einstein, *Essays in Science*, Philosophical Library, 1933, p. 2.

CHAPTER 11

Strategic Decision Making
The Conceptual Method

FOR A VARIETY OF REASONS, the most practical and ethical thing strategists can do in their careers is to focus on their *work role* in society. Strategic decision making—both strategy formulation and policy formulation—is the central activity that sets off the chain of events in the strategic system described in Chapter 10. These events act as intervening variables. They in turn cause the organization either to survive and grow in society or to break down and disintegrate. Strategy formulation and policy formulation are thus both the most important *work activity* and the most important *social or ethical responsibility* of general managers. This chapter will focus on these two types of strategic decision making. It will contain guidelines for formulating and solving strategic problems.

The dynamics of the system present strategists with what seems to be an impossible task. The three root causes of breakdown—intellectual complexity and chaos, human complexity and conflict, and the constant alignment tension between forces to stability and forces to change—are powerful obstacles to the kind of strategic decision making depicted in Chapters 3–5, the kind that requires creativity and clarity of conceptual logic. At the end of Chapter 10 we saw how easy it is for strategists, like all other human beings, to take easier courses of action, actions that may extricate the general manager from the chaotic situation but do not deal with the roots of the problem.

It is the purpose of this chapter to propose guidelines for making strategic decisions under conditions of such high uncertainty that existing decision methods in science are inappropriate. In such a situation what is needed is a strategic method, a combination of decision rules and attitudes that help "the strategic mind" to solve

319

unstructured problems very much as the scientific method and attitudes help "the scientific mind" to solve structured problems.

This chapter is divided into two parts. The first sections suggest certain *decision rules* of use to the strategic group. These are rules for bringing some order and meaning out of the chaos of the policy system. They are rules for formulating problems in an unstructured system. Later sections describe a *strategic-task-force process* that might accomplish diverse purposes with a single approach. It might (1) produce an approximate intellectual consensus within the strategic group, (2) produce an approximate emotional acceptance of a single strategy by members of the strategic group, (3) help the strategic group to obey the decision rules for use in chaos and unstructured systems, and (4) provide a common language, understandable to constituencies, with which strategists can communicate and secure cooperation of constituencies. This process is at the same time an intellectual process, an emotional process, a social process and a political process.

The decision rules for unstructured strategy situations may be of help to strategy groups regardless of whether they are coalitions held together by bargaining over self-interests, social groups held together by trust and authentic communication, or proximate policymakers held together by a variety of legal, extralegal, and habitual rules of the game. It is necessary to make this point at the beginning because such rules must be phrased in terms of operation of a single human mind, that is, as if there were only one policymaker. Though stated in this way, they should be understood to be of use to a single policymaker or to a group of policymakers, regardless of the motivations that hold the group together. It should be clear already that in this book we take the position that there is no such thing as a single strategist in the modern mature organization. If there should be such a strategist who attempts to make strategic decisions after inception (stage 1), the organization would either stagnate at early stages or disintegrate before it got very far into stage 2.

One other point must be clarified before we discuss decision rules. Some of them are more like attitudes of mind than they are like specific and structured rules in, for example, accounting. Rules about when to debit and when to credit are known and specific. It is precisely because the problem is unstructured that strategic rules must be stated in borderline terms, which in some cases are specific and in others more general. The rules should be taken as guidelines that will help to eliminate the root causes of confusion and to derive order and meaning from what looks at first like a chaotic situation.

Rules for Strategic Decisions

There are three guidelines that may help strategists formulate and solve strategic problems, regardless of whether they are strategy problems or policy problems. These will be discussed in this section. Following sections will show that these guidelines must be applied somewhat differently in strategic decisions and policy decisions. The guidelines are:

1. Recognize realities in the strategic situation.
2. Formulate the problem in a framework that matches the strategic situation.
3. Make final choice using the utilitarian criterion and the Pareto Optimum.

Realities in The Strategic Situation

John Dewey pointed out long ago that the very beginning of the decision process is a somewhat vague idea in the decision maker's mind. This Dewey called the *problematic situation*. In common terms, the problematic situation is simply "what's bothering you," "what's bugging you," or "what you are up against." For strategists, there are four aspects or characteristics of the strategic situation that should simply be consciously acknowledged and accepted. Such conscious acceptance is the first step toward eliminating the kinds of stress and uncertainty caused by the chaotic system.

First, the system is *comprehensive*. It is, like Galileo's famous diagnosis, "the world in buzzing confusion." Previous chapters have shown that the situation is a mixture of technological and human forces, a mixture of internal and external demands, a network of zones ranging from support to conflict. No other profession except those of statesmen and judges faces a situation like this. For strategists it is normal; it is a way of life.

Second, the system is indeed one of *conflict*, between things and people, between groups outside and inside the organization, between task goals and cultural goals. The psychology of individual differences tells us that in unstructured problems, and particularly in global problems, this will always be the case. The probability that diverse constituencies will agree on any one definition of the problem, to say nothing of any one solution, is virtually zero. The cause of this disagreement has been isolated in the psychology of individual differences as well as in political philosophy: the emotional (needs, self-interests) factor in perception often guides the intellectual or

321

cognitive way one views the world. As one important branch of the leadership literature has pointed out, leaders are simply "up against it." Unstructured situations are the most difficult in which to exercise leadership.[1]

Third, all parties to the situation assign a very difficult role to the strategic group: the role of *mediator between ethics*. In Chapter 2 this was called the "integrator role." As ethical mediators, strategists are expected somehow to reconcile, balance, trade off or otherwise produce an "ideal" set of decisions. Yet individual constituencies seem to phrase their own needs and interests in terms of absolutes.

Fourth, and most difficult of all, all parties who have a long-run view of social welfare assign to strategists a role that in Chapter 10 we recognized as one of the most controversial issues in organization theory and governmental theory: the role of *mediator between stability and change*. This exerts a great pressure on strategists. They are supposed to formulate strategies and policies that take into account both the present distinctive competences of the organization (stable systems that change slowly) and immediate short-term demands for change. In mediating between these two forces, strategists are supposed to add something to the decisions, not merely act as computers of popular demands. They are expected proactively to use their conceptual minds, to initiate that which is feasible in light of history (past mutations of the organization) and in light of the future. In practical terms, they are expected to maintain what is valuable to society in the way of products, services, markets, capital, organization structure, operating processes, and work designs, but also to forecast changing social needs and to change these to an ecologically viable new set of competences.

One side of the controversy is best known in the familiar question: should a United States senator compute popular opinion and then formulate laws that please the people? If so, the ethical criterion of choice is what will gain acceptance. The other side of the controversy is the question: should a senator compute popular opinion and then add his own judgment when he formulates laws that are best for the people?

In this book we take the latter position, agreeing with Nisbet, a modern political scientist who points out that James Madison and Edmund Burke knew well the role of mediator between stability and change.[2] Montesquieu revived this role in his famous *principle of intermediation*. According to Nisbet, strategists are indeed supposed to add something to popular opinion (the opinion of the mass, or the crowd). They are supposed to follow public opinion—the opinion that recognizes a need to mediate between what an organization might be to better serve society in the future. In Chapter 2 their role was called the role of organization builder. It emphasizes the need for time perspective, for a sense of evolution, and for viewing the future as history.

These four aspects of the problematic situation must be recognized clearly and accepted as the normal conflicts all strategists face. Without such recognition, the problematic situation becomes frightening, stressful, and anxiety-producing.

Formulating Problems: Strategic Methodology

All professions have methodological frameworks that enable them to attack the type of problematic situation faced by the profession. Scientists have one kind. They formulate hypotheses that isolate all parts of the world except the part under study, and then use the language of mathematics to either accept or reject the hypotheses. Medical doctors, lawyers, historians, psychologists, anthropologists, and accountants each have traditional methodologies that frame problems to match the particular problematic situation faced by the profession. Such decision frameworks serve very useful purposes. They help one to actually understand the situation, identifying problems in it and choosing between different alternative solutions. They provide a sense of order and meaning in the situation. Since every person does not have to reinvent the wheel, this eliminates a certain amount of unstructured anxiety. They allow persons to get on with the problem rather than wallowing around in initial confusion. Finally, they prevent the professional from trying to use some other profession's methodology that does not fit the situation.

The first rule of strategic methodology is to *focus the problem on the strategic concept that should receive the most weight (based on its importance to society) and the highest heuristic or sequential priority (based on the time available and limited attention span of the strategic group).* The first of these is explained here. The second will be discussed later because priority is one thing in strategy formulation and quite another in policy formulation.

In somewhat mechanical or superficial terms, a strategic concept is a typology of concepts found on the left side of the matrix presented in Chapter 1. The rule means to focus on:

TE. Product/markets (business organizations) or Service Constituencies (government organizations)
TI.1 Structural or Fixed Resource Competences
   TI.11 Physical Capital Competences

323

TI.12 Human Organization Structures at the Administrative Level
TI.2. Operating Level Resource Competences
TI.21 Operating Processes
TI.22 Human Work Designs (job designs, reward systems, work-group designs)

On first sight, the concepts in this typology seem simply to be the same marketing, capital investment, industrial engineering, personnel, and management concepts found in books on economics, accounting, management, industrial relations, operations research systems, and sociology of work design. As *strategic* concepts, however, they are that and more. They are richer constructs than those used in sociology, economics, or engineering. They embody three different and related meanings, each from the viewpoint of one of the actors in the strategic system (not from the viewpoint of an engineer, economist, or social psychologist). Thus, what may be a product in marketing or economics (TE), what may be a work design or reward system in social psychology (TI.22), an efficient allocation of capital in economics or accounting (TI.11), administrative organization structure in organization theory (TI.12), or an efficient manufacturing process or system in operations systems analysis (TI.22) becomes, in *strategic conceptual language*, these three things at once:

A demand, need, expectation or ethic of a *social constituency*.
A task performance goal (effectiveness, efficiency) for the *organization*.
A work role (responsibility) and an ethical role (responsibility) for the *strategist*.

A strategic concept is thus similar to a cultural concept: it is a concept that blends the meanings of products and resources into one central idea, an idea that is operational for the strategist (see Chapter 2) and that integrates the three parties in the strategic system: society, organizations, and strategists (Chapters 2 and 10).

Full understanding of the notion *strategic concept* can be achieved only by study of Chapters 3–9. In those chapters, when real-world characters (strategists, organizations, constituencies) act out their dynamic and joint actions, the idea of a strategic concept seems natural. A few case examples will also be given in the section immediately following, which discusses how to diagnose task responsibilities (TE, TI) in *strategic language*. Strategic language is like any other language, whether it be mathematics or English. It involves logically relating whatever concepts form its basic elements. In mathematics, basic elements are tied together in formulae. In English, words are tied together in sentences, models, and theories. In strategy, strategic concepts are tied together in conceptual schemes called strategies and policies.

Unfortunately, this difference between strategic concepts and concepts in different disciplines, between strategic methodology and other specialized methodologies, and between the ethics of strategic decision making and the ethics of scientific decision making is the most powerful reason why general managers and social scientists have difficulty in communicating with and in understanding one another. It is absolutely necessary that strategists have clearly in their minds their own place in the world, and their own methodology, if they are to recognize what is causing the problem and do what they can to improve communication.

The second rule of strategic methodology is to *search for alternatives that are value-rich, and outside the experience of the strategic group*. This rule requires two things. The first is to search for alternatives that at first may seem to be mundane "things" (products, or capital equipment and buildings, job descriptions) but that in reality are rich in human values. This is a matter of translating the technical "things" (TE, TI) in the system into organizational competences that have humanistic meanings to society. Ackoff has called this process *idealization*.[3] The second is to search for alternatives that are outside the past experience of the strategic group. This is necessary if strategists are to free themselves from the dysfunctional or ineffective leadership patterns described at the end of Chapter 10. This rule deliberately violates the heuristic rules by which most people *do* make decisions (see Chapter 4 for task heuristics, Chapter 6 for cultural heuristics). According to Simon's theory, human beings inevitably fall back on what they already have experienced. But if strategists act this way, the future of the organization, whether viewed through the paradigm of ecology and natural selection or through the paradigm of history, will be jeopardized. If they do give such weight to the organization's *past* products and services (TE) and to the resource competences (TI) that have built the organization, they will be unable to provide the kind of proactive, creative, and conceptual leadership that builds future strategic systems that fit future ecological conditions. How strategists might go about searching for alternatives outside their experience will be discussed in the last section of this chapter.

The third rule of strategic methodology is the *rule of diagnosis*. It advises: *diagnose the payoffs (outcomes) of any alternative strategy or policy in terms of (1) strategic language and (2) isolation of dominant payoffs.* The first of these will be discussed here. Because isolating payoffs is different in strategy formulation than in policy formulation, this process will be explained later in this chapter.

Strategic language is a crucial matter. It must be used at each step in strategy and policy formulation. When we come to diagnosis, a few examples recalled from Chapters 3–9 will help us to understand how the elements of strategic language can be diagnosed, that is, how they can be translated from their original meaning in one dimension (task performance) to their strategic meaning on all dimensions (organizational goals, constituency needs, and strategic responsibilities).

The *concept* of a lawnmower (Chapter 7) is not only something the organization produces as an output. Diagnosis reveals that it also affects the needs of persons who want to cut grass and persons whose physical health may be impaired by accidents. Strategists, as formulators of product/markets (Chapter 4) have both the work responsibility and the ethical responsibility to reconcile these two expectations or demands in society.

The *concept* of a gallon of gasoline (Chapter 3) is an organization output goal. It is also relief from boredom to one constituency, a way of earning a living in an industrial society to another constituency, and a source of profit to stockholders. Strategists are specialists in society who are expected to deal with and relate these needs.

The *concept* of a hydroelectric dam across a river (Chapter 7) is a task-efficiency goal of Seattle City Light Company (TI.11). Task constituencies (consumers, taxpayers) expect that the internal generation system will supply persons with low-cost kilowatts of electricity to protect them from the ravages of raw nature. Cultural constituencies (those who need tranquility in wilderness or the protection of the natural ecology) expect that the company will not generate electricity with a dam that will in turn kill 1000-year-old cedar trees, or upset the natural balance of wildlife and fish. Strategists who formulate capital equipment policies for the company are responsible for matching all of these needs.

The *concept* of work rules for New York City employees during the summer months, as well as the production-line job design in the Saab-Scania Company (Chapter 9) are efficiency goals of the organizations (TI.22). Resource suppliers (taxpayers in New York City, stockholders of the privately held automobile company) expect and demand that city employees and company employees will contribute enough *work* to justify their investment in the organization. Employees inside New York City government and inside the Saab

326

Company expect that both work hours and job designs will provide them with such values as freedom to engage in recreation, freedom to grow and develop as human beings, salaries to spend on other needs, and opportunities for self-actualization. Strategists must formulate working hours and design production lines that will meet the needs of all.

These brief examples are microscopic when compared to the rich and complex process of diagnosis depicted throughout this book. Every case history cited can and should be treated as these examples indicate. In summary, diagnosis is the process of converting what an organization does to the richer concept of what an organization is in a strategic system. It is a process, as Selznick reminds us,[4] that strategists cannot escape, whether they perform it by intuition or, as this book suggests, by more conscious effort. It is a process in which facts and values are mixed into a single concept. It differs radically from scientific investigation in which there is a deliberate effort to separate facts from values. It is a process important enough that strategists should recognize a single global term to identify the hallmark of their profession: *the conceptual method.*

Ethic 5: Criterion for Decision

In simple terms, four things are necessary to make any kind of decision: a problem focus, alternatives to consider, the outcomes or payoffs of various alternatives, and a rule for evaluating the total payoffs of each alternative. The criterion for choice that most nearly matches the strategic situation is the utilitarian principle. Here we label the rule Ethic 5. When added to the list presented in Chapter 10, it completes the notion of strategic ethics. The rule states, *When choosing strategies and policies, select that global strategy or that incremental policy which yields the greatest good for the greatest number of human beings in society.*

The utilitarian principle was first clarified by Hume, Bentham, and Mill in the eighteenth and early nineteenth centuries. Essentially, their problematic situation was to provide the British Parliament with a rule for choosing between alternative laws that would most "ethically" govern society. Since these writings, the utilitarian rule has been debated by philosophers, subdivided into schools of thought (e.g., hedonistic utilitarians versus pluralistic utilitarians, intrinsic-value utilitarians versus preference utilitarians), and criticized on various grounds (e.g., that it could lead to tyranny of the minority by the majority or tyranny of the majority by the minority; that neither the number of persons nor the utility valence of persons

327

can be measured; that it leads to hedonistic pleasure and ignores real values in life). In this book we cannot review all of these arguments and criticisms. We can, however, point out why the utilitarian principle is preferable to one of the other great ethical criteria, the categorical imperative. We can also show that the principle, when used in conjunction with other ethics and decision methods of strategic leadership, avoids the most serious abuses suggested by critics.

The other great ethical test that has received most attention in religion and philosophy is the rule proposed by Immanuel Kant. Known as the *categorical imperative*, this rule would require strategists in Organization A to *choose that strategy or policy which would be "good" or "right" if chosen by any other organization (organizations B, C, D), under the same conditions.* This is roughly equivalent to the golden rule: "Your organization has the ethical right to do unto constituencies as any other organization exactly like yours, and in the same situation as yours, would do unto identical constituencies." The problem in using this rule is evident to anyone who has studied the case histories in Chapters 3–9. There are no two organizations exactly alike at any one time, or in the same stage of historical development. Even if there were two identical organizations, they certainly could not face the same identical constituencies. No hydroelectric dam affects the same number of identical constituencies in exactly the same number of ways. No two job-design systems or merit-rating systems ever affect the same kind of employee, the same number of employees, or employees in the same cultural milieu (see Chapter 9).

One objection to the utilitarian principle is that it may be interpreted simply as amoral hedonism, advocating all sorts of pleasures ("wine, women, and song") without regard to the content of values. Though Bentham intended it that way, others have modified the principle to include intrinsic values. This of course was the purpose in Chapters 1–3, and again in Chapters 6–9, of dividing the responsibility matrix into quadrants and specifying the content of constituency needs and preferences. Without this framework of values in society, the use of the utilitarian rule may indeed be superficial.

Another serious criticism of the principle holds that it may be used either (1) by the majority to tyrannize the minority, or (2) by the minority to tyrannize the majority. These maladaptive acts can occur because there are two factors in the equation that yields the measure of "good" for any one constituency. One has to do with the *number* of people in the constituency. The other has to do with what expectancy theory in psychology calls *valence*. Traditional economic theory calls this "marginal utility."

328

Each constituency has a "strength of need," which indicates how much the value means to the group. One group of 1000 people may need low-cost electricity from a hydroelectric plant to heat their homes and another group of 1000 need a wilderness valley to satisfy their need for tranquility or natural ecology (Chapter 7). One group of 554,000 postal employees may need a 14 percent wage increase while another group of 554,000 citizens needs relief from inflation (Chapter 9). One group of 200,000 citizens may need low-cost automobiles, which can only be produced on a production line, while another group of 200,000 workers in automobile companies need relief from the mental stress caused by production lines (Chapter 9). In each case, the numbers are the same, but the constituencies' valences are different. How *much* does tranquility and natural ecology mean in the lives of Sierra Club members? How *much* does cheap electricity mean in the lives of low-income groups? There are questions of valence, strength of need, or marginal utility.

The majority can tyrannize the minority by ignoring valence altogether and simply counting numbers. Or the majority can simply fail to take the long-term development view of the strategic system required in strategic ethics. The British Parliament did these things once. In drawing up the colonial education budget, it assigned a high valence to education services (TE) for the constituency that lived in England. This was because school systems and education were judged to be a strong need of the people in England. It assigned a low valence to constituencies in colonial Africa. They reasoned that the Africans' needs for education (or at least the type of education offered in England), were not very great. Assuming that there were a million persons in England and a million in the colonies, and each were multiplied by a different valence, one can see that the final measurement of "the good of the constituency" came out to be high for England and low for Africa. Thus, the "greatest good for the greatest number" pointed to a large education budget for England and a small one for Africa.

In this example Parliament underestimated the valence for the minority. The utilitarian principle can also be used by the minority to overestimate their values and underestimate the valence of the majority. This actually happened in the Mount Rainier National Park case (Chapter 7). One minority, persons who wanted rugged wilderness areas for mountaineering hikes, numbered 23,945 people. They wanted 210,000 acres (90 percent) of the park's total acreage closed to all others. But as the case unfolded, it was found that 1.6 million other human beings used the park each year. These were divided into other constituencies: those who wanted automobile trips,

329

elderly people who wanted access roads for short walks in nature, handicapped people who could not endure mountaineering hikes in the wilderness, and working people who could not spare the time for week-long backpack trips as they could for day trips or weekend trips. Strategists in the National Park Service gave high valence to the needs of backpackers, ignoring the other minorities. They proposed to close the park. The inequity in the situation caused later strategists in the Park Service and the Department of the Interior to recognize the incorrect assignment of valences. The strategic decision was changed to more equitably distribute the park's resources on the basis of *both* numbers and *valences*, and to arrive at a new plan that more nearly represented the greatest good for the greatest number.

If strategists use the strategic ethic described in this book, the probability of either the majority or the minority tyrannizing the other is reduced. The strategic ethic requires not only a careful diagnosis of park strategy (services offered, constituencies served) in terms of the responsibility matrix explained throughout Chapters 3–9, but it requires a long-term developmental point of view, one that takes into account the development of both technical and human competences.

A final criticism of the utilitarian ethic is that no scientifically precise measures of either numbers or valences is possible. This criticism is correct—for scientists. However, the greatest economists, those who have a mastery of both the scientific methodology and the ethical questions involved, now know that it is impossible to use science to arrive at a real "welfare function," or a truly objective "cost-benefit analysis."[5] Kenneth Arrow, for example, acknowledges that this will be impossible because of the "incommensurability and incomplete communicability of human wants and values." He poses the problem in George Bernard Shaw's words: "Do not do unto others as you would have them do unto you. They may have different tastes."[6]

But what is an unworkable principle for one profession, science, is not only workable, but mandatory for another profession, strategy. We must remember that the language of strategy is conceptual logic, not mathematics. The concept of a hydroelectric dam includes both its factual engineering attributes (kilowatts) and its ethical attributes (an artifact with valences to human beings). This concept is used to focus problems, look for alternatives, and diagnose outcomes for constituencies. The concept of a constituency includes both a factual reality (human beings who consume products and services) and an ethical theme (human needs satisfied by products and services).

330

After problems have been focused, and after alternatives and outcomes have been conceptualized, it follows that *judgments* will be made in the same language. They will be made by estimating, as best strategists can, the greatest good for the greatest number. To expect strategists to articulate judgments already spelled out by mathematics would be as strange as requiring judges to serve simply as loudspeakers, announcing opinions mechanistically produced by an electronic computer.

Making judgments is, as we pointed out in Chapter 1, simply another way of looking at the work responsibilities assigned to the strategic group by society. Society cannot do without this kind of specialization. Strategists, whether they like it or not, and whether they do an effective or an ineffective job, do make judgments continually. They should be aware of their role, and of the rules by which it should be carried out.

Auxiliary Criterion: Pareto Optimum

One other criterion which is of use to strategists in searching for alternatives and judging between alternatives is a modified form of a rule proposed by the Italian economist and sociologist, Vilfredo Pareto. His most important work, *Mind and Society*, was published in 1916. His rule figures prominently in modern cost-benefit analysis using quantitative methods, but must be modified to fit strategic (conceptual) language.

Pareto proposed that in making decisions that affect a number of different individuals and groups, the rule to be followed is: *search for alternatives, and choose that alternative which will make everyone* better off. This is "the Pareto Principle." In game terminology, this means that strategists must play a nonzero-sum game, in which everyone wins, rather than a zero-sum game in which some are bound to win and others are bound to lose. Realizing that such ideal solutions are seldom possible, Pareto devised another rule, which should be pursued if the first one fails—"the Pareto Improvement." It holds that an alternative should be sought to make some people better off without making anyone worse off.

These two rules have practical significance for strategists. The first suggests that strategists should search for ideal solutions. Although these are never possible in practice, there are definitely alternatives that are closer to ideal and those which are farther from ideal. In practical terms, the principle holds that strategists should search for alternatives that increase the zones of support and acceptance, that also decrease the zone of indifference (by impacting constituencies not formerly actively concerned), and that *also* decrease the zone of conflict. Thus, the Pareto Principle urges a proactive role aimed at affecting all constituencies at once.

The practical application of the Pareto Improvement differs from that of the Pareto Principle. It urges strategists to "accentuate the positive and avoid the negative" rather than "accentuate the positive only." Using this principle, strategists would search for alternatives that expand the zone of support (clients, resource suppliers, and cultural constituencies that benefit directly from the organization's task performance) without affecting the needs of constituencies in the zone of indifference or the zone of conflict.

A recent case history of strategic planning at Seattle-Tacoma International Airport shows that strategists do indeed use these kinds of rules when designing the services to be rendered to different constituencies (cargo services, passenger services) and the internal resources for supplying these services (landing runways, gate entries, waiting lounges, parking garages.)[7] They considered policies that would increase the passenger-handling capacities of existing gates (better processes for bringing in aircraft in shorter time intervals) thus increasing the zone of support from both passengers and airlines. The same policies would decrease the noise generated in residential areas around the airport (by handling more aircraft in daylight hours, landings and takeoffs could be restricted from nighttime hours). Thus, "everybody wins." The zone of support is increased and the zone of conflict decreased. Incidentally, finding this kind of creative alternative is not easy. This particular "intuitive vision" (the logical relationship between technical tower procedures, the noise zone in private residences, and the use of a finite number of gates) was discovered in group creativity sessions to be described later in this chapter.

Strategists at the airport also searched for alternatives that would meet the Pareto Improvement's standard. Because noise from the airport cannot be completely eliminated, and because there will therefore, in the forseeable future, always be a zone of conflict, they sought to maximize the zone of support and convert constituencies in the zone of indifference to the zone of support. For example, they considered how they could eliminate access-road congestion, and improve both the capacity and the convenience of the parking garage, thus creating favorable attitudes in the minds of passengers. They considered approaching METRO, the mass transit authority of Seattle, to try to work out more convenient and useful services from downtown. They would thus gain not only passenger support, but the support of METRO and its constituencies, all of whom were

332

interested in such matters as low-cost transportation, the saving of gasoline in a time of shortage, and decreasing pollution on the freeways. Finally, they worked with small businesses in the adjoining town of Burien, which were interested in the flow of automobile traffic and in themselves serving passengers from the airport.

Why must the Pareto rules be modified for strategy and policy formulation? For the same reasons, previously explained, why the mathematical version of the utilitarian principle can be used by scientists but not by strategists. Pareto did not intend that the valences of human beings be included in his methodology. He refused to differentiate between the importance of one value or another to individual constituencies. Strategists, on the other hand, must use the strategic language rather than the mathematical language. They must judge the concept of a parking garage, or the concept of an airplane flying in an approach pattern in both engineering (factual) and ethical (valence) terms.

Strategy Formulation

Earlier we saw that the formulation of a framework for decision is a most important step in the decision-making process. The focus of the problem is in itself an act of conceptual logic and of ethical judgment. The choosing of *dominant constraints* (factors or outcomes to be considered) serves the same purposes. When one selects the most important factors to consider in the problem, one is actually choosing which variables and outcomes are most important to actors in the strategic system. Another way to say this is that the concept of the problem (what to focus on, what alternatives to consider, and what to treat as important constraints) is a powerful influence on everything else the decision maker does.

Problem Focus

Problem focus is determined by what is judged to be most important. "Most important" should be stated in two ways: (1) what has the highest payoff to society and (2) what represents the best use of the strategist's limited attention span, emotional energy, and time. The first is a matter of value weight in society. The second a matter of sequential attention. Strategists cannot "do everything at once."

When focusing comprehensive strategies, as contrasted with policy increments, the rule is: *Focus on the product or service concept (TE) as a long-term, evolutionary, distinctive competence, recognizing this concept as the ultimate* (primary) *mission of the*

333

organization in society. Product/market or constituency/service alignment then becomes not only the most important thing the organization can accomplish in society but the first sequential priority that strategists should attack. A brief word about both of these matters will provide further understanding.

Why should the product/market concept be weighted more than other values in society? The most powerful reasons lie in Chapter 10. The role of strategists in the organization, the role of the organization in society, and the slow evolutionary process of social alignment taken together mean that if outputs to society are not aligned today there may be no organization tomorrow. Enough has been said of the growth and breakdown processes, and of the social exchange process, and enough empirical evidence presented on these processes, that they can now be phrased as the first rule for strategic problem focus. Chapter 1 also pointed out, through simpleminded examples, that citizens get upset if they go to a symphony concert box office only to be offered there a bank loan. They get upset if the city fire department gives a charitable donation to a local art museum. Not only are citizens' functional needs thwarted but also their cognitive processes are interrupted when they try to cope through life in an industrial society.

It may seem at first that this rule is the same as that proposed in economics, namely, that the product or service goal of an organization is the ultimate end, and that all other goals are to be subordinated as means to this end. It is vital for the strategist to realize that the focus rule is *not* an argument from economics. Using strategic language, it is a *cultural* argument. It involves not only the economic welfare of society but the entire range of cultural values in society.

Why should the product/market concept have priority for general managers' time, emotional energy, and cognitive attention? Not only because of the reasons cited earlier, but because, as was pointed out in Chapters 4 and 6, human beings in unstructured situations *must* engage in heuristics; they must focus somewhere. Though strategists in the Boston Symphony seemed to "jump about" when they focused on a capital policy (TI.11), they were nevertheless focusing on output (TE). They were trying to align the music they offer to Boston society of the 1970s, rather than simply living with the music offered to Boston society of the 1920s.

Constraints

Having focused the problem on products and services, we may then ask what key factors must be considered in either creating

334

alternatives or predicting outcomes. This is a matter of judging which variables or outcomes are most relevant to the organization's primary mission. To use the language of mathematics, it is a matter of judging which factors will serve as constraints on strategists as they make decisions.

No substantive rule could ever answer this question. Everything in the strategic system depends on everything else. If strategists tried to attend to all constituency demands, their minds would be overloaded and they would be subject to such stop-gap methods as pointed out at the end of Chapter 10: putting new wine in old bottles, reverting to bureaucratic rules about past practices, or simply giving up and making ad hoc policies based on unguided self-interests.

Fortunately, though there is no substantive rule for isolating constraints, there is a set of process rules. Strategy formulation is a sequential decision process rather than an application of a formula. These process rules may be the best available to help strategists move through the complexity of the strategic system. They specify four steps, each of which yields "an answer" that becomes an input to solve the "next step." At the end of the chain of decisions, a comprehensive, global, logical, and ethical picture of the organization's future alignment emerges. This process is valuable for decision making by an individual human mind, but because it is even more valuable for arriving at a common strategic language, spoken by the entire strategic group, it will be discussed in the last part of this chapter.

Policy Formulation:
Focus and Constraints

Rules for structuring policy problems are different from rules for structuring comprehensive strategy problems. The reason is simple. Any methodology must fit the problematic situation. Policy situations are different from strategy situations.

Chapter 5 showed that policies are formulated to cover *parts* or increments of the strategy. They cover the twilight zone between strategic visions (comprehensive conceptual networks) and the brute facts of real alignments. They convert perceptions in the minds of strategists into real products, markets, services, capital equipment, and work designs. The policy method is experimental because strategists cannot forsee, predict, or control all of the technical and human events that might occur to block or change the strategy. Finally, policies have in one sense a shorter time perspective. They must deal with existing events and people rather than events and people that may exist in the future.

335

Problem Focus

For all of these reasons, the problem must be focused differently. It must be focused somewhat by reaction to events rather than by having visions of events in the future. Because of this, the rule for focusing the problem is: *Focus on that policy problem which other actors in the strategic system discover to be, for whatever reason, out of alignment with the rest of the system.*

Case histories in this book have shown that the *types* of dysfunctional alignments, the *constituencies* who discover the imperfections, and their *methods* for calling this to the attention of strategists differ from situation to situation. Sometimes a technical matter is out of alignment (Chapter 5: Sears, Roebuck parking lots may not hold enough cars to align with the new strategy on product lines; A&P grocery stores may not be located to fit with changes in population). In these cases, imperfections are usually discovered by consumers, clients, administrators, or work-level employees. At other times it is an economic efficiency matter that is out of alignment (Chapter 9: the taxpayers of New York City will not tolerate the large budget for manpower in various city departments; HEW in Washington will not tolerate the work procedures traditionally used by medical doctors in hospitals). In still other cases it is a cultural matter that is out of alignment (Chapter 7: citizens and OSHA Headquarters in Washington will not tolerate accidents and deaths due to lawn-mowers; Chapter 9: employees will not tolerate conditions on production lines).

Constraints

When we have the focus of the problem, what are the dominant constraints that must be taken into account? From all the confusion in the unstructured system, which variables are "most important"? There are five rules for choosing them: (1) make the master strategy the most important constraint, (2) satisfy immediate resource suppliers, (3) avoid nonremedial solutions, (4) use policy analysis to discover real outcomes, and (5) judge the timing of, and "system readiness" for change.

The first two of these rules are very different from the disjointed policymaking process. Disjointed policymaking is sometimes thought to be necessary for two reasons, one an intellectual matter and one a human conflict matter. It is argued that strategists cannot possibly predict the variables in the chaotic system; therefore they do not try. It is argued that constituencies have not only their own interests but their own way of formulating the problem; therefore

336

the most important outcome to consider is what will be accepted by diverse interests. Finally, it is argued that a comprehensive strategy, one that is best for society, will automatically emerge in the long run since any mistakes in alignment will be remedied in the future conflict process.

The *first rule*, stated earlier, is simply that successful strategists in government and in business do formulate comprehensive strategies. This was established empirically in Chapters 3–5. They may do this in a way that seems foreign to those committed to the language of mathematical science, but they nevertheless do it. They use a time perspective that is different from other professions and a method that fits the problematic situation. However, in policy formulation, what was formerly the focus of the problem now becomes the most important constraint. There is a logical reversal in the sequence of decision making. In focusing on immediate policies, the most important thing to take into account is the long-term strategy.

The *second rule* for isolating constraints is well known in social science literature. The resource-dependency approach explained in Chapter 1 tells us that in the last analysis no organization can survive for very long without resources from the outside world, and that strategists had better satisfy the parties in the immediate situation that supply resources. Another branch of literature discusses negotiating, bargaining, and coalition-forming processes that are necessary in dealing with resource suppliers.[8] Other authors have proposed a general framework for managing relationships with constituencies in order to secure greatest support from external parties.[9] The second rule for isolating key constraints is consistent with these perspectives. It simply says that the second most important factor to be considered in policy formulation is the power of those who supply resources to the organization. Strategists must, as the senator in Missouri stated in Chapter 5, "sometimes knuckle under."

This does not mean that strategists should weight this factor more than the primary mission. To do so would be ethically wrong. The resource-dependency model of policy formulation, if coupled with the disjointed-process model, results in an ethical principle that would violate five strategic ethics proposed herein. Pursued to the extreme, it means that if all parties in policymaking would simply be honest with themselves, as Nietzsche advocated, they would realize that in the last analysis *might makes right*. If they all recognize that the play of power is the strongest factor in the situation, they would, as Machiavelli pointed out, make power the most important variable. Not only would ranking power as the first constraint be ethically wrong, it would be factually ineffective for future growth and development of the organization.

The *third rule* for isolating important variables in the problem recognizes a characteristic of strategic systems that is similar to the process of *retention* in the evolutionary process. The nature of a cultural system, composed as it is of a vast network of stable technological and human patterns of action, is very difficult to change. It takes long time cycles of strategic action to add viable new competences to the system while retaining the delicate mechanisms that hold the system together. Policies that are made today inevitably affect the structure of the system tomorrow. Some are nonremedial. A large mistake in alignment at one stage of growth and development is equivalent to a large error in ecological selection, one that will be impossible to correct in the next stage of development. Organizations do die, and this is one of the most powerful reasons.

In earlier chapters, we saw that strategists in government locked the railroad industry into a set of policies that made it impossible for the industry to change into a form more viable for changing society. We saw that policy mistakes in the A&P Corporation made it nearly impossible for strategists to correct the errors made in past years. Here, we will simply raise two more examples to show the true nature of a cultural system, and to show that some policy mistakes cannot be remedied.

Picture the freeway system in Los Angeles. It is technically complex and technically stable (millions of tons of concrete). It is economically complex and economically stable (the sunk costs provided by county and federal governments, regardless of the rules of incremental capital investment, are compelling to taxpayers and government officials). It has determined the culture of the region: where private citizens build houses and how much they cost, what time a citizen must shave in the morning, or have breakfast. It has determined whether people can swim at beaches, get to work, visit sick relatives, or be together as families in the evening. It locates hospitals, apartment houses. In short, once the technological structures of the freeway are in place, and once the vast network of social customs has been formed and soldified, it is unrealistic to think that strategists in county and federal governments can simply decide they had made a mistake, change their minds, and change the whole cultural pattern.

One other case will show the nonremedial nature of certain policy decisions. Briefly, the situation is as follows. Strategists in California passed a law in 1974 that recognized the nonremedial principle. The law specified each county in the state draw up a comprehensive cultural plan for future development, one that would include all facets of the cultural system: technological structures, economic entities, and human life-style patterns. As this book goes to press, state officials have used various mechanisms to prevent counties from engaging in disjointed policymaking, to prevent them from making decisions that are nonremedial. In 1977, the state's attorney general notified strategists in Marin County and Sonoma County that he would file suit to halt *all* developments until master plans were drawn up. The city of Santa Barbara was actually placed under a moratorium to prevent all building permits until it complied with the law. In 1979 the attorney general halted *all* incremental developments in Lake County. The Office of Planning and Research banned all piecemeal subdivisions in Santa Cruz County and all construction in Mendocino County. Threatened with the same state of affairs in Monterrey County, Sam Farr, member of the Board of Supervisors, pinpointed the reason: "We are paying for the sins of past board of supervisors. The various permits being issued in the Carmel Valley may have to stop until there is more logic of overall development."

The *fourth rule* for determining the factors to be considered in any policy problem is: *Use policy analysis as a valuable instrument for predicting outcomes.* Scientific analysis is one of the most powerful ways for discovering what really happens when strategic visions are engineered. Although mathematical predictions are of limited use in strategy formulation (a logical/conceptual/ethical process) they are of great use in *policy formulation*. Thus, to the strategist, science has both powers and limitations. Knowing the difference between the two, and when to use science in proper perspective, is a key to effective strategic decision making. The range of policy-analysis techniques is so great that no book could possibly summarize them. They range all the way from use of social psychology to predict what kinds of production line actually will satisfy human beings who work on the line to use of engineering to predict whether or not the parking lots in Sears, Roebuck actually will support the weight of automobiles. The entire range of subjects offered in the modern business school curriculum, from cost-benefit analysis to discounted cash flow of incremental returns, represent techniques to find out what will happen if strategists decide that products should be improved, capital investments changed, organization structures designed differently, operating processes brought up to date, or human work designs altered. It is vital to recognize that policy analysis follows from strategic logic, not the other way around.

The *fifth* and last rule for finding constraints that must be observed is: *Judge the timing of and "system readiness" for change.*

339

Why is this a constraint? Simply because strategists, even though they believe they know the right policy that would integrate with the comprehensive strategy, cannot order it into effect without "system readiness." This concept means that changes must be prepared for in other ways than simply "making decisions" and that there is a proper time actually to make the decision. The concept is also related to the "demand for status quo" discussed in Chapter 8.

A wide variety of research from many social science disciplines supports the fact that effective strategists do observe the principle of timing. Mintzberg's study in the Volkswagen Company confirmed that there may be periods when the system is in flux, when it is stable, or when various actors in the system are actively demanding change (Chapter 5). Glazer found that in the history of the Supreme Court, the justices have engaged in "periods of activism" at certain times and "periods of quietism" at others. When they exceeded the ability of the system to absorb change, becoming too active, the results were the major catastrophes in American history. Wrapp (Chapter 5) found that strategists in business corporations behave the same way. He called this "muddling with a purpose." He found that during this muddling strategists explore corridors of indifference, and that they do this with a conscious sense of timing. Quinn (Chapter 5) saw the same thing in IBM, Control Data, and General Motors. In periods of quietism his strategists did not make clear policy decisions. They knew the comprehensive strategy well, but instead they engaged in activities such as "building awareness," "engaging in strategic dialogues" to broaden support for the strategy, or "creating pockets of commitment to the longer-term outlook." They were very careful to judge the time for crystallizing opinion and for actually making the policy decision. Toynbee found the same pattern of behavior in the history of civilizations. His leaders practiced a style similar to that of IBM and General Motors executives. Toynbee called it "withdrawal and return."

The Conceptual Method

In this section we will describe a method of comprehensive strategy formulation that is at the same time a cognitive method (it is based on conceptual logic), an ethical method (it reconciles pluralistic social ethics by means of the strategic ethic), and a social method (it involves interaction among the strategic group to learn a common strategic language).

Background

The following is not new. It is based on a methodology that was developed by policy professors at Harvard Business School over many years, as they wrote cases in business and government, diagnosed and solved these cases with students in the classroom, met each week to diagnose cases among themselves, and consulted with ongoing organizations. A brief history of how and when the method was developed, and some of the published works describing it, appear in Chapter 3.

The version that appears here has been modified in certain respects. The steps have been slightly rearranged. It is presented as a group method rather than an individual decision-making method. Interpretations of some of the intellectual and social processes that occur during its use are solely the responsibility of the author.

You may wonder where these interpretations come from and how they were derived. They were conceptualized partly by working with students in the classroom, but primarily from strategic planning projects carried out in eight organizations, five business corporations, and three government agencies.

Business corporations studied included Associated Grocers, an integrated wholesale-retail business with 300 branch stores; General Mining Company, the world's largest producer of uranium, and a leading producer of coal and gold; Recreational Equipment Company, an integrated manufacturer, wholesaler, and retailer of outdoor sporting equipment; SANLAM Insurance Company, a large life insurance company; and Shoe Corporation of South Africa, the largest manufacturer of shoes in the Southern Hemisphere.

Government agencies studied included the United States Navy Station at Keyport-Bangor, Washington, formerly a torpedo-testing station and now maintenance base for the Trident program; Port of Seattle, operator of marine facilities; and Seattle-Tacoma International Airport, serving approximately 9 million passengers per year and facing the uncertainties of a deregulated airline industry.

The strategic planning process was carried out in essentially the same way in each of these organizations, although there were variations in the timing within and between steps in the process.

Task force

A task force composed of 11 to 19 members was initially selected on the basis of two qualifications. First, each member was expected to have stored in memory a wide range of information about one major function or key policy area in the organization. The member was also expected to know such information as how the particular function relates to the final output (TE), how that function is structured internally (TI.11, TI.12), and how that function performs at the operating level (TI.21, TI.22).

341

Identifying major functions (key policy areas) was not an easy job. In most cases, the two or three top persons in the organization had some difficulty in using the existing organization chart. Two problems meant that the final task-force membership partly reflected the official chart and partially deviated from it. First, it was discovered in all organizations that some major functions were "buried" in existing divisions. The division head would be familiar with the broad picture of present operations, but, because his or her attention was spread so broadly, could not be expected to know the details. Second, there were times when a person was chosen to represent a division because he or she simply possessed the most complete storehouse of up-to-date information. These two factors of course created problems for the few top people choosing the team. But because they were choosing a decision-making group, and not a routine chain of command group, they found it impossible to avoid some selectivity when designating task-force membership.

One person, the project coordinator, was expected to perform three official functions and assorted informal functions. Officially, this person was (1) expected to keep the task force on its agenda, following the four steps listed later, (2) expected to serve as discussion leader at meetings, and (3) assigned the duty of writing long summary reports to answer the crucial questions raised in each step.

Informally, the coordinator served to overcome some of the maladaptive leadership patterns found in Chapters 8 and 10, particularly the feelings of insecurity generated by the chaotic policy system. For example, he or she was expected to watch for common threads of logic that might be expounded by two or three task-force members, each of whom put the matter in different terms. The coordinator was expected to use the questioning of a naive outsider to clarify the meaning of unclear logic. He or she used the agenda to remind members that they were "in the trees" but that the "forest will emerge if we just keep trying." He or she also used written reports to show members that what originally seemed to be an impossible situation in fact now adds up to a logical picture of solid accomplishment.

Over its entire 24-week schedule, the task force pursued a single goal: to arrive at an ideal comprehensive strategy for the organization — a logical network of interrelated policies, covering future outputs to society and future internal competences that would be required to produce those outputs.

At the end of the project, this strategy was to exist in two forms. By far the most important objective was to arrive at a *shared strategic language*, a framework in the mind of each member, a consensus of

342

the strategic group as a whole. It was the shared meaning, the shared comprehensive logic that was sought above all else.[10] In months following four of the projects, members commented openly that task-force members in many small ways were formulating real policies to carry out the spirit of the agreed-on strategy. They were doing this in their official departments (when elaboration was called for within a division) and in their official committees. When, for example, a capital budget or a new work design was called for it was the top capital budget committee or the top personnel committee that made policies to elaborate the strategy. Thus, the most important way in which policy was related to strategy was by the many proactive decisions that followed, somewhat on an ad hoc basis.

The second way in which the strategy existed was on paper. The official reports written by the coordinator were always fed back to the group for study before the following meeting. At the beginning of the next meeting, there was a time period often jokingly referred to as "corrections to the minutes." Members were completely serious about this, however; they felt that important decisions were being made and that if the coordinator had put erroneous facts or judgments into the report they should be corrected.

Timing of Steps

Timing of steps was spread over 24 weeks, with 6 weeks between meetings. This was important for two reasons, the nature of the work to be done and the busy schedule of general managers as they must continue day-to-day operations.

Strategic logic cannot be rushed. What is needed is an unhurried approach that allows for members' minds to be saturated with information yet free to mull over and absorb meaning before making final judgments. The six weeks between meetings also resulted in a large amount of informal interchange among executives. In all cases it was found that members who gathered for lunch or for official meetings would say to each other such things as "that subject of doing away with 'x' is a controversial one. What do you think about it?" Or, one might say, "I must confess I was fairly uninformed about that subject at our last meeting. I've since done some research on it and find that Joe was right."

The second reason for spreading the project over six months is that busy executives simply cannot, will not, and should not abdicate their ongoing responsibilities for a concentrated period of time. As one executive put it, "I won't interrupt my duties to engage in speculating about the future. It's got to be arranged so that we can do competent planning without it being a burden on my time."

Sequence of Steps

The method being described is a particular heuristic method especially relevant for strategy formulation. The focus of the problem shifts from step to step. The results (outputs) of one step are used as the basis for (inputs to) the next step. Thus the method involves a chain of conceptual logic. Logical heuristics is one thing but emotional heuristics is another. The method is valuable in generating certain feelings of security and accomplishment in one step that serve as a basis for moving on to the next step.

If the root causes of maladaptive leadership listed at the end of Chapter 10 are to be removed, it is vital that some way be found to progress from the insecurity of "open-field confusion" to the more secure feeling of "closure at each step." Starting with masses of facts, the method proceeds to structure each step so that the facts can be handled by the human mind without trying to "do everything at once." It is also designed to provide a sense of achievement and accomplishment, a feeling that the strategic group can indeed master the situation by using clear strategic logic. Finally, it is designed to overcome some of the problems of groupthink. It is arranged to provide an orderly interplay between the stability of the present (habitual) way of operating and the dynamism of the changing world outside the organization.

It is important to recognize that if the steps in the method are taken out of sequence, jumping to conclusions in step 1 before logical prior analysis in step 2 produces a readiness to do so, the emotional reactions of task-force members may be reversed. Such a short-circuiting of the process can cause the very emotions the method tries to prevent. It can generate insecurity in the minds of current strategists to the point where they may make a charade of the process. This is particularly true in step 3. Unless the law of the situation ("handwriting on the ecological wall") *out there* is firmly established in step 2, there is almost certain to be defensive behavior ("empire protection," "ego protection") in step 3.

Procedures within Steps

Five substeps were found to be useful within each step in the process.

Goal clarification for each step is accomplished six weeks ahead of

344

scheduled meetings. Goals are stated in two forms. First, the goal is stated as a declaration of work to be done. In the first step, for example, the goal is "to arrive at a statement of the present strategy of the Seattle-Tacoma International Airport." Second, the goal is stated in the form of a broad question: "What are the services being rendered to various constituencies, what statistical level of success do we enjoy with these constituencies, and what internal resource competences are causing this level of success?" The goal question is helpful to guide homework (policy analysis) of each member between meetings.

Policy analysis is the homework to be done between meetings to answer the goal question. This homework is performed by individual members. They are encouraged to go back to their departments and do two things: (1) gather facts and reasoning to answer the goal question and (2) consult with lower-level personnel to gather this information.

Meetings of the task force seem burdensome on first sight. For each step, the task force stays in continuous meeting for two days, or approximately 16 hours—when possible, at a location away from day-to-day work activities (and telephones). In all cases members reported that they initially dreaded such long meetings. But in all cases they have been surprised at the interest generated. Part of this is due to the agenda. The broad and open questions bring forth such comments as, "This is something I knew all the time we should be discussing but we have never found time to do it." Or, "I cannot believe that we could sit there and raise such vital topics—vital to the company and challenging in my career." In every case, *after* the project is completed, there are comments such as, "I have never known as much about what other departments are doing and what their place is in the overall success of the company." These comments are made in spite of the fact that the project is always treated as a decision-making project. It is never billed as an executive-development project or as a training session.

There are quiet periods during the 16 hours in which the task force seems to be getting nowhere. These are inevitably interrupted by "breakthroughs," in which some member will recall what another member said, add to it, and then conclude something like "this is the greatest threat to our success in the future." This in turn sets off another round of discussion in which other members clarify the issue, dig into homework notes to prove their point with facts, or slightly modify the logic of the original proposer.

The *report* of the meeting answers the goal question. It is written by the coordinator during five to eight days following the meeting. It

345

reflects the common threat arguments that seem to come up again and again among members, even though each member may phrase the logic of strategy in different forms. One member may focus on a different policy as a starting point at 10 o'clock this morning and then branch into the same reasoning another member used at 3 o'clock yesterday afternoon.

The coordinator uses a minimum of judgment in putting together arguments. Sometimes he or she may actually clarify a logic that was never articulated in the same words. A test of the coordinator's impartial role comes at the next meeting, in the "corrections-to-the-minutes" segment. In all cases general managers have not hesitated to challenge the report if they feel it has not captured the consensus logic, or if it fails to present factual proof of the logic.

Report writing of this type serves three vital functions. It puts the logical network of concepts on paper for all to see. It is a storehouse of facts to which members refer back not only at following meetings but also in months after the task force has disbanded. Finally, it serves as a benchmark of accomplishment, helping members marshall the great amount of energy to see the project through.

Phase I: History and Present Strategy

The goal in the first phase is to discover on the basis of facts and statistics how successful the company or agency is in the outside world, which products or services are causing this level of success (TE), and which internal resource competences (TI) are the key ones producing these products and services. The goal question is: What is the present strategy of the United States Navy Station at Keyport-Bangor, how successful are we in the outside world, and what resource competences are causing this success? An allied question is to trace the history of the organization to show by the same kind of analysis "how we got the way we are today."

Inevitably, members treat the history of the organization with some surprise. They begin to see how successive strategic groups have made certain decisions that propelled the organization forward, whereas others have engaged in periods of quietism. There is a great deal of speculation about which services and competences really are producing results. In this discussion members discover certain "myths" about current strategic logic. These myths are erroneous beliefs that a certain product, service, or internal resource is "the most important." They are natural in any organization. They mean that at one point in the past the mythical strategy did fit society. However, the organization has actually evolved new policies that, by

346

superceding older policies, have gone unrecognized as the corner-
stones of strategy.

On the positive side, many task-group members feel emotional
gratification from this phase. There are feelings of understanding of
one's part in the larger whole. For the first time, away from day-to-
day decisions, many persons understand what the whole strategy is
all about. There is an equally satisfying *social* feeling: "I see the logic
in it, they [peers] see it, and they [hierarchical bosses] see it." This is
a first step toward what some psychologists have termed "unfreez-
ing." An organization that has been frozen into stable beliefs and
practices needs some way to stand back and test which of these are
actually up to date and which are not.

Two opposite emotional feelings seem to stand out at the end of
phase I. On one hand, the task force discovers something that
provides a sense of security. It discovers that the organization has
been doing a number of things right. Some of its products or services, and some of its internal competences, have been successful in
the past and look as though they will be functional for present
society. These are the ones that generate pride in accomplishment.
At the same time, however, there is a feeling of anxiety when
members discover that certain polices are really not as important in
today's world as they believed. Both of these feelings are useful in
moving the group to the next stage. One says, "We're not going to
throw the baby out with the bathwater in this fancy strategic planning project." The other says, "But there are some things that are
worrisome."

Phase II: Environmental Analysis

The goal of phase II is to look *outside* the organization, analyze
predicted changes in the external environment, and conclude what
these mean to an organization with the strategic alignment depicted
in phase I. The goal question for homework guidance is: From your
vantage point, what future opportunities do you see for the Keyport
Naval Station and what threats do you see if it continues in its present
strategy?

In the informal assignment session at the end of phase I, the group
is told, "We are trying to read the handwriting on the wall; we are
trying to find out how constituencies in the outside world view us."
As Follett put it, the group is trying to find the *law of the situation*, a
series of changes in society that demand collateral changes in the
organization's strategy. This phase is in one sense the most crucial: It
prevents the organization from turning inward on itself. It protects

347

constituencies from a strategic group that could otherwise isolate itself and engage in the kind of groupthink described in Chapter 8.

Experience in the eight organizations reveals that each member approaches the meeting with a different perspective. This is a normal and highly useful situation. One member of the airport task force, for example, presents data on the overcrowded runways and opinions of airline constituencies. Another has done research on the access roads and parking garage situation. Still another has come prepared to show how the Civil Aeronautics Board or the Federal Aviation Authority has changed its posture on how airports ought to operate. As each member presents information, others, not specialists in that policy area, frequently add helpful insights for their colleagues and for the specialist presenting the report.

The emotional reactions to this phase are similar to those in phase I. There is a feeling of excitement and accomplishment as the team gets down to work facing the the realities of the future. There is also anxiety. However, this anxiety is "healthier" than sheer fear of the unknown. It is based on realistic acknowledgements of real-world threats. This feeling is best expressed as, "It's a tough world to operate in but at least we have identified the true situation. We have clearly identified the forces that we have to deal with." This is a very different attitude than one in which people feel as though the world is so full of chaotic events that they hardly know where to turn next.

Fortunately, the agenda tells the group "where to turn next." The next place to turn is phase III. In it, the group will learn to make use of the clear picture of the environment it has generated in phase II.

Phase III: Capability Analysis

Whereas in phase II the group looked outside the company or agency, in phase III it does the opposite. It turns its focus inward. Its goal is to take a clear look at the internal competences of the organization in light of the changing environment as discovered in phase II. The question posed for homework is: As we consider our present strategy (phase I), and what is facing us in the outside world (phase II), what are the most crucial strengths and weaknesses in our competences—those which will prevent future growth and success?

Here the typology from the responsibility matrix, as elaborated in Chapters 3–9, serves as a rough outline for the agenda. The task force must search its competences: its product/markets and service/constituencies (TE); the external cultural objections to these (CE); its internal technical resources (TI.11, capital structure; TI.12, administrative organization structure; TI.21, operating processes;

348

and TI.22, work designs); and the cultural objections to these (CI). In each case, the group is searching for signs that competences are out of date with future trends in society.

This is the most difficult emotional stage in the whole process. Many persons naturally fear to address the question because of the difficulties involved in making changes, or because of fear that one's own department will be exposed as a weakness. As with other phases, however, there is both a bright side and an anxious side of the picture that emerges. On the bright side, members of all of the organizations studied were somewhat amazed to find that they had hidden strengths—distinctive competences that were so well based in society's needs that they would serve as stabilizing forces in the future. On the other side of the picture, though there was considerable anxiety as to what to do about it. There was a feeling best expressed as, "I've known all along that some of these things that were concluded should have been talked about and resolved long ago. At least we now have the whole matter on the table rather than ignoring it or trying to devise piecemeal solutions."

Phase IV: The New Strategy

As with the bridge between other phases, the agenda for phase IV provides an orderly way to proceed. Its goal is to realign the organization starting with its present competences (phase I). It will use the environmental forecast from phase II to read the handwriting on the wall from outside constituencies. It will use the phase III analysis to concentrate on (1) using existing competences to pursue opportunities in society, (2) building new competences to meet opportunities and threats, or (3) somehow adjusting policies to avoid threats. The goal question to guide homework for this phase is: What actions (decisions, policies) do you think the organization must take if it is to maximize its strengths and deal with its weaknesses?

Experience in these eight organizations suggests that the best way to go about the final decision stage is to recognize freely that the task force is not going to make a series of full-blown concise decisions that can be put into practice immediately. What it will do is (1) phrase a list of priority issues that must be solved, (2) clarify the nature of the problem in each case, (3) list the most promising alternative that has been advanced, (4) cite reasons and research data to support this alternative, (5) estimate the date by which the final decision should be made, and (6) give advice to the normal hierarchical group as to *who* should solve the problem.

The last point deserves some comment. It was often found that

349

an existing department or division was the obvious one to do more analysis and elaborate the decision but that it had to work with other divisions that also would have to adjust their policies. This is not surprising, since all policy questions seem to affect other parts of the strategy. Occasionally, however, there was a problem identified as high-priority for which there was no equivalent department, division, or section. In these cases, the group had stumbled on the well-known problem Chandler pointed out. What it really discovered was that there was no existing resource capability, no distinctive competence, that could cope with the future.

Distinctive competences are not built overnight. Specializations must be brought in, or developed in existing personnel. There are political questions involved of the type discussed in Chapter 8. Fortunately, the key influentials in the organization have been members of the task force. There is at least the chance that organizational matters will, at this point, be viewed as "the law of the situation" rather than as matters to be avoided or to be fought over in protective skirmishes.

In all eight organizations it was possible to get agreement on the six items we listed. In each case, the task force had reached enough of a meeting of the minds that it had an overall, comprehensive vision of what must be done in the future.

The world's productive organizations have today reached a size and complexity that makes it exceedingly difficult to make strategic decisions "by the seat of one's pants." Everywhere we see private corporations and government agencies involved in what appear to be impossibly complex problematic situations. On one hand, these organizations are vital to the standard of living *and* to the cultural well-being of society. Society demands that they not only survive, but that they grow and prosper as it grows and prospers. On the other hand, a wide range of constituencies threaten their primary missions. Customers, clients, consumers, taxpayers, stockholders, external cultural constituencies, and even internal administrators and employees demand that organizations change their competences—their products, services, markets, or internal resource configurations.

If this kind of problematic situation cannot be structured by "the seat of one's pants," what can strategists do? Can they rely on decision methods from scientific decision making? Not likely. The methodologies of science were developed to match the kind of problematic situation faced in another profession. Although this book has shown that scientific analysis is powerful when used in a

350

certain way to help solve strategic problems, that same analysis has serious limitations when applied to a problematic situation it does not fit.

In this chapter we have proposed a decision-making philosophy to deal with the strategic situation. This philosophy includes decision rules for making strategic decisions in general, for formulating global comprehensive strategies, and for formulating policies. It includes a cognitive-social method for gaining consensus in the strategic group without the dangers of groupthink. It includes the ethical considerations and leadership principles found in Chapter 9.

If the last two chapters of this book do nothing else, perhaps they will convince practicing strategists, and those who study strategic planning in the classroom, that *the practice of strategy formulation and policy formulation is a profession in its own right, with its own ethical code, its own leadership roles and its own decision-making method.* Only by becoming self-conscious about these three things will the profession ever be accepted as such by the rest of society.

Notes

1. Fred Fiedler, *A Theory of Leadership Effectiveness*, McGraw-Hill, 1967.

2. Robert Nisbet, "Public Opinion versus Popular Opinion," *The Public Interest* 41 (Fall 1975): 166–92.

3. R. L. Ackoff, *Redesigning the Future*, Wiley, 1974.

4. Philip Selznick, *Leadership in Administration, op. cit.*

5. Kenneth J. Arrow, *The Limits of Organization*, Norton, 1974; Arthur Okun, *Equality and Efficiency*, Brookings, 1975.

6. Arrow, *Limits*, p. 24.

7. Seattle-Tacoma International Airport, Appendix.

8. Ian MacMillan, *Strategy Formulation: Political Concepts*, West, 1978.

9. John P. Kotter, "Managing External Dependence," *Academy of Management Review* 4:1 (January 1979): 87–92.

10. For a theory of organization based on conceptual language see L. R. Pondy, and I. I. Mitroff, "Beyond Open System Models of Organization," in *Research in Organizational Behavior*, JAI Press, 1979.

APPENDIX

Research Methodology
and Data Base

THIS APPENDIX will provide, for those interested in research methodology, a brief note on the method used to arrive at conclusions in this book. It will also contain a list of case histories that serve as factual bases for these conclusions.

Model of Strategic Behavior

In this book we have built a theory of strategic behavior (B). In briefest terms, this is a model of a strategic system as composed of three actors: organizations (O), society (S), and strategists (St). The action of each actor both causes and is influenced by the actions of the other two. This model can be expressed by the following formula. Behavior of a strategic system is a function of the interacting behavior of organizations, society, and strategists:

$$B = f(O, S, St)$$

The most essential features of an organization are (1) that it develops (grows and declines) depending on (2) whether it can maintain goals (distinctive competences in outputs and resources) that are aligned with the conflicting demands of society. This model can be expressed by the following formula, which expresses the relationship between organization and society. Organization development (O_d) is a function of conflicting demands of society (S) and the alignment of organization goals (O_a):

$$O_d = f(S, O_a)$$

The most basic function of strategists is to engage in strategic leadership (SL), a key factor determining whether or not the organization's resources are aligned with the demands of society (O_a). The following formula expresses the relationship between strategists and organizations.

$$O_a = f(SL)$$

Strategic leadership, you will recall, is composed of (1) strategic decision making (strategy and policy formulation) and (2) the acting out of power and influence roles, which themselves are partly the result of how strategists have formulated alignments in the past.

Simple Systems and Complex Systems

It may be helpful in understanding the research method used in this book to contrast it with one research method developed in natural sciences and later applied in the social sciences.

In hypothesis methodology, the scientist formulates a hypothesis about the interaction of a few forces (variables) in the system, designs an experiment to control out all other forces, and then uses mathematical techniques to record the affects of one variable on another. This can be called a "simple" system or a "closed" system of inquiry. It is simple and closed because it contains very few forces or variables (usually only two or three), and because all other forces are deliberately removed from the system by controlled experiments or controlled observations.

Typical examples are Charles's Law and Boyles's Law, prominent in the history of chemistry and physics. Combining these laws, experiments first set up an experimental apparatus consisting of a vessel filled with gas. This vessel is constructed so that it is expandable and contractable (to control volume) and so that all extraneous forces can be kept out of the system. The researcher next sets up a heating apparatus so that exact temperatures can be controlled.

The investigator then proceeds to analyze the behavior of the system in terms of the three variables: pressure (P), volume (V), and temperature (T). He or she may hold the size of the vessel constant (V) and raise the temperature (T), thus increasing pressure (P). Pressure, then, is a function of (directly proportional to) temperature: $P = T$. In common terms, if you heat a balloon or automobile tire it may burst. Scientists can perform other experiments in which one or the other variable is held constant and record the effects on the other factor in the formula.

For our purposes, the central characteristics of this method are (1) that it involves few forces or variables and (2) the reason it involves few forces is that the investigator *controls* what forces are in the system and what ones are kept out. Forces that might contaminate the pure interaction of a few variables are deliberately excluded.

354

Complex Systems

There is another view of systems, developed in physical science and later applied in social sciences, which more nearly matches the method used in this book.

Force-field theory, as postulated in physics, and as used by Lewin in psychology, holds that the behavior of an entity is caused by a complex, open system of forces operating within and around the entity. The system is complex in that it contains a very large number of forces or variables. It is open in that *all* of these forces play a part in determining behavior and none of them can be "closed out" or "controlled out" by the investigator. Consequently, the researcher must somehow use a method that is appropriate to complex, open systems. Lewin, in psychology, postulated a model in which behavior is a function of both what the person is (P, internal forces within the person) and what kind of environment surrounds the person (E, forces in the environment):

$$B = f(P, E)$$

In analogous fashion, in this book we hold that the behavior of an organization (O_d, its growth or decline) is a function of what the organization is (O_a, its alignment of distinctive competences) and the nature of the environment in which the organization is embedded. (S, forces generated by conflicting constituencies): $O_d = f(O_a, S)$. Further, whether or not an organization is aligned with society is a function of strategic leadership: $O_a = f(SL)$.

In Chapters 3–9 we saw that each of the entities under study is influenced by a large number of external and internal forces: task (technological-economic) forces and cultural (social, political, psychological) forces. These constitute the field of forces that has to be considered in explaining strategic behavior. There is such a large field of forces at work that strategic behavior cannot be accounted for by a hypothesis that explains behavior in a simple, closed field.

Data Sources: Case Histories

There are well known principles in academic research which hold that (1) there is no such thing as a universal research methodology, applicable to all types of research and therefore, (2) a methodology must be selected which *fits* the type of research in question.

Because the study of strategy and policy involve such a large force field, containing many interacting variables, case histories are the *only* form of data that can comprehend such a wide range of forces and such a wide range of causal effects (how each set of forces affects

355

others). It is no accident that case histories are used for research in law, in medicine and in cultural anthropology. Researchers in these professions, like those investigating strategy formulation and strategic leadership, are trying to explain the behavior of entities whose behavior is caused by a field of forces that cannot be *controlled* or *eliminated* without destroying the integrity of the system.

Given the fact that case histories are the appropriate source of data, the next question which must be answered is this: how does the researcher go about putting the data in orderly form? What methodology does he or she use?

Data Collection: Research Methods

Three research methods have been used to write this book, each of which has a rich tradition in academic fields other than the field of strategy and policy. The participant observer method has long been used in cultural anthropology. The case observer method has a rich tradition in legal research and medical research. The historical method has been developed for the study of history.

Cultural anthropologists have found that in order to gain a detailed and intimate knowledge of the forces at work in a given culture, the researcher must spend relatively long periods of time living in that culture and participating in its various forms of behavior. The researcher becomes a participant observer. As an outsider, he or she comes into the culture without having been trained to "take events for granted." This frame of reference frees the researcher to maintain a deeply inquiring mind, always asking, "what's going on here." But because the researcher is also a participant in the culture's events, he or she gains another frame of reference, one which reflects a deeper and more realistic understanding of what is happening and why.

This method was used in a number of cases in this book. The author in effect lived with strategists in a live organization which was responding to external and internal forces in a changing environment. He participated in discussions which were supposed to cope with such forces by adapting the organization to its environment. Cases compiled in this fashion are marked (*) in the list that follows.

A second research method used in this book is similar to methodology used in legal research and medical research. In the case observer method, the researcher performs one role in common with the participant observer. He or she spends extended periods of time living in the case situation, observing, and asking (1) what events are taking place and (2) what combination of complex forces are causing these events to take place. But the researcher is prevented from becoming a *participant* in the system either because he or she cannot participate (for example, judges do not participate in automobile accident cases, doctors do not contract diseases from patients) or because he or she deliberately refuses to become part of the system (most psychiatrists try not to become personally involved with patients).

The author acted as case observer in a number of cases listed below: AB Thorsten, British Commercial Investments Ltd., Mercury Stores, Metrocenter Ohio Police Department, Seaboard Chemical Company, Shoe Corporation of Illinois and Western Office Equipment Company.

A third method used in writing this book was the historical method. In historical research, the researcher values *primary source* data more highly than *secondary source* data. It is more accurate to rely on data compiled by a direct observer (one who acted as participant observer or case observer) than on information supplied by persons who in turn rely on direct observers. In the list which follows, the author draws heavily on cases written at Harvard Business School and by case observers such as Professor Quinn at Dartmouth. In doing this, he is drawing on primary sources who take seriously their responsibilities in terms of time, effort and factual reporting. In relying on these sources, the author is obeying one of the canons of historical research.

Other cases compiled by the author used as primary sources direct quotes from actors in the strategic system (strategists, constituency leaders) reported in the press or in hearings before government bodies: The High Ross Dam, Lincoln Rochester Trust Company, Mount Rainier National Park, SAAB Automobile Engine Assembly Department, Teachers Insurance and Annuity Association, University of Washington Law School, The Liberty Bank, and The New York City Fiscal Crisis.

A final method used in this book is the accumulation of case files as contrasted with the careful compilation of written case histories. This method has antecedents in medicine and law. Medical doctors, in analyzing forces at work in the health system of a human being, frequently find it necessary to keep files on the patient. These files may contain information gathered by the doctor as case observer or by the doctor as historian (the doctor asks other doctors or the patient himself or herself for prior history). Likewise, lawyers and judges frequently find it necessary to keep files on legal situations. Such files are accumulated by judges acting as case observers (they take notes on the plaintiff's behavior) or by judges acting as historians (they ask for facts and opinions of other judges).

Those cases listed below as "case files" were accumulated by the author to gather information on certain kinds of organizations (hospitals, city governments, business corporations) or certain actors in the strategic system (strategists, constituencies, or organizations). They include only data gathered from (1) primary historical sources (direct quotes of actors in the system), or (2) the author's own experience as case observer.

Published Cases

The following case histories have been published and are available to the public. Some are available in books. Others are available from the Intercollegiate Case Clearing House (ICCH) at Harvard Business School.

1. "AB Thorsten," by C. E. Summer and Gordon Shillinglaw, in C. E. Summer and J. J. O'Connell, *The Managerial Mind*, Richard D. Irwin, 1973, pp. 346–62. Copyright 1969 by Institute Pour l'Etude des Methodes de Direction de l'Entreprise (IMEDE), Lausanne, Switzerland.
2. "American Smelting and Refining Company," by David B. Jemison, University of Washington, Graduate School of Business, 1976.
3. "American Symphony Orchestras (History of)," by David B. Jemison and Charles E. Summer, ICCH, 1977.
4. "Anglo Norcross Shipping Company," by Howard H. Stevenson, ICCH, 1968.
5. "Bic Pen Corporation," by C. R. Christensen and E. L. Rachal, ICCH, 1974.
6. "The Boston Globe," by Daniel R. E. Thomas and Lina Carasso, ICCH, 1976.
7. "Boston Symphony Orchestra," by Malcom S. Salter, Thomas D. Steiner, and Jeanne Deschamps, ICCH.
8. "British Commercial Investments," by C. E. Summer, in Hugo Uyterhoeven, R. W. Ackerman, and J. W. Rosenblum, *Strategy and Organization*, Richard D. Irwin, 1977, pp. 742–52.
9. "California Federal Savings and Loan Association," by C. E. Summer, in C. E. Summer, J. J. O'Connell, and N. S. Peery, *The Managerial Mind*, Richard D. Irwin, 1977, pp. 149–75.
10. "General Mills, Inc.," by James Brian Quinn, Dartmouth

College, The Amos Tuck School of Business Administration, 1978.
11. "Harry Bridges and the I.L.U.W.," by Ira Goldstein and James P. Baughman, in J. P. Baughman, George C. Lodge, and Howard W. Pifer, *Environmental Analysis for Management*, Richard D. Irwin, 1974, pp. 442–59.
12. "Hart-Hanks Newspapers, Inc.," by Daniel R. E. Thomas and Steven Schiffer, ICCH, 1976.
13. "The High Ross Dam," by Peter T. Smith and C. E. Summer, in C. E. Summer, J. J. O'Connell, and N. S. Peery, *The Managerial Mind*, Richard D. Irwin, 1977, pp. 625–59.
14. "International Bulk Shipping Industry (History of)," by Howard H. Stevenson, ICCH, 1968.
15. "Lincoln Rochester Trust Company," by C. E. Summer, in C. E. Summer, and J. J. O'Connell, *The Managerial Mind*, Richard D. Irwin, 1964, 672–708.
16. "The Log Export Problem," by Frederick J. Truitt, ICCH, 1974.
17. "The Major Home Appliance Industry (History of)," by Joseph L. Bower and M. S. Hunt, ICCH, 1972.
18. "The Mechanical Writing Instrument Industry (History of)," by C. R. Christensen and E. L. Rachal, ICCH, 1974.
19. "Mercury Stores, Inc.," by C. E. Summer, in Robert N. Anthony and John Dearden, *Management Control Systems*, Richard D. Irwin, 1976, pp. 218–24.
20. "Metrocenter, Ohio Police Department," by C. E. Summer, University of Washington, Graduate School of Business, 1974.
21. "Mount Rainier National Park (National Park Service)," by C. E. Summer and Christopher L. Wolfe, University of Washington, Graduate School of Business, 1977.
22. "National Elevator Company," in J. D. Glover, R. M. Hower, and R. Tagiuri, *The Administrator*, Richard D. Irwin, 1973, pp. 53–56.
23. "The Newspaper Industry (History of)," by Daniel R. E. Thomas, Steven Schiffer and Lina Carasso, ICCH, 1976.
24. "Ontario Manufacturing Company," in J. D. Glover, R. M. Hower and R. Tagiuri, *The Administrator*, Richard D. Irwin, 1973, pp. 57–64, 425–28.
25. "The Pharmaceutical Industry in Iceland (A-C, R)," by C. E. Summer. Copyright 1968 by Institute Pour l'Etude des Methodes de Direction de l'Entreprise (IMEDE), Lausanne, Switzerland.
26. "The Recreational Vehicle Industry," by Michael Lovedal, ICCH, 1973.

27. "SAAB Automobile Engine Assembly Department," by C. E. Summer, David Hampton, C. E. Summer, and Ross Webber, in *Organizational Behavior and the Practice of Management*, Scott-Foresman, 1978, pp. 447–52.

28. "Scripto, Incorporated," by C. R. Christensen and E. L. Rachal, ICCH, 1974.

29. "Seaboard Chemical Company," by C. E. Summer, in C. E. Summer, J. J. O'Connell, and N. S. Peery, *The Managerial Mind*, Richard D. Irwin, 1977, pp. 205–27.

30. "Sears, Roebuck and Company: Appliances," by Joseph L. Bower and M. S. Hunt, ICCH, 1972.

31. "Shoe Corporation of Illinois," by C. E. Summer, in C. E. Summer, J. J. O'Connell, and N. S. Peery, *The Managerial Mind*, Richard D. Irwin, 1977, pp. 122–28.

32. "Tappan Company," by Joseph L. Bower and M. S. Hunt, ICCH, 1971.

33. "Taylor Wine Company," by J. W. Rosenblum and Michael L. Lovedal, ICCH, 1973.

34. "Teachers Insurance and Annuity Association," by C. E. Summer and Franklin T. Kudo, University of Washington, Graduate School of Business, 1977.

35. "Timex Corporation," by F. T. Knickerbocker, ICCH, 1970.

36. "Trans World Airlines," by J. J. O'Connell, in C. E. Summer and J. J. O'Connell, *The Managerial Mind*, Richard D. Irwin, 1964, pp. 326–58.

37. "U.S. Department of Health, Education and Welfare," by Stanton Peele and Thomas Reising, ICCH, 1972.

38. "United States Steel Corporation," in C. E. Summer and J. J. O'Connell, *The Managerial Mind*, Richard D. Irwin, 1964, pp. 563–612.

39. "University of Washington Law School," by C. E. Summer and Scott Hickey, in C. E. Summer, J. J. O'Connell, and Newman S. Peery, *The Managerial Mind*, Richard D. Irwin, 1977, pp. 595–624.

40. "The Watch Industries in Switzerland, Japan and the United States (History of)," by F. T. Knickerbocker, ICCH, 1970.

41. "Western Office Equipment Company," by C. E. Summer, in C. E. Summer, J. J. O'Connell, and Newman S. Peery, *The Managerial Mind*, Richard D. Irwin, 1977, pp. 352–83.

42. "Winnebago Industries, Inc.," by Michael Lovedal, ICCH, 1973.

43. "The Wine Industry (History of)" by J. W. Rosenblum and Michael L. Lovedal, ICCH, 1973.

360

Unpublished Cases

The following case histories have been completed in finished manuscript form but not published in quantity.

1. "Human Value of Oil," by Jerry Lee and C. E. Summer, 1975.
2. "The Liberty Bank," by Maurice Alexander and C. E. Summer, 1977.
3. "New York City Fiscal Crisis," by Gregory Dess and C. E. Summer, 1977.
*4. "Port of Seattle, Strategic Plan, 1977," by C. E. Summer, 1977.
*5. "Seattle-Tacoma International Airport," by C. E. Summer, 1979.

Case Files

The following case files have been accumulated to contain information on specialized aspects of strategic systems.

1. California Tax Revolt
2. Canadian Ministry
3. Capital Alignment in Government Industries
4. Capital Alignment in the Hospital Industry
5. Cleveland, Ohio
6. Conflict Between Cultural Constituencies
7. Conflicts Between Work Processes and Job Security
8. Cultural Constituencies
9. Cultural Demands for Capital Equipment Alignment
10. Cultural Demands for Operating Process Alignment
11. Cultural Demands on Product or Service Alignment
12. The Education Industry
*13. Family Service Association of America
14. Federal Entrepreneurial Organizations
15. Federal Industries
*16. General Mining Company, Strategic Analysis
17. Graduate School of Business Administration
18. IBM Corporation
19. Mobil Oil Corporation
20. The Nursing Home Industry
21. Professional Standards Review Organizations
22. Rainier Bank
*23. Recreational Equipment Incorporated, Strategic Analysis
*24. Roosevelt Hospital

*25. Sanlam Insurance Company, Strategic Analysis
*26. Shoe Corporation of South Africa, Ltd.
 27. Strategic Alignment
*28. United States Navy Station, Keyport
 29. Utility in Industrial Goods

NAME INDEX

SUBJECT INDEX